The Japanese Challenge to the American Neoliberal World Order

The Japanese Challenge to the American Neoliberal World Order

IDENTITY, MEANING, AND FOREIGN POLICY

Yong Wook Lee

Stanford University Press
Stanford, California 2008

Stanford University Press
Stanford, California

Printed in the United States of America on acid-free, archival-quality paper

Library of Congress Cataloging-in-Publication Data

Lee, Yong Wook.
The Japanese challenge to the American neoliberal world order : identity, meaning, and foreign policy / Yong Wook Lee.
p. cm.
Includes bibliographical references and index.
ISBN 978-0-8047-5812-3 (cloth : alk. paper)
1. Japan--Economic policy--1989- 2. National characteristics, Japanese. 3. Neoliberalism--United States. 4. East Asia--Economic conditions. 5. Globalization. I. Title.

HC462.95.L44 2008
337.52--dc22

2007045364

Designed by Bruce Lundquist
Typeset at Stanford University Press in 10/14 Minion

To My Parents,
Ik Beum Lee and Sook Il Yoon

CONTENTS

TABLES

ACKNOWLEDGMENTS

THIS BOOK WOULD NOT BE HERE without the generous support and encouragement I have received from my teachers, colleagues, and family over the years. The book was originally conceived in my doctoral dissertation, submitted to the School of International Relations at the University of Southern California. My teachers at USC—Hayward Alker, Saori Katada, and Gordon Berger—supervised my dissertation. Their guidance and scholarship importantly shaped my thinking about the subject and inspired me during and after my graduate study there.

First and foremost, I would like to express my greatest intellectual debt to Hayward Alker. When I began to grapple with the theme of this project, I had only an intuitive understanding of what I might do with what interested me. His perceptive comments and conceptual and methodological insights were invaluable in transforming my rough ideas into a viable project. Oftentimes, he reminded me of the value of my project in the field of International Relations when I was shaky about it. His encouragement right after my dissertation defense that "this should be a book" has sustained me through the revision process. Professor Alker's emphasis on an interdisciplinary approach to and the multiple possibilities of international relations will remain with me. I fondly recall sitting nervously in his office in late afternoons when he was reading the draft papers with me.

I was blessed to have Saori Katada as my adviser. She was always available whenever I needed her help and support. Her detailed comments and constructive criticisms significantly enhanced the quality of this book. She was finishing up her own book manuscript related to this book's analysis of the Asian financial crisis when I engaged in empirical research on Japan's policy toward the Asian Monetary Fund. Closely working with her at that stage immensely benefited me; I was constantly exposed to first-rate scholarship on the subject. Moreover, I could not have realized such fruitful research activities in Japan without her tireless support. Gordon Berger illustrated several ways of improving this book with his expertise in Japanese history and politics.

I would like to extend special thanks to J. Ann Tickner. Setting aside her contribution to my understanding of culture and identity issues in international relations, she gave me advice and inspiration at various stages in completing this book. Substantively, I could not have garnered enough courage to write Chapter 4 of this book had she not counseled me with her own article published in 1990. Her unflinching support and encouragement lasted until the book came to fruition.

I would like to express my gratitude to Sunhyuk Kim, Daniel Lynch, John Odell, and Apichai Shipper for their insightful comments and ideas for improvement. I also thank Hiwatari Nobuhiro in the Institute of Social Sciences at the University of Tokyo. He sponsored me during my research in Japan; I benefited from the research facility of the institute. I am also very grateful to the Center for International Studies at USC. I was a part of the CIS for five years (1998–2003), playing various roles. I greatly appreciate the CIS's support for my research. For the necessary intellectual and emotional context for development of this project at USC, my fellow graduate students deserve special thanks: Yooil Bae, Mara Bird, Eric Blanchard, Lyn Boyd-Judson, Jeany Choi, Gitika Commuri, Catia Confortini, Alba Hesselroth, Fei Hwang, Melissa Ince, Sung Jun Jo, Angeliki Kanavou, Wei Liang, Wendy Lords, Hye Mee Park, Geert Poppe, Anita Schjolset, Laura Sjoberg, Paul Steenhausen, Shinichi Suzuki, Pak Tang, and Leslie Wirpsa. The initial research presented in this book was funded by ACE-Nikkaido Fellowship in Japanese Studies. CIS also funded me through a dissertation fellowship and dissertation summer grant.

The considerable part of revising for publication took place at Brown University, where I was a Freeman fellow in the Department of East Asian Studies and the Watson Institute for International Studies. Colleagues there, including Peter Andreas, Thomas Biersteker, Natalie Bormann, James Der Derian, Leiwen Jiang, Hyun Wook Kim, Geoffrey Kirkman, Jae Ku, Catherine Lutz, Simone Pulver, Zlatko Sabic, Kerry Smith, Barbara Stallings, Nina

Tannenwald, and Kikuko Yamashita, provided intellectual stimulation and much-needed encouragement.

At the University of Oklahoma, where I currently teach and research, colleagues supported, encouraged, and cheered me as I completed this book. In particular, I would like to thank Robert Cox, Aimee Franklin, Paul Goode, Peter Gries, Suzett Grillot, Eric Heinze, Glen Krutz, Mee Young Lamothe, Scott Lamothe, Greg Russell, Mitchell Smith, and Ning Yu. I am grateful to Kevin Bobbett and Sara Sherman for their editorial comments and assistance.

This book also benefited from detailed comments and specific suggestions of two anonymous reviewers at Stanford University Press. They have my gratitude for balanced and insightful reviews. Additionally, I thank Muriel Bell, Kirsten Oster, and Joa Suorez of the press for their encouragement and effective assistance in the processes of editorial review and manuscript preparation. My gratitude also goes to Emily Smith and Tom Finnegan for their detailed and thoughtful editorial comments for the final shape of the manuscript. I am solely responsible for any remaining shortcomings of this book. Portions of Chapters 3 and 6 have been previously published in International Studies Quarterly.

Finally, I thank my family. I would like to dedicate this book to my parents, Ik Beum Lee and Sook Il Yoon. They have always had faith in me. They have encouraged and respected my independent thinking and choice ever since (or even before) they accepted my insistence on going to a local public elementary school when they wanted me to attend a renowned private one. This book would not have been possible without their love, sacrifice, and encouragement. I also deeply thank my parents-in-law, Jin Soon Jeong and Soo Ohk Hwang. My father-in-law shared with me his own graduate school experience, and this played a pivotal role in helping me tide over the ups and the downs of graduate school. My two sisters, Yoon Kyung and Dong Eun, have been unwavering as a source of support and encouragement. Dong Eun kindly agreed to listen to some part of this book for two years when she was an MBA student at USC.

Last but not least, my wife, Sun Hong, deserves my deepest thanks. The extent of her support throughout the entire process of writing this book is immeasurable and most gratefully acknowledged. With me, she went through both joy and anxiety emanating from the book. I also extend my heartfelt thanks to my two little girls, Jeong Haeng (Janice) and Eun Haeng (Erica), who wished to have more time to play with dad.

ABBREVIATIONS

ADB	Asian Development bank
ADBI	Asian Development Bank Institute
AfDB	African Development Bank
AMF	Asian Monetary Fund
APEC	Asia Pacific Economic Cooperation
APT	ASEAN Plus Three
ASEAN	Association of South East Asian Nations
BOJ	Bank of Japan
CMI	Chiang Mai Initiative
EAEC	East Asian Economic Caucus
EBRD	European Bank for Reconstruction and Development
EMEAP	Executives' Meeting of East Asia-Pacific Central Banks
EPA	Economic Planning Agency
ESF	Exchange Stabilization Fund
GATT	General Agreement on Tariffs and Trade
IDB	Inter-American Development Bank
IDE	Institute of Developing Economies
IDEA	Initiative for Development in East Asia
IFB	International Financial Bureau

IFIC	Institute for International Cooperation
IFIs	International Financial Institutions
IFMP	Institute of Fiscal and Monetary Policy
IIMA	Institute for International Monetary Affairs
IMF	International Monetary Fund
JCP	Japan Communist Party
JDB	Japan Development Bank
JETRO	Japan External Trade Organization
JEXIM	Japan Export Import Bank
JIIA	Japan Institute of International Affairs
JSP	Japan Socialist Party
LDP	Liberal Democratic Party
MDBs	Multinational Development Banks
METI	Ministry of Economy, Trade, and Industry
MITI	Ministry of International Trade and Industry
MOF	Ministry of Finance
MOFA	Ministry of Foreign Affairs
NIEs	Newly Industrialized Economies
NIFA	New International Financial Architecture
ODA	Official Development Assistance
OECD	Organization for Economic Cooperation and Development
OECF	Overseas Economic Cooperation Fund
PFP	Partners for Progress
PHRD	Policy and Human Resource Development
PRS	Poverty Reduction Strategy
RIDA	Research Institute of Development Assistance
SAL	Structural Adjustment Loan
SIT	Social Identity Theory
SMC	State Monopoly Capitalism
TICAD	Tokyo International Conference on African Development

UNCTAD	United Nations Conference on Trade and Development
VERs	Voluntary Export Restraints
WTO	World Trade Organization

The Japanese Challenge to the
American Neoliberal World Order

1 THE JAPANESE CHALLENGE TO THE AMERICAN NEOLIBERAL WORLD ORDER

Throughout this period [from the Renaissance to the middle of the eighteenth century], it was universally held that . . . the state should seek actively to promote the acquisition of wealth . . . the right way to make a country powerful was to stimulate production at home. . . .[1]

THE END OF THE COLD WAR, with the demise of socialism as a viable alternative for organizing the political economy of the world, reinforced the legitimacy of the U.S.-led neoliberal world order. This event has strengthened to a significant degree the political triumph of the "New Right" in the United States and Britain and seemingly confirmed a long-held conviction among neoliberals that the free play of market forces and a minimal role for the state in economic affairs would ensure efficiency and productivity of the economy. As was the case for the liberals' attempt to construct a global market society in the nineteenth century, proponents of the neoliberal world order invoked "the magic of the marketplace" while delegitimating the relevance of the role of the state in economic development as "dysfunctional and ahistorical." In so doing, they have advanced a liberal view of historical generalization that runs contrary to an understanding of history long held by critics of (neo)liberal doctrines. These critics argue that all modern economically developed states employed the practice of state-led economic development in one way or another when they began to industrialize.[2] Opposed to this is the position that all modern economically developed states have succeeded in their economic development by relying predominantly on self-regulating market forces.[3] Only these forces would generate the competition that promotes the most efficient use of resources, people, and capital.

In other words, on the basis of a particular historical generalization, proponents of a neoliberal world order have, on the grounds of economic efficiency, sanctioned liberal capitalism (or the liberal view of capitalism) as the only transhistorical, legitimate, and universal model of economic development.[4] In particular, the United States has spearheaded furthering of the globalization of the world economy along neoliberal lines. The neoliberal turn of the two Bretton Woods institutions, the International Monetary Fund (IMF) and the World Bank, in their policy prescriptions and lending conditionality has clearly indicated the influence of the U.S.-led neoliberal world order. These institutions have legitimated only one path to economic development: developing states are expected to adopt the free market blueprint, regardless of the conditions prevailing locally. In short, the U.S.-led neoliberal project has attempted to homogenize the shape(s) of the political economies of the world to an unprecedented degree.

The U.S.-led neoliberal world order, however, did not go unchallenged. Japan has challenged the foundation of the neoliberal world order by "bringing the state back in" for economic development since the mid-1980s, and Japanese attempts to resuscitate the fortunes of state-led economic development were intensified in the 1990s.[5] These efforts resulted in confrontation with the United States in numerous international financial and economic development forums, such as the Asian Development Bank (ADB),[6] the World Bank (the famous controversy over publication of *The East Asian Miracle*),[7] and the Asia-Pacific Economic Cooperation (APEC).[8] The Japanese challenge arguably culminated in Japan's Asian Monetary Fund (AMF) proposal that intentionally excluded the United States from membership during the Asian financial crisis. Furthermore, in the aftermath of the Asian financial crisis, Japan established the Tokyo-based Asian Development Bank Institute (ADBI) as "a center for alternative development and monetary paradigms" challenging the IMF's global prescriptions.[9] As such, the Japanese challenge cautions against a still-simplified perception that the postwar Japanese foreign economic policy is nothing but strategic pursuit of, or a free ride on the benefits of, the U.S.-led (neo)liberal world order. This is particularly so considering that despite the historical truism touted by critics of the neoliberal historical generalization noted above, Japan has remained the *only*[10] developed state in the entire post–Cold War era that has directly and officially questioned the universal validity of the so-called Washington Consensus (neoclassical economic orthodoxy[11] or neoliberal doctrine). In both synchronic (only Japan) and diachronic (defying the timeless postwar "checkbook" diplomacy) considerations, the Japanese challenge constitutes one of the most provocative Japanese foreign economic policies in the postwar era.

In this context, this book offers a historically informed, holistic account of the recent Japanese challenge to the American neoliberal world order and incorporates the interaction between Japanese domestic politics in the political-intellectual milieu and the international environment over the last 150 years. By "the Japanese challenge" I mean a set of Japanese foreign economic policies at the bilateral, regional, and global levels that since the mid-1980s have promoted a state-led alternative model of economic development. The Japanese challenge is aimed at undermining U.S.-led neoliberal attempts to delegitimate the role of the state in economic development through promulgation of the universal validity of the magic of the marketplace. Two interrelated research questions, to be discussed here, are designed to give a detailed and theoretical account of the nature, emergence, and policy developments of the Japanese challenge. Central to this book's analysis are the historically and socially constructed Japanese conceptions of Japan's economic development and the associated identities and meanings that have shaped Japan's interest in challenging the American neoliberal world order. In so doing, this book builds on the insights of a constructivist theoretical framework in the field of International Relations.

The first question is "constitutive": What made it possible for Japan to challenge U.S.-led neoliberalism? Addressing this question is fundamental to understanding the nature of the Japanese challenge. The answer uncovers deep-seated meaning structures that the Japanese themselves have historically attached to the role of the state in Japan's economic development, and that enabled the Japanese challenge to be conceivable, plausible, and compelling in the first place. Using a longitudinal intertextual analysis, I inductively examine three major Japanese economic development discourses—Marxism, economic liberalism, and developmentalism—to empirically ground the meaning structures that allow the very possibility of the Japanese challenge. In other words, explicating the ontological question of "how possible" (or what makes it possible) helps connect the historicity of identity (understanding of self) and agency (social conditions of possibility for action).[12]

These are the book's findings:

1 Despite Japan's different politico-economic-historical settings since the late nineteenth century, all three discourses have interpreted Japan's economic development in terms of "normal-abnormal" meaning structures.

2. These discourses have determined their normal-abnormal claims by locating Japanese economic development experience in the context of their *respective* interpretations of the role of the state in the history of economic development of the West (or Western advanced economies).
3. Developmentalism, which became the dominant discourse in the 1980s (with the rise of Asia) on which the Japanese challenge was established, has claimed a historically informed generalization that state-led economic development was the *normal* practice for all the successful industrializers (including even the first industrializer, Great Britain).
4. By extension, Japan's postwar state-led economic development is nothing but normal (not unique or idiosyncratic) in the context of the history of the world economy and is thus transferable to developing countries.

In this vein, the Japanese developmentalists have dismissed the neoliberal evocation of the magic of the market as "hijacking" the history of the world economy. What is *truly* normal or universal is the proven validity of state-led economic development across time and space. In a nutshell, I argue that the discursive, deep-seated meaning structure called normalcy enabled the Japanese developmentalists to challenge U.S.-led neoliberalism by offering a justificatory foundation for the international validity of state-led economic development.

Having established the ontological condition of the Japanese challenge in terms of the deep-seated, historically constructed meaning structures, I relate it to one of the most provocative foreign economic policies in postwar Japan. The second question I ask is "causal": Why did Japan propose to create the AMF during the Asian financial crisis in 1997 while intentionally excluding the United States from membership? The sheer importance of Japan's AMF proposal in the history of Japanese foreign policy is that this proposal constituted Japan's first-ever attempt to intentionally exclude the United States from an international institutional setting in the postwar era.

This book's primary original claim is that the conception by officials in the Japanese Ministry of Finance (MOF) of Japan and the United States as leaders of two different models of economic development provided the basis on which Japan proposed to create the AMF. Such identity topography on the part of MOF officials (or the MOF as an institution) was internalized when they confronted the United States (the Treasury Department) on proper models of economic development in various international forums such as the ADB, the APEC, and the World Bank. In particular, I show that the MOF's effort to publish *The East Asian Miracle* in the World Bank in 1993 was a pivotal moment for the MOF to consolidate this binary identity conception internationally and domestically. Thus, Japan's AMF proposal was not an isolated policy choice. A fuller account of the primary reason for Japan's AMF proposal is established only in the historical context of the politics of economic development between Japan and the United States.

More specifically, I explain the development of Japan's AMF proposal, from initial *cooperation* to *conflict* with the United States and the IMF, as emerging out of Japan's (more precisely MOF officials') *interpretation* of the structure of its interaction with the United States and the IMF. The structure is social, that is, not as "an environment that is external to and independent of the agent [the MOF on behalf of Japan], but as a social context woven from rules and meanings, which define relationships between the self and others and give interactions their purpose."[13] MOF officials' identity conception of Japan and the United States in the sphere of economic development played a central role in producing Japan's AMF proposal by giving Japan its interaction purpose when Japan confronted the U.S.-led IMF bailout operation in Thailand.

Tracing closely the detailed processes and timings of the social interaction between Japan and the U.S.-led IMF bailout operation, I demonstrate how the AMF proposal was deemed most compelling over the range of other possible policy actions by MOF officials according to their understanding of the structure of their interactions with the U.S.-led IMF bailout operation. I argue that the immediate cause of Japan's AMF proposal lies in Japan's interest in defending the Asian (or Japanese) model of economic development, as the MOF *interpreted* the U.S.-led IMF bailout operation in Thailand as unduly rolling over the Asian model. The AMF proposal was a Japanese attempt to institutionalize a financial mechanism for quick disbursement of funds to help the crisis-affected Asian economies fight against the U.S.-led IMF imposition of a neoliberal economic model. As such, exclusion of the United States from AMF membership was a key factor in realizing such an interest.

In answering these two questions, I theoretically and methodologically draw on a constructivist approach to International Relations in two important senses.[14] On the one hand, constructivists take ideas and discourse seriously: *discourse, or how we think and talk about the world, largely shapes practice.* This facilitates the first, constitutive question I have for the Japanese challenge. Of equal importance is the commitment of the constructivist approach to opening up the black box of actors' interests. It endogenizes actors' interests by connecting the actors' interpretation of their social and material environment to their choice of action. Thus, it stresses how actors' social identities, for example, affect their interests and the strategies they employ to realize those interests. This crucial insight stems from constructivist conceptualizations of agent and structure in world politics.

In contrast to a realist world of international relations, where the identities of both actors (states as unitary actors) and structure are fixed as egoistic utility maximizers and anarchy respectively, the identities of both actors and structure(s) in a constructivist world of international relations are socially and interactively constructed to the extent that they can vary, as evident in Wendt's "Anarchy Is What States Make of It."[15] This notion of agent and structure takes constructivists to focus on the social, interactive processes of agent-structure that transform actors' identities and their associated interests. One should not make a priori assumptions about actors' interests. Neither interests nor identities (of actors) can be conceived of prior to their interaction with others; this is in opposition to realists' transhistorical emphasis on guarding against the moral and idealistic pretenses of actors and uncovering rational power calculations behind their moves. Interests are always to be acted out in the context of socially constructed collective meaning. By endogenizing formation of interests through *problematizing actors*, constructivism is able to offer a better way of dealing with overdetermination of given interests as well as underspecification of the kinds of interests at stake to which rational theorizing of international relations is often vulnerable. The answer to the second, causal question benefits from this identity-based constructivist theorizing of interest formation.

Yet constructivism (or constructivist empirical works), as it stands now, shows some limitations to fully delivering on its own promise. Two major charges stand out inside and outside constructivist scholarship. The first charge is its relative neglect of a constitutive analysis that explores actors' social conditions of possibility for a particular course of action at a given moment. This shortcoming is reflected in constructivist self-criticism. As Ruggie puts it, "They [constructivists] do not begin with the actual social construction of meanings and significance from the ground up."[16] Or, in Cederman and Daase's words, this practice leads to "premature ontological closure" in analyzing the structure of identity and interest.[17] By skipping over the how-possible (or what makes it possible) question,[18] constructivists only partially live up to their aspiration to holism in explaining social and political action.

Despite constructivists' stress on the importance of actors' consciousness in defining their identities and interests, the absence of constitutive analysis makes it hard for constructivists to explain the *emergence* of the actors themselves.[19] This is related to explication of a deep-seated meaning structure ("particular interpretive dispositions" in Doty's words[20]; "deep-seated cultural mentalities" in Reus-Smit's words[21]) that enables possibilities for a certain course of action and constrains others. In other words, before any policy possibility is deemed valuable, it has to be made "thinkable" in the first place on the part of actors.[22] Weldes makes this point clear, saying:

> Meanings . . . for states are necessarily the meanings . . . for . . . individuals who act in the name of the state. . . . And these . . . officials do not approach international politics with a blank slate onto which meanings are written as a result of interactions among states. . . . Their appreciation of the world, of international politics, and of the place of their states within the international system, is necessarily rooted in collective meanings already produced, at least in part, in domestic and cultural contexts.[23]

In this regard, Peter Hall's illustration is instructive in clarifying the connection between a deep-seated meaning structure and a state's policy development. He argues that the emergence and persuasiveness of new ideas and identities engendering a particular policy stand in a conditioning relationship with a *terrain* already defined by a prevailing set of what he calls the "political discourse of a nation."[24] The deep-seated meaning context (of a particular issue area) within which political actors are embedded affects the possibility of developing particular policies.[25] For example, the flip side to the Japanese challenge is that, so long as the predominant interpretative disposition of economic development held by the United States remains discursively constructed on the basis of the magic of the marketplace, any possibility of the United States becoming an *agent* that practices exporting state-led economic development to the world is precluded. Without constitutive analysis, one has yet to explain how *Japan*, not others, comes into being in the first place as a challenger to an American neoliberal world order. In other words, what would be an enabling, permissive environment for the Japanese challenge? To fully materialize the constructivist commitment to holism in explaining social and political action, it is necessary to begin foregrounding, say, the Japanese challenge by exploring the "terrain" of the Japanese agency in the politics of economic development. Empirically, this requires "grounding" or "historicizing"[26] the domestic discursive meaning structures that the Japanese themselves have historically attached to the role of the state in Japanese economic development experience. This is logically prior to the domain in which Japan causally develops a set of foreign economic policies challenging neoliberalism.[27]

The second charge against constructivism is concerned with causal indeterminacy in relation to the *why* question and is largely due to constructivists' analytical processes, which tend to take social structures in their inquiry as exogenously given. Rather than examining a detailed process of social interactions that shape identities and interests of actors, certain social structures (whether they be ideas, norms, or identities) are already given. Empirical constructivists sequentially measure changes in state behavior as effects of the already-given normative or identity structures.[28] As such, few constructivist research projects empirically demonstrate the interactive process through which identities and interests are defined, redefined, and transformed in the process of policy making.[29]

This analytical bracket engenders the problem often associated with "revealed preferences": there is no independent measure of the impact of the already-given social facts on behavior, apart from the behavior itself (this also gives rise to the issue of circularity). Without a clear analytical path and independent measure of the structure of identity and interest, constructivists are unlikely to establish more than a correlative relationship between an identity and an outcome.[30] A specific causal mechanism or link between identity and interest remains to be fully developed.[31] In addition, exogenously given social structures also invite the criticism that "operationalizing mutual constitution is a dilemma for all empirical constructivists."[32] Constructivist empirical works are still individualist in practice.[33] Taken together, underspecification of the process generated by exogenously given social structures elicits theoretical and methodological gaps that might undermine the constructivist ontology of interest as a product of intersubjective and contingent social interactions.[34]

This book is designed to fill these gaps. There is no single work offering an account of both constitutive and causal analyses of foreign policy.[35] I offer this account of the Japanese challenge on both constitutive and causal terms as has been summarized here. In developing a causal analysis applied to Japan's AMF decision, I do not take as exogenously given the social identity structure of Japan and the United States in the politics of economic development. I shed light on the processes by which Japan (or MOF officials), since the mid-1980s, has internalized the binarization of itself and the United States as the leaders of different models of economic development. Analysis of the processes of identity formation not only is important in its own right as part of an ongoing process of agent-structure interaction, with historical insights into the origin and development of the formation of identity constructs, but also significantly contributes to explaining how Japan built the AMF proposal that intentionally excluded the United States from membership. As I demonstrate, the MOF's own understanding of its conflict with the United States during the process of identity formation played a key role in actualizing Japan's AMF decision. In particular, Japanese experiences with the United States at the World Bank crucially affected MOF officials in terms of how they defined the institutional purpose of the AMF.

Furthermore, I develop an identity-intention analytical framework that offers an empirically testable microfoundation for a causal mechanism between an identity and an interest. I draw on analytical philosophy, social psychology, and constructivism in establishing such a microfoundation. The analytical framework I advocate in this book is anchored in an "interpretivist notion of identity."[36] As will be discussed in greater detail, the interpretivist notion of identity differs from the social identity theory (SIT)-based in-group and out-group action theory and role identity theory in its adherence to causation in explaining choices of action. The crux of the identity-intention framework is that identities, as a cognitive heuristic, constitute the basis for interpretation of unfolding events, which in turn affects valuation of incentives by informing actors as to which actions are valuable, necessary, and compelling.

In this book, I adopt Wendt's definition of identity as "a property of intentional actors that generates motivational and behavioral dispositions."[37] This definition resonates with the analytical framework already briefed, which emphasizes the intersubjective quality of the formation of actors' interest. In the context of Japan's AMF proposal, this basically means that *the emergence of what Japan wanted (AMF establishment) depended on its interpretation of what the U.S.-led IMF bailout operation wanted* ("demolishing the Asian model of economic development"[38]). I test the validity of this framework against the formation of Japan's interest in the AMF proposal. The analytical focus is on the role of identity in this interpretative function.

As I have noted, this analytical effort is a response to criticisms leveled against constructivism for its failure to specify a causal link. Together with a process-tracing technique facilitating detailed analysis of policy making, I construct a theoretically rigorous and empirically rich account of Japan's AMF proposal. Even though the identity-intention framework is tested against one specific instance of Japanese foreign economic policy, the framework is in principle applicable to analysis of interest formation emerging out of any social interaction, with some scope conditions (as is noted in Chapter 3).

Throughout this book, I do not take Japan as a unitary actor but rather open up the black box. In the task of grounding the discursive meaning structures attached to the Japanese economic development experience, three major economic development discourses are identified and discussed: Marxism, economic liberalism, and developmentalism. Each discourse, operating within its respective historical interpretation of the role of the state in economic development, interprets in its own way the role of the state in Japan's economic development and its associated meanings in the history of the world economy. The analysis illustrates divergent, seamless Japanese efforts to make sense of their economic development experience in the historical context of the world economy. On this basis, I examine how the developmentalist thread[39] won out over the other contending visions and became the basis of Japanese foreign economic policy. Moreover, I shed light on the role Asian economies' success played in empowering the developmentalist notion of normalcy.

With respect to Japan's decision to propose the AMF, I scrutinize the interactions between MOF officials and others, such as the Ministry of Foreign Affairs (MOFA) and big business in Japan. In particular, given the private (both financial and trading sectors) sectors' high exposure to the Asian financial crisis, their posture on the AMF proposal is carefully explicated vis-à-vis MOF officials. The interplay of the domestic and the international looms large, as these domestic actors work with the United States and the IMF under different relational contexts. The MOFA, for example, traditionally defines its top priority in terms of maintaining a good relationship with the United States. This has not been the case for the MOF. Even within the MOF, there is a pro-IMF faction that has a close tie with that institution. By linking analysis of domestic discursive meaning structures attached to Japanese economic development to Japan's actual policy choice of the AMF proposal, this book treats domestic and international structures and processes as two faces of a single sociopolitical order that shape the emergence and development of the Japanese challenge.

PUZZLES

Japan presented itself as a leader of "antiparadigmatic" views on economic development ideas when it pressed the World Bank to publish *The East Asian Miracle* in 1993. What is behind this Japanese challenge? This simple question remains enmeshed in many apparent contradictions. First, the Japanese challenge theoretically runs counter to Krasner's provocative hypothesis on states' preferences of regime "types." He argues that small, poor states in the South tend to support those regimes that allocate resources authoritatively, while the richer states in the North favor those regimes whose principles and rules give priority to the market mechanism.[40] Was or is Japan a small, poor state in the South?

Second, the Japanese challenge seems to go against Japan's economic interests. If all developing states truly applied a Japanese model of economic development, it would not be in the best interest of Japan or in that of the most internationally competitive Japanese multinational corporations. This is because the Japanese model implies a protectionist tendency. Put another way, Japan had no incentive to turn the tide; it could have continued its free ride on the U.S.-led neoliberal world order.[41] Japan previously adopted the policies of a developmental state (tariffs, subsidies, government administrative guidance, and so on) in order to catch up to the West. However, economic liberalization is now beneficial for Japan since it has caught up.[42] From a realist or economic nationalist perspective, one would expect that Japan would encourage other developing states to liberalize in order to further its own economic interests. In this respect, Lanciaux predicted that Japan would not continue to promote the model that is not in its best economic interests.[43] The Japanese challenge is thus puzzling even to those critics of free trade liberalism, who have long criticized the dual standards of economic development that developed states apply to themselves[44] and to other developing states.

Third, Japan's coming out (clear articulation of its model by the Japanese themselves) had the effect of making Japan more vulnerable in bilateral trade negotiations with the United States. One effect of this situation was manifested in U.S. adoption of a "result-oriented" approach in bilateral trade negotiation with Japan.[45] Lastly, the Japanese challenge has, since the mid-1980s, taken place in a political-intellectual milieu that globally tones down any positive social standing for the "state." Put another way, as Japan has become economically more powerful in the world market, why does it not endorse free trade and discard the mercantilist element in its own history (like everybody else, from the point of view of critics of free trade liberalism)? This is particularly troubling because there exists *within* Japan a liberal interpretation of Japanese economic development (see Chapter 4).

Surprising many observers, in 1997, four years after World Bank publication of *The East Asian Miracle*, Japan proposed to create the AMF in the midst of the Asian financial crisis. This is an unexpected call, considering that the proposed institution was supposed to be financed and run by *only* Asian countries, thus excluding the United States from membership. At the annual meetings of the World Bank and the IMF on September 21, 1997, Japan explained that the AMF was necessary to help governments in trouble cope with the currency crisis. Intentionally excluding its all-time postwar ally (or patron), the United States, from membership in such an international institution was Japan's boldest and most independent policy initiative in the postwar era. With the exception of the wars fought against the Western powers (that is, the Russo-Japanese War and the Pacific War), this could arguably count as the second (in conjunction with Japan's challenge to the World Bank) *civilian* revolt against the West since Japan was forced to open up by Commodore Perry in 1853.[46]

The question of why Japan proposed establishment of the AMF with exclusion of the United States also poses challenges to the accepted wisdom of the day on Japanese foreign policy. First, the Japanese proposal stands in stark contrast with its earlier East Asian Economic Caucus (EAEC[47]) back-off. Despite its initial interest, Japan, the assumed center of the EAEC, semiofficially refused to join the grouping by not attending the April 1995 proposed ASEAN (Association of Southeast Asian Nations)-sponsored meeting in Thailand. Japan was known to be dragging its feet on the issue mainly because of pressure from the United States, which did not want to be left out in the cold with the emergence of a new economic bloc centered on Japan. This elusiveness on the part of Japan seems to reconfirm that Japan is a reactive state,[48] an assessment that would also be endorsed by the realist account, given Japan's market and security dependence on the United States.[49] In addition, this evidence seems to enhance the notion of Japan's aversion to regional economic institutionalization.[50] Japan's AMF proposal seems to defy its aversion proposition, as well as policy behavior expectations borne out by the realist account. Aware of U.S. opposition to any economic institution restricted to East Asia, how could a reactive state such as Japan possibly propose such an exclusionary regional institution, and even exclude the United States from it?

Second, the Japanese proposal does not seem to derive from Japan's economic interests, *material interests narrowly defined as immediate, short-term economic gains.* Despite Japanese banks' high exposure to the Asian economies in trouble, many of them supported solution (of the crisis) through the IMF. They argued against the AMF because "such a fund as the financial last resort creates a psychology of dependence."[51] Moreover, many businessmen, particularly from the manufacturing or exporting sectors, demonstrated their doubts about the AMF. They were aware that it would be dangerous to supply easy money in the name of an Asian rescue that could undermine the reforms and adjustments that the stringent conditionality of the IMF usually provided. They were also aware that such action (creating an AMF that would allow the affected countries to have more maneuvering space with the IMF) might result in loss of golden opportunities for further liberalization of the Asian markets.[52] Such opposition from the private sector evidently invalidates the claim that Japan would use such a fund to help Japanese industrial and financial sectors withdraw from Thailand and possibly from other financially troubled countries in Asia without accruing significant losses. Who could calculate the utility of the AMF better than a Japanese private sector that had risked its assets in the troubled economies in Asia?

Lastly, the Japanese proposal came abruptly after Japan's initial cooperation with the IMF in managing the Thai crisis. When the financial crisis hit Thailand in May 1997, Japan hosted an international conference in Tokyo to help facilitate concrete terms of an agreement between Thailand and the IMF. By August 4, 1997, Thailand and the IMF had reached a basic agreement. Japan began to participate in an IMF bailout operation after $17.2 billion for Thailand was agreed on August 11. In less than forty-five days of working with the IMF, Mitsuzuka, Japan's finance minister at that time, put the idea of the AMF, the "Asian only institution," on the table on September 21. What happened around and after Japan's participation in the IMF-led bailout? What made it imperative for Japan to set up an AMF that intentionally excluded the United States?

Given the unusually assertive nature of Japanese foreign economic policy, manifested in the Japanese challenge in general and the AMF proposal in particular, many studies have explored these problems. With respect to emergence of the Japanese challenge, for example, Yasutomo explains that in the 1980s there were three specific catalysts for the Japanese challenge to neoliberal doctrine: "the assumption to office of the Reagan administration, with its strong ideological commitment to a universal development philosophy; the intensification of the accumulated debt crisis in Latin American states; and the impressive accomplishments of state-led economic development in Asian states."[53] The track records of structural adjustment loan (SAL) programs in both Latin America and Africa gave Japan instructive case studies of a failure of the neoliberal doctrine. In contrast, the emergence of an economically successful Asia offered an alternative answer to the question of sustainable development. In short, these two phenomena together triggered in Japan a reassessment of its own development experience.[54] Along with it came amplified doubts about the Reagan administration's seemingly inflexible universal development approach. This explanation, which explicitly or implicitly relies on the concept of "learning" defined as "changes in belief systems or cognitive structures as the result of experience and study,"[55] however, might produce necessary but not sufficient conditions for the emergence of the Japanese challenge. That is to say, it does not explain why the learning derived from these *objective* realities did not take place in other developed states. Since the mid-1980s, Japan has remained the only developed state to explicitly challenge neoliberal doctrine.

More specifically, Wade offers four plausible reasons for the Japanese challenge: ideological conviction of its own or an Asian-state–led model of economic development; the MOF's organizational interest in preserving its positive role in Japan's economic development against the World Bank's criticism of Japan's concessional and directed aid practice; national material interest promoting "interventionist" policies as a cloak to facilitate economic collusion between Japan and developing countries; and nationalism as part of a wider attempt by the Japanese elite to overcome a sense of being inferior (that is, "economic superpower and political pygmy" or "dinosaur with a huge body but a tiny brain") to other states and assert its own views on appropriate rules for the international economy. In other words, the last reason points to Japan's desire to develop "an ideology that goes beyond Japan's uniqueness and yet remains distinct from free trade and orthodox liberalism."[56]

Even though these four plausible reasons are suggestive for explaining the emergence of the Japanese challenge, there are two problems in this account. On the one hand, they are underspecified in terms of the relative importance of the four.[57] Empirically, for example, Wade himself suggests that the best way to gauge the degree of Japan's material interest in promoting state-led economic development is to study what Japan does in the ADB. Japan has had a great deal of influence in the ADB since its foundation, and he argues that one can infer the relative importance of these reasons from the pattern of the ADB lending.[58] In this respect, Wan reports on an interesting empirical result. In his study of Japan's policies toward the ADB from the early 1960s to the mid-1990s, he finds that as Japan became more powerful in the ADB it has also become less concerned about its tangible and immediate economic gains from the bank.[59]

On the other hand, Wade's suggested reasons eventually face the same predicament as Yasutomo's three specific catalysts mentioned earlier. They are incomplete in that they unquestionably accept that the challenge takes place in Japan. That is, why does *Japan* challenge the neoliberal doctrine but not others, such as France and Germany? In the end, it is well known that Japan patterned its state-led economic development after the French and German models (even the Hamiltonian American model) of economic development when it began to call for "enriching the nation, strengthening the army" in the late nineteenth century.

Thus, any developed state could have challenged the neoliberal doctrine in the face of such unfolding events in the world economy of the 1980s. Any of them could have done it out of a desire to make an ideational or ideological contribution to international society. Any of them could have done it to exercise a leadership role by becoming a source of metapolicies for developing states as well. The possibility was open to any who shared the historical experience of state-led economic development,[60] but only Japan did it. Why does the idea of state-led economic development resonate more in Japan than in other states? As such, the question of why Japan challenged the American neoliberal world order could not be fully addressed without answering the question of what made it possible for Japan to challenge it.

When it comes to Japan's AMF proposal, three plausible reasons have so far been suggested by previous studies.[61] The first, a material explanation, stems from the exposure of Japanese private sectors (banks and manufacturers) to troubled Asian economies. Japan could take advantage of the AMF on its mission to rescue their private sectors. The second is "ideational": the AMF could have been a perfect mechanism for Japan to put into practice its own version of a crisis management solution. The third is linked to Japan's ongoing efforts to build its influence in Asia through playing a regional leadership role.

As is discussed in my examination of these explanations in detail (Chapters 2 and 6), however, they are at best underdetermined in accounting for the nature of Japan's interests in creating the AMF, let alone furnishing causal mechanisms of how *their* definitions of the Japanese interests were formed and projected as a foreign policy. This is partly because this research does not focus solely on the AMF per se. In addition to some empirical evidence undermining these explanations, I claim that their indeterminacy pivots on their failure to pay due attention to Japan's intention to exclude the United States from AMF membership, as the institutional purpose of the AMF was inseparable from its exclusion of the United States. In other words, emergence of the AMF and exclusion of the United States are two sides of the same coin in Japan's decision-making process. At a substantive level, they do not capture an important turning point in Japan's policy choice toward the AMF proposal: the Japanese proposal came after Japan's initial cooperation with the IMF in managing the Thai crisis. A fuller account of Japan's AMF decision emerges from the relaxation of bracketing the social processes that influence formation of identity and interest of Japan as an agent in the politics of economic development.

ALTERNATIVE EXPLANATIONS

Against the arguments so far discussed, I explore a number of alternative explanations, collected from the existing literature on Japanese foreign policy. I identify here three approaches; variants within each approach are considered as well. They are "interest group," "state-centered," and "systemic" approaches. These three show a striking parallel to rationalist International Relations theories on foreign policy. The interest-group approach is reflective of liberalism (not neoliberalism), while domestic grand strategy reflects the state-centered approach. The systemic approach resembles the two neo-utilitarian theories (neoliberalism and neorealism).[62] They all assume policy actions arising from exogenously determined interests that define the ends actors intentionally pursue by choosing from among available alternative courses of action. Simply put, policies can be understood primarily on the basis of plausibly inferred material interests of key actors. These approaches differ, however, on who the key actors are and which level of analysis should be prioritized. By deductively drawing inferences from these alternative explanations, I test them against empirical evidence to see whether they are persuasive in accounting for the Japanese challenge in general and Japan's AMF proposal in particular. Previous explanations for this book's research questions are explored in detail within each theoretical approach. In addition, rationalist treatments of the influence of ideas on policy choice are also discussed in relation to the research questions.

METHODOLOGY

This book is based on a constructivist approach that problematizes Japan as an actor in the politics of economic development in a holistic way. Doing so methodologically requires specifying an empirically testable, clear path of analytical steps that connects in an orderly way meaning-oriented domestic discursive practices, through formation of identity and interest to actual policy choices.[63] In other words, the holistic approach *foregrounds* the constitutive analysis of Japan's agency and links it to causal analysis of Japan's AMF decision to deepen the endogenization of Japan's interest in challenging the American neoliberal world order.

What brings the two analyses under a holistic analytical perspective is to make the case that the MOF, which has spearheaded the Japanese challenge as the major decision-making body, is institutionally part of the developmentalist discourse.[64] The holistic analytical perspective calls for two interrelated empirical demonstrations. To establish the condition of possibility of the Japanese challenge (constitutive analysis), it must be shown that the MOF subscribes to the normal-abnormal meaning structures, embedded in developmentalism, of the role of the state in economic development. As for causal analysis exploring the structure of identity and interest in the AMF proposal, evidence should point to the MOF's deeply internalized binary perception of Japan and the United States as two rivals promoting different models of economic development. Elucidating the processes of identity formation on the part of the MOF is important as this identity topography resulted in Japan's interest in the establishment of the AMF without the United States.

That said, I present specific qualitative and quantitative techniques of data collection and analysis aimed at addressing the two research questions noted at the outset: discourse analysis, economic data gathering, process tracing, and interviews. The different types of research question inform particular methods by which to answer them. Depending on the type of research question, some methods and evidence are more logically and empirically plausible than others. In this vein, this book entails a multimethod research design.

What made it possible for Japan to challenge neoliberalism?

This book uses discourse analysis to identify and explicate deep-seated meaning structures within Japan that allow the very possibility of the Japanese challenge. It is grounded in the notion of "discourse productivity." In Milliken's words, "discourses make intelligible some ways of being in, acting towards the world, and of operationalizing a particular 'regime of truth' while excluding other possible modes of identity and action."[65] Discourse productivity takes the form of "ontological narratives" in a sense that connects identity (understanding of self) and agency (the conditions for action).[66]

Discourse analysis takes certain specific, interrelated analytical steps to address the question: (1) identifying inductively[67] Japanese economic development discourses, namely three schools of economic thought in Japan (Marxist, economic liberal, and developmental); (2) investigating *how* each discourse offers an understanding of Japan's economic development, as well as that of other states; (3) uncovering meaning-oriented interpretative dispositions (through the second step) in which the three discourses organized, interpreted, and developed their understanding of Japan's economic development in the historical context of the world economy (that is, normal-abnormal meaning structures), this "thick" contextualization bringing to the fore "the origins of condition" for the Japanese challenge; (4) examining how the developmentalist discourse (and its associated meaning structure) became dominant over the others as a force shaping and defining the nature of the Japanese challenge[68]; and (5) empirically demonstrating that the MOF in fact shares the normalcy meaning structure (normal-abnormal) embedded in developmentalism.

The core feature of the technique for discourse productivity in this book is a longitudinal, intertextual analysis. The book demonstrates that despite Japan's different politico-economic-historical settings, all three discourses have since the late nineteenth century contextualized Japan's economic development in terms of normal-abnormal meaning structures. Such an intertextual treatment of longitudinal analysis enables this book to escape the trap of deriving a meaning-based argument from behavior or policy outcome, which tends to lead to the kind of tautological, ad hoc rationalizing of which meaning-oriented analysis (broadly cultural analysis) is often accused. Based on extensive consultations with Japanese economic historians and economists, a rule of thumb for choosing texts (and authors) in conducting an intertextual analysis is to select those most widely read and cited. My final selection derived from those authors known to be most actively participating in the making of economic policies of the Japanese government. In this way, this part of the analysis is able to reduce the gap between economic ideas and discourse and actual policy choices as much as possible. All the authors introduced in Chapter 4 for developmentalism, for example, either were directly involved in Japan's economic policy making as career bureaucrats or indirectly influenced it as economic advisors.

Why did Japan propose to create the AMF during the Asian financial crisis while intentionally excluding the United States from membership?

An identity-intention approach to action assumes that "social action can only be intelligible if we recognize that people are guided to act by the relationships in which they are embedded [rather] than by interests we impute to them."[69] This assumption leads to an empirical focus on how actors characterize themselves and the actions they produce. As such, the identity-intention analytical framework requires analysis of how actors organize, process, and interpret information toward achieving their relationally defined goals when it explores the endogenization process of actors' interests.[70]

Given the identity-intention analytical framework's emphasis on explaining social action by probing what actors think and why they are doing so, the method employed for this question combines interpretation with a process-tracing technique. It takes the form of an analytical causal explanation couched in active, self-directing, and self-monitoring human agency capable of social actions deriving from the meaning(s) ascribed to a particular situation.[71] This way of using process tracing is not a deterministic pattern matching between the configuration of conditions and the configuration of outcomes.[72] Rather, it traces the sequence of events or actors' moves by identifying intrinsic sociohistorical objects meaningful to historically located individuals who participated in the events subject to analysis. On the grounds of the *verstehende* project, such a combination allows explication of the intentional actions of particular individuals and groups through an intrinsic narrative approach.[73] The identity-intention analytical framework guides minute tracing of the explanatory narrative by supplying key meaning constituents needed for construction of the social realities that eventuate actors' choice of action.

Methodologically, the challenge for the identity-intention analytical framework is thus how to empirically deal with "internal" matters (or what John Hall calls "intrinsic objects"[74])—that is, actors' practical interests in relation to the intersubjective content of the world they interpret. Put another way, how can one construct nontautological, falsifiable, and independent measures of the reasoning processes used by MOF officials when they were deliberating on creation of the AMF? Can the framework effectively assuage the "other-minds" problem of which interpretation-oriented scholarship is often accused?

A key to solving this challenge is to devise a clear path of analytical steps, borne out of the identity-intention analytical framework, that demonstrate the influence of identity on actors' reasoning processes with respect to what they want. To do this, one should keep identity, preferences, and strategies (to materialize given preferences) analytically and empirically distinct, as Abdelal notes.[75] This is also a way to avoid the pitfall of the "fallacy of imputed preference."

I offer such analytical steps in Chapter 3 after a theoretical explication of the identity-intention analytical framework in detail. Along with it, I specify what evidence or theoretical expectations would demonstrate that the framework indeed works empirically. Nonetheless, I note here the important first step toward application of the framework to empirical analysis of Japan's AMF decision. It is to show that decision makers (Japan's MOF officials) are indeed embedded in a particular conception of their identity in relation to others (such as "the conception of Japan and the United States as the two rivals promoting different models of economic development"). If one assumes (as advocated here) that human beings act on the basis of their interpretations of the world, one needs access to these interpretations in order to explain what they do and why they do it. Ultimately, one tries to explain actions by looking for meanings the actors *themselves* made, not the meanings one wishes to assign. It is thus imperative to demonstrate whether or not MOF officials discursively and conceptually associate themselves with the hypothesized identity conceptions. Locating MOF officials in their identity contexts enables one to have crucial access to the social meaning underlying their choice of action, because it leads to an understanding of the action's meaning and its significance to the decision makers. Other than that, there are few ways to empirically ground the identity-based reasoning processes leading to a particular policy decision. Explaining action means "elaborating, justifying, or possibly excusing the action rather than simply 'refuting' the hypothesis,"[76] through reconstruction of actors' goals, purposes, and reasons behind their intentions.

Keeping this in mind, I address these two research questions by means of a comprehensive survey of the existing scholarly works on the topics, combined with close content analysis of various primary sources, including government documents and official and unofficial statements from key state policy makers in Japan. Newspapers are a significant source as well. Particular attention is to be paid to interviews with key officials at the MOF in Japan and their counterparts in the IMF for cross-examination.[77] These interviews, along with government white papers, help trace the reasoning processes behind state preferences. The information obtained from those interviewed, as well as that from primary and secondary sources, is carefully examined in its proper context so as not to be mistakenly blended.

PREVIEW OF CHAPTERS

Chapter 2 explores alternative explanations. It examines how existing theories on Japanese foreign policy, such as interest-group, state-centered, and systemic approaches, which show a striking parallel to rationalist IR theories, could account for the two main research questions posed in the book. In addition, rationalist treatments of the influence of ideas on policy choice are empirically scrutinized. Previous explanations for this book's research questions are examined within each theoretical approach. This chapter demonstrates the indeterminacy of these alternative explanations.

Chapter 3 introduces the identity-intention analytical framework, designed to establish the causal link between identity and interest. Drawing on analytical philosophy, social psychology, and IR constructivist literature, this chapter offers a way to connect meaning-oriented discursive practices through formation of interests to actual policy choices by specifying an empirically testable, clear path of analytical steps. It also discusses methodological issues related to validity and reliability when the proposed analytical framework is applied to Japan's AMF decision.

Chapter 4 explicates the question of what made it possible for Japan to challenge neoliberalism. It analyzes three main economic discourses in Japan—Marxism, economic liberalism, and developmentalism—to address the question. The last section of this chapter explores a domestic version of the politics of economic development in the late 1980s and early 1990s in Japan. The Japanese developmentalists had to win over the other two contending approaches domestically before international projection of their preferred model of economic development could be realized. This part of the discussion demonstrates how the rise of Asian economies in the 1980s empowered the Japanese developmentalists. The rise of Asia played a key role in increasing the intellectual authenticity of their normalcy claim, essentially arguing that any country wishing to industrialize rapidly must adopt a state-led economic development strategy in one way or another.

Chapter 5 sheds light on the processes of identity formation to endogenize the structure of identities that later shape Japan's interest in the AMF proposal.

It examines how MOF officials have since the mid-1980s internalized the binarization of Japan and the United States as two leaders of different models of economic development. The focus is on Japan's clash with the United States in the politics of economic development at the ADB, the World Bank, and the APEC. In particular, this chapter shows how Japan's pressure on the World Bank to publish *The East Asian Miracle* in 1993 not only constituted a formative moment when Japan officially established itself as the leader of state-led economic development but also sowed the seed of Japan's AMF proposal in 1997. In addition, this chapter gives an account of how the MOF has institutionally nurtured developmentalism through promotion, internal education, and research and publication. Together with the MOF's external interactions with the United States, these institutional practices make the MOF the agent that has constituted Japan as a leader of an alternative model of economic development.

Chapter 6 examines why Japan proposed to create the AMF, which intentionally excluded the United States from membership. The identity-intention analytical framework developed in Chapter 3 is empirically tested against the MOF's decision to propose the AMF. The empirical focus is on the interactions between the MOF and the U.S.-led IMF bailout operation in Thailand. With the aid of process tracing, this chapter offers a detailed analysis of the MOF's decision-making process.

Chapter 7 summarizes the overall findings, drawing out implications of the Japanese challenge for Japan's foreign economic policies at the bilateral, regional, and global levels (after touching on the current status of the Japanese challenge at these levels). This concluding chapter offers, by extension of empirical findings in Japan's AMF proposal, an analysis of how the proposal has constituted the beginning of the postcrisis "New Asian Regionalism." The main characterization of New Asian Regionalism is more formalization and institutionalization of economic integration among East Asian states, which tends to exclude the United States from membership, such as ASEAN Plus Three (China, Japan, and Korea) and the East Asian Summit Meeting. ASEAN Plus Three (APT) made an official proclamation of the East Asian Community, as a goal to be pursued in the declaration that followed the summit meeting of Japan and ten ASEAN members held in Tokyo in December 2003. Recent development of the AMF is also discussed in this context. Finally, the chapter highlights the theoretical, empirical, and methodological contribution of this book to social science in general and the field of International Relations in particular.

2 ALTERNATIVE EXPLANATIONS

One thing we must learn is that the national interest is a variable and not a constant. . . . Within wide limits, this is a subjective variable.[1]

IS IT WORTHY TO STUDY an actor's preferences in terms of "those interests of a given actor that determine how the actor rank-orders the possible outcome"[2] in a field such as International Relations? Realists say it is not necessary.[3] International politics differs fundamentally from domestic politics in its anarchic character. It is not in the realm of normal relationships and calculable results; anarchy is a condition of rule in which states interact.[4] In other words, anarchy perennially causes states to be *defensive positionalists*,[5] and it is thus futile to make a distinction between state interest and state preference. Morgenthau maintained that "a realist theory of international politics . . . will guard against two popular fallacies: the concern with motives and the concern with ideological preferences."[6] A theory of international politics must be focused on "the concept of the national interest,"[7] but not the national *preference*. Waltz added that "to say that a country acts in its national interest means that, having examined its security requirements, it tries to meet them."[8] International politics is the realm of recurrence and repetition, where the theory of survival is appropriate.[9] Anarchy, the offensive capabilities of others, and their uncertain intentions combine to leave states with little choice but to compete aggressively with each other.[10] One can thus deductively assume that states have one ultimate, prior interest—"survival"—while power and plenty (wealth) are immediate interests or the necessary means enabling states to ensure such an ultimate goal. For Morgenthau, national security is the cornerstone of the nation's interest,[11] while for Waltz states can afford to seek other goals such as tranquility, profit, and power "only if survival is assured."[12] As such, state interests are materially christened in terms of the distribution of capabilities. Realists' utility function should not incorporate such ideational factors as ideas, identities, and norms. They are the sources of "organized hypocrisy"[13] that stand in the way of objectively seeing problems of international politics as they are.

Constructivists say it is necessary to investigate the formation of state (or national) interest to make better sense of the concrete actions of states. Realist renderings of the national interest, defined as "the security and survival of a state," are so general as to be indeterminate.[14] If one agrees with the assumption that interests imply choices, a realist analysis of international politics is not very helpful for explaining and understanding the choice of one policy over another for achieving, say, security. The dictates of power and survival are never clearly manifest by themselves in international politics.[15] Part of the reason might be that realism deals with "the perennial conditions that attend the conduct of statecraft, not with the specific conditions that confront the statesman."[16] But more fundamental to the constructivist argument concerning the indeterminacy of state action in realism is that realism ignores the centrality of processes of interpretation on the part of actors (or state officials) in choosing a course of action.[17] As Waltz himself admits, "we cannot predict how states will react to the pressures of structure without knowledge of their internal dispositions."[18] *Defining* the particular situation faced by a state necessarily takes place prior to *defending* the "correct" national interest with respect to that situation. Without this interpretive labor, realists' purely naturalistic empirical analysis can be *more* exposed to the pitfalls of what Bourdieu once termed "the scholastic bias"—the tendency of social analysts to project their own relations to the social world into the minds of the people they observe.[19]

As a way of studying social action by means of interpretive approaches,[20] constructivism can be a better way of theorizing states' action, precisely because it concerns the issue of human (or actors') consciousness capable of reflecting or learning in the web of social relations. This emphasis on the human capacity as a social being better positions constructivism to interpret the meaning and significance that actors ascribe to the situation in which they find themselves. In this way, constructivism offers analytical means for studying the historically and socially contingent content of the national interest as identified and pursued by actors in social relations.

Because constructivism studies the social processes that influence the formation of interests, this makes constructivism neither materialistic (or rationalistic) nor idealistic.[21] In a constructivist world, actors are rational, in the sense that they have goals and make choices accordingly. These goals reflect actors' needs and wishes in light of their social and material circumstances. They order preferences, which requires them to compare the possible outcomes of choices. The question then to be posed to constructivists who are not willing to treat actors' interests as exogenously given is, How can an actor reason about what to want in the first place? More specifically with respect to international relations, "How do states reason about what to want?" After all, Adam Smith himself, the champion of the claim that "self-interest dominates the majority of men," discussed extensively the prevalence and important social role of such values as sympathy, generosity, public-spiritedness, and other affiliated concerns: "We do not need to invoke 'benevolence' to explain why the *butcher*, the *brewer*, or the *baker* wants to sell their products, and why the *consumers* want to buy them."[22]

In what follows, I explore alternative explanations to the identity-intention analytical framework in order to establish the usefulness (or marginal utility) of efforts to study the formation of national interest. In other words, this is an exercise to determine if policies can be understood primarily on the basis of plausibly inferred interests of key actors without recourse to a sophisticated analysis of the formation of identity-informed national interest. To that end, I employ a number of alternative hypotheses that have prominently been used to explain Japanese foreign economic policy: interest group, state-centered, and systemic approaches, all of which place little emphasis on the role of identity in the formation of interests. I test each hypothesis by asking the two specific questions central to this book: What made it possible for Japan to challenge neoliberalism?[23] and Why did Japan propose to create the AMF while intentionally excluding the United States from membership? I deductively draw empirical expectations from each theoretical approach and match them to empirical findings with regard to the questions under investigation. To further scrutinize these alternative explanations, I also examine the possibility that rationalist treatments of the influence of ideas on policy choice can account for these research questions.[24] I conclude this chapter by rationalizing the necessity of the holistic analytical approach (incorporating both constitutive and causal analyses) for a fuller understanding of the nature, emergence, and policy development of the Japanese challenge.

INTEREST GROUP APPROACH

The interest group approach focuses on the influence of societal actors (vis-à-vis the state) in economic and political development. It attributes adoption of economic policies to the pressures of powerful economic interests, usually the industrial class or big business.[25] It points out that policy choices are the result of competition among groups or individuals for political and economic benefits. In this theoretical framework, the state per se does not determine a policy choice but tends rather to play the role of a referee.[26] In other words, this approach views policy as either reflecting the preferences of the dominant group or class in society or resulting from the struggle for influence that takes place among various interest groups or political parties. A state, therefore, does not have much autonomy from societal pressures. In either case, the approach explains foreign economic policy as a function of domestic politics and renders the system-society nexus flexible, less deterministic, and more situational,[27] though it does not discount the importance of systemic factors under certain circumstances.[28] As such, national interests themselves are internally determined and deducible from the preferences of societal actors within the domestic political economy.[29]

When it comes to Japan's foreign economic policy making, this economic interest group approach shows a strong tendency to emphasize the shift in the balance of power between the state bureaucracy and big business in Japan.[30] The main claim is that the internationalization of Japanese industry and finance sharply enhanced the influence of the private sector vis-à-vis the bureaucracy and politicians (the transition or regime shift argument). Pempel in particular argues that "the centripetal politics of Japan Inc. had been superceded by a centrifugal politics of numerous pockets of pluralist power."[31] Even in the sphere of financial policy,[32] widely considered the most powerful tool the Japanese state used to influence industrial outcomes, it has been argued that private sector strategic interests are at the center of policy outcome. The Japanese state merely constitutes one of several forces shaping Japan's policy, and not even a major one.[33]

Within this framework, the Japanese challenge to neoliberalism, with its emphasis on the role of the state in economic development, can be portrayed as the ideology and project of the Japanese internationalized industrial classes (or big business) and of their technocratic allies in the state. It clearly seems to be in the interests of Japanese internationalized big business to support an active role for the state in the economic development of developing countries. State-led economic development proposes prioritizing industrialization by offering incentives and subsidies for industrial development and improving financial and exchange policies to facilitate industrial growth. It explicitly and implicitly presupposes a considerable degree of state autonomy (strong state) vis-à-vis society for successful implementation and consolidation of industrial policies.[34] From the point of view of successfully internationalized Japanese big business, interventionist policies in developing countries can potentially help them secure and consolidate profits and influence in those interventionist countries more easily than otherwise. For example, Japanese big business, in collaboration with the Japanese government, influences and enables a certain interventionist developing country to give special support to it (or the host country's joint venture partner of it) directly through targeted loans and protection. In this way, Japanese business elites could vertically integrate, say, Asia into their production network by supporting interventionist policies in East Asian and Southeast Asian developing countries.[35] Thus, for the economic interest group explanation to be convincing, one needs to show a pattern of industrialist (big business) support for, and championing of, state-led economic development in developing countries, and a pattern of alliances between state technocrats and industrialists that facilitated the developing countries' adoption of state-led economic development.

The results of my research on the Japanese challenge to neoliberalism and its policy toward the AMF proposal increasingly call into question the validity of the economic interest group approach. Particularly problematic for this interpretation was that most Japanese big businesses failed to facilitate, or did not even support, promoting the Japanese alternative to neoliberalism. For example, in the mid-1980s Japan began to seriously consider and promote an alternative to neoliberalism. At the same time, early revisionist writings[36] (about Japanese political economy) appeared, suggesting that Japan should be recognized as having deviated significantly from neoclassical free market principles; MOF officials and intellectuals, often faced with an uncooperative business elite as well as such other ministries as the Ministry of International Trade and Industry (then the MITI; now the Ministry of Economy, Trade, and Industry or METI) and the MOFA, began to promote state-led developmental ideas. Whether out of fear that the revisionist Japanese practice (that is, the Japanese challenge to neoliberalism with a state-led mercantilist element) would backfire on them in the world economy or from a genuinely different understanding of the Japanese political economy, Japanese industrial elites, in cooperation with the MITI and the MOFA, often tried hard to prove that the Japanese economy was squarely within the neoclassical framework; Japan simply operated the neoliberal model more efficiently.[37] One of the leading economists in Japan commented on the revisionist argument: "Although their analysis is correct in some respect, overall the revisionists' viewpoint lacks balance and is inappropriate, and the object of their policy is not constructive."[38] In the early 1990s, both Sony Chairman Akio Morita and Gaishi Hiraiwa, the powerful head of Japan's big business alliance (*Keidanren*),[39] endorsed free trade and urged abandonment of mercantilism, which they thought was an obstacle to efficient market operation in Japan and elsewhere. In other words, the Japanese model of economic development is the source to be discarded, not promoted for emulation.

Furthermore, the Japanese financial and manufacturing sectors that heavily invested in the crisis-laden Asian region expressed strong reservations about the MOF's AMF proposal. Despite many Japanese banks' high exposure to the Asian economies in trouble, they supported a solution through the IMF. They argued against the AMF because "such a fund as the financial last resort creates a psychology of dependence."[40] Moreover, businessmen from the manufacturing and exporting sectors who opposed the AMF claimed that it would be dangerous to provide easy money, in the name of an Asian rescue, that could undermine the reforms and adjustments that the stringent (market-based) conditionality of the IMF usually required.[41] Additionally, they recognized that such action (creating an AMF that would allow the affected countries to have more maneuverability with the IMF) might result in the loss of golden opportunities for further liberalization of the Asian markets.[42]

Taken together, empirical evidence shows that Japanese business elites were either indifferent to or occasionally involved in moves to undermine the MOF's attempts to promote a Japanese economic development alternative, and by no means can it be claimed that they pressured the Japanese government to propose the AMF for the sake of their own profit. There is no evidence of formation of an alliance between industrial and financial elites and state bureaucrats that could help explain the Japanese challenge to neoliberalism. As such, it is hard to argue that societal preferences are aggregated into state preferences for the Japanese challenge to neoliberalism in general, and Japan's AMF proposal in particular.

State-Centered Approach

The state-centered approach postulates a state as an autonomous political actor that is relatively independent from societal pressures in determining policy outcomes[43]: "The state is at least relatively autonomous and an active participant in the policy-making or supply process. The government, therefore, does not simply respond to societal demands (and international pressure). Rather, the state possesses interests and makes choices that are central to understanding policy."[44] In other words, it is the state that mobilizes societal actors (including business elites) to achieve its goals, rather than the other way around. In this approach, the state is, with its own mind and will, associated with instrumental institutions capable of influencing and structuring society, rather than with a system that is subjected to that apparatus.[45] The state is capable of setting the agenda of policy making and subsequently mobilizing required social resources to achieve its policy goal in the context of domestic and international structures and constraints. To control policy outcomes, the state can use both offensive and defensive strategies that create new rules of the game, mitigate damage, and adapt to or avoid changes altogether.[46] It is the state, through public policies (domestic and foreign), that shapes societal preferences, which are frequently uncoordinated among the societal actors. To the extent that societal actors shape the choices of government policy, the parochial nature of their interests could not determine the state's overall policy, even in a specific sector.[47] In a nutshell, the state is the purposive entity that can envision and implement policies contributing to an overall increase of national wealth and power. It has the ability to use its military and economic resources to overcome resistance by the interests and actions of other actors (including other states and societal interest groups).[48]

When applied to the making of foreign economic policy, this state-centered approach generates an analytical distinction between strong and weak states in the tradition of comparative foreign policy.[49] Depending on the degree of state autonomy from societal pressures in the process of defining and materializing its prescribed goals, some states such as France and Japan are considered strong while others, such as the United States, are seen as weak.[50]

The usefulness of the distinction between strong and weak states, however, has been questioned for a number of reasons. First, a state's ability to impose its own interest on policy outcomes is constant neither over time nor across issues areas.[51] Second, such a distinction may confuse state capacity (which is about state flexibility in controlling policy outcomes and extracting social resources for its policy goals) with state strength (which is measured by the degree of state intervention in society). The ability to impose a market, for example, can be as powerful an indicator of state capacity as the ability to intervene in the economy.[52] Lastly, a state can be strong vertically while weak laterally. A state may be insulated from sectoral pressures (strong state vis-à-vis society) but nevertheless, as in the case of U.S.-Japanese negotiations on Japan's market liberalization, produce a policy outcome that is no different from the outcomes of a weak state.[53]

Despite the weaknesses of the strong-weak state distinction as an analytical tool, the idea that Japan is a strong state has been widely endorsed. The state-centered approach to Japanese foreign policy making was often associated with the elitist model of the "iron triangle." The elitist model depicts a Japanese state in which decision-making power is concentrated in the hands of the bureaucracy, the ruling Liberal Democratic Party (LDP), and big business, which constitute the iron triangle as a whole, although power is not evenly distributed among them. This definition of the Japanese state privileges the bureaucracy, which presides at the top of the power triangle supported by the two other powerful actors, the LDP and big business. As such, the bureaucracy controls and determines national policy, with the LDP and big business playing secondary roles.

At the same time, this model posits the Japanese state as "a unitary, interest-maximizing, rational actor."[54] The Japanese state is thought to relentlessly pursue economic growth, supported by a consensus among those three actors in an iron triangle (as a merchant or trading state).[55] The Japanese state makes economic policies and imposes them on society. In this context, Chalmers Johnson's contention that Japan was a "developmental state" led by the MITI gained great influence in the study of Japan's policy making.[56] It is the highly trained state bureaucrats who plan and direct the Japanese foreign economic policy, the sole purpose of which is "unflinching pursuit of economic gain (of Japan as a whole)" through strategic participation in the world economy. In short, Japan's model of action is the epitome of what Schmiegelow calls "strategic pragmatism," in which Japanese public and private leaders (usually big business leaders as a junior partner) unite in one direction, which is called "strategic," and they derive that direction from the nature of the changing problems (affecting the distribution of the economic and technological resources of Japan) to be solved, called "pragmatism."[57]

For this state-centered explanation to convincingly address the question of why Japan challenged neoliberalism (and Japan's subsequent policy toward the AMF), one needs first to show a pattern of strategic consensus among the bureaucracy, the LDP, and big business (led by the bureaucracy) in their joint efforts at propagating and justifying its development alternative to positively affect the distribution of economic and technological resources of Japan as a whole. Second, the emphasis in this approach on the strategic nature of Japanese foreign policy, derived from a narrowly drawn materialist conception of interests, leads one to expect to see an uneven geographical distribution of Japanese efforts to implement (not just verbally challenge) policies that encourage adoption of its state-led alternative in developing countries. Japan would be far less concerned about spreading its alternative to Africa, where its economic interests are least salient.[58] Third, and more specifically, one needs to show a pattern of Japan's tangible and immediate economic gains from influencing the institutionalization of policies and prescriptions of such a Japan-dependent development institution as the ADB. Institutionalization of Japanese alternative development ideas at the bank would be the best justified means by which a mercantilistic-cum-strategic Japan expresses its material interests.

The empirical results do not support a state-centered approach that associates Japanese foreign economic policy with relentless pursuit of global market shares and natural resources (the so-called economic animal). First, when Japan challenged neoliberalism, there was no clear pattern of strategic consensus among the state bureaucracy, the LDP, and big business. A state-led economic development alternative was promoted mainly by MOF (international bureau) officials and intellectuals.[59] In contrast, the MITI, whose main institutional focus is to represent Japanese business interests by bringing economic benefits to Japanese firms, even opposed self-promotion of the Japanese model on the grounds that it would further increase friction between Japan and the United States. For example, Makoto Kuroda, the MITI's best known hardline negotiator to the United States, commented on the Japanese challenge to neoliberalism: "We must not provide a dangerous basis for the argument that says Japan conducts itself by a different set of rules and must be treated differently. . . . For some time I have repeatedly stated that we should avoid expressions such as 'Japanese-style practices.'"[60] As was discussed earlier, internationally competitive Japanese big business was either indifferent to or opposed the possible protective walls that the Japanese development alternative would establish inside and outside Japan. It was thus clear that the Japanese challenge to neoliberalism (orchestrated by the MOF and intellectuals) often faced uncooperative business and intragovernmental elites, not to mention a pattern of strategic consensus among elites in the iron triangle.

As for the AMF proposal, the MOF faced a continuum of support and opposition within the Japanese government.[61] The MOFA responded negatively to the proposal, paying careful attention to the negative reaction from the United States, while the MITI remained neutral.[62] There was some support from political leadership, evident in Prime Minister Ryūtarō Hashimoto's call for a more vigorous Japanese foreign policy toward Asia.[63] However, this alliance alone does not explain why Japan intentionally excluded the United States from the AMF.[64]

Nor does an explanation connected to Japanese domestic politics capture Japan's AMF decision, which claims that the AMF emerged out of the conflict between the MOF and politicians. In this view, the MOF's idea of establishing the AMF is closely tied with domestic political disputes over administrative reform.[65] The debate concerning separation of budget and finance was a contentious one. A large number of politicians, concerned about the size and power of the too-big and too-powerful MOF, were demanding that matters under its jurisdiction be divided. Specifically, they suggested that jurisdiction over financial matters should be transferred to the newly established independent agency, an eventuality that greatly concerned the MOF. Thus creation of the AMF as a means to deal with the Asian financial crisis presented a golden opportunity to the MOF to justify its sole jurisdiction over both budget and finance. Nonetheless, this domestic dispute gives no explanation for the exclusion of the United States. More important, this exclusion was decided even after the United States pressured Japan to abandon the AMF proposal.[66]

Second, there is no indication for the uneven geographical distribution of the application of Japan's challenge. For example, on the basis of interviews in Japan's aid agencies and analysis of a dataset on Official Development Assistance (ODA) to African countries from 1959 to 1994 (using a series of multiple regressions), Stein argues that although Japanese economic interest, as represented by investment in Africa, has been far less clear in its relationship to the overall pattern of Japanese bilateral aid to Africa, imposition of neoliberal structural adjustment packages on African countries has had a significant impact in shifting Japan's bilateral aid pattern to Africa.[67] Particularly after 1986, Japan began to openly criticize the adjustment package and refocus its bilateral aid on infrastructure and production assistance, which was closely linked to Japan's commitment to a state-led economic development alternative.[68] Therefore, no clear correlation can be found between the size of Japanese economic interest and the geographical distribution of the Japanese challenge to neoliberalism.

Third, the empirical results do not show a pattern of tangible and immediate economic gains for Japan from influencing the institutionalization of the policies and prescriptions of the ADB.[69] Japan has made significant efforts to keep U.S.-led neoliberalism from penetrating the policies and prescriptions of the ADB while further promoting its development alternative at the bank.[70] At the same time, Japan has been providing more while gaining less in the ADB. In other words, as Japan has become more powerful in the ADB (by contributing more money to the institution), it becomes less concerned about its tangible and immediate economic gains from the bank.[71]

In sum, even though there is much that is convincing about the state-centered approach for Japanese foreign economic policy making in the context of a historically developed particular state-society relationship in Japan, this approach suffers from some of the same problems that International Relations rational choice theories do, namely, assumption of the state as a unitary actor[72] and a universalistic notion of interest. Rational choice theories focus on individual policy makers (the equivalent of the state as a unitary actor in International Relations), arguing that policy makers (states) are rational and would choose policies that maximize their *goals*. Rational choice theorists are, however, silent on how actors themselves construe and define their goals, a priori assuming that interests are universal in the function of a materially determined utility.

To be fair, proponents of the state-centered approach claim that it neither takes the state as the most important actor nor assumes that the state always acts as a rational, unified entity.[73] Nonetheless, regardless of whether they take an institutional approach or analyze the power of politicians and civil servants in influencing foreign economic policy, their empirical analyses presume a priori that the state (or state officials) is readily equipped with a particular set of "objective" national interests, often tied to national security and welfare maximization (however they define them). As such, their analyses illuminating the causal importance of the state as an actor in formulating and implementing foreign economic policy end up focusing on institutional stickiness or the state's capacity to impose its pregiven interests on society in policy-making processes by manipulating the domestic political environment, mobilizing domestic and international coalitions, and effectively defining certain issues in national security terms.[74] It is one thing to argue that the interests and capabilities of groups and individuals are mediated by the state institutional structures within which they operate. It is another to analytically specify how, say, state officials come to define national interests as such in the first place. Without this analytical effort, the state-centered approach is limited and indeterminate in explicating the nature and content of interest that actors hold in concrete historical contexts. For example, how and why did the MOF (state actor) define Japan's national interest in terms of creating the AMF when most of the Japanese financial and industrial sectors that were themselves highly exposed to the troubled Asian economies[75] support a solution through the IMF? Surely, this might be the case for imposition of the state actor's interest on societal actors. But it invites a question in a circular fashion: On the basis of what interest did the MOF do it?

Systemic Approach

Reflective of the dominance of the two neosystemic rational choice theories in International Relations, the systemic approach has attracted most attention from experts on Japanese foreign policy making. This approach, compared to the other two, most forcefully takes the state as a unitary actor and expresses foreign policy making in terms of the rational "action and reaction" of the state in its interaction with a fixed strategic environment characterized by "anarchy." Following these lines of thought, the two conceptions of Japan—namely as a "reactive state" (a variant of neorealism) and a "supporter state" (a variant of neoliberalism)—have played a predominant role in characterizing Japan's postwar foreign policy at the systemic level.[76] More recently, deriving from the economic statecraft literature, Japan as a "normal proactive" state has increasingly become a significant part of the systemic-level understanding of Japanese foreign economic policy.

First, with respect to the notion of Japan as a reactive state,[77] although this approach does not ignore domestic factors,[78] it adopts the core tenet of Waltz's version of systemic theory, neorealism. According to neorealism, the international system is anarchic without an overarching government. This generates an action-reaction world of states attempting to maximize their own power at the expense of others. Waltz asserts that each state arrives at policies and decides on actions according to its own internal processes, but its decisions are shaped by the very presence of other states as well as by interactions with them.[79] Most important, therefore, is distribution of power in the international system as a whole, and the place of a given state in that distribution.[80]

One significant implication of this position is that there are two types of states in this world: laterally strong and weak states, as determined by the distribution of power in the anarchic international system. A weak state's foreign policy tends to conform to the preferences of a strong state.[81] There is a causal relationship between power and compliant or subservient behavior.[82] Therefore, given Japan's asymmetric market and security interdependence on the United States, Japan is a weak state while the United States is a strong state powerfully influencing Japan's foreign policy. As the neorealist version of the "coercive" hegemonic hypothesis[83] maintains, for the less powerful state there is no choice but to acquiesce, out of fear of punishment (for example, the United States closes its markets to Japanese exports if Japan does not respond) to the demands of the hegemonic power. In the end, Japan becomes a reactive state vis-à-vis the hegemon or patron, the United States.

The notion of Japan as a "supporter" state derives directly from the theories of interdependence or transnational relations. They suggest that growing economic interdependence, defined as "situations characterized by reciprocal effects among countries or among actors in different countries," has a deep impact on economic policy making.[84] Proponents of Japan as a supporter state therefore claim that "Japan engages in 'the politics of interdependence,' which means that actors make strategic use of interdependence with enough self-restraint not to jeopardize the system of interdependence itself."[85] Faced with a barrage of pressures from the United States and other industrial countries, Japan accommodates the needs of other governments to the extent that the accommodation serves Japan's national interests.[86] Japan supports, rather than challenges, the postwar U.S.-led international system (including regimes) because it is advantageous to Japan.

The third approach, which presents Japan as a "normal proactive" state, claims, in an attempt to explain Japan's past reactivism and increasing proactivism, that Japan used to be reactive under the shadow of the United States, but that it is now taking more active foreign policy initiatives. On the basis of the economic statecraft literature that stresses the evolutionary positive correlation between power and plenty and the proactivity of a state's foreign economic policy,[87] proponents of this view argue that Japan has pursued independent, active policies since the 1970s, spurred by various factors, including the U.S. defeat in the Vietnam War, Japan's impressive economic development, and the declining economic power of the United States.[88] Japanese foreign economic policy has followed a progressive transition from reactive to proactive.

How, then, would these systemic explanations help one to understand the Japanese challenge to neoliberalism? The reactive model, based on Calder's characterization of Japan as "more deferential to American pressure than have [been] most middle-range powers such as major European countries,"[89] is most limited in explaining the Japanese challenge, one of the most proactive foreign economic policies in postwar Japan. On the contrary, this book asks why, despite the fact that all modern developed states in this century undertook state-led economic development at least in the beginning of their industrialization, Japan has been the only developed state to seriously challenge neoliberalism on the basis of different ideas about economic development. The reactive model asks about the peculiar reactive nature of Japanese foreign economic policy; this book asks about the strong proactivity of Japan.

In contrast to the reactive state model, both the supporter and the normal proactive model open the possibility for the Japanese challenge. First, the supporter model essentially argues that Japan supports, rather than challenges, the U.S.-led international system because it is beneficial to Japan. Therefore, Japan could decide to challenge the U.S.-led international system (or international regime) if the system worked against Japanese national interest. For this model to convincingly address the question of the Japanese challenge, one has to show a pattern of Japanese economic loss under the U.S.-led world market economy when Japan started to challenge neoliberalism.

The empirical evidence does not support the implication. Japan's economic power in the world market has significantly and incessantly increased throughout the 1980s. For example, with output equivalent to only one-twentieth of the U.S. Gross National Product in 1945, and surpassing its prewar level of industrial production only as recently as 1959, Japan's wealth was equal to one-half of the U.S. GNP by the 1980s.[90] The marvel of Japan's economic power could also be signified by its extensive capital exports to the United States (which effectively financed half of the U.S. government's annual budget deficit), its global position as the largest aid donor (since 1989), and the fact that the top ten international banks and the largest stock exchange were Japanese by the end of the 1980s. In short, no evidence whatsoever indicates Japanese economic loss under the U.S.-led international system, and as the most internationally competitive nation-state Japan was still arguably the largest beneficiary of the liberal world market when it began to challenge neoliberalism.

As for the AMF proposal, the supporter model is not very helpful in explaining Japan's change of posture from "cooperation" to "conflict" with the

U.S.-led IMF bailout operation in Thailand. There is no apparent evidence of a shift in distribution of Japanese material incentives that would support a policy change (cooperation to conflict). Given the high exposure of the Japanese financial and manufacturing sectors in the troubled economies, it clearly seemed to be in the interests of the Japanese government to set up such a fund to help them. However, by the time Japan proposed the AMF the so-called Asian financial crisis, which later engulfed almost the entire region (by the contagion effect), remained an unlikely possibility. As discussed in greater detail in Chapter 6, the MOF's focus was thus rather on having a regional monetary fund able to respond to the Thai crisis quickly without much concern about saving Japan's investment. The greater concern was that undue intervention of the IMF-led universal approach (under U.S. influence) could exacerbate the situation. For example, in September 1997, Japan offered Thailand a soft-loan package of $900 million. It was the second largest amount in the history of yen loans to Thailand. In contrast to the IMF loans, the Japanese offer did not come with any reformist strings attached, and it made the Thai government fully responsible for using the funds.[91]

When it comes to the evolutionary normal proactive model, the model seems to best fit the Japanese challenge, given its focus on growing Japanese proactivism while at the same time recognizing the existence of reactivism in Japanese foreign economic policy. Attributing the shifting pattern of Japanese reactivism-proactivism to bilateral relations (or bilateral power configurations) with the United States, this model can explain the Japanese challenge that came in *only* in the mid to late 1980s, despite the early success of state-led economic development. The Japanese challenge to neoliberalism, by criticizing the structural adjustment model, was nothing more than a by-product of the increasingly acrimonious negotiations between the United States and Japan over the trade deficit.[92] Growing weary of U.S. accusations concerning Japanese practices, Japan, for example, issued a white paper openly criticizing American commercial policies. Subsequently, among other things Japan refused to commit itself any longer to import targets in semiconductors and automobiles,[93] arguing that Japan "has rolled back formal tariff barriers and quotas farther than any other countries, including the U.S."[94]

Why, then, did the Japanese challenge not emerge until the mid-1980s, especially considering that tension between Japan and the United States over trade practices (including nontariff barriers in the Japanese market) was a source of official concern since at least the 1970s? As this model positions

Japanese reactivism-proactivism with regard to bilateral power relations with the United States, it can explain the emergence of the Japanese challenge in the context of the decline of U.S. hegemony and the rise of Japan. By pointing out the shortcomings of market-based neoliberal economic policies, Japan aimed in the short run to get more bargaining power in trade negotiations with the United States and in the long run to preserve existing economic practices (such as tariff and nontariff barriers) currently found in Japan. In short, the Japanese challenge was nothing but an indirect yet strategic way of materializing Japanese economic interests.

For this model to convincingly address the question of the Japanese challenge along with this line, one has to show that the most critical proponents of the state-led Japanese alternative must have been those who insisted on leaving mercantile Japan intact, because they believed that a mercantile regime featuring power concentration and bureaucratic intervention for unflinching pursuit of relative gains in the world market always had worked and always would work marvelously for Japan. Any serious changes in the Japanese mercantile regime would hurt Japanese national interests.

Again, empirical results do not confirm this implication. The bureaucrats and intellectuals who argued most enthusiastically for a state-led alternative as a more useful way of undertaking rapid economic development for developing countries were those who most critically evaluated the current practice of the Japanese politico-economic regime (featuring power concentration–iron triangle–bureaucratic intervention). They proposed the dissolution of that regime, which had worked so well during the periods of rapid economic development (the "high growth era" from 1953 to 1973). What proponents of the state-led alternative basically claimed was that it could not be an *ideal* economic practice that all societies should ultimately realize. Rather, it was a *transitional* political economic practice (or system) for the purpose of rapid economic development.[95] Therefore, once the purpose (rapid economic development) was achieved, the system should be dismantled—just like "the booster rockets that must be detached at a certain altitude in a Space Shuttle launch."[96] According to this argument, Japan should have dissolved the state-led politico-economic regime and instituted a freer and more open system a long time ago. Measured by per capita income, Japan had already caught up with the Western industrial economies by the early 1970s. These bureaucrats and intellectuals considered the current hardships of Japanese economy to be derived from "institutional fatigue" resulting from Japan's failure to dismantle the once wildly successful developmental regime. To ensure further economic development, they argue, Japan should initiate bold reforms toward a freer and more open system.[97] After all, Sakakibara, who spearheaded the AMF proposal, was the one who substantially liberalized the Japanese financial market in the 1980s against the insular view favored by Japan's financial elites.[98] The argument that the Japanese challenge was a "hook" by which proponents of the state-led alternative expressed their material interests is therefore not empirically defensible.

In sum, each model at the systemic level can help one understand the peculiar nature of Japanese foreign economic policy in relations with the United States. In particular, the third model, of a proactive normal state, is useful in that much of Japanese foreign economic policy since the rise of Japan involves making policy postures to further and more aggressively express what Japan wants independently of the United States. Yet the proactive model cannot furnish a satisfactory explanation of the decision to challenge neoliberalism, because it is, like the rational state-centered approach just discussed, unable to deal with the question of the state's preferences. If international politics is all about survival, and the logic of survival in turn reproduces "like units" with preferences largely fixed by the material capability the units can dispose of in the anarchic international system, why have major European countries such as France and Germany been more receptive or deferential to the spread of U.S.-led neoliberalism than Japan, despite their original contribution to state-led economic development and similar international position as middle-range powers? Systemic theories alone are not adequate in explaining variation in preferences across units.[99] Wendt, for example, identifies four categories of national interest even at the systemic level: "physical survival," "autonomy," "economic well-being," and finally "collective self-esteem."[100] Which of these is more salient in Japan than the others, and under what conditions? More important, what structures preferences? Many types of policy activity can plausibly be construed as preferences structured by the desire to survive in an anarchic world. But how does one explain why one survival strategy is adopted instead of another? In the case of the Japanese challenge, how does one explain why Japan chose policies that appeared to be irrational, in the sense that they exacerbated the bilateral relationship with the United States with no immediate material gains? The Japanese challenge was much more than what was required for survival.

So far, this chapter has explored several alternative explanations, not to dismiss them but rather to point out some of their limitations in trying to answer the two specific questions posed in this book: What made it possible for Japan to challenge neoliberalism, and why did Japan propose to create the AMF while intentionally excluding the United States from membership? Each alterative explanation, which has frequently been used to explain the process of foreign economic policy making in Japan, explains policy outcomes on the basis of plausibly inferred interests of the relevant key actors without questioning the basis on which the key actors themselves defined their interests. As a result, they do little to determine, within a set of equally plausible strategies for furthering the interests of the relevant key actors, why one policy is chosen instead of others, let alone specifying the content of interests themselves.[101]

RATIONALISM AND IDEAS

Can then some ideational-based (or less materialistic) rational actor framework, which attempts to examine a causal connection between ideas and interests without sacrificing rationalist assumptions of how actors behave in uncertain conditions, help us illuminate a mechanism through which an actor's preference is structured? I now briefly describe rationalist accounts of the role of ideas. After briefly addressing the bias and shortcomings of these accounts, I rationalize the necessity of approaching the Japanese challenge from a deep historical perspective to understand its nature and evolution in a fuller way.

In rationalist explanations of ideas, Goldstein and Keohane present a framework for analyzing the impact of ideas on policy outcomes. They argue that ideas are assumed to influence behavior through one of three causal pathways.[102] First, ideas may serve as *road maps*. Out of the universe of possible actions, decision makers select those that best fit their normative and analytic understandings. Principled beliefs help define actors' goals; causal beliefs strongly influence the choice of means to achieve these ends.[103] Different choices under apparently similar circumstances can thus be explained by varying ideas or belief systems of actors. Second, widely shared ideas may facilitate cooperation in the absence of a unique equilibrium, serving as *focal points* that help define acceptable solutions to problems of collective action.[104] Third, the impact of ideas is often mediated and enhanced by *institutional* rules and norms that are created under the influence of widely shared beliefs. Once ideas have become embodied in institutional frameworks, they constrain public policy so long as they are not undermined by new scientific discoveries or normative changes.[105]

What then are the problems with these three causal pathways, through which ideas may influence policy outcomes? There are two important shortcomings, biased by their material precepts. First, as in the case of the alternative explanations discussed earlier, these causal pathways, fully positioned in a policy-making and problem-solving mode, fail to deal with the question of preference formation. By saying little about the impact of ideas on state identities and corresponding interests, Goldstein and Keohane tend to reduce the role of ideas strictly to that of a tool used in a process of elimination or selection to better execute the already given interests.[106] The utility of ideas rests on resolving particular policy problems. For example, the fate of institutionalized ideas (the third category) depends very much on the sunk costs embedded in institutions. As Ruggie aptly puts it, "The heavy lifting in the Goldstein-Keohane scheme ends up being done by principled and causal beliefs functioning as focal points in multiple equilibria situations."[107] The ideational frameworks offered by Goldstein and Keohane can therefore tell much about how actors with plausibly inferred interests go about their business with ideas, but not about how multiple equilibria are defined as such by actors. By arguing that interests are defined on the basis of a set of preferences shaped by ideas that best embody interests, Goldstein and Keohane's interest-based ideas framework tends to generate a circular reasoning.[108] The question of what structures actors' preferences still remains to be answered.

Second, the utilitarian framework viewing ideas merely as a means to better effect a given interest undermines the impact of human subjectivity on agentic behavior. As discussed in Chapter 3, what matters is not so much the objective conditions as how actors understand them. Between objective conditions and human volitions lies interpretation.[109] Before choices can be made, circumstances must be assessed and interests identified. Interpretation that shapes the perception of reality and informs actors about the meaning and significance attached to the particular situation in which they find themselves is in turn largely a function of the self-conception or identity that actors hold at a given time and place (constituted by cognitive as well as material structures). Silence on the role of ideas in constituting actors' identities therefore contributes to presenting a political world in which actors are treated as *objects* rather than *subjects*. The silence denies negotiated and redefined intersubjective frameworks of meaning anchored in social action. Except in circumstances that require little interpretation on the part of the relevant key actors—because the environment is placid, because shared knowledge prevails, or because coercion determines outcomes—political actors make a choice as much from the meanings they attach to it as from bare facts that materialism attributes to interest. Simply put, physical objects or variables cannot *will* things to happen; within limits (international and domestic constraints and opportunities), human agency can.[110] Interpretive frameworks enable one to trace the process of how certain meanings emerge around policies, ideas, and identities. To the question of what made it possible for Japan to challenge neoliberalism, for example, the emergence of such successful Asian state-led developing economies as the Newly Industrialized Economies (NIEs) in the 1980s empowered the proponents of a state-led alternative within Japan to augment their normalcy claim (attached to state-led economic development) for international validity. The rise of Asian economies critically contributed to materializing the Japanese challenge. The impact of ideas on policy outcomes is not limited to instrumental dimensions. It includes a constitutive function that shapes the subjectivities of actors and creates the very possibility for them to define and develop their new interests and ideals.[111]

In sum, the limitations of the rational account of the role ideas play on actors' behavior result in leaving the fundamental assumption of interests unquestioned and unchanged. Regarding understanding of the interrelationship of ideas and interests, most research in this vein in fact follows the rationalist path of assuming material interests as given and employs ideas as "intervening variables" between interests and political behavior.[112] This position is exemplified in Peter Hall's assertion that new ideas enter a terrain already defined by a prevailing set of political ideas (which he refers to as the political discourse of a nation).[113] What makes new ideas persuasive is the way they relate to both political priorities at that time and a prevailing set of ideas in a given political system.[114]

This important observation necessitates developing an alternative strategy of foreign policy analysis. To achieve a fuller understanding of the nature, emergence, and policy development of particular foreign policies in a given issue area, both constitutive and causal analyses are called for. Using Peter Hall's words, constitutive analysis offers a way to uncover "a terrain or political discourse of nation" on which particular foreign policies rest. Causal analysis analytically equipped with explicating the formation of actors' interests critically addresses the question of why one policy is chosen over other policy options in a particular time and place, precisely because such a causal analysis works on the basis of the content and kinds of interest actors develop in a given situation. The next chapter offers an analytical framework that problematizes formation of actors' interests.

3 IDENTITY AND INTENTION FRAMEWORK

We might suppose that the "I" is the agent. However, this is surely mistaken. . . . The constitution of the "I" comes about only via the "discourse" of the Other . . . but the "I" has to be related to the body as the sphere of action. . . . The contextuality of social "positioning" determines who is an "I" in any situation of talk.[1]

IN THIS CHAPTER, I present the identity-intention analytical framework in order to illuminate how identity causally leads to social action in the name of national interests. I develop the framework by unpacking the constructivist claim that "identities are the basis of interests."[2] In so doing, I theoretically and conceptually chart a causal mechanism between an intersubjective identity conception and a foreign policy outcome. As is discussed in detail, this framework emphasizes the causal importance of the relationship between interpretation and a choice of action on the part of reflective actors. The crux of the framework is that identities provide the basis for interpretation of unfolding events, which in turn affects valuation of incentives by informing actors about necessary actions.

Some conceptual and analytical clarifications are called for. Conceptually, I use the term *national interest* with the understanding that it is constructed and projected by some human agents (or institutions) in charge of particular issue areas on behalf of a national entity, such as Japan. As such, specification of both actors and issue areas is important in understanding how a certain national interest is forged, developed, and later implemented. Thus I maintain the utility of employing the concept of national interest in studying international relations but oppose its "transcendental" and strictly "objectivist" usage in a priori fashion. Analytically, by *causation* I mean here a constructivist notion of social causation that takes *primary reasons* as causes (see Davidson's definition of primary reason later in this chapter). It is not meant to be a notion of causation that statistically establishes a cause-and-effect relation subsumed under covering laws.[3]

That said, I first discuss the framework in the context of the agent-structure problematique in International Relations, because it cannot be fully understood outside of its relation to this debate. Drawing on analytical philosophy, social cognition, and international relations literature, I then present the framework itself. To compare it effectively and explicitly with two other traditions of action schema—objective and subjective rationality—I use the logical scheme of each action framework comparatively and demonstrate their core differences in the formation of interests. Spelling out a logical scheme of the identity-intention framework that analytically links the interpretative function of identities to a choice of action also helps to make this framework explicitly testable. Lastly, I specify a clear path of analytical steps to demonstrate the framework's empirical validity. I have validity and reliability issues in mind for this part of the discussion.

CONSTRUCTIVISM AND ANARCHY

As I have just noted, one of the most common criticisms of rationalist approaches to social science is their exogenous treatment of interests, as though a researcher could assign them from the choices actors make. Critics of rationalist approaches thus claim that this treatment leads to backward induction from the choice to the interest, resulting in the "fallacy of imputed preference."[4] In International Relations, both neorealism and neoliberalism take on a homogenizing assumption that states have the same a priori interests, called self-interest. The assumption is rationally justified by pointing out the implications of anarchy in international relations. The structural condition of anarchy, here defined as "the absence of an overarching authority in world politics that imposes limits on the pursuit of sovereign interests," is so constraining that the logic of survival determines the behavior of actors. This ontological rendering of anarchy gives all units in international politics only one meaningful identity, that of self-interested state.[5] With respect to theorizing international relations, this leaves little room for agency. The implications of anarchy are constant across all relationships and issue areas of international politics, thus allowing only a particular set of interests or preferences with respect to choices of action before actors. In Axelrod and Keohane's words, anarchy "remains a constant."[6] Self-interest, which is thus a structurally determined behavior of actors, manifests itself in the form of self-help: "States are subject to no superior government. The resulting system is sometimes referred to as one of 'self-help.'"[7]

States, according to neorealism, are destined to strive for (and should be striving for) relative power and relative gain in order to guard their security and economic autonomy (or independence) whenever possible.[8] Likewise, neoliberalism also considers states to be self-regarding units in the pursuit of exogenously given economic incentives. They can be less concerned with self-help only when economic relations among them are mutually beneficial or satisfying.[9] Even in a reformulated version that is designed to deal with the formation or origin of states' preference, according to neoliberalism states are still locked in the configuration of exogenously given economic interests. In the reformulated version, the state is no longer a unitary actor. Individuals and firms are the key actors, but they are *assumed* to follow economic incentives. State preferences are simply the aggregation of societal preferences mediated by domestic institutions.[10] Given the fixed identities and interests of key actors, in reformulated neoliberalism a state merely enacts in the end stable preferences, like its predecessor under the condition of anarchy (though it should be mentioned that a proponent of this position has argued persuasively that the propositions one can derive from anarchy are almost entirely indeterminate[11]).

Taken together, the rationalist treatment of anarchy sees no disadvantage to treating the identity and interests of actors as exogenously given.[12] Anarchy keeps reproducing a fixed actor's identity as an egoistic utility maximizer, and a particular set of interests or preferences are assumed to go along with such. Problematizing the identities and interests of states as a way to better theorize their choice of action is not worthy of effort in a field called International Relations, in which "political action is most regularly necessitous."[13] Little is to be lost by analytically assuming the actors (for example, states) to be subordinate to anarchy without the "possibilities of doing otherwise."[14] Anarchy makes it permissible to conceptualize the "thin" actors or agents as solely pursuing material interests encapsulated in instrumental reasoning.[15] In Jackson's words, under the presumption of anarchy actors are "essential agents who lack the ability to make meaningful choices." Ironically, these essential agents "become mere throughputs for environmental factors, ending up as the very cultural and structural dupes that the turn to [rational] individualism was supposed to avoid."[16]

In contrast, the constructivist approach to international relations advanced in this book attempts to endogenize actors' interests by treating actors' identity as a variable. It empirically considers how the identities of specific states shape the conditions that make one particular conception of national interest prevail over others. It explores "what happens *before* the neo-utilitarian model purportedly kicks in."[17] Endogenization assumes the "thick" conception of actors with a rich psychological makeup and contextual sensitivities.[18]

This way of problematizing identities and interests of actors is premised not on the presumption of anarchy as having a single eternal constituting meaning for international relations, as described earlier. Alker, for example, objects to the use of anarchy in International Relations on two grounds. When anarchy is meant by a "confused," "disordered," "lawless," "unregulated" state of affairs, it is not historically correct. When anarchy is meant by a state of affairs "without rule, authority or government," its causal argument incorrectly denies the possibilities of order, law, and regulation inherent in pluricentric or polyarchic sociopolitical systems.[19] Onuf goes so far as to say that "international relations was never a matter of anarchy, any more than domestic society could have been."[20] Simply put, constructivism does not accept that the purely material implications of anarchy permeate all relationships and issue areas of international politics. Whether anarchy as such organizes international politics depends largely on dynamic intersubjective interpretations of the nature of repeated interactions among political actors in a given issue area.[21] A more nuanced approach posits a continuum of *anarchies*[22]: "Self-help and power politics do not follow either logically and causally from anarchy, and . . . if today we find ourselves in a self-help world, this is due to process, not structure."[23] Constructivists thus view the international structure as a *social* structure, made up of socially knowledgeable and discursively competent actors who are nevertheless subject to constraints that are in part material, in part ideational: "The manner in which the material world shapes and is shaped by human actions and interactions depends on dynamic normative and epistemic interpretations of the material world."[24] It means, in Popper's three-worlds vision of the universe of reality that affects individual human decision making and actions, that world two (the psychological and interpretive thought process, the decision-making level) is always mediated by world one (the physical world) and world three (the knowledge world invented by human agents) through reflective "feedback" processes.[25]

Constructivists' treatment of the international structure returns actors to the making of international relations.[26] Regardless of the level at which they sit, human actors cannot be compared with billiard balls in physics.[27] The actor is capable of being caused to act by the beliefs, desires, and other psychological states that give him or her *reason* to act. As Aristotle puts it, "The origin of action—its efficient, not its final cause—is choice, and that of choice is desire and reasoning with a view to an end."[28] In other words, the actor is an embodied unit and as such a possessor of causal powers that he or she may choose to employ to intervene (or not) in the ongoing sequence of events in the world.

> What is the nature of the logical connection between action and power? . . . To be able to "act otherwise" means being able to intervene in the world, or to refrain from such intervention, with the effect of influencing a specific process or state of affairs. This presumes that to be an agent means to be able to deploy [chronically, in the flow of daily life] a range of causal powers, including that of influencing those deployed by others. Action depends upon the capability of the individual to "make a difference" to a pre-existing state of affairs or course of events. An agent ceases to be such if he or she loses the capability to "make a difference," that is, to exercise some sort of power.[29]

However, human consciousness of the possibility of doing otherwise always stands in a mutually conditioning relationship with social structures, whose ontological status is endowed with possibilities of *becoming* otherwise (other than anarchy), but not of *being* (anarchy). Thus, in constructivism's account of structure and agency, states are conditioned by three factors: (1) they are expected to have a far wider array of potential choices of action before them than is assumed by realism; (2) these choices will be constrained by social structures that are mutually created by states and structures via social practices[30]; and (3) structural constraints always operate via actors' motives and reasons.[31] As such, what matters in understanding a choice of action in terms of initiating, mediating, and controlling events is to explore the socially conditioned mind that actors bring to bear on the circumstances they confront in their material and ideational environment.

Not taking anarchy for granted enables constructivism not just to permit a greater degree of agency. On the basis of the notion that any foreign policy is the outcome of an international process viewed as "a chain of temporally related and spatially interdependent intersections of decisions made by two or more actors in the global system, which pertain to a particular set of issues, over a relatively long period of time,"[32] constructivists' characterization of the international structure as social also opens up a space for the importance of the *relational* sensitivities of actors in interaction. States act differently toward enemies than they do toward friends because enemies are threatening and friends are not.[33] U.S. military power has different meanings for Canada and Cuba, despite their similar structural positions, just as British missiles have a different significance for the United States than do Chinese missiles. As much as agency is socially and relationally constructed, formation of the actors' interests is processual and relational.[34] As such, actors make a choice of action within a processual and sequential movement of relationships. Relationality is, as I discuss in detail, an analytic variable that *meaningfully* guides actors' choice of action.

Taken together, despite a variety (or variants) of constructivism,[35] common to all are two basic principles[36]:

1 What people do, publicly and privately, is intentional, that is, directed to something beyond itself, and normatively constrained, that is, subject to such assessment as correct or incorrect, proper or improper, and so on.
2 What people are, to themselves and to others, is a product of a lifetime of interpersonal interactions superimposed over a very general ethological endowment.

In other words, constructivism operates on the basis of the fundamental principle that "people act towards objects, including other actors, on the basis of meanings that the objects have for them."[37] Material facts themselves are indeterminate; norms, cultures, and identities give meaning to material facts so that actors can interpret and react to them.[38] With respect to choices of action in relation to formation of foreign policy interests, the state's choices are enabled and constrained by the webs of understanding of the practices, identities, and interests of other states that prevail in particular sociohistorical issue contexts. As Max Weber famously puts it, "Action is *social* insofar as its subjective meaning takes account of the behavior of *others* and is thereby oriented in its course."[39]

Given the interactive nature of foreign policy making, the key to addressing a particular foreign policy choice under constructivism is thus explication of the influence relational identities have on formation of interests. That is, identities are the basis of interests, which are endogenized rather than exogenously given. Interests are assumed to go along with identities. An actor "chooses from among available representations of the Self who one will be, and thus what interests one intends to pursue."[40] From an analytical point of view, the issue is to infer implied or associated interests from "available" identities (these are potentially the sites for domestic politics; alternative identities can compete for relevance) and then to see if they are in fact present at the moment of choice.[41] By extension, changes in identity result in corresponding changes in interest.

However, this conceptually parsimonious Wendtian mapping of the identity-interest nexus has been criticized as theoretically underdeveloped in addressing the causal mechanisms behind identities, interests (preference ordering), and conceptions about ends-means relationships.[42] Its empirical applications do not establish more than a correlative relationship between an identity and an outcome.[43] It thus does not establish a theoretical basis for understanding why one identity rather than another is chosen and becomes institutionalized.[44] Simply put, at the most basic level, is a foreign policy decision based on a chosen identity? Do state officials (or decision makers) talk about identities, if not interests (of any kind), at the moment of choice?[45] If not, is it not another type of "scholastic fallacy"? How does having an identity *causally* lead to action?

In what follows, I develop an identity-intention (or reason) analytical framework to address these questions. The framework offers an empirically testable causal mechanism though which identity shapes national interest. In developing the framework, I also establish a theoretical and conceptual microfoundation for such a mechanism by drawing on the empirical findings of social cognition literature. Empirically, the framework is designed to explore the intersubjective meanings (or the *socially conditioned* actors' mind) attached to a particular choice of action borne out of historically and relationally constructed identity relationships of actors in interaction, and the associated *contents* of their interaction experiences; interests are meaning-laden under the influence of identity conceptions.

Analytically, the framework marries a notion of social causation that takes *primary reasons as causes* to the constructivist insight that national interest emerges out of the representations (or out of situation descriptions and problem descriptions) through which state officials and others make sense of the world around them. Following Davidson, a primary reason can be defined:

> Rationalization is a primary reason why an agent performed the action *A* under the description *d* only if *R* [rationalization] consists of a pro attitude of the agent towards actions with a certain property, and a belief of the agent that *A*, under the description *d*, has that property.[46]

Along with developing the framework, I also discuss scope conditions for the framework to be precise on the analytical range the framework covers. Finally, I relate the framework to the agent-structure debate with a focus on how the framework puts together social structure and agency to produce social action. I illustrate this point with a concrete example from Japan's AMF decision.

THE IDENTITY-INTENTION FRAMEWORK

How does having an identity lead an actor to choose a particular action? If having an identity in fact affects an actor to take one course of action over another by helping to form the actor's preference, is the relationship between an identity and an action said to be causal? Incorporating important insights from social cognition literature, I develop the identity-intention analytical framework to illuminate how having an identity causally leads to an action in the name of national interest. By *causation* I mean here a constructivist notion of social causation that takes primary reasons[47] as causes. It is not meant to be the notion of causation that statistically establishes (or sanctions) a cause-and-effect relation subsumed under covering causal laws.[48] In addition, this framework assumes an actor reflectively communicating with his or her sociohistorical contexts when choosing an action.[49] By this I mean that actors "act in terms of their interpretation of, and intentions towards, their external conditions, rather than being governed by them."[50]

What follows from this is the causal importance of the relationship between interpretation and a choice of action on the part of reflective actors.[51] The crux of the identity-intention framework is that identities provide the basis for interpretation of unfolding events, which in turn affects valuation of incentives by informing actors as to which actions are "valuable, appropriate, and necessary."[52] Analytically, the framework is simple and straightforward. It is ingrained in a typical pattern of decision making: an actor observes an event (observation); the actor *interprets* the event normally in terms of who did what and why (interpretation); then, from this *interpretation*, the actor makes a decision as to how to respond (decision). The conception of identities works at the second level by helping the actor interpret the event in a certain way over others. In other words, in terms of the actor's interpretation of who did what and why, the question *who* (and the answer for it) guides interpretation of what, and eventually why. For the purpose of making the framework explicitly testable, I present a logical scheme that analytically links the interpretative function of identities to a choice of action. This scheme is also compared to two other action schemes, the reason-based intentional scheme and the rational action scheme, to elucidate its difference and its evolutionary intellectual root.

Identities, Situation Description, and Action

A theoretical account of identity argues that to the extent individuals' cognitions are socially constructed, the self and the other mutually need their identities to understand each other and act on such understandings.[53] Here identities, which are relational social constructs resulting from social interaction, work like categorizers that help people understand and predict their own and others' actions.[54] The basis of this theoretical account is the idea that because of the limited capacity of the human brain, a human being must rely on various cognitive economizing devices to be able to process the sheer volume of information received,[55] and that identities, as a cognitive economizing device, help make sense of external realities. This in turn informs people how to respond to them. In other words, identities offer "templates for interpretation that reduce the amount of cognitive processing an individual has to undergo in order to account for events" through selective processing of information.[56] Given multiple identities associated with the individual, "A particular identity becomes activated/salient as a function of the interaction between the characteristics of the perceiver (accessibility) and of the situation (fit)."[57]

The experimental psychology literature has demonstrated the role identities play in perceiving the external world. In Hopf's words, "an individual's identity acts like an axis of interpretation, implying that she will find in the external world what is relevant to that identity: What an individual understands himself to be, whether a man or a worker, helps determine what information he apprehends and how he uses it."[58] Identities, as a cognitive heuristic, conventionalize the objects, persons, and events one encounters in terms of the identity of the self by making them perceived in a mode that is resonant with already set patterns of comprehension, expectation, and perception.[59] In this way, actors' identities become fundamental to the process of defining and interpreting external realities on the part of actors involved in interaction, in which interests eventually develop. Once one categorizes the other as having a certain identity, for example, he or she tends to interpret the other's action in terms of assumed intentions, motives, and interests associated with the categorized identity[60]; humans categorize themselves and others, and this categorization affects their judgment and action.[61]

As such, reality develops through social interaction in which "conceptions of self and interest tend to mirror the practices of significant others over time."[62] Individuals' processing goals are determined in a social context "by the nature of the relationship between self and the other social categories evident in that context."[63] Because stable identities and expectations about each other are developed through repeated interactive processes, social cognitive and social identity processes function together to produce contextually meaningful and relevant judgment and behavior.[64]

These findings of experimental psychology are useful for the constructivist theoretical emphasis on the intersubjective relationship between interpretation and action. Simply put, "Between international structures and human volition lies interpretation." Before choices can be made, circumstances must be assessed and interests identified.[65] In the making of national interest, this line of reasoning analytically and conceptually suggests that the choice of a particular foreign policy in the form of national interest is always in conditioning relationships with how the cognitive dimension of identity shapes how an actor describes and defines a situation he or she faces. Given that any foreign policy emerges out of interactions between states and the understandings (and misunderstandings) that underlay the "moves" they made in response to one another's actions, the key to this linkage lies in one state's giving *meaning* to another's action through situation description. To give meaning is to make sense of the situation in light of who did what and, eventually, why. As so far discussed, understanding what and why for the situational description depends largely on the workings of the cognitive dimension of identities (who), because identities, which presuppose social relations, give each state that is in interaction a meaningful understanding of the other state, including "its nature, motives, interests, probable actions, attitudes, and role in any given political context."[66] Once a situation is defined in a certain way over others, the interests of the state are already entailed within the situation description in which the identities of and relations among the relevant actors or objects are established.[67] The situation descriptions created by state officials make clear both to those officials themselves and to others "who and what 'we' are, who and what 'our enemies' are, in what ways 'we' are threatened by them, and how 'we' might best deal with those threats."[68] In essence, what the self wants is constituted by understanding what the other wants.

How actors formulate their interests is thus dependent on how they intersubjectively interpret the situation, not on something inherent in material and ideational imperatives. Reicher and Hopkins effectively capture this insight:

> The point that we wish to stress is that context should not be seen as some passive ground on which human actors operate. . . . The context in which we act and the constraints imposed on us are either constituted or mediated by *the practices of others.* When I [in the sense of either the individual or the collective self] seek to shape the world in one way, I am confronted by other people seeking to shape the world in different ways, and my attempt to mold them is confronted by their attempts to mold me. Thus, even if "context" is external to my subjectivity, it is not independent of subjectivity itself because it is at least partially made through the subjectivity of others.[69]

It is on the basis of these interpretations that actors present various policy options to themselves. The cognitive function of identities provides a theoretical account of how actors' identities constitute a meaning-oriented social structure that makes threats and opportunities, enemies and friends intelligible, which in turn helps to form actors' reasons and goals for their action in response to a prevailing political context. In this way, identities become the basis of reasoning about what to want. If this account is correct, then the logical scheme of what I call "the identity-intention analytical framework," whose conception of human interest is emerging and historically contingent (not pretheorized), is as follows:

> A judged his situation to be C (interpretivist identity-dynamics works here)
> A was resolved to achieve the end E in the context of C
> A judged that E could be achieved in C if he did x
> Therefore A did x

This scheme builds on the "reason-based intentional scheme (or subjective rationality)" advanced in the tradition of the classical model of practical reasoning,[70] which offers a microfoundation on which action rests.[71] The two schemes share three things in common: (1) there is no ultimate criterion of rationality[72]; (2) the Hempelian sense of deterministic covering law models for human action is thus improbable in the social world; and (3) primary reasons made up of desire and belief can be causes, given that they foster an analysis of "because."[73] Its logical scheme is as follows:

> A was resolved to achieve the end E at all costs (preference E is given)
> A judged his situation to be C

A judged that E could only be achieved in C if he did x
Therefore A did x[74]

As Elster notes, however, this intentional scheme does not offer a theoretical basis for understanding an actor's reasoning process for *formulating* a feasible set of subjective alternatives (preference E is still given).[75] The feasible set of alternatives is assumed (or "structurally given" in Elster's words) or becomes known to an actor *somehow* in a given situation. On the basis of the assumed subjective goals, the actor is just doing his or her best to achieve subjective goals with whatever means are made available to the actor. In other words, the intentional scheme is mainly concerned with a matter of deliberating about *means* to achieve *given* (subjective) ends. Although the intentional scheme can substantially reduce the fallacy of imputed preference often found in the N-D rational action scheme (to be discussed) by not presupposing that an actor's resolution or his or her judgments are rational, the current status of the intentional scheme is fairly limited in offering a fuller understanding of human action. As Giddens puts it, "doing something for reasons means applying an understanding of 'what is called for' in a given set of circumstances."[76] However, the intentional scheme just above does not offer a way (mechanism) to discern "what is called for" in a given situation. The identity-intention framework is helpful in this regard because it offers a way to fill such a missing link for the emergence of feasible alternatives. For the comparative perspective, the scheme of the rational N-D model explanation would be:

A was in a situation of type C
A was a rational agent
In a situation of type C, a rational agent would do x
Therefore A did x[77]

Whether or not the identity-intention analytical framework in fact works as discussed here is an empirical question. The question of why Japan proposed to create the AMF, excluding the United States, is particularly tested against the framework (Chapter 6). Three caveats regarding the scope of this analytical framework should be mentioned before discussing how to empirically test the framework. First, the framework works best when two parties in interaction have substantially developed each other's identity construct, such as Japan and the United States, two rivals promoting different models of economic development. The flip side of this is that the analytical strength of the framework is relatively weak when it deals with actors' interaction without such mutually well-developed identity constructs. Second, the framework is not in tune with an actor's decision or policy in isolation from other specific actors—for example, a decision to follow a rule or norm (such as international human rights).[78] Lastly, a particular structure of identity and interest affecting a particular choice of action in a given time should not lead to the misperception of its components as having a fixed and static relationship. As will be discussed, any relationship is open to change in response to various forms of interaction.

Testing, Analysis, and Evidence

As has just been discussed, the identity-intention framework endogenizes actors' interests rather than treating them exogenously. When it is shifted from the theoretical to the empirical realm, the framework is methodologically committed to the interpretivist[79] tradition. This means that the endogenization process requires finding out what the actors think they are doing, necessitating an account of social action in terms of the actors' reasoning processes.[80] Given the framework's reliance on actors' processes of identity-based reasoning as the data for causal claim, at stake is how to empirically deal with "internal" matters (or what John Hall calls "intrinsic objects"[81]) of actors' practical interests in relation to the intersubjective content of the world they interpret. Put another way, what would be the analytical steps and evidence (or theoretical expectations) demonstrating that the framework indeed works empirically? Can the framework effectively deal with the "other-minds" problem of which interpretation-oriented scholarship is often accused?

Methodologically, the framework's focus on the relationship between the identities and situational descriptions that help to form actors' interests critically reduces the other-minds problem. Because identity-based situational descriptions and actors' actual respect for those situational descriptions (as indicated by their actions) are both observable phenomena, one can arrive at plausible conclusions without much access to actors' internal processes, which are extremely difficult to observe. Of importance is to demonstrate a significant degree of consistency between the two phenomena.[82]

When the framework is applied to Japan's AMF decision, several analytical steps are necessary to demonstrate its empirical validity. First, one has to make the case that decision makers (MOF officials) indeed associate themselves with or are embedded in a particular conception of their identity in relation to others (such as "the conception of Japan and the United States as two rivals promoting different models of economic development"). Second, given the temporally sequential, interactive processes of foreign policy making, one has to identify the critical "raw material" (or data or information) that decisively affects the future course of action. In Japan's AMF decision, the U.S. Treasury Department's involvement in the IMF operation in Thailand, for example, plays such a role. Lastly (and perhaps most important for empirical analysis), one has to ask if MOF officials' internalized binarization of identity conceptions indeed operated in their reasoning processes in making the AMF decision, as the identity-intention framework specifies. In relation to the second step noted earlier, the framework expects that such a binary set of identity conceptions leads MOF officials to interpret the U.S.-led IMF operation in Thailand in a certain way (such as "the demolition of the Asian model of economic development"[83]) over others, which in turn impels them to reason that "the AMF proposal excluding the United States" is the most compelling course of action. In essence, the identity-intention link can be inferred with confidence if the MOF's AMF decision derives from its own articulated identity-*filtered* (or *enabled*) reasoning of the nature of the U.S.-led IMF operation in Thailand.

On the basis of the identity-intention framework developed here, the social interaction processes between Japan and the U.S.-led IMF in the Thai bailout operation are broken down into four major sequences. I break down the social interaction processes between Japan and the U.S.-led IMF in the Thai bailout operation into four major sequences. First, the IMF, acting on its definition of the situation (the evolving nature of the Thai crisis, including the causes of the crisis), signals to Japan (MOF officials) *both* which action the IMF is planning to take in the interaction and *which* corresponding action it envisages for Japan. In the second sequence, Japan interprets the meaning of the IMF action in relation to its own perception of the situation (the evolving nature of the Thai crisis, including the causes of the crisis). In the third sequence, Japan—from its interpretation, which may involve its socially and historically constructed identity conceptions of itself and the United States as leaders of different models of economic development—now engages in an action of its own (the AMF proposal that excluded the United States from membership). This constitutes a signal to the IMF in the same way in which the IMF action (demolition of the Asian model) signals Japan in the first sequence. Finally, in the fourth sequence, the U.S.-led IMF responds with opposition to establishment of the AMF.

This is the basic interactive structure that outlines the evolution of Japan's AMF proposal. However, because the question of the role of identity in influencing actors' definition of interests is not only one of shared or collective identity but also one of opposed and contested identities that are the basis of differing conceptions of Japanese national interest, I also take into account the domestic political contention leading up to the AMF proposal.

DOUBLE AGENCY IN CHANGE AND CONTINUITY

Finally, I conclude this chapter by locating the identity-intention analytic framework in the agent-structure debate in the social sciences. The major concern here is how the framework can bring new insight to the constructivist claim that agents and structures are mutually constitutive of each other in producing political action or practice. In particular, I suggest a need to theoretically and analytically explore the concept of "double agency" to account for the change and the continuity of mutual constitution.[84] As Jackson aptly summarizes, by *mutual constitution* it is meant that "in any given concrete situation, the agency which actors exercise is shaped by social structures, but that at the same time social structures have no independent existence apart from human social activity (or human consciousness)."[85] Despite its theoretical premise, the notion of mutual constitution has been criticized on empirical grounds. Constructivist empirical works tend to prioritize the influence of the already-given social structure (whether it be based on ideas, norms, or identities) on state behavior without sufficient attention to the other pillar of explanation, the role of actors' *choice*. Checkel, for example, suggests that "operationalizing mutual constitution is a dilemma for all empirical constructivists."[86] This dilemma is in large part related to the constructivist (somewhat practical but reluctant) choice of the "bracketing" analytical method. Again, Jackson succinctly notes this predicament:

> Constructivist analyses are supposed to locate action within its social context, showing how that context gives rise to the action at the same time as the action reproduces or transforms the context. The problem with this position is that it is virtually impossible to demonstrate both of these things at the same time. Many constructivists opt for some form of analytical "bracketing," concentrating first on either actors exercising agency or on structures, and then reversing the analytical lens and focusing the opposite.[87]

A major problem that arises from this bracketing analysis, without a further theoretical and conceptual elaboration on the notion of mutual constitution, is that constructivist literature is, in the end, too static. By static I mean that the current status of empirical constructivism can account for the continuity of political action or practice under social structures (the continuity of the mutual constitution of agent and structure) but may not be able to theoretically and conceptually reveal how changes in social structures occur simultaneously with changes in agency (change in the mutual constitution of agent and structure). For example, Finnemore, along with Keck and Sikkink, relies on "[external] norm entrepreneurs" to explain the change(s) in social or norm structures within domestic societies under their studies.[88] Their norm entrepreneurs have to be, however, "(internal) domestic agents" for the sake of fully observing the change of mutual constitution of agent and structure. Simply put, the norm entrepreneurs are external to this change, because they themselves do not go through a process of, say, normative change. Sending similarly captures this point:

> Granted that it is held the LoA [logic of appropriateness] best describes the action-orientation of different actors *before* such processes of normative change start, how does such a process of normative change ever get off the ground? The LoA can hardly account for such changes—it cannot convincingly account for the process by which changes in norms come about, as it portrays actors as being internally related to prevailing norms as they constitute their very identity. Invoking the "dictates of identity" to explain action, and excluding the use of judgment and reflection upon the adequacy of the relevant norms [as in the case of a motivational externalist position], the LoA cannot account for the agency implied in changing those norms that it treats as constitutive for actors' identities.[89]

As I have suggested earlier, the constructivist failure to offer a way to capture the change in the mutual constitution of agent and structure may at worst unwittingly point to the case for the "cognitive miser": actors follow the dictates of identity and norms without a true agency involving choice.[90] This caveat can be applied to the identity-intention analytical framework, which heavily emphasizes the causal importance of the relationship between interpretation and a choice of action. Because the actors' choice of action is guided by the identity-based interpretation, the framework may end up presuming an automatic chain of action and reaction. Thus, even in a framework that allows far more agency than the rational choice model by incorporating the actors' own interpretation of the external world as a factor in shaping their choice of action, one can argue that full agency is not attained. Marx's observation might often be true: "Men make their own history but they do not make it just as they please; they do not make it under circumstances chosen by themselves."[91] This does not, however, preclude the possibility of change in the mutual constitution of agent and structure, insofar as social structures do not fully exhaust the possibility of choice. Some constructivist scholarship has empirically tackled changes in social structures and their associated political practices.[92] What is lacking, however, is a conceptual apparatus to precisely capture this possibility. I suggest the notion of double agency to analytically accommodate change in the mutual constitution of agent and structure. I sketch this out in relation to the identity-intention analytical framework.

Double agency presupposes an ideal type of full agency. By *full agency*, I mean that an actor is *always* in a position to evaluate, reflect on, and choose how to act: "None was more foundational than the human capacity and the will to take a deliberate attitude towards the world and lend it *significance*."[93] As the term *double* indicates, there are two levels of agency working to generate a choice of action. At the first level, agency functions in forming what actors want by helping them interpret their political contexts. This is where the identity-intention analytical framework operates. As a result, a feasible set of alternatives is presented to the actors. In other words, the actors now know what they want.

This is where the second level of agency comes in. In Greenwood's words, "The fact that my actions can be regularly predicted (because actors regularly act in accord with conventional rules and reasons) . . . does not entail that I cannot refrain from any of these actions."[94] In the case of the ideal type of full agency, the actors still have a choice to act out or refrain from their perceived interests.[95] In the case of the MOF's decision to propose the AMF, for example, the MOF still had a choice between nonaction (not proposing) and action (proposing) even after it interpreted the nature of the U.S.-led IMF operation in Thailand as rolling over the innocent Asian model of economic development (Chapter 6). At this second level, the function of agency is closely related to capacity and the will. On the one hand, the actors require "capacities" that enable them to translate what they want into action. Capacities embody ideational as well as material resources. In the case of Japan's AMF proposal, for example, Japan had the financial capacity (or the resources) to found such a regional institution. On the other hand, it is the will that enables the actors to act in light of their grasp of their perceived interests.[96] Between the perceived interests and the will, there are always some exogenous possibilities that the actors could act otherwise. Hollis lucidly illustrates this possibility when he makes the connection between reason and role. To quote him at length:

> The notion of judgment which I am after is both normative and positive. A particular decision-making game opens with a situation and a problem. For instance the CIA reports that Nicaragua is importing Soviet weapons, and the President, having summoned a dozen principal advisers, asks the Secretary of State for his view of this threat to national security. The Secretary of State must judge quickly not only whether he agrees that there is a threat to national security but also whether he is *willing* to say so. The former question is positive, in the sense that it is an empirical matter whether the movement of weapons constitutes a threat, and also quasi-normative, in the sense that interpreting the situation involves understanding several sorts of norms. The latter question is normative in different sense that to accept a posing of a problem is to accept an agenda. *If he is at odds with the Defense Department, he will not want the problem defined in terms which invite military solutions*; on the other hand to redefine the problem in a way which could seem soft on communism is to risk losing influence over its solution, if the others present still believe in a threat to national security. Meanwhile the latter question is also positive in that, if he makes the wrong move, experience can demonstrate his error.[97]

Given the could-have-acted-otherwise condition, one preliminary hypothesis regarding the connection between the perceived interests and the will might be gleaned from Erikson's two typologies of individual identity development, "developmental individualization" and "default individualization."[98] The former refers to an active trajectory of identity development in which the individual acquires a given identity by deliberately and consciously defining himself or herself in relation to the social milieu. The latter represents a passive trajectory of acquiring identity options and attributes without much effort. As such, the two trajectories are likely to produce differing degrees of individual commitment to the identity-driven perceived interests. Simply put, the individual in the former trajectory would be more likely than the individual in the latter one to adhere to the perceived interests flowing from the identity-interpretation nexus, and vice versa. This is at the individual level. When it comes to collectivities, one should take into account more contingencies in both type and kind, as implied in Hollis's illustration. Thus one might observe the less tight connection between the perceived interests and the will when it involves the collectivity.

To sum up, this discussion suggests that insufficient capacity and weak will (whatever reasons) at the second level of agency can be the sources of change in the mutual constitution of agent and structure: change begins to take shape with the actors not engaging in flow-producing activities reflecting the prevailing constitution of agent and structure. The resulting new practice constitutes a means of a different or new construction of the self and other, which reflects or embodies the newly constituted agent and structure. Of course, this is not the only way to produce a new mutual constitution. New practice, for example, would emerge with the arrival of new actors in office who are embedded in another set of structures of identity and interests in a given issue area (for instance, Gorbachev's New Thinking and Kim Dae Jung's Sunshine Policy).[99] This occurs at the first level of agency, but even in this case a final implementation has yet to pass (at least theoretically) the test of capacity (sufficient) and the will (strong). Taken together, the notion of double agency is conceptually useful to chart the possibilities of both change and continuation in the mutual constitution of agent and structure. Production, reproduction, and change of agent and structure are dependent on the self *and* others acting in ways that produce, reproduce, and change their embedded social relations. Because agent and structure within a given issue area are involved in a continuous process of construction, it is ultimately an empirical question to discern whether a choice of action reflects or ruptures a prevailing set of agents and structures constructed via the self-other nexus.

As such, empirically locating or embedding actors in a particular structure of identity and interests is the most important analytical step to make the tight connection between their choice of action and the source(s) of that choice. For a fuller understanding of that choice on the basis of double agency, the empirical task is not only to investigate how the actors acquire a given identity (developmental versus default individuation; implications for the will) but also to bring to light what choices are available to the actors, and how and why one particular choice wins out over others. As discussed in detail in Chapters 5 and 6, the MOF as an institution followed the trajectory of developmental individuation in the process of acquiring its institutional identity as a challenger to the U.S.-led neoliberalism. In particular, Sakakibara, who as vice minister of the MOF spearheaded Japan's AMF decision, was one of the most outspoken critics of neoliberalism in the 1980s and 1990s (and still is). The MOF had three choices available when it deliberated on the AMF proposal. The AMF was a choice rather than automatically given. The notion of double agency can conceptually amount to an initial window for integrating the change and continuity of political practices by enabling analysts to shed light on each decision point that can potentially affect the future course of action.

4 WHO AND WHAT IS NORMAL IN THE HISTORY OF THE WORLD ECONOMY?

Marxism, Economic Liberalism, and Developmentalism

Despite the claims of liberals that laissez-faire was a natural, organic development, there was nothing natural about laissez-faire; free markets could never have come into being merely by allowing things to take their course. Laissez-faire capitalism was enforced by the state, which resulted in an enormous increase in its administrative and bureaucratic functions.[1]

The seeming victory of the state-as-referee conception has given American social science in particular an ethnocentrism and an ideological quality that seem to have erased all Western memory of the state from Plato's Republic to Hobbes's Leviathan.[2]

INTRODUCTION

What made it possible for Japan to challenge neoliberalism? The Japanese challenge was forged in the mid-to-late 1980s, when Japanese domestic politics in a political-intellectual milieu interacted with an international environment characterized by the emergence of an economically successful Asia and intensification of the debt crisis in Latin America. The Japanese challenge was clearly manifest when Japan pushed the World Bank to publish *The East Asian Miracle* (1993). After all, with some qualifications, Japan has remained the *only* developed state in the entire post–Cold War era to question the universal validity of the so-called Washington consensus as its *official* foreign economic policy.[3]

Of course, a simple answer to the question can be found in the fact that the Japanese, with their own method (state-led rather than market-led), succeeded enormously in their own economic development in the postwar era. Proud of themselves, they wanted to be a leader of the "unorthodox" economic development paradigm. This is unquestionable. Moreover, by challenging neoliberalism Japan claimed the international validity for the Japanese or Asian model of economic development. But international validity does not follow from uniqueness or idiosyncrasy; that is, idiosyncrasy does not give the Japanese proponents of state-led economic development sufficient rationale to challenge universal neoliberalism.

The task of this chapter is thus to inductively uncover the deep-seated meaning structures that the Japanese themselves have historically attached to the role of the state in the Japanese economic development experience. These meaning structures enabled specific types of political action (such as the Japanese challenge to neoliberalism) to be conceivable, plausible, and even compelling. In other words, deep-seated meaning structures are equivalent to Searle's "constitutive rules," which "create the very possibility of certain activities."[4] As will be discussed in detail, this constitutive analytical approach draws on the insights of constructivist possibility ontology; meaning-oriented discursive practices (in both written and spoken forms) can produce social effects.

Because meanings (or meaning structures) are embedded in discourse and discourse itself competes for policy relevance, answering the question at the heart of this chapter requires three central empirical tasks. First, it is necessary to investigate and specify the range of economic development discourses within Japan. Three major development discourses are identified: Marxism, economic liberalism, and developmentalism. I use Murakami's definition of developmentalism throughout this chapter:

> Developmentalism is an economic system that takes a system of private property rights and a market economy [in other words, capitalism] as its basic framework, but that makes its main objective the achievement of industrialization [or a continuous growth in per capita product], and, insofar as it is useful in achieving this objective, approves government intervention in the market from a long-term perspective. Developmentalism is a political-economic system established with the state [or a similar polity] as its units.[5]

By examining all three discourses without prioritizing a particular one, the analysis remains as inductive as possible in establishing the thick contextual basis for the meaning of Japanese economic development. This also helps explore the divergent interpretive meaning structures that were historically constructed by the Japanese, while reducing the chance of premature closure on differences in them, within and across discourses. As will be demonstrated, each economic development discourse interprets differently the role of the state in Japan's economic development. The diverging meanings of Japan's experiences are therefore threaded through discourses.

Second, the analysis empirically grounds the meaning structures that create the very possibility of the Japanese challenge. It is the inductive process of uncovering each economic development discourse's interpretive framework that shapes the ways in which each has given meaning and significance to Japanese economic development experiences. Here are the findings of this chapter: (1) despite Japan's different politico-economic-historical settings since the late nineteenth century, all three discourses have interpreted Japan's economic development in terms of normal-abnormal meaning structures; (2) these discourses have determined their normal-abnormal claims by locating Japanese economic development in the context of their *respective* interpretations of the role of the state in the history of economic development in the West (or Western advanced economies); (3) developmentalism, which in the 1980s (with the rise of Asia) became the dominant discourse and on which the Japanese challenge was established, has claimed a historically informed generalization that state-led economic development is a *normal* practice for all the successful industrializers (including even the first industrializer, Great Britain)[6]; and (4) by extension, Japan's postwar state-led economic development is nothing but normal (not unique or idiosyncratic) in the context of the history of the world economy so as to be transferable to developing countries. In this vein, Japanese developmentalists have dismissed neoliberal evocation of the magic of the market as a practice of hijacking the history of the world economy. What is *truly* normal or universal is the proven validity of state-led economic development across time and space.[7] In a nutshell, I argue that the discursive, deep-seated meaning structure called normalcy enabled Japanese developmentalists to challenge U.S.-led neoliberalism by offering a justificatory foundation for the international validity of state-led economic development.[8]

As this chapter demonstrates (and related to the second point in the preceding paragraph), however, each discourse reads the world (mostly Western) history of economic development in its own way. This is because the discourses themselves are at least partially built on their worldviews in general and theories of state in particular. Each discourse's conceptualization of what is normal therefore varies; what is normal for Marxism differs from what is normal for economic liberalism, and likewise for developmentalism.

Third, the analysis examines how the rise of East Asian economies empowered developmentalism, thus transforming Japan's silence to "voice." Despite the fact that the Japanese developmentalists began dispensing advice in Asia as early as the 1960s,[9] the Japanese challenge came only in the mid-1980s. The dominant neoliberalism (or neoclassical orthodoxy supported by the Western material hegemonic position) remained strong and continued to suppress the developmentalists' claim of normalcy. It was difficult for Japanese developmentalists to fully develop a positive sense of their normalcy argument both domestically and abroad. Against this backdrop, the rise of Asian economies in the 1980s gave them an intellectual authenticity on their normalcy claim, essentially arguing that any country wishing to industrialize rapidly must adopt a state-led economic development strategy in one way or another.

That said, I begin the analysis from Marxism and proceed through economic liberalism to developmentalism. For each discourse, I uncover the late-nineteenth-century origin of normal-abnormal meaning structures in Japan. This is followed by an exploration of each discourse's interpretation of Japan's era of high economic growth (1956–1973), which was the nucleus, particularly for the Japanese developmentalists, of the challenge to neoliberalism. On this basis, the next section examines how the rise of Asia empowered and reinforced the developmentalist conception of normalcy. Lastly, I discuss the contribution of constitutive analysis in studying international relations. In the context of this chapter's inquiry and constructivist possibility ontology, I note how constitutive analysis can increase our understanding of the *nature and emergence* of a particular foreign policy.

MARXISM AND JAPANESE DEVELOPMENT

This section is divided into two parts. I first deal with the prewar normalcy debate within Marxism, and in the second part I explore Marxist interpretation of Japan's era of high economic growth within the context of the normalcy debate.

Origins of the Debate

Radical thinkers in Japan were drawn to Marxism[10] by its claim to be scientific and by its radical critique of Western capitalist society. In the 1880s, the growth of *Zaibatsu* (prewar Japanese conglomerates) promoted a capitalist economy, which was inevitably accompanied by social problems. By the 1890s, urbanization and industrialization polarized Japanese society in terms of massive inequality of economic distribution (city versus country, industry versus agriculture, and mental versus manual-labor work). Disputes among workers and peasants (the *Musan*, or propertyless, class) occurred in various parts of the country.[11] It was against such a background that Marxist ideas were introduced and found a home among radical intellectuals.[12] The Japanese Marxists intellectually inherited the traditional (or pre-Meiji) Japanese approach to economic problems as connected to questions of power, justice, and morality.[13]

However, it was not long before Japanese Marxists realized that in order to work toward a socialist revolution it was necessary to understand how Japan would fit into the Marxian scheme of economic and social development. Marx, after all, had envisaged the transition to socialism as occurring only after a long period of capitalist development and decay, while Japanese Marxists confronted a capitalist system whose origin was relatively recent. In addition, a more complicated picture emerged from their view that Japan, in terms of its political and economic institutions, fell somewhere between the feudal and the capitalist stages of Marxist schematic history: a highly organized and concentrated capitalist economy in coexistence with an emperor system, primitive agriculture, feudalist social and economic relationships between landlords and peasants, and a close link between economic and political elites.

It was not until the mid-1920s that Japanese Marxists began to critically apply the Marxist paradigm to uncover and interpret both the universal and the unique aspects of Japan's economic development since the Tokugawa era.[14] There emerged two factions within Japanese Marxism, namely the *Kōza-ha* (the "Lectures faction," connected with the Japan Communist Party) and the *Rōnō-ha* (the "Worker-Farmer faction," later connected with the Japan Socialist Party). Their debates revolved around the so-called feudalist controversy (*Hōken Ronsō*) in the development of Japanese capitalism and developed respectively along particularistic and universalist lines. Central to the entire debate was the nature of the Japanese state. Both the Kōza-ha and the Rōnō-ha agreed that the most notable particularity of Japan's industrialization lay in the fact that the state played a key role: the Meiji Restoration, which inexorably developed a pattern of economic growth while simultaneously constructing a capitalist state, was a "revolution from above."[15] The central role of the state in Japan's economic development was, however, in apparent contradiction to the Marxian axiom that it was the economic base that determines the superstructure. Thus the character of the Japanese state—whether it was to be viewed as essentially feudal or bourgeois—would determine if the revolutionary transition to socialism in Japan required one step or two.[16]

The Kōza-ha, led by Ōtsuka, Noro, Hirano, and Moritarō Yamada, interpreted the heavy involvement of the state in Japan's capitalist economic development as an indication of "feudal remnants" in the political superstructure.[17]

In the process of economic development and industrialization, the semifeudal ties between landlords and peasants were not dissolved but rather incorporated into the Japanese capitalist system. On the one hand, there was no general transformation in social relations differentiating the post-Meiji from the pre-Meiji Restoration; modern capitalism was "founded on the exploitation of rural life under a sort of pseudo-feudalism . . . original accumulation of capital, imperative for the establishment of capitalistic industry, was realized by legalizing (the Land Tax Act of 1873) the traditional feudal status in agriculture."[18] On the other hand, the Meiji Restoration did not generate a genuine bourgeois regime; Japanese industrial entrepreneurs and large landlords did not emerge as an independent political force *as they had done in Europe*. Instead, they remained dependent on the support of the imperial bureaucracy and military.[19] Bourgeois political and economic institutions that had begun to form with the Meiji Restoration were weak, and a retrograde consciousness persisted among the peasantry. Instead of bourgeois democracy, a state power that was semifeudal in character remained intact.[20]

Japan's capitalist economic development was clearly particularistic in the Kōza-ha's analysis. It was a deviant type manufactured from above, in which elements of a bourgeois system were enmeshed in the *ancien régime*. Moritarō Yamada most concretely captured the abnormal character of "Japanese-type" capitalism.[21] From his comparison of Japanese capitalist economic development with that of five other countries (England, France, Germany, Russia, and the United States in historical sequence), Moritarō Yamada concluded that "Japanese capitalism represents a departure, or deviation, from a (generalized) structural grasp."[22] In all five cases, capitalist economic development began with some kind of bourgeois revolution against an absolute monarchical order. It rang true even in the Prussian model, of which Japan was one particular variant, where capitalist or bourgeois forces would have to compromise with the feudal elements to survive a hostile international environment as a late industrializer.[23] In Japan, the "absolutist" Japanese state formed the pivot of developing industrial capitalism.[24] The incompletion of Japan's bourgeois revolutionary transition made its path to capitalist economic development deviant from the normal model of capitalist development depicted by Marx in his analysis of western European capitalism.[25]

In contrast, the Rōnō-ha (Kushida, Yamakawa, Tsuchiya, and Sakisaka are the main figures in its early development), which emerged as critics of the Kōza-ha, insisted that the Meiji Restoration, despite some feudal elements, together with Japan's status as a late-industrializer constituted a complete bourgeois-democratic revolution. The evidence for this includes the existence of the Diet, competitive political parties, cabinet rule, and constitutional government.[26] More important, the Meiji Restoration brought about fundamental change in how agricultural rent and industrial wages were determined. Competition among tenants and insufficient expansion of industrial employment (taken together, capitalist logic), for example, better explains high agricultural rent, the low standard of living of the peasants, and low industrial wages than does the remaining feudalistic semiservile system (as the Kōza-ha claims).[27] As Sakisaka put it, "Even though high rent in this country in the early years of Meiji inherited feudal practices [remained intact], the principle of rent determination changed, as feudalism was formally and substantially abolished with the development of capitalism, in other words, as commerce invaded the villages."[28]

Although these theorists, like those in the Kōza-ha, recognized the impossibility of applying European models directly to Japanese capitalist economic development, they argued that the Kōza-ha exaggerated the differences and underestimated the similarities between Japanese capitalism and capitalism in Europe and America. For example, Tsuchiya attacked the Kōza-ha's notion of "remnants of feudalism (or semi-feudalism)" as meaningless, arguing that it would be groundless to assert a resemblance between the Japan of the 1930s and the feudal Japan of the seventeenth or eighteenth century.[29]

The Rōnō-ha's emphasis on similarity resulted from its interpretation of the pre-Meiji origins of Japanese capitalist economic development. According to Tsuchiya and Hattori, commercial exchange originated already in the late Tokugawa age, and manufacturers in Marx's sense of the word reached a relatively advanced level of development in Tokugawa Japan.[30] In a similar vein, Sakisaka also suggested gradual transformation of the peasantry into a modern proletariat since the late Tokugawa era.[31] All this boils down to the claim that the way in which Japan proceeded toward Western-type industrialization in the late nineteenth century was not so deviant or different (as the Kōza-ha argued) from the normal model of capitalist economic development represented by Britain. In other words, because of the bourgeois monarchy character of the Japanese state and pre-Meiji Japanese capitalism that laid the foundation for Japan's rapid adoption of Western industrial techniques in the late nineteenth century, the fact that the Japanese state led the industrialization of Japan did not particularize the Japanese experience.[32] Japan showed the universal character of capitalist economic development as one of a number of imperial finance capitalisms.[33]

Marxism and Japan's High Economic Growth Miracle

In 1956, just one decade after the military defeat, the White Paper on the Economy declared: "We are no longer in the postwar."[34] By 1955, Japan had recovered to its highest prewar levels. The Japanese economy thereafter enjoyed an average annual real growth rate of around 10 percent for some twenty years, an exceptionally high sustained rate. This period (1956–1973) is often called the era of high economic growth. This growth raised serious questions for Japanese Marxist theorists, who continued to anticipate the collapse of the Japanese economy in the postwar era: (1) How could they explain Japan's high economic growth? and (2) How could they understand why Japan brought about rapid economic growth while others did not?[35] In what follows, three major interpretations within Marxism are discussed. All three are built on the debate of the Kōza-ha and the Rōnō-ha and continue to focus on the question of the normalcy of Japanese experience in the historical stage of capitalist economic development. The role of the Japanese state occupied the center of the debate.

The first interpretation was offered in close connection to the concept of "state monopoly capitalism" (SMC), first conceived by Lenin.[36] SMC refers to "the stage of capitalist development in which the economy comes to be dominated by large oligopolistic firms, whose productive power induces chronic tendencies to underconsumption and economic depression. To combat these tendencies, the state takes on an increasingly active role in the maintenance of demand and of general conditions for the survival and growth of the capitalist system."[37] Following Lenin's prediction of an era of "general crisis (in addition to the crises of world wars and the Great Depression)," Inoue and Usami, who succeeded the particularistic Kōza-ha,[38] argued in 1951 that under intense pressure monopoly capitalism became unable to sustain itself without transforming into SMC. In other words, because of capitalism's inherent internal contradictions, monopoly capitalism had to rely on the state's specific "strengthening" policies to keep it from imploding. Thus SMC reveals "the last aspect" of capitalism ready to fall away for the establishment of socialism.[39] This crisis version of SMC theory treated Japan's high economic growth as a brief "exception" to the basic tendency of crisis and stagnation of twentieth-century capitalism.

Uno,[40] within the universalistic Rōnō-ha tradition, understood as normal a Japanese SMC for high postwar economic growth. Also influenced by Lenin, Uno identified three sequential, universal stages of capitalist development (mercantilist, liberal, and imperialist: *Dankairon*), and within each stage a cycle of tripartite growth (genesis, growth, and maturity) defining the technology and organization of capitalist production in each successive economy.[41] The transition from one stage to the next is made possible only if the tripartite cycle is completed within each stage. Uno placed Japanese capitalist economic development since the Meiji Restoration in line with such a schema. He argued that Japan had gone through all three stages in the prewar era, and postwar Japan was ready for the emergence of socialism. Japan's early postwar high economic growth was anything but unique, he argued by pointing to an end of the last, ephemeral succession of the tripartite cycle in the last stage of capitalist economic development.[42] Continued high economic growth in Japan, however, forced these two earlier interpretations to be replaced with the two modified versions called "the socialization theory of SMC" and "the crisis theory of SMC."[43]

The socialization theory of SMC explained SMC in terms not of the general crisis of capitalism but of the "socialization of productive relations." That is, as "socialization of productive forces" develops in a capitalist system, productive relations also must necessarily become socialized. This socialization was expressed in formation of joint-stock companies and monopoly corporations. SMC constituted the ultimate development as states were increasingly led to intervene in their economies to forestall the contradictions that had recently emerged out of socialized production forces. Thus SMC is a product not of the crisis of capitalism but of a certain degree of capitalist development.[44] In this view, SMC-driven high economic growth in Japan was transitorily normal but destined to be brought to an end (or crisis) sooner or later.

Ōuchi, who succeeded the Rōnō-ha via Uno,[45] advanced the crisis theory of SMC. According to Ōuchi, the essence of SMC lies in the role of the state in mediating the relation between capital and labor by controlling the economy through fiscal policies and wage management.[46] The ultimate objective of the state under SMC consists in preemptively escaping from crises. Two principal methods employed by the state for this purpose are reduction of real wages through inflationary measures and perpetuation of rural poverty (and the rural polarization between large and small landowners developed later).[47] High economic growth in Japan, according to this version of SMC, was explained exclusively by the "backwardness" (meaning "an abundant existence of low-wage labor") of the Japanese economy and the "postwar factor" (new possibilities for expansion of investment and the domestic market owing to the end of the war). This combination resulted in generation of "exceptional" growth that should have occurred not only in Japan but also elsewhere in Europe. Backwardness and the postwar factor were, however, only temporary phenomena that would disappear before long, and thus high economic growth based on these particular conditions was nothing but abnormal or peculiar.[48]

Despite these efforts to revise and restructure SMC to confront the fact of high economic growth, its continuation (high growth without, for example, backwardness and the postwar factor) made Marxists themselves abandon the concept of SMC to account for postwar Japanese economic development. Marxists realized that the true roots of SMC failures consisted in the very concept of SMC, which is inseparable from a historical scheme of "more and more contradictions and the final collapse of capitalism." The sustainable high growth of 1960s capitalism cannot be accounted for by the concept of SMC. For this reason, before long Marxists declared that they would cease using the term *SMC*.

The second interpretation came from the "civil society theory" (*Shimin Shakai-Ron*).[49] Operating within the context of the Kōza-ha's adherence to the prewar assertion that Japan required a two-stage revolution, the civil society theorists posited that economic growth would stand in a mutually conditioning relationship with economic democratization on the basis of creation of liberated and equal individuals. Capitalism or high growth without civil society was just an unlikely possibility. Thus the fact that Japan achieved such exceptional economic growth during the 1960s and 1970s posed a big theoretical challenge to civil society theorists, precisely because the undemocratic (premodern or feudal) elements of Japan's polity appeared to them to have survived unchanged. After the war, as a result of the American Occupation civil society did achieve considerable development. But ironically, it was the continuing weakness of elements of civil society in Japan that permitted the exceptionally rapid growth of the Japanese economy in the 1960s. Uchida, the founder of this theory,[50] metaphorically characterized Japan as "capitalism without civil society." He explained the difference between Japanese development and the Western European experience thus: "In Europe, God created the rights of man and afterward, man created the rights of the state. Conversely in Japan, God first created the rights of the state, and then the state created human rights."[51] This meant that it was precisely the lack of democracy and individual rights in production and social relations that made possible Japan's postwar economic development. In his words, "there is a degree of premodernity in both social relations and thinking patterns. It is precisely this premodernity that has made our startling leaps in production possible."[52] Simply put, the premodern elements in the formation of the Japanese economy or society did not hamper Japan from developing but helped realize excessively high growth so as to create "the supermodern without the modern."[53]

Building on Uchida's observation, Hirata put forward the concept of the "enterprise state" (*Kigyō Kokka*) to capture the distinctive pattern of Japan's high postwar economic growth.[54] By enterprise state he meant the hegemonic role of the Japanese state in controlling both micro and macro aspects of Japanese political economy to ensure the needs of the state. Japan's enterprise state worked by using strong bureaucratic guidance over economic decision making and by nurturing close networks with major firms at the expense of a fragmented labor force. Like Uchida, Hirata argued that the enterprise state was only workable in Japan, where "precapitalist social relations integrated within capitalism itself."[55] In the Japanese experience of economic development, only the power of capital and the state manifested themselves, while human rights and civil society remained marginalized.[56] This is the sole reason Japan developed so rapidly. In Toshio Yamada's words:

> It was only under the Fordist compromise of the decades after 1945 that sustained economic growth based on high productivity was realized through the fair distribution of productivity. The lesson of Fordism was, without fairness, no efficiency. Under the enterprise state [or Toyotist regime], it was no fairness, yet efficient leading to unfair, therefore efficient.[57]

For the civil society theorists, Japan's high growth through the weakness of civil society was nothing but paradoxical or abnormal.

The third interpretation of the role of the state in Japan came from Makoto Itō within the vein of Wallersteinian world system analysis.[58] Makoto Itō points out four major factors explaining sustained economic growth of the postwar capitalist world: the economic hegemony of the United States and its dollar expenditures, a long wave of technological innovation, relatively cheap primary products (especially crude oil) from Third World countries, and the availability of comparatively inexpensive workers. He argues that these four factors simultaneously helped create capital accumulation in advanced countries throughout a considerable part of the postwar era, which in turn led to the consistent process of high economic growth in virtually all advanced countries.[59]

In Makoto Itō's view, Japan's miracle was just one of those examples. That is, Japan's higher economic growth compared to other advanced countries had more to do with its higher degree of backwardness than "the legacy of the state control of the economy." Those who explained Japan's miracle in the framework of national economy (that is, the Japanese developmentalists to be discussed later) were just "carving out bureaucratic monopoly space."[60] Following Uno's general crisis theory, Makoto Itō conversely predicted that any erosion of the four factors would be a great challenge to the entire world. Japan would be no exception.

I have so far discussed the three major interpretations of Japanese economic development stemming from Marxist traditions (the Kōza-ha as well as the Rōnō-ha traditions) and showed the dynamics of normal-abnormal claims under a Marxian theoretical perspective (see Table 4.1 for a summary). Marxian political economy had great influence in the field of economics until at least the 1960s. The reasons for this strong influence were (1) its demonstration of considerable analytical power during the Japanese capitalism debate in the 1930s, (2) the high prestige it accrued as a science that confronted poverty and war directly and bravely, and (3) the great distance between the realities of Japanese society and the theoretical world depicted by Anglo-Saxon neoclassical economics. However, the influence of Marxist or Marxian economists, who constituted the majority of economists in Japan from 1945 until the late 1960s, severely decreased throughout the period of high economic growth. Continued rapid industrial growth from the mid-1950s onward sustained faith in the ability of capitalism to generate economic prosperity. In contrast, Marxian political economy failed to adjust to the conditions of the postwar era, despite various efforts to revise and restructure it to account for economic growth. For example, general crisis and SMC theories completely lost their validity and were abandoned by almost all the Marxian economists themselves, let alone the general public. Marxian political economy found itself marginalized within the economic world. As a result, Marxian economists gradually began to lose the ability to participate in planning economic policies at the government level.[61] In this way, Marxian political economy, which entirely lost track of actual political concerns in some cases, became an abstract discourse of criticism against capitalism in general.[62] Japan's prolonged high economic growth made Marxism the first losing side in the politics of economic discourse in Japan.

Table 4.1 Marxism, Japan's High Growth, and Normalcy

Variants	*General Historical Scheme*	*Main Factors of Japan's High Growth*	*Normal or Abnormal*
SMC (state monopoly capitalism)	General crisis → SMC → collapse of capitalism → socialism	Low-wage labor manipulated by the state; postwar factors	Transitorily normal but destined to collapse sooner or later
Civil society theory	Feudalism → capitalism → socialism	Repressing workers' rights and civil society	Abnormal
World system analysis	Feudalism → capitalism → socialism	Postwar factors (U.S. hegemony, technical innovation, cheap raw materials and labors)	Normal; Japan just did it better than others

ECONOMIC LIBERALISM AND JAPANESE DEVELOPMENT

This section first explores how Japanese economic liberals historically developed their conceptualization of normalcy in prewar Japan. Then, their interpretation of Japan's era of high economic growth within the context of normalcy debate is discussed in detail.

Origins of the Debate

As the first Western economic theory imported to Japan, economic liberalism played a pivotal role in the earliest stage of modernization in Japan. No other political economy existed outside economic liberalism, and Adam Smith's *The Wealth of Nations* was regarded as "the first great work on political economy."[63] From the outset, the role of the state occupied the center of debate among economic liberals: Should the Japanese state apply laissez-faire policies when Japan engaged in foreign trade? Should the state not intervene in domestic economic matters? Following the fundamental theme of laissez-faire economics as well as the "invisible hand," economic liberals first fought against the remnants of feudalism, as evidenced by the dispute over land reform.[64] They then confronted not only the state's protectionist policies but also the views and arguments of those who supported the interventionist role of the state. Japan's place in the world economy as a late industrializer (or unequal partner to the Western powers), however, led these economic liberals to be in tension between the ideals of laissez-faire and invisible hand and the power and plenty of Japan as a nation.[65] Economic liberals often promoted liberal principles or ideals of economy as a means to increase Japan's national welfare without necessarily presuming that the ideals should take root in Japan at the expense of national independence. In addition, economic freedom ensured by the practice of liberal economic ideals was a means to achieve national prestige as a criterion for the level of modernization and enlightenment Japan had achieved.

Reflective of the influence of the laissez-faire views of Western economists, Japanese economic liberals argued against state interference with trade and industry.[66] As early as 1867, Fukuzawa argued in his bestseller *Seiyō Jijō*:

> The government cannot provide for the subsistence of the people at large; for the extent of the remuneration which workers should receive for their labour, or the extent to which they should work for the wages they obtain; for the extent to which commodities of any kind—such as food, clothing, &c.—should be procured, the manner in which they should be sold, or the price that should be paid for them: generally speaking, government should not interfere with trade.[67]

Fukuzawa further elaborated on the idea of the appropriate role of the state in economic affairs, capitalizing on "the principle of competition" to suggest what the government could and should do. Other than "great public affairs," such as railways, telegraph, gas and water supplies, and iron mines, all of which cost too much to be run privately but which cannot be left undone for Japan, the government should not intervene in "practical affairs," either by encouraging or protecting them. With faith in the principle of competition and belief that the nation's future depended on the rise of a business middle class,[68] Fukuzawa argued in *Minkan Keizairoku*:

> They [all ordinary people] are equally concerned with comparing expenditure with income, thus competing with each other on the prospect of being a winner. On the other hand, the conduct of the government . . . which spends without due consideration of gain tends not only to be spendthrift and wasteful but also to interfere with mutual competition among individuals, thus resulting in double losses.[69]

Therefore,

> It would be a great mistake to misunderstand the principle and to believe that the government may do anything in order to enrich the nation, running ordinary works and even competing with people in industry and trade. Only

> competition can lead industry and trade to average prices and can induce in the parties concerned every exertion. If someone should do something without due consideration of profit or loss . . . the effect would be disastrous.[70]

Similarly, Nishi saw protectionism, mercantilist systems, and government interference as three elements that could restrict the potential advantage of laissez-faire in Japan.[71]

Free trade was encouraged for similar reasons based on the ideals of economic liberalism. Katō praised the benefit of free trade, saying that "as there are nice things in the Western countries that are not available in Japan and there are commodities in Japan that are attractive to the Westerners, it is useful and enriching for both sides to trade freely."[72] Against the claim that free trade caused an outflow of gold,[73] Tsuda argued:

> How then will the equilibrium be restored in the imbalance between exports and imports? I would respond that there are but two ways—through an increase in the level of exports or through a decrease in the number of imports. Now under recent conditions in our country, exports exceeded imports for several years after the opening of the ports, and imports exceeded exports for three or four years thereafter. I would judge that exports should also exceed imports for some years to come. Exports and imports thus will never lose their equilibrium, as they circulate according to the laws of nature, never ceasing recurrently to rise and fall. Such being the case, enlightenment will progress with advancing technology. I say that one should never worry groundlessly.[74]

In the preface that he wrote for Hayashi's translation of Bastiat's *Sophismes économiques*, Nakamura argued that the outflow of gold was "not so much by the import of foreign goods as by the much heavier government expenditure in sending students abroad, in employing foreigners, and in purchasing weapons, warships, and the like."[75] In a similar vein, Kanda, facing the fears and criticisms of the scholars and officials who believed that Japan's engagement with free trade was draining its precious reserve of specie, argued that the main cause of this problem was not the existence of free trade per se. Instead, the causes were the Meiji government's hasty enlightenment projects and its attempts to fill its empty treasuries by printing large amounts of unconvertible paper money.[76] In addition to "wasteful expenditures on supernumeraries and nonessential construction," the printed paper notes were unacceptable as a means of international payment. As such, they provoked domestic inflation, making it more difficult for Japan to sell its products overseas.[77] As Kanda put it, "Specie is sent abroad because of temporary disturbances to commodity prices, because of hasty [programs] for enlightenment, and because it is driven out by paper. There is no other way to prevent paper from driving out specie than to reduce the amount of paper money."[78]

What was more fundamental for Japanese economic liberals' opposition to state intervention in the economy was, however, their *universalist* approach to interpretation of Western economic development. They based their interpretations of the subsequent processes of successful Western economic development and industrialization on the principles of private property and market competition. As opposed to the developmentalist interpretations that will be discussed later, Japanese economic liberals understood that Britain represented the normal model of capitalist industrialization, and that all other subsequent Western industrialization was more or less patterned after Britain. Nishi compared Britain's success with Spain's failure in these terms: "Spain cannot thrive because it has prohibited the importation of foreign goods, seeking to acquire gold and silver only by the export of its own produces. . . . Protective duties in agriculture, manufacture and commerce are what stand accused most in political economy."[79] As for Tsuda, protective duties rarely benefited a nation.[80] Economic freedom maximizes national wealth:

> Why is it that Britain has attained such wealth? . . . But it also results from its people, who compete with each other both in intellect and labour. . . . How is it that they can expand their knowledge and strive so hard? It is mainly on account of their government's securing for their people unrestricted freedom.[81]

For Taguchi, who launched Japan's first economic journal, *Tokyo Keizai Zasshi*, economic liberalism was a universal principle working beyond the constraints of time and place for national as well as individual wealth. For the Meiji economic liberals, Japan should follow *the* normal model in order for Japan to truly modernize itself in a progressive fashion. Their universalist thoughts and writings were embedded in, and reflective of, their extreme liberal interpretations of European experiences.[82]

In sum, like its competitors Marxism and developmentalism, the early stage of economic liberalism in Japan was understood as a means to assist the nation in its pursuit of *true* "civilization and enlightenment."[83] As early as 1886, however, there emerged an urge among Japanese economic liberals to discriminate between theory and actual policy. The essential character of this urge was that, while pursuing laissez-faire in principle, the state should be more active in nurturing infant industries relating to the national and military security necessary for Japan's independence.[84] Disillusioned with Western imperialism, the Meiji economic liberals came close to a perspective that financial and military power would be essential to the realization of liberal ideals in Japan. It was not until the late 1960s and 1970s that economic liberalism (this time in the form of neoclassical and Keynesian theories, or the synthesis of those theories) acquired a new position of influence in both academic and administrative spheres. This was partly related to the demise of Marxian theories and partly to the emergence of a new generation of Japanese economists[85] who absorbed the ideas and concepts of neoclassical economic theories.[86]

Economic Liberalism and Japan's High Economic Growth Miracle

In the face of the longevity of exceptional economic growth in Japan, Japanese market-oriented economists intensively discussed the relationship between trade and development and the characteristics of the Japanese economy using their comparative observations of economic and political policy practices around the world (but mostly in comparison to other advanced states). The earliest writings of the market-oriented approach on interpretation of Japanese economic growth were empirical and practical in nature without relying much on coherent theory or thought in their ongoing arguments. Characteristically neoclassical (neoliberal) interpretations began to emerge in the late 1960s. The earliest of them did not engage in comparative analysis but focused solely on understanding Japan's experience. They were concerned about the economic stability and growth of Japan, though paying some attention to the possibility of transferring Japan's experience to other developing countries. Thus, whether Japan was an exception or normal was largely outside their consideration. In contrast, later neoclassical-oriented interpretations made attempts to squarely put Japan's high growth experience in the normal-abnormal interpretive framework in light of their theoretical and empirical understanding of Japan and other advanced economies.

The first of the market-oriented interpretations came from Shimomura, who in his eponymous thesis[87] argued that the size of *private* fixed investment in production innovation as a percentage of GNP (rather than any particular government policies) determines the growth rate.[88] He drew this conclusion on the basis of his observation and calculation of trends in the Japanese economy rather than abstract model building.[89] In the case of Japan, he observed that the private sectors' heavy investment in production equipment in the 1950s ("effective demand") led to Japan's high postwar economic growth by increasing both productivity and the import capacity of the Japanese economy ("supply capacity"). In other words, the dynamics of economic growth parallels "entrepreneurial investment in production innovation."[90] He later added that the nature of economic development lies in promoting productivity (or "promotion of production forces") by increasing private fixed investment.[91]

Given his sole empirical focus on the cause(s) of Japan's economic growth, Shimomura did not attempt to translate Japan's experience into a comparative analysis, either theoretically or historically. Whether or not the private fixed investment that led to Japan's economic growth had a "universal validity" across other states' economic development experiences was outside his consideration. The most he did in this regard was to point out that the factors influencing economic growth and development would differ from one state to another in the function of supply capacity and effective demand.[92]

Under the influence of Kuznets's empirical research program,[93] which was guided by empirical generalization based on the historical growth and transformation experience of developed countries, Shinohara criticized the Shimomura thesis on the grounds that the input-output ratio (of private fixed investment) was in fact high in countries with a low rate of economic growth and low in countries with a high rate.[94] Instead, he emphasized "the parallel expansion of domestic and external markets" enabled by low wages and technological adaptability in explaining Japan's high economic growth.[95] As Shinohara put it, "The fact is that the high growth rate in Japan was not merely export-led: aided by vigorous increases in investment in plant and equipment in the domestic market, investment-led features were also marked. Growth was attributable to a combination of export- and investment-led developments."[96] As discussed later in detail, the essence of his interpretation or explanation is anchored in his explication of how low wages became the basis for Japan's high economic growth. Shinohara derived his low-wage thesis from Japan's dual industrial structure, called *Nijō Kōzō*, first coined by Arisawa.[97] But it was connected to the Kuznets hypothesis that the process of economic development was likely to be accompanied by a substantial increase in inequality, which would reverse itself only at a relatively advanced stage of development; economic inequality can generate growth (when combined with technology inputs) rather than obstruct it.

For Shinohara, industrial dualism in Japan meant the symbiotic coexistence of large firms paying relatively high wages and small unsophisticated workplaces paying low wages.[98] Large firms, having easier access to bank loans and new technology, achieved a high level of efficiency and were able to pay relatively high wages, which was just the opposite of small firm sectors. He argued that this duality or dichotomy prevented the wage level of the more efficient large firms from placing upward pressure on wages in their smaller, less productive counterparts. It was thus a dual structure that enabled the Japanese economy to combine increasingly advanced industrial technology with comparatively cheap labor and thus contributed to the growing competitiveness of Japan's manufactured exports.[99] Economic growth gets off the ground with export and domestic market growth through a combination of cheap labor and high-level technology, enabled by the dual structure.

Shinohara's explanation of Japan's economic growth was thus two-sided on the normalcy claim. On the one hand, technological adaptability, spurred by low-wage and economic inequality, in increasing both domestic and export market implies that the Japanese experience did not considerably deviate from that of other developed states. This is in tune with Kuznets's historically generated hypothesis. On the other hand, his treatment of industrial dualism (generating the low-wage explanation by connecting import substitution to export promotion in a "feedback" fashion) as "peculiar" to Japan points to an idiosyncratic characteristic of the Japanese experience.[100] As Shinohara put it:

> Japan was able over time to effectively connect import substitution, by introducing foreign technology, with export promotion. This was due, first, to the fact that private industry had a high degree of capability and vitality. It was also due to the fact that MITI created a good environment in which these private firms could demonstrate those capabilities to the highest. . . . Even if the policies derived from theoretical systems [neoclassical economic systems] . . . have been beneficial to advanced countries in achieving a high economic standard, this does not mean that the same thing will have a validity in the emerging nations. . . . In this sense, then, Japan's postwar road to industrial development is *heretical* compared to that of other advanced nations.[101]

Komiya was the first to clearly articulate the normalcy claim under a neoclassical economic mode. He was highly skeptical of the positive effects of state intervention on economic growth in Japan.[102] Komiya attributed Japan's success, as the most important factor, to the unusually high level of savings in Japan, which provided the capital for investment in the newly expanding industries of the 1950s and 1960s.[103] In his view, Japan's high economic growth was well accounted for by neoclassical growth theory, which emphasized the critical role of capital accumulation in economic growth; higher investment and savings rates better allow a country to increase the capital it leaves to its future workers, thus raising their productivity and income over time.[104] Citing the so-called threshold thesis, which ultimately postulates that once a country reaches a threshold point (in terms of capital accumulation made possible by savings) income per capita can grow only as far as improvements in technology, and then applying it to Japan's growth experience, Komiya was skeptical about the benefits of government planning and intervention.[105]

Komiya did not deny the existence of industrial policy. Nor did he completely discount some positive role the government played in supporting Japan's economic development through "indicative planning." But this assessment was limited to the indirect role of the government. For example, the Japanese government had played a positive role in helping to speed dissemination of economic information, thus assisting rational decision making for each economic player by bringing business people, officials, and others together to discuss the state of the economy.[106] However, he cast serious doubt on the effectiveness of industrial policy in fostering industries for economic growth, a core tenet of the developmentalists' attribution of the role of the state to economic development. In Komiya's view, the notion of the success of Japan's postwar industrial policy was more ideology than actual reality. He argued:

> During the period of rapid growth and into the next period, quite a few industries developed, many of which achieved remarkable success in exporting. Early on were the industries that produced such goods as sewing machines, cameras, bicycles, motorcycles, pianos, zippers, and transistor radios. . . . These industries developed without any dependence on industrial protection and promotion policies. . . . It would undoubtedly be the executives of these firms who would disagree with the most vehemence to the statement that industrial policy in Japan was extremely strong, systematic, and comprehensive.[107]

In contrast to those successful industries that developed on their own, many industrial policy measures did not deliver on their promise. The famous infant industry protection policies, which were wholeheartedly regarded by Japanese developmentalists as a positive effect of government intervention, are a case in point. Komiya argued that these policies had frequently become a means of supplementing mature but inefficient industries, while the areas of manufacturing that flourished were often the ones that had received little encouragement or support from the government.[108]

As recently as 1990, Komiya argued that those responsible for industrial planning and policy in the Japanese government had a tendency to exaggerate the importance of the role of the state (and therefore their own roles as well) in bringing about Japan's miracle.[109] He pointed out that the effects of economic planning and industrial policy had remained very limited throughout the entire period of high growth, and he added that this has been particularly true since the mid-1960s, with the gradual deregulation of trade, licensing of foreign-owned patents, and inward foreign investment.[110] As he put it, "despite wide coverage in the press and the pervasiveness of various catch phrases, throughout this period the reality of industrial policy was that intervention declined in importance and the price mechanism and the autonomous decisions of enterprises in the face of competition came to play the central role in allocating resources."[111] Regarding the Income Doubling Plan that was known to have had an enormous impact on Japan's growth in the early 1960s:

> What was important was not so much the contents of the national plans as the political will to promote industrial growth. Even without national plans, if the government would have made clear its willingness to promote growth, and fiscal, monetary, and industrial policy measure for that purpose, almost the same effect would have been obtained. The situation would then have been similar to West Germany in postwar years.[112]

In this vein, Komiya forcefully asserted, "National Income Plans in postwar Japan, including the Income Doubling Plan, were substantially little more than official forecasting."[113] The Japanese miracle was thus "far from being the outcome of the planning of a small elite. Japan's high economic growth was achieved only as a result of the high rate of savings by the people, by their will to work, and by the vigorous efforts of Japan's entrepreneurs."[114]

In sum, Komiya explained Japan's high economic growth by a synergic linkage between the high savings rate and capital accumulation. In so doing, he put the sources of Japan's success squarely within neoclassical economic growth models. The mode of the Japanese success was thus just as normal as for other developed states that had shared the successful experience of postwar economic development. He observed in this regard:

> By and large, Japan's postwar economy has been of the "classical" [as against the "Keynesian"] model. . . . In such a situation, "saving is a virtue," and, *ceteris paribus*, the greater the supply of saving, the higher will be the rate of

> capital accumulation and economic growth. . . . Therefore, an analysis of the causes of the high rate of personal savings may aid us in understanding Japan's postwar growth . . . a survey of countries such as Japan, West Germany, and Austria [particularly after 1955] strongly suggests that the high rate of saving in these countries is closely related to their rapid economic growth.[115]

Essentially, in Komiya's view, Japan operated the neoclassical model more efficiently thanks largely to the incessant efforts of the Japanese private sectors' entrepreneurship and hardworking workers.

Since Komiya's publication, there has emerged a chain of normalcy claims about the interpretation of Japan's miracle under the rubric of a neoclassical economy. Using standard macro and growth tools and simple data processing, Ohkawa, like Shinohara, attributed Japan's high economic growth to flexible, low-cost labor supplies and to the technology gap between Japan and the West.[116] In addition, Ohkawa tested his claim on Japan against Korea and Taiwan, the two most successful industrialization cases in the postwar era, and confirmed it.[117] Later, Ohkawa (with Kohama) made it clear that "Japan's experience is not a unique but a common process of late-comer economic development."[118] By "a common process of late-comer economic development" he meant "the operation of the competitive market in the domestic private economy" that would ensure technological progress indispensable for industrialization.[119]

Minami, Ohkawa's student, also explained Japan's high growth in term of the neoclassical economic theory of "the turning point." Following his predecessors, the Japanese turning point (meaning here "enough capital accumulation" for modern industrialization) was realized by the industrial dual structure and abundant low-cost wage supplies (these two factors also led technological innovation in Japan).[120] Comparing Japan's experiences of industrialization with those of Britain (and other developed and developing countries), he concluded that Japan was no more normal (or "not unique," in his term) than any other country in comparison.[121] He maintained that

> to a certain extent the government's industrial policies did contribute to rapid economic growth. But the real engine of this growth was the huge investment in equipment and the active introduction of new technology by private enterprises. Government policies encouraged this tendency but were no substitute for it. In other words, high growth can be attributed to the private sector's dynamic response to the government policies.[122]

Table 4.2 Economic Liberalism, Japan's High Growth, and Normalcy

Variants	*Normalcy Under Liberal Economics*	*Main Factors of Japan's High Growth*	*Normal or Abnormal*
Shimomura (1962)		Successful private fixed investment (initiated by private sectors)	
Shinohara (1962) and followers	Kuznets's income inequality hypothesis	Low-wage from Japan's dual industrial structure and technological adaptability	Normal in low-wage thesis, but abnormal in dual industrial structure
Komiya (1966–) and followers	Threshold thesis	High savings; most skeptical of the effectiveness of industrial policy	Normal

In line with Komiya, Kosai and Ogino—firmly dismissing the role of the government—emphasized the role of savings in explaining the high growth era.[123] Nakamura went further than anybody, arguing that the government started to play a certain role *only after* the initial growth (through private initiatives) had already begun. Moreover, its role was limited to the extent that rather than spurring growth the government made an effort to sustain it and strove to remove obstacles to it.[124] Shimada, commenting on the revisionist writings of the United States à la Johnson, argued, "Although their analysis is correct in some aspects, overall the revisionists' viewpoint lacks balance and is inappropriate. . . . Japan is well within the confines of the neoclassical model."[125]

DEVELOPMENTALISM AND JAPANESE DEVELOPMENT

This section is divided into two parts. First, I explicate the origins and development of normalcy claim in prewar Japan's developmentalism. I then illuminate the developmentalist interpretation of Japan's era of high economic growth in the context of the normalcy debate.

Origins of the Debate

Japan's developmentalism[126] emerged in opposition to free trade economic liberalism.[127] This order was reversed in the development of economic thought in the West.[128] Carey and List figured prominently in the shaping of the early Japanese developmentalists.[129] From the beginning, the Japanese developmentalists attacked the theory of free trade on the grounds that for a national economy free trade was good enough in theory but not in practice.[130] They based their attack as much on their empirical observations of Japan's adverse balances of trade and industries in relation to foreign countries (such as Britain and the United States) as on their particular interpretations of economic development in the West.

Reminiscent of the pre-Meiji arguments against the opening of foreign trade, Wakayama was the first to bring out a protectionist treatise in Japanese.[131] Only three years after the Meiji Restoration, Wakayama wrote in 1871 "An Explanation of Protective Tariffs (*Hogozeisetsu*)" to question the validity of free trade arguments, particularly for such a backward country as Japan to survive international competition. He essentially argued for the need for Japan to use protectionist policies by attacking the rosy promises found in the principles of free trade (or Ricardo's comparative advantage). Free trade, he asserted, would produce the wealth and strength of a nation *only* if the nation was sufficiently capable of competing with other countries in trade and industries.[132] By the same logic, he warned that Japan, whose trade and industrial capabilities were far behind those of the Western powers, could conduct free trade only at the expense of Japan's prosperity and security. In addition to empirical evidence of Japanese trade and industries hard pressed by foreign competition, Wakayama supported his argument comparatively by citing numerous historical examples of successful use of protectionist policies by foreign nations.

It was, however, not until six years later (1877) that Wakayama firmly located his argument within a comparative historical point of view. In the translator's introduction of Byles's *Sophisms of Free Trade and Popular Political Economy Examined* (1849), Wakayama pointed out:

> No country had ever achieved wealth without exercising protective methods; look at France, Germany, Switzerland, Denmark, America or any other country. . . . When a baby is born, is it not the duty of the parents to take care of it in every possible way until it grows old enough to be independent of them?. . . . It is as [clear] as day that an economic policy suitable to one country is not necessarily so to another, and accordingly, that it is absurd to believe that there is one general rule that applies in any country.[133]

Following Wakayama, other prominent early developmentalists started to elaborate on protectionism within a comparative historical perspective, with attention to the state's intervention of or control over foreign trade. For example, Sugi made an infant industry argument by drawing on French (Jean Baptiste) as well as English (Oliver Cromwell) protectionism.[134] Ushiba tried to contradict economic liberalism:

> Even the free trader Mr. Mill once said that the recent rise in the price of land and product in *America* was a result of the rapid growth in industry there. This is enough to prove the effectiveness of the protective system, since the country has been trying to protect its own industry by means of customs. . . . So this is clearly a free trader contradicting himself.[135]

In this vein, Nishimura went so far as to argue that even Britain had followed "mercantile" theories:

> Even a country like England, initially following the "mercantile system," prevented the reckless export of hard currency and stimulated her national industries by levying heavy import duties and by granting bounties on exports. . . . I know that Adam Smith would never have asserted free trade principles had he been born three or four hundred years earlier. . . . I earnestly beg that, having now an opportunity to correct the trade policies, we adopt protective tariffs in emulation of the *American* methods, on the one hand to prevent the reckless export of hard currency and on the other to stimulate industrial progress.[136]

Inukai and Ōshima, the respective translators of Carey and List, expounded a theory that government intervention in trade and industries is essential for any country wishing to claim its place as a modern industrialized nation. Inukai launched *Tōkai Keizai Shimpō* in 1870 to compete against *Tokyo Keizai Zasshi* (a premier journal for economic liberalism). He historicized the role of the state in late industrialization on the basis of his theoretical exposition of "disadvantage" placed on agriculture in world trade.[137] Ōshima (who was known to spearhead "Japanization of economics") asserted that state-led late industrialization was *the* lesson or historical truism for Japan to put into practice for the survival of Japan as a nation. He claimed that "we have to seriously take into consideration the fact that India became colonized with its rejection of the lesson [state-led industrialization] when *America* aggressively pursued it."[138]

Perhaps more important than these developmentalist theoretical (and empirical) critiques of economic liberalism was the fact that such a view was widely shared by many of the Japanese policy makers of the period. These policy makers came to agree with such a view after their extensive travels to

Europe and the United States. This was particularly the case with Okubo. The historical importance of Okubo is that, as the minister of finance, he implemented the "industry and trade" policy that prepared the way for Japanese industrialization. Okubo traveled to Europe and the United States from 1871 to 1873, along with many leading governmental figures, to learn the political and economic systems of the advanced countries.[139] On his return to Japan, he urged the Japanese government to adopt a forceful policy of encouraging domestic industries:

> Generally speaking, the strength and weakness of a country is dependent on the wealth or poverty of its people, and the people's wealth or poverty derives from the amount of available products. The diligence of the people is a major factor in determining the amount of products available, but in the final analysis, it can all be traced to the guidance and encouragement given by the *government and its officials.*[140]

Okubo explicated his argument this way:

> Nothing is more urgent for the government than the promotion of industry and trade. An unsatisfactory state is due partly to the backwardness of the people, but more so to an insufficient effort by the government to lead them. From the production of industrial commodities to the means of transport by land and sea, the government should maintain the facilities already established and initiate what has not yet established.[141]

However, it was not Germany but Britain that Okubo, in his "Memorial," recommended to the emperor as the model that Japan should follow. Okubo turned to the Navigation Acts in the British mercantile system. He argued that the acts increased the number of British ships and trained the nation in the art of navigation on the one hand, while barring foreign commodities from rushing into the country and protecting the domestic industries on the other. After this, the Navigation Acts were removed and free trade was permitted. British wealth and power was made possible only in this sequence, not the other way around. Okubo concluded his Memorial by saying, "Following the British example, the government should encourage and induce the docile nation of Japan to industriousness and endurance in pursuit of trade and industry."[142]

If all of these earliest developmentalist writings were in the final analysis about "what Japan should do" to survive as a nation in the competitive international system of the nineteenth century demanding free trade (except perhaps Okubo, because he himself formed the basis for promotion of industry owing to his overseas experiences),[143] Fukuda wrote the first serious study of Japanese economic development from a comparative perspective and was the first to literally use the term *normal* for the Japanese historical experience.[144] Conceptually influenced by Karl Bucher (*Die Entstehung der Volkswirtschaft*), Fukuda metaphorically divided the evolutionary processes of social and economic development into two categories, normal (*Seijō*) and abnormal (*Hiseijō*) paths. In Fukuda's evolutionary scheme, any nation that had gone from "inward family economy" through "city economy" to "national economy" belonged to the normal path on which most of the Western countries built their societies and economies.[145] He then applied this historical schema to the history of Japanese social and economic development. He concluded that the Japanese experience showed a striking parallel to those of Western countries.[146] For him, in particular, state-led economic development (since the Meiji Restoration) that produced the emergence of the national economy was a clear example of Japan's normalcy.[147] Asia stood on the other end of the spectrum (thus abnormal) because he defined it to consist of agricultural social economies.[148] Japan was normal in comparison with the West but unique (or abnormal) in Asia.

If Fukuda made the normalcy claim deductively (from the West to Japan), Akamatsu, a student of Fukuda, did it inductively in an inverse fashion.[149] On the basis of his empirical studies of import, domestic production, and export of such manufactured goods as cotton yarn, cotton cloth, spinning, weaving machinery, and general machinery industries over the period of 1870 to 1940, Akamatsu noted that the import curve usually increased until it reached some peak and declined with the increase of domestic production, at which time exports increase. This finding enabled him to put forward a general principle of economic development for late industrializers, coined "the flying geese pattern theory (*Gangō Keitai Ron*) of industrial development" or "the catching-up product cycle theory of development."[150] Akamatsu's theory accentuates "dynamic" rather than "static" Ricardian comparative advantage. The state's industrial policy plays a pivotal role in creating dynamic comparative advantage.

With the help of the flying geese theory, Akamatsu attempted to explain how an underdeveloped country could become developed relatively quickly. In his flying geese schema, an underdeveloped country adopts suitable labor-intensive industries from more developed countries. It then produces first for the home market but starts to export as soon as industries have grown strong enough. Initially, products are simple, crude, and cheap, but gradually the level of quality is elevated. This sort of procedure is repeated over and over again, finally leading to rapid process of national economic development. This three-stage development of import, domestic production, and export constituted the core of the flying geese pattern of development. In particular, Akamatsu stressed the role of the state in facilitating the transition from import to domestic production (the second stage).[151] He stated, "It was often necessary for the state to apply protective measures, such as the use of tariff policies and import restrictions, to make the expansion of local production large enough to compete with foreign manufacturers."[152]

As noted above, Akamatsu inductively developed his three-stage flying geese theory on the history of Japan's industrialization. He further expected that his findings for Japan could be generalized into a theory for late industrializers. In other words, he believed that his "historical theory" should be able to depict the industrial development of *any* less advanced country that entered into extensive trade relations with more advanced countries after the age of a closed self-sufficient economy. He thus started to apply his theory not only to European late industrializers (including the United States after its independence) but also to several Asian countries (notably China, Korea, Hong Kong, and India). He confirmed his theory and subsequently generalized the Japanese experience in the context of historical normalcy.

From a historical point of view, Akamatsu argued that Japan was no different from other advanced Euro-American countries in terms of the contribution the state's industrial policy made to development of technological sophistication. In the Asian context, Japan was *only* the first to fully harness the state's industrial policy to move to the position of advanced industrial states. It follows that even though a long time is needed as a rule for any late industrializer to attain the level of technological sophistication of the leading countries, it is possible for the country to achieve economic development in the long run with *appropriate industrial policies.*[153]

The influence of Akamatsu's theory on the modern Japanese developmentalists has been so enormous that they embraced Akamatsu's ideas as their theoretical baselines. This is evident in the fact that the contemporary Japanese developmentalists' core methods of economic development are almost identical with Akamatsu's emphasis on the growth of real sectors (production-based), long-term planning, stage-based trade policies, and national autonomy for successful industrialization. Perhaps more important, Akamatsu's theory itself was regarded as influential in the making of Japan's own postwar industrial policies as well as Japan's postwar economic policies toward Asia.[154]

DEVELOPMENTALISM AND JAPAN'S HIGH ECONOMIC GROWTH

In postwar Japan, economic development became the top priority in Japan's public policy. It was somewhat natural to believe that the government should do something to secure imports (such natural resources as crude oil, coal, iron ore, bauxite, and other mineral materials, which would supply the basis of an industrial economy) in exchange for exports and thereby raise the standard of living for the Japanese people. Toward that purpose, the MITI was established in 1949 to promote exports to acquire foreign currency in order to pay for essential imports in the short run. The Economic Stabilization Board was replaced by the Economic Council Board from July to August 1952. The latter was reorganized into the Economic Planning Agency (EPA) in May 1955. Since its establishment, the main task of the agency has been to draft long-term economic plans. Also in 1952, the Economic Council and the Japan Development Bank (JDB) were established by the government. The Economic Council had been an auxiliary organ of the Economic Council Board (later the EPA). The agency was to conduct surveys and deliberate on important economic policies and plans in response to inquiries by the prime minister. The JDB was designed to play crucial roles such as being the guarantor in borrowing funds from the World Bank and foreign private banks for national projects and massive capital projects by private companies.[155]

As such, the existence of the government's industrial policies and central planning for Japan's economic development has not been in dispute. The question was, To what extent was Japan's high economic growth the result of conscious policy decisions made by the government rather than by private initiatives (as claimed by the Japanese economic liberals such as Komiya)? Or was Japan just lucky in fortuitously favorable postwar economic circumstances (as claimed by some Japanese Marxists such as Makoto Itō)? In interpreting the causes of Japan's miracle, the Japanese developmentalists did not have much contention with such explanations claimed by economic liberals as "private fixed investment" (Shimomura thesis), "dual structure-led low wages" (Shinohara), and "high savings" (Komiya).[156] Where they disagreed with economic liberals was that the government facilitated the emergence of such conditions in the first place. The developmentalists emphasized the fact that Japan's postwar pattern of industrialization ran counter to conventional notions of Ricardian static comparative advantage. In short, Japan's miracle was achieved with strong government support and guidance, exercised primarily through the MITI, the MOF, and the Bank of Japan (BOJ). Included in the instruments of government intervention were, they argued, tariff protection, tax concessions, preferential allocation of loans and foreign currency to selected industries by dividing the industries between "sunrise" (*Shinkō Sangyō*) and "sunset" (*Shayō Sangyō*), and the famous "administrative guidance" (*Gyōsei Shidō*). Japan's prolonged economic success enabled them to reassert the normalcy claim in a way not much different from how their predecessors constructed the role of the state in economic development, as discussed earlier. Given the total collapse of the Japanese economy in the early postwar era, the Japanese postwar developmentalists thought of industrialization as a "fresh new start" from scratch. Like their predecessors, they showed a tendency to anchor their normalcy claim by placing Japan in the context of the early industrialization processes of Western developed countries.[157]

An early developmentalist interpretation of Japan's high economic growth came from Kojima, a student of Akamatsu.[158] Kojima rejected Shinohara's low-wage explanation on the grounds that cheap labor had been a significant factor only for brief periods in Japan's industrialization history. Instead, in the footsteps of Akamatsu, Kojima attributed Japan's success to Japan's flying geese-based successful export expansion in the world market. In the vein of historical normalcy, he claimed that Japan's experience was typically found in late industrializing countries well positioned to take advantage of the dynamic comparative advantage.

While Kojima focused his attention on applying the trade aspect of Akamatsu's theory to postwar Japan, Ókita,[159] one of the most influential government economists (*Kanchō Ekonomisuto*) in postwar Japan, clearly articulated the importance and efficacy of the government's role in analyzing the causes of Japan's high economic growth. Although he was not so much opposed to the analyses of Shimomura and Shinohara as evident in his endorsement of such aspects as surplus labor and the dual industrial structure, he credited the role of the government's economic planning and policy. His particular emphasis was on the role of the government in combining a free market structure with indicative planning and initiating the political and social reforms that accompanied Japan's high economic growth.[160] Dissolution of the Zaibatsu, improvement of wages and working conditions, and above all abandonment of large-scale military expenditures were, he argued, the foundations on which Japan's economic miracle was built.[161] All of these conditions could not have been put in place without the government's long-term planning for economic development. He stated, "In Japan, the government has continued to exercise strong leadership over the private sector of the economy since the beginning of modernization."[162]

In his earlier publications, Ōkita did not fully put into a historical perspective Japanese development experience. Rather, he focused on exploring the lessons of Japan's industrialization for less-developed Asian nations.[163] Nonetheless, he made some effort to place the Japanese experience in a comparative perspective. In a chapter titled "Comparison of Two High-Growth Economies: Brazil and Japan," Ōkita found some similarities between the two countries from an institutional point of view. He pointed to the positive role of the government in economic development:

> These [similarities] include the mixed economy system of private and governmental initiatives, the importance of the role of the government, political stability, continuity in the government's policy, a "growth-first" orientation in economic policy, and so on. . . . In Brazil the government leads the process of economic development by various policy measures including state ownership of basic industries such as iron and steel and petroleum. Since 1964 in Brazil, under the strong leadership of the technocrat government, continuity of policies has been maintained. In Japan, the continuation of the Conservative government for more than 20 years has contributed to the stability of policies. Both governments have relatively efficient bureaucracies.[164]

In his later writings, Ōkita cultivated the normalcy claim by calling Japan's postwar economic development "catch-up capitalism" or "late-comer capitalism." At the same time, he confidently recognized that the high rate of economic growth of the NIEs and ASEAN resulted from state-led economic policies *similarly* exercised in postwar Japan. He asserts, "Late-comers to industrialization *must* lay particular stress on the need for government intervention, not just to compensate for failures in the market, but because their private sector economic agents are still immature and their markets underdeveloped."[165] In the flying geese pattern of state-led, catch-up economic development, not only was the Japanese experience normal but also the economic successes of the

East and Southeast Asian countries were firmly placed alongside historical normalcy in grounding the role of the state:

> With Japan as the lead goose . . . the nations of the region engineer successive take-offs and are soon moving on their way to higher stages of development. It is akin to a V-formation, and the relationship among the countries in the formation is neither horizontal integration nor vertical integration as they are commonly known. Rather it is a combination of both. And because the geese that then go off later are able to benefit from the forerunners' experiences to shorten the time required to catch up they gradually transform the formation from a V-formation to eventual horizontal integration.[166]

Murakami,[167] who figured heavily in postwar Japanese developmentalist discourse, interpreted Japan's high growth experience in his originally explicated theory of "dynamic increasing returns" or "decreasing costs." He visibly (perhaps most visibly) located the Japanese experience in the historical context of state-led late industrialization.[168] In brief, Murakami's growth theory of decreasing costs is based on his historical observation (what he calls "the undeniable fact") that the costs of industrial production have been declining since the beginning of industrialization in Europe and ever more rapidly today as technological progress continues at an accelerated pace. He argues that this is how industrial economies have grown and why real wages have risen.[169] Technological progress results in decreasing costs (the flip side is increasing returns) by lowering production costs.[170] In Murakami's words, "believing that industrialization means a trend of decreasing costs is a straightforward economic judgment based on what we observe. An economics of industrialization has to be an economics of decreasing costs."[171] However, the technology-driven decreasing costs do not take place evenly across all economies. Their presence is historically frequent in the rapid industrialization process of latecomers while rare in mature industrialized economies. Again, in Murakami's words, "A tendency toward dynamic increasing returns [for example, decreasing costs] has been *the rule* rather than the exception in the process of [modern] industrialization."[172]

Murakami's emphasis on the role of the state in leading industrialization derives directly from his decreasing costs argument. Because modern industry in latecomers tends to exhibit dynamic increasing returns and decreasing costs, it is the state's industrial policy as "direct policy measures to preserve and promote the growth potential of industries which are supposed to exhibit a tendency toward decreasing costs."[173] Given the limitations of technological as well as financial resources facing a developing country, the most crucial industrial policy is thus to select "targeting" industries that are best able to adopt new technologies (and that thus enjoy the maximum benefit of decreasing costs).[174] Without such a policy (industries left unattended by the state), even the industries easily benefiting from decreasing costs would be unable to fully realize their latent potential for growth. As such, technology, incentive structures, and finance constitute the three most important contents of industrial policy, in addition to such traditional protective measures as trade protection, subsidies, and price regulation.[175] Decreasing costs were crucial in Japan's postwar economic growth. Successful Japanese industrial policies helped industrial firms realize the gains of decreasing costs.[176]

More important, state-led decreasing costs were observable in the long history of industrialization of all modern developed countries. In Murakami's view, even Britain, which is considered "the cradle of modernization," was no exception: "In the European countries between sixteenth and eighteenth centuries, the phenomenon frequently referred to as industrialization before the industrial revolution, or proto-industrialization, made progress under absolute monarchy hand in hand with mercantilism."[177] Britain was the first developmental state under absolute monarchy that attempted to link nation-states and capitalism, followed by France, Germany, the United States, Russia, Sweden, Turkey, and Japan.[178]

On the basis of this historical understanding of the origin of developmentalism, Murakami added, "The historical characteristics of industrialization were self-evident. There was no room for doubt; Western civilization had created the history of industrialization and by so doing had dominated the world. But the intellectual orthodoxy of Europe and North America was unable to deal with the actual facts of industrialization."[179] He subsequently claimed that:

> What causes developmentalism to be regarded as heretical when seen from other perspectives is its historical perspective [as opposed to ahistorical liberal conception of industrialization]. . . . Japan, which did not fit well into this widely accepted analysis [classical economic analysis], was explained as an exceptional case. . . . Japan [including NIEs] was heretical when seen only from the standpoint of classical economic liberalism.[180]

In sum, Murakami accounted for Japan's high growth experience through industrial policy-driven decreasing costs. Japan was not an atypical case. The

Japanese experience was normal in the sense that the Japanese state helped to harness a historically generalizable method of realizing decreasing costs.

Though sharing many ideas about industrial policy with Murakami, Takatoshi Itō[181] elaborates further on Akamatsu's flying geese theory (what he calls "industrial sequencing"). He attempts to empirically elevate it to the historical truism of successful economic development.[182] Against some views (mostly cultural explanations) that defined Japan's success as an idiosyncratic miracle (thus implying that Japan's success could not be duplicated elsewhere), Takatoshi Itō finds that one interesting common feature of all successful economic developments (including NIEs) is the industrial sequencing or flying geese pattern. In other words, all successful industrialized countries have upgraded their industries in an orderly fashion. First, textile industry flourishes. Light industry follows. Usually, heavy industries—such as steel, shipbuilding, automotive industries, and various chemical industries—must wait until the textile and light machinery industries find success in the world market.

As such, Takatoshi Itō finds the historical pattern of successful economic development in effective implementation of industrial sequencing. Thus, he (like Akamatsu, Ōkita, and Murakami) argues that the biggest challenge to developing countries is in deciding which industries to promote. It is difficult to wisely select the correct industrial sequencing. Takatoshi Itō writes, "However, for a developing country that follows the flying geese pattern, it is easier to pick an industry that is losing competitiveness in countries similar in factor endowments and economic environment, just ahead of these countries."[183]

Japan's postwar success resulted precisely from the government's (MITI and MOF) successful selections of industrial sequencing in the flying geese pattern.[184] In his words, "Japan has constantly upgraded its main engine from textile to light manufacturing, to heavy manufacturing and to high-tech industries. The sequencing of industries was important."[185] The NIEs followed roughly (Table 4.3), but not exactly, the path that Japan took some years ago (but the commonality was that each country started with light industries and then moved to more sophisticated ones). However, the pattern, he asserts, was "initiated by England, the first nation to achieve industrial revolution, and was copied by late-industrial countries."[186] Takatoshi Itō's answer to his own question, "Japanese Economic Development: Idiosyncratic or Universal?" is "What appears unique in Japanese economic development, from the 1950s to the 1980s, in fact makes economic sense and is replicable by other developing countries given the right initial conditions."[187]

Table 4.3 Flying Geese Pattern (Sequencing of Star Industries)

	Japan	*Korea*	*Taiwan*	*Hong Kong*	*Singapore*
Textile	1900–1930	1960s		Early 1950s	Early 1960s
	1950s	1970s		(dominant)	1970s
Clothing, apparel	1950s	1960s		1950s–1960s	
Toys, watches	1950s	1960s		1960s–1970s	
Footwear		1970s			
Refining		(promo) early 1960s			
Steel	1950s–1960s	(promo) late 1960s–early 1970s			
Chemicals	1960s–1970s	Late 1960s Early 1970	1970s		
Shipbuilding	1960s–1970s	1970s			
Electronics	1970s	Late 1970s 1980s	1980s		1970s
Automobile	1970s–1980s	1980s			
Computers, Semi-conductors	1980s	Late 1980s			
Banking and finance				Late 1970s 1980s	1980s

SOURCE: Japan, Korea, Taiwan: author's elaboration; Hong Kong, Singapore: Young (1992); the table is reproduced from Itō (1994). Adapted from Takatoshi Itō (1998, 21, Table 2.1).

Lastly, Ohno and Ohno's volume is devoted to explicating the role of the state in economic development theoretically and historically. The volume as a whole is intended to offer a major thesis of postwar Japanese developmentalists' views on economic development by systematically challenging the primacy of the market in economic development. Above all, the importance of the volume lies in the fact that it compiles key writings of officials and scholars who have shaped the philosophy of Japan's Official Development Assistance (ODA). Many of the writers directly participated in the Japanese challenge to neoliberalism at the World Bank and other forums of international finance and development.

Ohno and Ohno's volume asserts that development of a market economy requires many conditions that do not automatically arise through hands-off economic policy. These conditions must be built by conscious efforts on the part of the government. In short, adoption of a state-led development strategy is *unavoidable* for any country wishing to industrialize rapidly.[188] Incorporating European, American, Japanese, and now East Asian experiences of late industrialization, the volume firmly establishes the historical normalcy of state-led economic development:

> To initiate the industrialization process, the state must assume a principle role in developing industrial vehicles able to mobilize resources, induce and organize industrial development. The Credit Mobilier of France, the world's first investment bank, and German banks that provided long-term financing for the industrial sector were the key institutional instruments of industrialization in the European continent, which initially fell far behind England. In late developer Russia, where the banking system was underdeveloped, the state itself assumed the role of the primary agent, propelling industrialization through fiscal policy. Similarly, in Meiji Japan the state played a leading role in promoting industrialization. . . . "State-led capitalism" was typically adopted in latecomers as vehicles for industrialization.[189]

> The active role of government is particularly important in the early states of development. . . . This was already recognized clearly in the nineteenth century when Japan began its transformation from a feudal samurai society to a modern, industrialized one. Returning from the two-year official mission to America and Europe, the Meiji government's high official Toshimichi Okubo wrote in his back-to-office report: "the strength of a country depends on the prosperity of its people which, in turn, is based on the level of output. However, no country has ever initiated the process of industrialization without official guidance and promotion."[190]

So far, I have expounded the Japanese developmentalists' conception of state-led economic development within the context of historical normalcy. As has been made evident, the Japanese developmentalists do not seem to agree with every aspect (or specificity) of the exact causes of Japan's miracle, let alone their historical generalization of the causes of successful late-industrialization.[191] Nonetheless, what they all acknowledge is the active role of the government as an initiator of change in the early stage of economic development. In particular, the common ground is their positive assessment of the

Table 4.4 Developmentalism, Japan's High Growth, and Normalcy

Variants	*Normalcy Under Developmentalism*	*Main Factors of Japan's High Growth*	*Normal or Abnormal*
Ōkita (1975–)	Industrial policy, competent bureaucracy	Government's long-term economic planning and policy autonomy of bureaucracy	Normal
Murakami (1975–)	Technology-led; decreasing costs; initiated by the government	Successful selection of target industries that maximize the benefit of decreasing costs	Normal
Kojima, Takatoshi Itō, and Ohno and Ohno	Flying geese pattern of economic development (production cycle theory; import → domestic production → export) initiated by the government	Industrial policies that promote successful sequencing of industries (from textile through light through heavy through high-tech industries)	Normal

state's pursuit of long-term real targets (production-based) and technology-led stages of development (see table). As the normalcy claim clearly indicates, the Japanese developmentalists historically and comparatively supported their state-led thesis and later challenged U.S.-led neoliberalism. The tenets of neoliberalism are ahistorical and valid only in deductively formed mathematics. In the eyes of the Japanese developmentalists, the neoliberal commitment to a universal development philosophy is no more than a practice of hijacking the history of the world economy. State-led economic development, rather than just an alternative possibility to industrialization, has been a normal (or universal) practice for all late-industrializers.

ASIA AND EMPOWERED NORMALCY

The Japanese developmentalists, however, had to prevail over their rival economic liberals domestically before they could project their state-led economic development vision internationally.[192] The clash of the two camps was observed in the early 1990s when a great deal of discussion occurred about what Japan, as the largest ODA donor in the world, could contribute to the economic development of developing countries. Economic liberals insisted that Japan should guide its ODA policy along the lines of Washington's drive for privatization and free markets. This meant that Japan should drop its traditional ODA practice of "request-based procedures," which assumed the recipient country (or government) would best know its own needs. In place of that, Japan should place rigid conditions on aid to developing countries.[193]

In opposition to economic liberals, the Japanese development economists and some policy makers within the confines of developmentalism argued that Japan should shape its ODA policy along the lines of lessons learned from its own economic development.[194] In other words, Japan's ODA policy should be directed at stressing the role of the state in economic development, meaning Japan should maintain its request-based ODA policy. The policy calls for recipient government leadership to initiate the development strategy, as it is implemented through a financial mechanism known as "two-step loans," which funnel capital or aid to private sectors through public agencies.

At this critical juncture, the successful economic development experiences of Asian countries helped the Japanese developmentalists articulate and advocate the Asian development model. They emphasized the common features of state-led economic development strategies of the Asian region. At the same time, the Japanese developmentalists did not forget to question the viability of a purely unregulated market mechanism for sustainable economic development. In the end, the Japanese or Asian development model became the basis for Japan's ODA policy, which increasingly focused on the role of the state in economic development strategy, as proponents of state-led economic development began to coalesce the Asian development model into concrete policy proposals.[195] Japan has since then become the principal advocate of the Asian development model in multilateral development banks and other international forums.[196]

In short, the Japanese developmentalists were greatly empowered with the rise of Asia and the failures in Latin America and Sub-Saharan Africa. They believed these failures were clear examples of the failure of neoliberalism. The rise of Asia has reinforced their conception of the historical normalcy of state-led economic development being a prerequisite, particularly for late-industrializers. Of course, the Japanese developmentalists recognize the similarities and differences between Japan and Asian followers. They also see the differences between East Asia and Southeast Asia. For example, Japan has not relied on foreign capital for its investment, while most Asian countries (particularly Korea and the nations of Southeast Asia) have borrowed extensively from abroad. Nonetheless, they interpret that Japan's Asian neighbors patterned their economic ɔpment after Japan. To them, the role of the state was indisputable.[197]

The rise of Asia has also played an indispensable role in dispelling the Japanese developmentalists' small specter of doubt on the historic normalcy of Japan. This doubt arose from the fact that until the 1980s Japan was the only non-European country that had succeeded in industrialization. As early as 1990, the MOF's Committee on Asia Pacific Economic Research officially recommended, "It is necessary that what Japan used to do should be done by the Asian NIEs, what the Asian NIEs used to do should be done by ASEAN countries."[198] This partly explains the question of why it was not until the mid-late 1980s (with the arrival of the successful Asian state-led developments) that Japan began to somewhat aggressively promote its development model.[199] The rise of Asia also empowered the Japanese developmentalists to domestically win over the remnants of the culture-driven uniqueness view.[200]

Perhaps more important, the developmentalists' interpretations of Asia's success were not confined to the theoretical level. Japanese exportation of its development model to Asia began in the early 1960s (for example, to Korea and Taiwan).[201] In the 1960s and 1970s, Japan advised developing Asian countries to adopt the industrial sequence that it followed in the rise to great economic power status: solidification of the country's agricultural basis, a shift to light and then to heavy industries, followed by a shift to tertiary industries. By the mid-1980s, Japan (particularly the MITI and the MOF) was already advising many Asian economies on development of export-oriented industries, in addition to indirectly influencing the industrial policies of Asian economies through education and technical assistance.[202] The Japanese developmentalists thus regarded the rise of Asia as their intellectual success as well. As such, the rise of Asia played a pivotal role in giving the Japanese developmentalists sufficient rationale to challenge neoliberalism on the basis of their (now more empowered) conception of historical normalcy. With the aid of the rise of Asia, the Japanese developmentalists had stronger theoretical and empirical justification for the role of the state in economic development in the 1990s when challenging the Washington consensus in various international settings.

CONSTITUTIVE ANALYSIS

So far I have grounded Japanese conceptions of the role of the state in economic development in the meaning structure called normalcy. I have done so by answering the question of what made it possible for Japan to challenge neoliberalism. This type of question is not classified as *causal* in a traditional social scientific sense. Rather, it calls for constitutive analysis that explores the actors' social conditions of possibility for a particular course of action at a given moment. In the constructivist vein, social conditions of possibility are closely related to discourse and associated meanings in a given issue area (as was emphasized in Chapter 1, discourse, or how we think and talk about the world, largely shapes practice). In this analysis, normalcy captures the relevant pattern of how Japanese developmentalists think and talk about the relationship between the role of the state in the history of the world economy and Japan's own experience. From outside constructivist scholarship, however, one might wonder about the contribution of this kind of constitutive analysis for understanding foreign policy. Because of space limitations, I address this issue only briefly here.

The aim of constitutive analysis is to offer an insight into what it is that creates the very possibility of the Japanese challenge. Simply answering the question of why the Japanese challenge came about limits fuller understanding of the *emergence* and *nature* of the Japanese challenge. First, the absence of constitutive analysis makes it difficult to account for the emergence of Japan as an actor challenging neoliberalism (or Japanese agency as a challenger).[203] In other words, before any policy possibility is deemed valuable by actors, it must be made thinkable in the first place on the part of the actors. In Doty's words: "The possibility of practices presupposes the ability of an agent to imagine certain course of action. Certain background meanings, kinds of social actors and relationships, must already be in place."[204] In the case of the Japanese challenge, I have demonstrated that the normalcy interpretative disposition of the Japanese economic development experience made it conceivable, plausible, and even compelling for the Japanese developmentalists to challenge universal neoliberalism. That is, the historically constructed normalcy meaning structure engendered Japanese agency with the disposition of challenging neoliberal universalism.

In this regard, Peter Hall's illustration (as noted in Chapters 1 and 2) is instructive in clarifying the connection between a deep-seated meaning structure and states' economic policy development. He claims that the emergence and persuasiveness of new ideas and identities engendering a particular policy stands in a conditioning relationship with a *terrain*[205] already defined by a prevailing set of what he calls the "political discourse of a nation."[206] The social meaning context in which a particular issue is embedded in a given state affects present and future conditions for the pattern of a particular policy development. A useful example of this is the constitutive effect of social meaning in shaping the specific forms that Japan's economic liberalization has taken over the last twenty years.[207] For example, the flip side of the Japanese challenge is that, so long as the predominant interpretative disposition of economic development of the United States remains discursively constructed on the basis of the magic of the marketplace, this precludes a possibility of the United States becoming an *agent* that practices exporting state-led economic development to the world. Without constitutive analysis, one has yet to explain how Japan, not another, comes into being in the first place as a challenger to U.S.-led neoliberalism.

The Japanese challenge was forged in the mid to late 1980s with an international environment witnessing emergence of an economically successful Asia and intensification of the debt crisis in Latin America and Africa. In contrast to the Asian development economies, those of Latin America and Africa were considered clear examples of the failure of neoliberal prescriptions. As such, any industrialized state could have challenged neoliberalism in the face of such *objective* realities in the world economy of the 1980s out of a desire to make an ideational contribution to the international society. Any of them could have done it to exercise a leadership role by becoming a source of an alternative development paradigm for developing countries. The possibility was open to any of them who shared the historical experience of state-led economic development,[208] but only Japan did it. Why did such an idea of state-led economic development resonate more in Japan and less in other nations? Had I just questioned why Japan challenged neoliberalism, I would have taken as unproblematic the possibility that the challenge could take place in Japan. Without constitutive analysis, any answer to the question of why and how the Japanese challenge occurred is only partially successful, because such an answer fails to offer the very ground on which Japanese agency as a challenger is based. Constitutive analysis is logically prior to the domain in which Japan causally develops a set of foreign economic policies that challenged neoliberalism.[209]

Second, constitutive analysis offers an insight into the *nature* of the Japanese challenge. Had I not uncovered the normalcy meaning structure, I might have pointed to, for example, intensified trade conflict between the United States and Japan during the 1980s and 1990s as an explanation for the fact that only Japan challenged U.S.-led neoliberalism. The two countries blamed one another's economic system as a root cause of their economic conflict (overconsuming United States versus predatory Japan).[210] However, my findings suggest the Japanese challenge goes much deeper than that. Theoretically, this explanation still considers unproblematic the *possibility* of the Japanese challenge in that Japan (or the Japanese developmentalists) does not challenge any alternative economic system from which Japan differs and with which Japan has a trade conflict. Substantively, the level of conflict does not determine the Japanese challenge either, even in the context of U.S.-Japan economic relations. The U.S.-Japan trade conflict was arguably no less severe in the 1960s than in the 1980s over, for example, Japan's textile exports to the United States. The United States applied Voluntary Export Restraints (VERs, which represent a symbol of U.S. accusations about Japanese economic practice) to Japan as early as 1956 in cotton textiles. Trade conflicts have continued in steel (1968 and 1974), televisions (1977), automobiles (1981), semiconductors (1986), and machine tools (1987). In short, the blaming game was nothing new. However, the Japanese challenge took place only in the late 1980s, with promulgation of neoliberal universalism.

This historical timing of the Japanese challenge is further confirmed by Stein (see also Chapter 2 in this regard). The Japanese challenge has been observed in Africa as well, where Japan's economic and strategic interests were least salient. From interviews in Japan's aid agencies and analysis of a dataset on the ODA to African countries from 1959 to 1994 (using a series of multiple regressions), Stein argues that Japanese economic interest has been far less clear in its relationship to the pattern of Japanese bilateral aid to Africa. Instead, imposition of neoliberalism-based structural adjustment packages on African countries has had a significant impact in shifting Japan's aid pattern to Africa.[211] Particularly after 1986, Japan began to openly criticize structural adjustment packages and refocus its bilateral aid on infrastructure and production assistance. This refocus was closely linked to Japan's commitment to the state-led economic development alternative. As such, the Japanese challenge has been a global phenomenon, not confined to the U.S.-Japan bilateral relationship. Had I not engaged in constitutive analysis, I never would have spelled out the *nature* of the Japanese challenge with the alternative *universalism* (who and what is normal) entrenched in the role of the state in economic development.

All in all, explicating this ontological question of what makes it possible, or how possible, contributes significantly to a fuller understanding of the emergence and nature of a particular foreign policy by empirically furnishing the properties of agency. In light of constructivist theorizing of the endogenization of actors' interest,[212] answering the constitutive question helps fully materialize the constructivist commitment to holism in explaining social action, as discussed in Chapter 1. As has already been noted, the absence of constitutive analysis makes it difficult for constructivists to explain how Japan came into being in the first place as a challenger to the U.S.-led neoliberalism. Toward fuller endogenization of Japan's interest in the Japanese challenge, it is necessary to begin foregrounding the challenge by exploring the constitutive possibility of Japanese agency in the politics of economic development. Constitutive analysis helps connect the historicity of identity (understanding of self) and agency (social conditions of possibility for adopting a particular foreign policy).

To conclude, here is a reformulated, shortened version of "Japanese View on Economic Development" in Ohno and Ohno's volume, which compiles key writings of officials and scholars shaping Japan's ODA policies.[213] This systematically rationalizes the role of the state in economic development.

GOVERNMENT AS THE INITIATOR OF CHANGE

The Japanese view is based on the belief that a market economy does not grow automatically in developing countries even if the macroeconomy is stabilized, prices and economic activities are liberalized, and state-owned enterprises are privatized. More is required for development of the market economy. What is additionally needed is well-designed activism on the part of the government in the production sphere. Though incompetent government will surely stunt growth potential, withdrawal of government does not solve the problem either. The ability to formulate appropriate long-term development strategy is the key to economic development; there is no way around it.

The fundamental difficulty of government in the developing world stems from its dual role as the subject and the object of reform. Nonetheless, the first thing we must recall is that a market economy will not automatically grow in a developing or transition economy. In those countries, the market mechanism is intentionally introduced by the government to raise productivity and living standards. There are no internal dynamics within the existing social structure that will generate the institutions and attitudes needed to support the market economy. In other words, the market economy is a very demanding economic system. Its proper operation requires a large number of conditions to be satisfied: property rights, a contract system, economic freedom, firms and entrepreneurs, labor and capital markets, transportation and communication, technical absorptive capacity, and so on. Provision of these conditions is not automatic, and only those societies that happen to be equipped with them—or those that deliberately adapt themselves to be compatible with the market mechanism—can successfully adopt it. In the latter case, the government must take the initiative to marketize the economy, or it will not be marketized. Laissez-faire policy will not work. Hence, the role of government becomes crucial; the initial impulse for marketization must come from government (assisted by an international donor group). Active government is absolutely necessary because without it the base society will not turn into a market economy.

There is another reason government action is essential. Marketization is a process that must be undertaken with the nation-state as the implementing unit. It requires enforcement of laws, rules, and standards consistent with market exchange; scarce resources must be mobilized into selected projects on a nationwide scale; geographically integrated markets with supporting infrastructure must be built; personal and regional income inequality must be corrected by taxation, subsidies, and public investment; and foreign diplomatic and economic relations must be managed properly. The private sector, ethnic groups, and local governments are incapable of handling these tasks. The central government, with concentrated political authority for mobilizing people and resources, is the only viable alternative at an early stage of development.

As the initiator of change, the government must implement policies that create the necessary institutions and attitudes for the market economy. Typically, this takes the form of (1) setting long-term national goals (that is, creating a certain number of new jobs within five years, doubling income in ten years, building certain industries from scratch, achieving industrialization by 2020, and so on) and (2) designing comprehensive and concrete annual steps toward these goals, identifying bottlenecks, appropriating budgetary resources, and establishing implementing bodies. Working backward from long-term goals thus determines action required today. The process often materializes in five-year plans and similar indicative official blueprints. These plans are not rigid but remain quite flexible, allowing modification as circumstances change. These long-term visions and accompanying official guidance are deemed necessary for underdeveloped countries in order to concentrate available resources in a few key sectors that can bolster overall growth. Igniting economic growth requires such resource concentration. The free market mechanism based purely on individual economic incentives tends to dissipate limited human and nonhuman resources over too many projects and sectors.

Japanese development economists believe that the "appropriate" development strategy differs fundamentally from one country to another, and from one stage of development to another. Thus we reject generalization at the level of individual policy measures. The validity of import substitution, agricultural price support, industrial policy, privatization, and thousands of other policies cannot be ascertained in the abstract. They are good or bad depending on the particular situation of the country in question. The path to the market is unique to each individual country. Hence the main task of the economist is to uncover the relevant unique characteristics of the country and propose a set of comprehensive and concrete policy measures suitable for its initial conditions.

For this reason, the Japanese aid community is extremely ill at ease with the universal policy orientation of international financial institutions, which can be summarized as simultaneous pursuit of macroeconomic stability and "structural adjustment" (liberalization and privatization). Although these institutions argue that all adjustment programs are designed differently, the difference extends only to the intensity of individual measures in the preset menu of policies: tight budget, subsidy cuts, monetary restraints, positive and internationally competitive real interest rates, exchange rate devaluation, price and trade liberalization, higher public utility charges, and so on. The original menu does not change. This approach ignores the fact that each country requires its own menu and the effectiveness of each policy is case-dependent. Careful diagnosis is needed before treatment. The same medicine can cure or kill, depending on the condition of the patient.

5 BINARIZATION OF ECONOMIC DEVELOPMENT IDENTITIES

Japan and the East Asian Miracle

I wish to emphasize in this book [Sakakibara's] that there is, at least, one legitimate model of capitalism that is different from the American or neo-classical economic model . . . Although I called the Japanese system a non-capitalistic market economy in this book, I would not mind renaming it Japanese capitalism, as long as different versions of capitalism are recognized as legitimate alternatives that a country may choose or develop according to its own historical and cultural evolution.[1]

THE PRESENT CHAPTER and the next one together address why Japan proposed to create the AMF in the middle of the Asian financial crisis while excluding the United States from membership. Chapter 2 showed that the existing theoretical approaches on Japanese foreign policy—interest group, state-centered, and systemic analyses—did not furnish a reliable explanation for the question. Chapter 4, with its longitudinal analysis of domestic discursive meaning structures, uncovered the normalcy claim in which the three economic discourses of Marxism, economic liberalism, and developmentalism located the Japanese development experience in the context of their views on the role of the state in the history of development of the world economy. It also illuminated how the rise of the Asian economies in the 1980s empowered and enabled the developmentalist thread to win over the other contending interpretations and become the foundation for Japanese foreign economic policy. On the basis of these findings, I account for Japan's decision to propose the AMF by using the identity-intention analytical framework introduced in Chapter 3.

To reiterate the framework in brief, national interest emerges out of "situation or problem descriptions" through which state officials and others make sense of the world around them. Once a situation is defined in a certain way, the situational description informs state officials as to which actions are valuable, necessary, and compelling. Here identities, which are inherently relational and emerge out of repeated interactions among actors (states), are central to the situational description in giving each actor (state) meaningful understanding of the actions of others, including their nature, motives, interests, probable actions, attitudes, and roles in a given political context. Identities thus become the basis of *reasoning* what a state wants in the name of national interest; what actors want depends on their intersubjective understanding of what others want.

That said, using this framework I intend to empirically demonstrate how Japanese state officials' (International Finance Bureau officials at the MOF; hereafter MOF officials) conception of Japan and the United States as two rivals challenging each other's preferred model of economic development provided the basis on which Japan proposed an AMF. As will be discussed in greater detail, however, Japan's road to the AMF was not direct, but indeed rather circuitous. At the beginning of the financial crisis in Thailand, Japan refused to give bilateral assistance to the Thai government, insisting instead that Thailand negotiate with the IMF first. Indeed, Japan seemed willing to play a subordinate role in supporting the IMF. Japan's AMF proposal aimed to reverse that course, questioning the authorities of the IMF. I account for this variation in Japan's actions in terms of how MOF officials' fundamental (re)interpretation of the nature of the U.S.-led IMF operation in Thailand led them to propose the AMF as the most compelling action over a range of alternative policy actions. The aforementioned binary identity conception facilitated MOF officials in developing their new understanding of Japan's national interest.

As noted in Chapter 1 (the methodology section) and Chapter 3, however, there are a number of interrelated analytical steps that must be completed before one can successfully apply an identity-based analytical approach to a specific empirical problem such as Japan's AMF proposal. They are necessary to avoid tautological reasoning and ensure falsifiable research. First, one has to make the case that Japanese decision makers (MOF officials) were indeed part of the developmentalist discursive structure that interpretively accentuated the essential role of the Japanese state in the nation's economic development and shared its associated social meaning ("normal") in the history of the world economy. Locating MOF officials in the developmentalist discourse is indispensable to understanding their choice of a specific policy action, because this analytical effort (in the spirit of the constitutive analysis in Chapter 4) helps connect the historicity of identity (understanding of self) and agency (social conditions of possibility for adopting a particular foreign policy). In other words, this analytical process establishes the MOF as an institution with agency with respect to the politics of economic development.

Second, if Japan's decision to propose the AMF relates to previous events, one must specify those events and trace the decision's intrinsic relationship to them. Since the identity-intention analytical framework posits that an interest depends on a particular construction of self-identity in relation to the conceived identity of others, tracing the sequence of events that brought about the AMF proposal necessarily involves inquiring into the processes by which the definitions of self (Japan as the leader of state-led economic development) and other (the United States as the leader of neoliberal economic development), which MOF officials politically and socially constructed, have been produced and reproduced in international politics. As MOF officials continued to confront the United States in various international finance and development forums such as the World Bank, the ADB, the IMF, and the APEC, they internalized this binarization of self and other as a constitutive part of Japan and the United States in this given area. In terms of collective identity formation, this is a classic example of social and relational identity formation, defined by MOF officials' interaction (on behalf of Japan) with, and relationship to, their U.S. counterparts.[2]

Lastly, one has to examine whether MOF officials' internalized binarization of self and other indeed operated in their reasoning processes when they proposed the AMF, as the framework specifies. The focus is on tracing the detailed processes and timing of the MOF's policy change in relation to its interpretation of the IMF approach to the financial crisis. In other words, in order to account for the variation noted earlier, the empirical analysis is expected to explicate when and how such a binarization set in and subsequently came to lead MOF officials to interpret the U.S.-led IMF operation in Thailand in a certain way, thus leading them to consider "the AMF proposal excluding the United States" the most compelling course of action.[3]

This chapter deals with the first and second steps of this analytical process; the next chapter is devoted to the third step. The first section of this chapter locates MOF officials (or the MOF as an institution) in the developmentalist discursive structure. Emphasis is placed on MOF officials' construction of the so-called Asian model in the 1980s and 1990s by merging their interpretation of Japan's economic development with the lessons of the Asian experience. Special attention is paid to Eisuke Sakakibara, who muscled up the AMF proposal. This is followed by a section dealing with the processes by which these officials (and others in Japan) have since the mid-1980s internalized the binarization of Japan and the United States as leaders of different models of economic development. The focus here is on Japan pushing the World Bank to publish *The East Asian Miracle* in 1993. Not only did this event constitute a formative moment when Japan officially established itself as the leader of state-led economic development but it also sowed the seeds of Japan's AMF proposal in a path-dependent fashion. Following these analyses, the next chapter examines Japan's AMF proposal.

MINISTRY OF FINANCE: DEVELOPMENTALISM AND CONSTRUCTING THE ASIAN MODEL

What would MOF officials of the 1980s and the 1990s think of the role of the state in the success of Japan's economic development? The answer seems to be self-evident if one considers the MOF (formerly called *Okurasho* in Japanese, it is now called *Zaimusho*[4]), often referred to as the "ministry of ministries." This reflects its status as the most powerful and prestigious ministry at the apex of the Japanese bureaucracy. The MOF has itself been an integrated part of Japan's postwar interventionist economy with a political, economic, and intellectual force.[5] As evident as this may be, MOF officials have not shied away from claiming their own indispensable contributions to making possible what they call "the world's first economic miracle" or "an inspiration and model for all the later 'miracle' economies of East Asia." They normally point out two particular contributions of the MOF to the Japanese miracle:

> First is the doctrine of a balanced budget. Although Japan's early postwar stipulation of balanced budget was imposed by the U.S. to contain inflation, it was embraced by the Okurasho [MOF]. Even when the politicians of the Liberal Democratic Party managed to effectively end the policy in 1965, when the Diet authorized the issue of government bonds to finance deficit financing, the ministry remained powerfully attached to the doctrine of fiscal discipline. By limiting government spending, the ministry was able to keep tax rates low and give the private sector easier access to the national savings pool. Second is the emphasis on exporting. The national system of industrial finance operated by the Okurasho—both through the banks and through the Fiscal Investment and Loan Program, or *Zaito* system—funneled low-cost financing into Japan's industrial base and its export sector. The money channeled through these systems was used to build up the industrial infrastructure and fund government-designated priority industries and sectors. This was a critical element in Japan's successful export drive.[6]

Setting aside taking such an interpretation as an act of self-validation, what is more conspicuous about it lies in the fact that MOF officials' general interpretation (as exemplified in the excerpt) parallels that of the developmentalists in their assessment of the role of the state in Japan's miracle. As noted in Chapter 4, the Japanese developmentalists do not have much problem with such explanations, put forward by economic liberals as "private fixed investment," "dual structure-led low wages," or "high savings." Where they disagree with economic liberals is in their contention that the government *made possible* such conditions in the first place; they thereby emphasize the fact that Japan's postwar pattern of economic development ran counter to conventional notions of Ricardian static comparative advantage and was achieved with strong government support and guidance (for example, tariff protection, tax concessions, preferential allocation of loans and foreign currency to selected industries), exercised primarily through the MITI, the MOF, and the Bank of Japan. In other words, somewhere between the almighty market mechanism and the completely planned economy, the Japanese state wielded influence in leading private sector development through subsidizing and targeting credits to specific industries ("directed credit" policies[7]). The MOF indeed finds Japan's success in its defiance of U.S.-style capitalism. As such, it would be fair to say that not only have some, if not all, MOF officials been consciously or unconsciously embedded in developmentalism; they have also been the agents of embedding Japan within developmentalism.

From an institutional point of view, however, the source of MOF officials' embeddedness in developmentalism does not derive just from how they implement and interpret Japan's postwar economic development in a circular fashion. Perhaps more fundamental than that is the historically institutionalized status of free-market–oriented neoclassical economics within the MOF, which makes such a circularity possible in the first place. Historically, MOF officials have never fully acknowledged the self-organizing property of an impartial market providing efficient allocation of goods and capital.[8] Instead, they have viewed the market as being held aloft by two pillars: "one is the pillar of routine daily investment activity, and the other is the pillar of official support to keep the market behaving in an *appropriate* manner."[9] Along this line and speaking in general terms, Sakakibara, a prominent MOF economist and thinker, contrasts the Anglo-Saxon approach of allowing markets to fall and institutions to fail with the MOF attempts to keep all participating players in operation: "It is a question of relative social costs, a question of preserving order in the markets."[10] In other words, the market itself has been regarded as an entity to be nourished and developed in the Polanyian sense. Japan's prolonged economic success during the high growth era was believed to testify to the validity of their concept of market.

Such a traditional conception of the market has been responsible for two particular institutional practices of the MOF. First, MOF officials are trained to view neoclassical (or neoliberal) economic principles as a set of ideas and techniques to be used as one reference among many. The principles should not be taken as paramount but as one set of considerations within a larger framework of administrative and legal principles.[11] The MOF wants its staff to understand economics but not be possessed by it.

The second practice is manifested in the MOF's hiring (and perhaps promoting) practices. Maintaining its prewar tradition, the MOF employs a handful of neoclassical economists, but the bulk of men appointed to the top echelons of the MOF are graduates of Tokyo University's department of law, not economics. As such, Komiya and Yamamoto were able to articulate in 1979 that "there is not one professional economist employed by the Government of Japan."[12] In 1995, they reaffirmed their earlier position that "nothing had changed" in the case of the MOF.[13] Komiya, who has taught many MOF officials, believes that the economic sophistication of the MOF is slowly improving, but he thinks overall that its bureaucrats "don't have much faith in the market mechanism, and they like to intervene in the market."[14] Likewise, Miyao Takahiko of Tsukuba University argues that the ministry has "no belief in what might be called economic principles."[15] In contrast, if the World Bank begins the art of paradigm maintenance (neoclassical economy) with a hand-picked staff (about 80 percent of whom are U.S.- or British-trained neoclassical economists, thus most of them sharing the preconceptions of mainstream Anglo-American economics),[16] the MOF does it by training its staff to be aware of the undisciplined nature of the free market.

In this institutional context, the rise of the economically powerful Asian developmental states in the 1980s played a pivotal role in preparing the MOF to challenge neoliberalism in two important ways. First, it created a space for MOF officials to make a strong case for the international validity of state-led economic development by merging their interpretation of Japan's development with the lessons of the Asian experiences. As MOF officials contrasted the Asian experiences (including the Japanese) with their observation of the track record of those of Latin America, they came to question the effectiveness, universal application, and rigidities of the neoliberal model.[17] The impressive accomplishments of state-led economic development in Asia thus bolstered MOF officials' opinion that Japan's experience is neither unique nor irrelevant beyond its own borders:[18]

> After seeing Asian countries' experience—Korea, Taiwan, Malaysia, Thailand, Indonesia—there was much stronger confidence in that model as viable and applicable. The crux of that model is the ingenious combination of private and public sector dynamism. Japan feels that Japanese success has something to do with this mixture. When the U.S. came up with its strong preference for private sector initiative and its clear dislike for the public sector, conflict developed between the two approaches.[19]

Going beyond Japan's uniqueness, MOF officials started to represent state-led economic development in terms of the Asian model,[20] as opposed to that of Anglo-Saxon (or neoliberal)[21] economic development. Thus, presenting their approach as a viable alternative, MOF officials focused on a positive market-guiding role for the state, developed a cautious attitude about rapid privatization, saw the utility of protectionism at early stages of development (thus enabling the flying geese model to work), and questioned the viability of a purely unregulated financial market mechanism. As they increased their doubts about the universal applicability of the neoliberal approach, they did not hide their considerable lack of confidence in the practitioners of the neoliberal approach in the World Bank. Taking issue with World Bank economists' preoccupation with short-term results and universal application of the neoliberal model rather than consideration of the long run and differences in each country's developmental stage and economic situation, MOF officials expressed their resentment:

> Something may be okay in theory but not in reality. Top management understands this, but the problems are the economists who don't understand this. There are many American academics who are stupid about this.[22]

And:

> The United States and Britain speak in loud voice about market mechanism. This is the Anglo-Saxon way, uttered by American Ph.D.s who talk with strong voices. . . . U.S.-educated Ph.D.s have no experience with government-led economics. Thus they favor laissez-faire.[23]

In a similar fashion, the MOF-seconded ADB officials asserted:

> The United States emphasizes program lending. That's not a bad direction, but the question is, what kind of policy dialogue do they want? U.S. policy dialogue is based on the belief in the market, liberalization, private sector. That is, if only countries liberalize, everything will be all right. But developing countries are in different stages, especially in Asia. Each has distinctive characteristics. This should be the basis of policy dialogue.[24]

> It is not good to do what the United States does by pressuring DMCs [developing member countries in the ADB] based on ideology. Asia is not Latin America. There the United States acts as a consultant or doctor and intervenes in a country's management—and look what happened. Latin America followed U.S. philosophy, and it has become the world's baggage.[25]

As such, the rise of Asia has updated Japan's model and coalesced into the Asian model. It offered the basis on which the MOF justified its challenge to neoliberalism.

Second, the rise of Asia has become a catalyst for, or literally helped, the "Asianists" take up influential positions in the International Financial Bureau (IFB), which holds jurisdiction over Japan's external financial affairs in the MOF.[26] The emergence of the Asianist-based lineup on the international side of the MOF took root in the MOF's personnel policy changes in the 1970s, and the lineup eventually contributed to the ministry's 1990s reputation as Asia-oriented.[27]

In the 1970s, the MOF revised its personnel policy programs to strengthen the capacity to deal with international financial and development issues. At the core of the revised personnel program were (1) dispatching MOF officials abroad early in their careers for periods ranging from a few months to two years for studying, as has already been noted; and (2) promoting appointment of some of these officials, on their return to Japan, to the international financial institutions (IFIs) such as the IMF, the World Bank, the Inter-American Development Bank (IDB), and the ADB. The MOF felt these were the best training places for increasing these officials' capacity to understand international finance and development issues.[28] The effect of this policy shift was the emergence of a cadre of more internationally minded and experienced officials who returned from the IFIs to take up influential positions in international finance affairs. They brought back to the MOF foreign language skills, expertise in development issues, expanded personal contact abroad, knowledge of foreign financial markets, familiarity with the cultures of various regions of world, insights into the workings of international financial institutions, and perhaps greater wariness of the U.S. and Western approach to economic development and associated diplomacy. As such, they were resources the MOF could rely on when it began departing from the traditional diplomacy of "silence, smile, and sleep" in the IFIs.[29]

The impact of these personnel exchanges or rotations, however, was not distributed equally across the IFIs. Indeed, it was greatly skewed to the ADB when ex-ADB personnel returned to the MOF to assume positions pivotal for international finance and developmental affairs. ADB veterans have been conspicuous in the vice ministry for international affairs and in the IFB.[30] For example, the MOF's lineup in 1993, when *The East Asian Miracle* was published by the World Bank, would illustrate this point: through the first half of 1993, Tadao Chino held the vice ministership for international affairs, the top international post and number three in the ministry, subordinate only to the minister of finance and the administrative vice minister,[31] while Kosuke Nakahira directed the IFB.[32] Nakahira then succeeded Chino in July 1993 as vice minister. Among the ADB executive directors (director, or *Kachō*, level at the MOF), Takatoshi Katō, executive director from 1985 to 1987, served as Nakahira's IFB assistant director general and succeeded Nakahira as IFB director-general; Shoji Mori, ADB executive director from 1987 to 1990, served a stint as director of the IFB's Coordination Division before being sent to Washington as financial attaché; and Ken Yagi, ADB executive director from 1990 to 1992, served as director of the IFB's Development Finance Division, which oversees bilateral ODA.[33]

As such, it was no coincidence that Japan embarked on propounding the Asian development model and its direct challenge to the United States in the World Bank at a time when these ex-ADB officials (nicknamed "the Asian Mafia") dominated the IFB and the vice ministership for international affairs. These officials were intimately familiar with the workings of the ADB and the development record of the Asian economies, had first-hand knowledge of Asian development processes, and understood the proclivities of the United States on development issues. In this vein, it is not surprising that the knowledge and expertise gained through the experiences of the Asian development process enabled "Asianist" MOF officials such as Masaki Shiratori and Isao Kubota to later assert with confidence that the neoliberal approach was inferior to a now well-tested Asian development model.[34]

The predominance of the Asianists on the international side of the MOF has continued to the present, with officials in favor of the neoliberal approach constituting a minority faction.[35] In this institutional context, Sakakibara, who virtually launched the AMF proposal, was promoted to vice minister for international affairs in July 1997 from his director-general post at the IFB. The promotion was granted by Prime Minister Hashimoto, who would also be classified as a pro-Asian politician in Japan's political circle.[36] Hashimoto supported the view that Japan must have an independent policy on Asia.[37]

Sakakibara was one of the most outspoken Japanese critics of neoliberalism in international finance and development in the 1990s.[38] A good example of his uneasiness about the universal precept of the orthodoxy was his attack on Yukio Noguchi, a former comrade in radical left-wing activities in the heady days of 1960 (student protests against the AMPO, the 1960 revision of the U.S.-Japan security treaty) and professor of economics at Hitotsubashi University. In his response to Noguchi's claim[39] that Japan's economic structure was a historical aberration (abnormal) even in the history of Japan—a "1940 economic structure" based on the needs of World War II, "a total war economy"—Sakakibara wrote:

> The first action [Noguchi's participation in the radical student protests] was based on Marxism and the second on neoclassical economy. The thinking pattern at work in both events was his belief that there was a universal model to be found and "reform" to be aimed at, based on comparing that model with Japan's current conditions. . . . In other words, it is an advocacy backed by the impatience that comes from immaturity, arrogant elitism, and complex passions mixed with a kind of inferiority complex toward Europe and the U.S.[40]

Sakakibara's draconian criticism was firmly anchored in his developmentalist interpretation of a positive market-guiding role that the Japanese and other Asian states played in their respective economic development. He specified the successful role of the Asian states in realizing the "flying geese pattern of development headed by Japan, then followed by Singapore, Taiwan, Korea, and Hong Kong, and then followed by the rest of Asia,"[41] which strikes at the core of the Japanese developmentalist discourse (see Chapter 4). Like Funabashi, who characterized the disputes between the United States and Japan over models of capitalism and economic development as the "new cold war,"[42] he (Sakakibara) envisioned as early as 1990 that, although the end of the Cold War might have closed one chapter of ideological competition between two extremes, it opened a new era of subtler competition between the United States and Japan.[43]

At the same time, Sakakibara himself attempted to challenge the concept of Japan as abnormal internationally: "In Japan, Fukuyama's universalism/revisionism is dominant in the press, as well as in political and administrative circles. . . . At this point we thought it necessary to verify the truth about universalism/revisionism."[44] Sakakibara marshaled the resources of the MOF and assembled a panel of sixteen experts—thirteen academics, two bureaucrats, and a private sector economist—through the ministry's Institute of Fiscal and Monetary Policy[45] and asked them to compare the Japanese political, economic, and social systems with those of the United States and Europe. Setting aside cultural differences, the group's specific task was to "examine whether or not Japan, in spite of such differences, is well equipped with modern mechanisms institutionally."[46] The group concluded that Japan was not abnormal, but torn between the European and the American model: "What is important is to cast aside the reform view based on *the outlier-Japan* concept and then to position Japan as a model or as a civilization in thinking about what direction it will take."[47]

Furthermore, in addition to focusing his attention on the role of the state in economic development, Sakakibara has explicitly linked his efforts to promote the Asian model to the debate over structural adjustment policy. In a speech in Washington, D.C., in September 1996, he argued that "the 'Washington consensus' on the need for thorough and rapid deregulation, along with liberalization of capital flows, drastic curtailment of the role of government in influencing credit allocation and a shift from bank lending to equity-based financial systems, may not be appropriate for developing countries following different development paths."[48] In May 1997, only two full months before the Thai crisis, Sakakibara launched another severe attack on the Washington consensus at an ADB-hosted private luncheon, calling it "blind application of a universal model of capitalistic fundamentalism" by Washington and by the multinational bureaucracies that subscribed to it. Scandalizing many of his Western listeners, he declared:

> Asia is resonating with overoptimistic Washington-generated market expectations. . . . Euphoric expectations have been generated by inflows of foreign capital which are market-oriented and sensitive to short-term changes. . . . It might lead to the latter day of *colonization* of Asia via the promotion of neoclassical economic paradigms.[49]

Did he prophesy the impending doom known as the Asian crisis?[50]

ASIAN VERSUS ANGLO-SAXON: *THE EAST ASIAN MIRACLE*, BEFORE AND AFTER

With the MOF's embedded economic developmentalism in mind, this section illustrates several of Japan's key confrontations with the United States in the politics of economic development at various international stages.[51] The aim is to present the processes by which Japan (or MOF officials) established itself as the leader of antiparadigmatic state-led economic development in relation to the United States. It was in the ADB in the mid-1980s that the clash between the United States and Japan first played out, a milestone for the emerging binarization of identities on both sides. The regionally bounded clash was replayed at the World Bank, the world center for controlling economic development discourse, in the early 1990s. Japan's decision to challenge the World Bank constituted what one calls a formative moment when Japan internationally (that is, going beyond Asia) consolidated its identity as the leader of state-led economic development. Japan's questioning of the universal validity of the neoliberal approach continued right up to the outbreak of the Thai crisis in July 1997.

First Clash: Japan vs. the United States at the Asian Development Bank

With the inauguration of Ronald Reagan in 1981, the United States geared up a powerful drive promoting the magic of the marketplace for economic growth and development.[52] The positive role of the state in economic affairs was denied, and it was asserted instead that the state should not be a player in the market, but a referee ensuring the necessary institutional framework within which individuals are free to pursue their own economic activities.[53] In support of the market thesis, the United States universalized the effectiveness of the market mechanism, arguing that any "societies that have experienced the greatest success in terms of economic growth relied on the magic of the market,"[54] which is most vividly demonstrated by the American experience in its early industrialization.[55]

With respect to construction of the universal model, the United States not only adopted liberalizing and deregulating economic policies for itself (Reaganomics, or supply side economics) but also reasserted the centrality of the market in international development.[56] The United States claimed that past government intervention in developing countries had often had malignant effects and that aid applied within a distorted policy framework was likely to be wasted. As such, the United States demanded that developing countries follow the three basic policies laid down by the universal model, which were to become the basis of the Washington consensus in 1990: encourage free and open international markets by lowering tariff and other trade barriers, reduce barriers to the flow of private capital investment, and encourage sound economic policies that allow the market to operate and limit the role of government in the economy.[57] In short, economic development was attributed to free market forces, while government intervention was blamed for underdevelopment and stagnation. As a result, the United States shifted its bilateral aid programs (USAID) toward projects that emphasized the developments of private sectors in developing countries. Simultaneously, the United States influenced the IMF and the World Bank, the two most powerful Bretton Woods institutions in the realm of international finance and development. These institutions started to reflect the rise of liberalizing, deregulating, and anti-Keynesian policies in their lending practices.[58] The World Bank, which was created to encourage economic development, lost its earlier enthusiasm for policies that emphasized a role for the state: nationalization of industries, state planning of the economy, or tariffs to protect emerging domestic industries. Instead, it started to put a high priority on privatization of state enterprises and private sector development in developing countries.

Along with the United States pushing the IMF and the World Bank to the far right of economic theory, there emerged structural conditionality attached to these institutions' loans to developing countries.[59] Until the end of the 1970s, the only substantial policy conditionality applied to developing countries in search of assistance was that of the IMF, which was established to smooth world commerce by reducing foreign exchange restrictions and helping out countries experiencing temporary balance-of-payment problems. The World Bank had yet to move far into "policy-related" lending; the same was true of, for example, other regional multinational development banks (MDBs).[60] Moreover, IMF conditionality at that time was of quite limited scope, confined to a few macroeconomic policy variables such as the exchange rate and domestic credit.

U.S. insistence on the magic of the marketplace in the 1980s transformed the entire picture. As for the IMF, the scope of conditionality was greatly extended. The previous principle of restricting it to a few macroeconomic variables was abandoned in favor of a far more ambitious neoliberal agenda.[61] The IMF broadened the content of its conditionality into such areas as reduction or elimination of public subsidies and removal of price controls. Operation of the market mechanism was also promoted through liberalization of trade and payments. The realm of the private sector relative to the public sector was extended by numerous requirements for privatization of public enterprises. The efficiency of the private sector was additionally promoted through stipulations requiring some chronically inefficient public enterprises to go into liquidation. Domestic resource mobilization was promoted by tax measures, and by provisions for reform and deregulation of the financial sector, including recapitulation and restructuring of banking institutions and deregulation of interest rates.[62] In other words, the IMF "unobtrusively introduced microconditionality,"[63] and with this broadening of conditionality it proceeded to take a more active role in the sphere of economic development, which had not been its primary institutional concern.[64]

Once the World Bank began to impose policy conditionality, it was also on par with the IMF. The World Bank launched economywide SAL programs emphasizing in a similar fashion privatization, cutting government subsidies, dropping trade protectionist measures, reducing regulation of the private sector, and creating incentives to attract foreign capital.[65] The fallout of U.S.-driven application of the neoliberal model did not stop at the World Bank but spread to other MDBs, namely the IDB and the African Development Bank (AfDB).

Until the end of the 1970s, all MDBs more or less converged in terms of lending policies, priorities, and prescriptions.[66] Because of the World Bank's adoption of structural adjustment-type lending practices, the early 1980s were years of growing divergence, particularly between the World Bank and other MDBs. By the end of the 1980s, however, the general tendency of a growing convergence among MDBs was restored, despite debate that still occurred about application of structural adjustment-type lending practices. Restoration was made possible through changes in power configurations made at both the IDB and the AfDB, the two MDBs created and controlled by the borrowing countries (contrary to the World Bank and the ADB) in their respective regions; negotiation between the donor and borrowing members had led to parity in voting shares at the IDB and to pressure for parity at the AfDB.[67] As a result, the two MDBs' lending activities and operations became almost indistinguishable from those of the World Bank.

Swimming against this tide was the ADB, which was the most passive with respect to this general tendency. For example, even though the ADB also initiated policy-based lending in 1987, it restricted its operations to sectoral adjustment loans (thus not demanding the World Bank style of structural adjustment).[68] Furthermore, in terms of lending policies and prescriptions, the ADB still focused on project loans, recognized the importance of infrastructures, and (perhaps most important) allowed for state guidance, most notably in the form of making two-step loans[69] to recipient members, all of which had become almost obsolete at other MDBs. The ADB's continuing lending practice of preferring (now-old-fashioned) loans to governments for big agricultural and public works projects instead of significant help for the development of private sectors in recipient countries led to increasing friction with the American executive directors at the ADB. Japan firmly resisted U.S. pressure because the U.S emphasis on structural reforms clashed with Japanese priorities, which rested on financing social overhead through each recipient government—in the sphere of public transport, communications, and energy facilities—to enable private investors to establish manufacturing enterprises.[70] The tussle at the ADB marked the first clash of the politics of economic development between the United States and Japan.

As was the case for the IDB and the AfDB, the American conception of the ADB's proper role was that of a regional incarnation of the World Bank, making loans conditional on adherence to policy reforms, such as privatization and liberalization in the financial and commodity realms.[71] As such, the American executive directors at the ADB had since the early 1980s embarked on assertive promotion of the neoliberal model, which was deemed universal and applicable to all regions and all MDBs. These officials, in alliance with the ADB's European shareholders, vociferously criticized the public sector orientation of the ADB's lending policies at the 1985 annual meeting.[72] They accused the ADB of doing business the Japanese way by declaring that the Japanese officials involved in the ADB's strategic planning work entertained a "zen-like theory of economics" [referring to these officials' proclivity for the flying geese model; see Chapter 4].[73] The American executive directors aggressively struggled (with arrogance and inflexibility, in the eyes of Japanese ADB officials) to get the principles of market forces and privatization established in the ADB's lending policies. They insisted, for example, that any capital increase at the ADB must be predicated on encouraging private sector development and that loans be given on condition of adherence to policy reforms such as those that support financial liberalization.[74]

This posed a big problem for the Japanese ADB officials (most of whom were seconded from the MOF, as has been noted). It was not just because these officials feared that the excessive U.S. emphasis on private sector versus public could cause irreparable damage to the ADB's reputation and operation as the most successful (in terms of mobilizing resources and channeling them to developing member countries) project-based (as opposed to policy-based) lending MDB.[75] More important than that were their serious doubts about the neoliberal model's appropriateness for the needs of Asian economies. It was not that the Japanese officials disagreed with U.S emphasis on the importance of market forces, privatization, and liberalization. Rather, they thought it was too early for the Asian countries to adopt such neoliberal measures. As such, Japanese officials, often in collaboration with the ADB's Asian directors, found U.S. efforts to apply the neoliberal model universally, in textbook fashion, to Asian countries out of step with the Asian reality. Most of those countries still depended heavily on strong government guidance and a degree of protectionism for infant industries and lacked a strong private sector that could carry out and sustain policy reforms envisioned by the universal model. As Fujioka (a Japanese president of the ADB from 1981 to 1990) argued, there should not be "an arbitrary difference between the public and private sectors."[76] Japanese officials increasingly criticized American executive directors' assertiveness with respect to universal principles at the ADB as dogmatic or too idealistic, particularly in light of "their suspicious knowledge and expertise of Asian and Asian development experience."[77] To quote two arguments made by Japanese ADB officials:

> America's support for policy dialogue was tough. This is the Anglo-Saxon approach, the World Bank approach. But the ADB should take an Asian approach. The World Bank deals with the world and does not especially understand Asian thinking. It has a Western philosophy: yes-no, give-not-give. They have brilliant young economists, but they don't understand Third World societies or psychology at all.[78]

> Policy dialogue is important, but you must base it on Asian experiences. Then it's okay. But nonregional countries look at Asian development in a textbook fashion, with textbook knowledge. The United States asks Japan to cooperate on this basis, but Japan takes a lukewarm attitude.[79]

However, this initial clash of the United States and Japan at the ADB did not occur in the form of a clear distinction, an Asian versus Anglo-Saxon development approach. At this stage, Japan still did not have a clear conceptualization of the Asian model; the Asian experiences had yet to coalesce into a model supported by specific policy proposals. As such, Japan's advocacy of Asian development tenets during this time was primarily designed to offer a counterpoint to the American directors' aggressive drive for application of the neoliberal model.[80] Japan thus attempted to maintain the status quo at the ADB by supporting its lending practices (as noted earlier), which accorded well with Japan's preferred development strategy. Japan's financial power at the bank[81] made it possible for the ADB to remain (as it still remains) the only MDB left unscathed by neoliberalism as a project-based lending institution.[82]

Japan's first clash with the United States at the ADB generated three important developments for its later challenges in the World Bank and elsewhere. First, the clash gave Japanese officials a unique opportunity to seriously study the development experiences of Asian countries when they confronted the U.S. push for the neoliberal model. The studies of the Asian experiences matured (or refined) these officials' previous conception of a proper development model based largely on Japan's experience and eventually led to emergence of an Asian model stressing government leadership (or the role of the state) in forging private and public sector cooperation. Second, the initial Japanese experience of defending an Asian-type development strategy at the ADB imbued Japanese officials with an embryonic sense of Japan's "mission" as "the source of technology and knowledge for Asia, just as the advanced Western states had served that function for Japan in the past."[83] Third, and not least important, because of the strong institutional linkage between the MOF and the ADB many of these officials, who served the ADB during a period of great contention with the United States, returned to the MOF in influential positions, in charge of Japan's external finance and development affairs. Thus the MOF started to be called "Asian-oriented," and such a lineup enabled it to speak out on the Asian development experience in the World Bank and elsewhere with greater knowledge and self-confidence than before. Taken together, it was no accident that toward the end of the 1980s Japan began to clearly articulate an Asian (distinct from Anglo-Saxon) model. Japan stressed the role of the state in industrial and credit-allocation policies while questioning the viability of a purely unregulated market mechanism. Moreover, it asserted the utility of protectionism, as opposed to rapid privatization, at early stages of economic development.

Second Clash: Japan vs. the United States at the World Bank and The East Asian Miracle

Japan's tensions with the United States over a proper model of economic development culminated at the World Bank in the early 1990s.[84] As tensions increased, they generated numerous attacks and counterattacks between Japan and the World Bank (Japan always thought the United States was behind World Bank operations). During this turbulent period, Japan firmly established itself internationally (going beyond Asia) as the leader of state-led economic development approach, first by establishing the theoretical precepts of state-led economic development (see the Overseas Economic Cooperation Fund or OECF Occasional Paper No. 1) and second by literally forcing the World Bank to look into the importance of the Asian alternative to the Anglo-Saxon orthodoxy (*The East Asian Miracle*).[85]

Despite growing uneasiness with the World Bank's SAL program, however, Japan was not the one that initiated the tussle. Japan did not openly carry its development agenda to the World Bank until 1989, partly because it viewed the World Bank as "America's bank," just as it thought of the ADB as "Japan's" or "Asia's" bank. It was also in part because Japan had yet to put together a coherent rendition of the Asian model.[86] It was not until the end of the 1980s that MOF officials began to openly express their reservations about the effectiveness, universal application, and rigidity of the neoliberal approach, having studied and found contradictions between their observations of the SAL program's track record (especially in Latin America) and the Asian experience. These Japanese reservations, together with Japan's defense of an Asian-type development strategy in the ADB, started to get attention from the IFIs (including the World Bank), which realized that Japan was promoting a different set of development strategies that emphasized the role of the state in guiding markets, including managed trade and financial policies.

The uneasy peace between Japan and the World Bank was dismantled in September 1989 when the World Bank strongly criticized Japan's largest aid implementing agency, the OECF,[87] for its two-step loan policies in Southeast Asia.[88] In the late 1980s, Japan established the ASEAN-Japan Development Fund, as part of recycling Japan's large current account surplus, to support private sector development in the Southeast Asian region. The OECF administered the fund. As usual, it was dispensed in the form of two-step loans, first to the development banks of aid recipient countries, which then lent to targeted industries at below-market interest rates. In other words, the loans were targeted, subsidized credits to be used for selected industries. Focusing on the case of the Philippines, the World Bank criticized Japan's two-step loan practice on the grounds that it was inconsistent with financial sector reform in a country that the World Bank was helping to restructure with the aim of eliminating subsidized credits. A senior-vice president of the World Bank wrote the president of the OECF asking him to reconsider the policy of subsidized targeted loans: "Passing these funds to the banks and final beneficiaries at below market interest rates could have an adverse impact on development of the financial sector and hence would create unnecessary distortions and set back the financial sector reforms which had been supported by the IMF's Extended Fund Facility and the Bank's Financial Sector Adjustment Loan."[89] The World Bank, in line with strict financial sector liberalization for client countries, insisted that credit should always and everywhere be at market or nonsubsidized rates.

The World Bank's criticism provoked Japan, because it amounted to nothing short of annihilation of Japan's aid philosophy, which was built on its experience of economic development. In Japan's view, subsidized targeted credits were "the nerves of the developmental state."[90] The credit policies were the Japanese state's pivotal means of successfully developing selected industries (that is, assisting some businesses more than others, given limited resources), which would otherwise have had to pay very high interest rates.[91] Thus Japan's executive director at the World Bank strongly protested to senior management and to the board of executive directors from member governments, insisting that financial sector deregulation should only be a means of attaining economic development rather than an objective in itself, but to no avail.[92] The World Bank refused to back down, continuing to voice skepticism on state guidance of development processes while theoretically refining and justifying the Washington consensus through publication of its annual *World Bank Reports*.[93] Nonetheless, it had to find a way to account for the rise of the Asian economies, particularly NIEs, with respect to their recent prosperity, and address what other countries should learn from their experiences.

The 1991 World Bank Report, which was titled *The Challenge of Development* and released in June, did just that. Unlike the two earlier reports that advocated extreme neoliberal prescriptions for developing countries' economic development,[94] the 1991 report made the famous "market-friendly" conclusion regarding the development experiences of Japan, Singapore, Korea, and Taiwan. This phrase was coined by Lawrence Summers, who joined the World Bank as chief economist and vice president in January 1991 and who later countered Sakakibara in the Asian financial crisis management as deputy secretary of the U.S. Department of Treasury. By "market-friendly" the 1991 report meant that these Asian countries were successful economically largely thanks to "effective but carefully delimited government roles" in facilitating adequate investments in human capital, provision of a competitive climate of enterprise, openness to international trade, and stable macroeconomic management. The 1991 report also acknowledged cases where market mechanisms were either lacking or inadequate to the task of economic development, and where privatization required caution and prudence. As such, the 1991 report seemed to endorse "enlightened, selective, and moderate" state guidance of the development process.

The 1991 report's conclusion, however, brought everything back to the old position. It argued for increased withdrawal of the state from the development process in favor of market forces (limiting the role of the state as the provider of a regulatory framework for private-sector developments—the state not as a director or a player but as a referee of market exchanges) and urged a change from the "old" state-centric paradigm. The report concluded:

> No one argues that there is a better economic system for the production and distribution of goods and services than competitive markets. . . . But markets cannot operate in vacuum—they require a legal and regulatory framework that only governments can provide.[95]

It thus restated a largely free-market view of appropriate public policy for development under the label "market-friendly." From Japan's point of view, market-friendly still reflected too closely the Washington consensus. To Japanese eyes, the 1991 report was what Wade would call the origin of "the Art of Paradigm Maintenance."

In response to all these adverse developments, Japan issued a sweeping critique of World Bank policy. Thirty years after its foundation in 1961, Japan's OECF (in charge of the ASEAN-Japan Development Fund) issued its first occasional paper, titled "Issues Related to the World Bank's Approach to a Structural Adjustment: Proposal from a Major Partner," in October 1991.[96] Here is Wade's summary of its main points:

1. For a developing country to attain sustainable growth, the government must adopt "measures aiming 'directly' at promoting investment."
2. These measures should be part of an explicit industrial strategy to promote the leading industries of the future.
3. Directed and subsidized credit has a key role in promoting these industries because of extensive failures in developing countries' financial markets.
4. Decisions about ownership arrangements, including privatization, should relate to actual economic, political, and social conditions in the country

concerned, not to the universal desirability of privatizing public enterprises. For example, there may be legitimate national sentiments about the desirability of foreign ownership.

5 Japanese fiscal and monetary policies in the postwar era may be worthy of consideration. They were centered on preferential tax treatment and development finance institutions' lendings.[97]

Focusing on these points, the paper concludes:

> It is impossible to achieve optimum allocation of resources solely through market principles regardless of the level of development. There are many areas which cannot be handled by market mechanism [market failure], and government intervention is necessary to cope with such conditions. . . . We wonder whether privatization is always the solution for improving efficiency of public sector. Various conditions in individual countries must be taken into account very carefully. Unfortunately, the World Bank's approach seems to be almost similar for every country.[98]

The OECF paper made clear that trade liberalization and financial deregulation, the twin pillars of World Bank prescriptions for developing countries, should be a subordinate part of industrialization and industrial strategy rather than objectives themselves. To support each point summarized above, the paper walked through a step-by-step criticism of World Bank policy. On the financial deregulation front, the OECF paper pointed out that the World Bank's rigid insistence that capital be allocated only at market interest rates correctly reflecting its scarcity values was likely to prevent capital from flowing to socially desirable economic activities that were too costly or risky for the private sector to undertake. On the trade liberalization front, it argued that too-hasty liberalization measures could cause balance-of-payments difficulties and make it impossible for developing countries to gain a competitive and comparative advantage in higher-value-added industries. This was reminiscent of Ōshima's critique of free trade policy in 1891, which argued that "the ultimate implication of the theory of free trade is that agricultural nations must remain agricultural, and industrial nations must remain industrial."[99] On the privatization front, the paper cautioned that in some developing countries government officials were better managers and entrepreneurs than those in the private sector, and that unqualified pursuit of privatization thus represented degradation.

Even though the OECF paper was designed to question several basic tenets of the SAL program (according to the program's track record so far accumulated) from Japan's point of view, it was hardly separable from Japan's desire to respond to the World Bank's earlier criticisms. Apart from the political nature of the paper, the significance was twofold: first, Japan "officially" spelled out at the international level what a state *must* do for economic development as a player in, rather than a referee of, market exchanges. By the same token, Japan "officially" merged (or molded) its development experience into the Asian model internationally by firmly articulating that industrial policy played a central role in the economic development strategies of East Asia (including Japan).

Japan reaffirmed commitment to the Asian model by furthering its criticism of the World Bank's blanket prescription for economic development—trade liberalization and financial deregulation—at the expense of government industrial and credit allocation policies. At the annual meeting of the board of governors of the World Bank and the IMF in Bangkok in 1991 (the same place where the OECF paper was circulated), Yasushi Mieno, the president of the Bank of Japan, standing in for Japan's finance minister, argued that government intervention can complement market mechanisms to "create the kind of environment in which free markets can function effectively."[100] Addressing the role of the state, Mieno did not forget to mention the *Asian* experiences:

> Experience in Asia has shown that although development strategies require a healthy respect for market mechanism, the role of the government cannot be forgotten. I would like to see the World Bank and the IMF take the lead in a wide-ranging study that would define the theoretical underpinnings of this approach and clarify the areas in which it can be successfully applied to other parts of the globe.[101]

Mieno challenged the World Bank to study the Asian experience. MOF officials at the annual meeting called the World Bank's approach "simple minded," resting on "outmoded Western concepts that fail to take account of the successful strategies pursued by Japan and some of its Asian neighbors in developing their economies."[102] In private, these officials accused World Bank economists of gross arrogance, of presuming to lecture them that Japan was doing the wrong things while at the same time asking for more Japanese money. They also added privately that even though they directed their criticism at the World Bank they were not blind to the fact that the World Bank was under U.S. influence, and that World Bank economists, regardless of nationality, were dominated by U.S.-trained neoclassicists.[103]

Having presented an unusually sharp critique of World Bank policies, the

MOF took issue with the 1991 World Bank annual report, expressing frustration with the report's tendency to underplay the importance of the Asian alternative to Anglo-Saxon orthodoxy. The MOF pressured a reluctant World Bank[104] to pursue a thorough study of Asian development experiences. By "Asia," Japan broadened the study this time to include Japan, NIEs (Korea, Hong Kong, Taiwan, Singapore), and Indonesia, Malaysia, and Thailand; the 1991 World Bank report covered only four Asian countries (Japan, Korea, Singapore, and Taiwan). At the insistence of Japan, and with $1.2 million from Japan's Policy and Human Resource Development (PHRD) fund, the World Bank finally agreed to study the Asian experiences. It was agreed that the study was to focus on the two key questions Japan had so far posed: "Did state intervention—such as subsidized targeted credit, protection of selected industries from imports, and export promotion—contribute to the rise of the Asian economies?" and "Can policies that worked in Asia be used in the rest of the developing world?"

The study got under way in January 1992 and was to be written over eighteen months for publication at the time of the annual meeting of the World Bank and the IMF in September 1993.[105] Lawrence Summers and Nancy Birdsall (the director of the research department) were appointed to direct the study.

The political significance of Japan's initiative in publishing *The East Asian Miracle* study was such that Japan firmly consolidated internalization *and* externalization of its identity as the leader of state-led economic development in relation to identification of the United States as the leader of the neoliberal economic development approach, a situation that had been developing in various confrontations with the United States since the mid-1980s. In terms of symbolic interaction theory,[106] by making its Asian neighbors the "positive" reference group ("us"), from which Japan would derive the sense of legitimacy and leadership indispensable for promoting its own development experience abroad, Japan at the same time constituted a "negative" reference group (the proponents of neoliberalism, "them"). Yasutomo's commentary on this event suffices to illustrate this point:

> This initiative constituted the strongest challenge to date of the IBRD's [the World Bank] orthodoxy and the clearest indication thus far of Japan's intention to contribute "ideas" rather than only money and personnel. Although couched in terms of raising questions about the relevance of the Asian experience for other developing nations, Japan's prime motive appeared to encom-

> pass taking a leadership role within the bank on development philosophy. One Japanese government official claims that *only* Japan and the United States engage in philosophical discussion of development approaches on the board.[107]

In the meantime, once the momentum of the politics of development set in, both Japan and the World Bank were unable to apply the brakes on their differences. While *The East Asian Miracle* was being prepared for publication, Lawrence Summers (then the World Bank chief economist and the vice president who had openly expressed that Japanese economists would be regarded as "second rate") firmly rejected each point made in the OECF Occasional Paper No. 1. In his reply to the OECF paper, Summers concluded:

> The capabilities of governments in most developing countries were not sufficient to: implement successful industrial promotion campaigns; utilize targeted, subsidized, interest rate systems; prepare and carry out protection regimes for infant industries; and adequately improve the efficiency of most state enterprises in place of privatization. . . . For most developing countries, relying on imperfect markets—rather than imperfect governments—has the greater chance for promoting sustainable growth.[108]

In the same month, April 1992, Japan made another statement against the neoliberal approach, this time targeting IMF policies. With the MITI's *Blueprint for Economic Reconstruction and Development in Russia*, which takes an approach that is in "stark contrast" to that of the IMF, Japan advocated that its postwar economic renaissance could be used to formulate appropriate policies in, for example, designing emergency measures to halt the plunge in output, and developing priority production programs to ensure the supply of essential industrial goods. Japan expressed doubts about whether macroeconomic approaches, such as those advocated by the IMF, were sufficient to meet the chief need of revitalizing the production of Russia. Japan warned that "the worst choice would be to diversify investment in all-out manner, because what is now most needed is focus on specific sectors of particular importance as a way to increase overall production."[109] Japan advocated a sector-specific industrial policy, the hallmark of state-led economic development.

On September 26, 1993, the 1993 World Bank Report (titled *The East Asian Miracle: Economic Growth and Public Policy*) was published at the annual meetings of the World Bank and the IMF. To Japan's great disappointment (especially in the MOF), the report's conclusion predictably (given Summers's critic of the OECF paper in 1992) repeated the market-friendly conclusions of the 1991 World Development Report, as evident in a preface by Lewis Preston (then World Bank president): "The authors conclude that rapid growth in each economy was primarily due to the application of a set of common, market-friendly economic policies."[110] By market-friendly, the World Bank meant only a limited role (for example, export promotion) of the state in fostering the East Asian miracle, while the bulk of the report gave strong endorsement to the established Washington consensus.

MOF officials, who spearheaded publication of the report and were in Washington for the annual meeting, did not hesitate to reveal their uneasiness with the World Bank's responses to the challenge from Asia. Along with Sakakibara, they complained that "Japanese financial officials' attempt to spread the word on East Asian development had been hijacked by the bank's mainstream neoclassical economists and that the output was not worth the investment."[111] At the same time, they added that they were not surprised by the outcome of the report, given the World Bank's basic acceptance of what they term "Anglo-Saxon dominance" in its management, staff, and organizational culture.[112]

Because *The East Asian Miracle* did not produce the desired outcome for Japan, perhaps naturally the country supported numerous publications and projects that questioned the World Bank's interpretation of Asian experiences and promulgated the Asian model in other parts of the developing world (particularly in formerly socialist transitional economies, notably Vietnam, Russia, and Poland). As will be observed, however, Japanese pressure on the World Bank to respect the Asian model was weakened, though not because Japan lost interest in exporting the Asian model to other parts of the developing world. Rather, it was because *The East Asian Miracle* gave a good lesson to MOF officials in particular, who realized that they could never penetrate the structural power of the United States in the World Bank. In other words, MOF officials felt that Japan's chance of advancing its development agenda would be slim with the presence of the United States,[113] a situation that resulted in changes to Japan's strategy in promoting the Asian model. Japan began to employ *independent* measures to fulfill its development agenda. The Japanese challenge to neoliberalism continued in various forms well into the Asian financial crisis in 1997.

The first manifestation of this challenge came shortly after publication of *The East Asian Miracle*.[114] Unsatisfied by the outcome of publication, the OECF commissioned a comparison of Korea and Thailand, two countries with diverse patterns of development with respect to the role of government and private sector responses.[115] In the spring of 1994, the OECF selected twenty-six economists from Britain and Asia (and one from the United States) who were widely recognized as critics of the neoliberal interpretation of Asian development to solicit their views on the World Bank's interpretation of the Asian successes. Predictably (like *The East Asian Miracle*), their views tended to affirm OECF criticisms of the World Bank's publications on the Asian experience, and the OECF published it as a discussion paper.[116]

Other ministries and aid agencies joined the OECF with similar efforts. The MITI's Japan External Trade Organization (JETRO) organized an Asian NIEs Newly Industrial Policy Study Group and published a report presenting the favorable impact of industrial policy in Korea, Taiwan, and Japan in the areas of textiles, electronics, and automobiles.[117] Another MITI agency, the Institute of Developing Economies (IDE), has since 1993 sponsored a twelve-country study of industrial policy in developing countries in many regions, one of which was a study on Nigeria as the case for critical failure of the World Bank's SAL program.[118] Not confining itself to publications, the MITI was active in selling Asian interventionist industrial policies to transitional economies such as those in Poland,[119] Vietnam,[120] Kyrgyzstan,[121] and Russia.[122] In March 1996, the Japan Trust Fund for International Development sponsored through UNCTAD (United Nations Conference on Trade and Development) a conference on East Asian Development in Kuala Lumpur, Malaysia.

The last push (before the Thai crisis) of Japan's efforts to build international consensus on the legitimacy of the Asian model came in October 1996, when the OECF hosted a joint Bank-OECF workshop in Tokyo to discuss the 1997 World Development Report titled "*The State in a Changing World*." Led by Ishikawa, a renowned development economist who had earlier been involved in developing a strategic industrial policy for Vietnam, Japan emphasized the need to go beyond the market-failure role of the state to encompass policies aimed at market formation and development in countries with a rudimentary private sector. The World Bank agreed to reevaluate some of the issues raised in *The East Asian Miracle* report, but to no avail. By early 1997, the OECF indicated its growing frustration that "in spite of all the discussions they had not yet found common ground" with the World Bank on what polices would lead to development.[123]

Furthermore, Japan was not averse to deploying its antiparadigmatic leadership in such forums of international finance and development policy as the

G-7, ASEAN, and APEC. Japan placed greater emphasis than the United States did on development issues regarding North-South cooperation. For example, Japan introduced its proposal for Partners for Progress (PFP) in February 1995, aiming at mobilizing foreign aid under the auspices of APEC to be dispensed to the organization's developing members.[124] Japan explained that the purpose was to narrow the developmental disparities among APEC members and thus prepare the less developed members for, and make them more amenable to, liberalization. As such, the United States complained that Japan's emphasis on development cooperation was at the expense of the relative weight assigned to APEC's trade and investment liberalization processes. Japanese officials defended the PFP as reflecting more accurately the preferences of APEC's developing members, and as restoring balance to the overall APEC agenda, which they thought had become too heavily skewed toward liberalization.[125]

In this context, Japan's policy toward APEC's Osaka meeting offers an interesting illustration of Japan's leadership in the politics of economic development in alliance with other Asian countries (which is observed in the AMF proposal). Since the APEC came into being in 1989, a difference of emphasis (if not a conflict of interests) between the United States and Asian member states on APEC's main institutional purpose has been observed. Although the United States prefers to use the APEC as a forum that facilitates trade and investment liberalization processes by negotiating binding trade and investment rules, Asian states assign a relative weight to APEC's role in development cooperation. The United States increasingly pushed for institutionalization of the APEC along liberal lines in the early 1990s, and its efforts bore fruit with the Bogor Declaration in 1994, which laid out a liberalization timetable for member states. The declaration was, however, not wholeheartedly entertained by every member state. Malaysia, Thailand, and China (along with some other states) did not hesitate to express their reservations about the declared liberalization processes, and Japan and the Philippines were not enthusiastic about it. In this context, Japan hosted the APEC annual meeting in Osaka in 1995. The major issue in Osaka was whether or not to further expand and spell out more specific goals for APEC liberalization processes that had gained a sizable momentum from the Bogor Declaration. Many Asian member states became increasingly wary of U.S.-led liberalization agendas that essentially meant a considerably reduced role of the state in organizing both international and domestic economic activities. As such, the choice presented for member states in the Osaka meeting was whether or not to endorse U.S. (or Western) free market ideals. Depending on the negotiated outcome(s), the Osaka meeting could have been a defining moment not only for the future of the APEC in terms of its main institutional purpose but also for Asian regionalism: liberalization or development cooperation?

What came out of the Osaka meeting was the first embryonic form of an East Asian developmental alliance that "succeeded in eviscerating virtually all traces of the type of liberalization program sought by the United States." Instead of the more structured, rule-binding liberalization processes advocated by the United States and Australia, the liberalization process that emerged from the Osaka meeting was "voluntary, unilateral, consensus-based, non-binding, lacking common timetables, and uncertain as to comprehensiveness and comparability of members' effort." Apart from ASEAN countries, the meeting saw China, Japan, and South Korea (the "Plus Three" members) joining forces to restore balance to the overall APEC agenda, which they claimed had become too heavily skewed toward liberalization. In effect, Yoshiro Sakamoto, vice-minister of international affairs of the MITI, argued that "Japan should keep step with the rest of Asia by agreeing only to those U.S. proposals that are acceptable to the whole of Asia."[126] According to an internal MITI memo, the economic liberalization initiated and pushed by the United States seemed to be "forcing Minor league players to play in Major league games."[127]

All this demonstrates Japanese agency as a challenger to the American neoliberal world order. As discussed in Chapter 6, Sakakibara played (as a prominent individual agent) a decisive role in launching the AMF proposal. This analysis, however, suggests that Sakakibara had broad institutional support when he deliberated the AMF. In crude terms, Sakakibara was standing on top of the dominance of the Asian faction in the MOF; he was an institutional product rather than an idiosyncratic ideologue. The MOF developed its institutional agency with respect to the politics of economic development. Japan's national interest in creating the AMF was constructed and projected by the MOF on behalf of Japan. Insofar as the MOF's institutional identity is socially and politically constructed in relation to the United States on the grounds of proponent and opponent of the U.S.-led neoliberalism, the very social condition that generates the MOF's institutional identity has the effect of challenging the American neoliberal world order.

6 JAPAN AND THE ASIAN MONETARY FUND

And despite the evidence of the inherent risks of free capital flows, the Wall Street-Treasury complex is currently proceeding on the self-serving assumption that the ideal world is indeed one of free capital flows, with the IMF and its bailouts at the apex in a role that guarantees its survival and enhances its status.[1]

ON THE BASIS OF THE IDENTITY TOPOGRAPHY of Japan and the United States in the realm of international finance and development developed in Chapter 5, this chapter demonstrates how the MOF's conception of such binary identities shaped Japan's interest in proposing the AMF and excluding the United States from membership. As discussed in detail here, Japan made a major break in terms of its policy change around mid-August 1997, from "supporting the U.S./IMF-led Thai crisis management" to "pursuing its own independent measures of the crisis management." The break was manifested in the AMF proposal.

Hence in this chapter I offer an empirical account of this policy variation by systematically testing the identity-intention analytical framework. The application of this framework to Japan's AMF decision involves several analytical steps to demonstrate its empirical validity. First, one has to make the case that decision makers (MOF officials) indeed associated themselves with, or are embedded in, a particular conception of their identity in relation to others (such as the conception of Japan and the United States as two rivals promoting different models of economic development). This was shown in Chapter 5. Second, given the temporally sequential, interactive processes of foreign policy making, one has to identify the critical raw material (or data and information) that decisively affects the future course of action. In Japan's AMF decision, the MOF's realization of the U.S. Treasury Department's involvement in the IMF operation in Thailand, for example, plays such a role. Lastly (and what is perhaps most important for empirical analysis), one has to probe whether MOF officials' internalized binarization of identity conceptions indeed operated in their reasoning processes when making the AMF decision, as the identity-intention analytical framework specifies. In relation to the second step, the framework expects that such a binary set of identity conceptions leads MOF officials to interpret the U.S.-led IMF operation in Thailand in a certain way (such as "the demolition of the Asian model of economic development"[2]), precipitating a kind of reasoning that saw an AMF proposal that would exclude the *United States* as the most compelling course of action. In essence, the identity-intention link can be inferred with confidence if the MOF's AMF decision derives from its own articulated identity-*filtered* (or *enabled*) reasoning of the nature of the U.S.-led IMF operation in Thailand.

That said, this chapter is divided into three sections. The first is an account of Japan's initial decision to cooperate with the IMF bailout operation in Thailand. The second section is devoted to Japan's decision to propose the AMF, along with the U.S. response to such. The last section analyzes the findings to show how the framework empirically works and provides a better explanation of Japan's AMF decision in comparison to three major previous explanations pertinent to Japan's AMF decision. I explore these explanations *after* I offer my identity-based analytical argument. In this way, the identity-based analytical leverage might be better measured in comparison to previous explanations, because one can evaluate the weight of each approach with the evidence already available.

Throughout this chapter, the empirical focus is on tracing the detailed processes and timings of Japan's interactions with the United States and the IMF in the management of the Thai financial crisis. Of particular importance to account for the variation in Japan's policy choice is a period before and after the bailout package agreement between Thailand and the IMF on August 11, 1997, in Tokyo. Here are the major chronological lines:

Major Chronological Points in the Asian Monetary Fund in 1997

July 2, 1997: The Thai crisis breaks out.

July 11: The Thai government asks Japan to offer bilateral assistance.

July 18: Japan refuses to offer the Thai government bilateral assistance and asks it to go through the IMF framework.

August 11: Japan hosts negotiation between Thailand and the IMF in Tokyo. The bailout package is agreed.

September 21: Japan proposes to create the AMF at the annual meetings of the World Bank and the IMF in Hong Kong.

November 17: The AMF ideas are assimilated into the Manila Framework.

There are thus four key questions to be answered regarding Japan's road to the AMF proposal:

1 Why did Japan refuse to offer its bilateral assistance to Thailand?
2 What made Japan go against the IMF?
3 What were the policy choices or alternatives available to Japan when it began to consider the AMF proposal?
4 Why did Japan exclude the United States when it proposed the AMF?

STAGE ONE: JAPAN DECIDES TO SUPPORT THE IMF

The miracle economies of Asia were abruptly dismantled by a series of attacks on the stock, currencies, and banking markets in the regional economies. The crisis of 1997–98 began in Thailand in May 1997. Through the summer and fall, it swept through some of the most important and stable economies of Southeast Asia: Malaysia, Indonesia, the Philippines, and Singapore. By early December, the crisis reached Korea and subsequently engulfed Brazil and Russia. In its scope and depth, the crisis of 1997–98 proved to be far more disruptive and less tractable than its Latin American predecessors.

The first of these spiraled crises erupted in Thailand on May 7, 1997, when the Thai currency, the baht, came under pressure from speculators who began selling off their holdings of the currency. On a single day, May 13, $6 billion exited Thailand. In response, the Bank of Thailand intervened in the currency markets, spending $6.3 billion on the same day to defend its pegged currency. On May 14, the central banks of Singapore, Malaysia, and Hong Kong also supported the baht with $10 billion in the currency market, adhering to the promise made among the Asian countries eighteen months before.[3] By May 15, the Thai government was trying to stem speculation against the baht by increasing interest rates (and hence raising the cost of borrowing funds to purchase baht), implementing selective capital controls aimed at making it prohibitively expensive for foreigners to purchase baht offshore, and buying baht with its own currency reserves.[4] Stability was achieved, and the Thai prime minister hosted a party at his official residence on May 16 to celebrate the success of the defense of the baht. But the tranquility was short-lived; investors were not calmed by these measures. In fact, as Thai interest rates rose, stock and land prices fell because borrowing became more costly, and major Thai financial and real estate firms began declaring bankruptcy. On June 27, 1997, the Thai government announced suspension of sixteen finance companies (out of ninety-one Thai finance companies; forty-two more were added to the list on August 5, shortly before the announcement of a Thai deal with the IMF), giving them thirty days to implement merger plans. The sell-off of baht and baht-denominated investments continued.[5]

Finally, on July 2, 1997, rather than devalue the baht the Thai government ended its efforts to defend the currency's fixity and announced that the baht would float with market forces. The currency came under severe attack that day and lost about 17 percent of its value against the U.S. dollar; it continued to depreciate throughout the week. Fearing further sales of baht and baht-denominated assets, the Thai central bank and government took action to try to defend speculation by raising the discount rate by 2 percent, to 12.5 percent, and restricting sales by foreigners of Thai stocks.[6] Following pressure from the government, Thai private banks refused to provide short-term credit to speculators.[7] Given the intense demand for funds to borrow baht and given the government's efforts to curb such borrowings, offshore interest rates rose to 1,300 percent annum. The rise in Thai and foreign interest rates and the collapse in property values led to loan defaults and losses for Thai banks. The baht's depreciation compounded debt and bank distress as Thai borrowers faced dramatic increases in the domestic currency value of their hard-currency repayment obligations.

Despite the financial panic, it was not until July 28 that the Thai government finally turned to the IMF to request a bailout. The main reason for its reluctance to do so was that it did not want IMF money with stringent conditionality. Behind this was Thailand's expectation that Japan would demonstrate "leadership" by stabilizing the crisis if asked to. Japan's money would come with fewer strings attached, given its request-based bilateral ODA implementation.[8] Furthermore, the Thai government also recognized Japan's high economic stake in the stability of the Thai economy. After all, more than two thousand Japanese companies were operating in Thailand, and it owed Japan \$37.5 billion (out of a total debt of \$70.2 billion). The collapse of the baht meant that Thai companies would face a tougher time servicing their foreign debt. In addition, Japan accounted for 40 percent of total foreign direct investment in Thailand, after Japanese firms increased their annual level of investment by 72.5 percent from 1994 to 1995, and 22.2 percent from 1995 to 1996.[9] With the collapse of the baht, Japanese parts imported for final assembly by Japanese manufacturers in Thailand now became more expensive, hurting the export competitiveness of the Japanese transplants. In the meantime, domestic demand for Japanese products in Thailand would threaten to contract with the Thai economy.[10]

Thus the Thai government's first response was to seek bilateral assistance from Japan. Japan reacted favorably, hinting on July 11 that it would take steps to fulfill the Thai request for emergency funding.[11] Following this, Thailand's finance minister, Thanong Bidaya, and the president of the Thailand central bank, Rerngchai Marakanond, visited Tokyo from July 16 to July 20 to meet not only with government officials but also with twenty-one Japanese commercial bank representatives to explain the economic situation in Thailand and perhaps finalize Japan's bilateral assistance.[12] To the Thai government's great disappointment, Japan almost completely changed its position on July 18 after Thanong's meeting with his counterpart, Japanese finance minister Hiroshi Mitsuzuka. Even though Japan agreed to closely cooperate with Thailand if necessary to intervene in the foreign exchange markets, Japan reiterated that it "would only provide assistance if the IMF participated in the bailout."[13] By this, Japan made clear its position to the Thai delegation that a Thai agreement with the IMF would be a precondition for additional support from Japan. The Japanese refusal eventually led the Thai government to turn to the IMF on July 29, as the attack on the Thai currency and outflow of foreign capital continued.

Table 6.1 Japan's Foreign Direct Investments, FY 1992–FY 1996 (Millions of Current Dollars)

	FY 1992	*FY 1993*	*FY 1994*	*FY 1995*	*FY 1996*	*Accumulated by March 1997*
Total	34,138	36,025	41,051	51,398	49,728	564,732
Asia	6,425	6,637	9,666	12,361	12,027	100,064
Indonesia	1,676	813	1,759	1,605	2,500	21,086
Hong Kong	735	1,238	1,133	1,147	1,540	16,568
PRC	1,070	1,691	2,565	4,778	2,600	15,807
Singapore	670	644	1,054	1,185	1,155	11,875
Thailand	**657**	**578**	**719**	**1,240**	**1,453**	**9,988**
Malaysia	704	800	742	575	592	7,524
South Korea	225	246	400	449	430	6,147
Taiwan	292	292	278	455	540	4,992
Philippines	160	207	668	718	579	4,114

SOURCE: Japan's Ministry of Finance. Adapted from Altbach (1997, Appendix, Table 2). Bold added.

Table 6.2 Japan's Bank Lending in Asia, Year-end 1996 (Millions of Current Dollars)

	Japanese Bank Loans	*Share of Total Foreign Lending (%)*
Total to all countries	633,253	
Asia	265,000	
Hong Kong	875,000	42.2
Singapore	588,000	31.1
Thailand	**37,525**	**53.4**
South Korea	24,324	24.3
Indonesia	22,035	39.6
PRC	17,792	32.4
Malaysia	8,210	36.9
Taiwan	2,683	11.9
Philippines	1,558	11.7

SOURCE: Bank for International Settlement. Adapted from Altbach (1997, Appendix, Table 3). Bold added.

By choosing not to offer Thailand its independent bilateral assistance, Japan decided to play a "supportive" role in IMF management of international financial crises, as it had done before in Latin American crises. The decision looked odd, at least in the eyes of the many Asian countries that came to expect Japan's regional leadership, in the context of its previous confrontations with the Bretton Woods institutions. The questions, then, were, Why did Japan shift its policy? Why did Japan give up on an "unprecedented" opportunity to demonstrate its "regional leadership or responsibility" toward Thailand?[14] Where was Japan's high economic stake in the stability of the Thai economy in such a decision? Was it pressured to be subsumed under the IMF by the United States? Did the Japanese government still need the IMF to afford cover against domestic criticism of Japanese taxpayer money going to foreign debtors, as Green argues?[15] What was the relationship of that shift with another one—the AMF proposal, Japan's most prominent display of regional leadership—in September 1997?

Japan's decision to support the IMF initiative was largely due to Thailand's refusal to supply the MOF with the Thai economy's macroeconomic data, including information on foreign exchange reserve and the status of the Thai government's intervention in currency markets. The Thai government turned down the MOF's request three times during a period of about two months. The first refusal came around May 18, 1997, while the second one took place between July 9 and July 11. The last refusal came during the Thai delegation's visit to Tokyo. Each refusal increasingly undermined the position of the Asian faction vis-à-vis the IMF faction in the International Financial Bureau of the MOF, although the Asian faction constituted a majority. In particular, the Thai government's third refusal in Tokyo critically weakened the voice of the Asian faction calling for Japan's independent role.

The MOF's involvement in the Thai crisis began shortly after more than $6 billion worth of baht was sold on May 13, 1997. The MOF dispatched to Bangkok two high-ranking officials, Watanabe (director of the Treasury Department of the IFB) and Kimura (deputy director of the Foreign Currency Department), on May 18, to check the Thai economic conditions first-hand with the possibility of extending Japan's bilateral assistance.[16] MOF officials had extensive meetings with high-level officials in the Thai government, including the vice minister of finance and president and vice president of the Thai Central Bank. The Thai government "unofficially" requested bilateral assistance from Japan to help recover market confidence in the baht. In response, MOF officials asked the Thai government to give detailed information on the current status of the Thai economy, such as foreign exchange reserve and the Thai currency market situations, so that Japan could decide, for example, the size of bilateral assistance. The Thai government, perhaps out of a feeling of confidence in defending the baht (consider the Thai prime minister's party on May 16, just noted), did not reveal the requested information to MOF officials. Even though the MOF figured out that the refusal derived largely from the Thai government's domestic political concerns, the MOF subsequently decided not to consider supporting Thailand bilaterally. This was not only because the MOF felt that it could not properly spell out its plan for bilateral assistance without such detailed information on the Thai economy but also because the Thai government's refusal gave the MOF the impression that the situation was not serious enough to mandate Japan's direct involvement.[17] Furthermore, the MOF had to take into account its relationship with the IMF, which had been urging the Thai government to adopt its program since March 1997.[18]

Bringing all of these ingredients to a boil, however, was the fact that the Thai government's refusal aroused the suspicion of pro-IMF MOF officials while draining the power of the Asianists. Simply put, the pro-Asian MOF officials could not persuade the reluctant pro-IMF officials to agree to offer an uncooperative Thailand Japan's bilateral assistance.[19] Eventually, the internal division grew skewed toward the pro-IMF MOF officials, and the MOF decided to advise the Thai government to look to the IMF program if necessary. Behind this pro-IMF stance (or what Sakakibara calls the "orthodox" stance) were two assumptions. First, the MOF would have access to the Thai economic data *only* with the IMF, and it could thus be well prepared for further action. Second, even if the MOF worked within the IMF framework, it could maintain a relationship with the IMF as an equal partner rather than a subordinate one by cofinancing the Thai bailout.[20] The Thai government's refusal to turn to the IMF in May 1997 was repeated two months later.

In the meantime, through meetings with the Thai government, the MOF learned that a considerable portion of Thailand's foreign exchange reserve had already been lost, many banks and financial firms were on the brink of collapse, and thus the Thai government did not have much room for maneuver if speculative attacks were to resume. The MOF continued to work on the possibility of extending Japan's bilateral assistance upon the Thai government's requests. Before that, however, another massive wave of speculation struck the baht in July, forcing the Thai government again to seek critical help from outside. The Thai government decided to elicit Japan's help and applied for a delegation visit, which was scheduled to last from July 16 to July 20.

On receiving the Thai government's unofficial request to discuss establishment of a credit line and the size of yen-denominated loans, the MOF again dispatched to Thailand a mission headed by Watanabe from July 9 to July 11. The purpose was to fine-tune the two governments' positions prior to the Thai finance minister's visit to Tokyo. More important, however, on the part of the MOF was to request from the Thai government disclosure of such indispensable information as the total amount of the necessary loan size, the actual conditions of the Thai government's intervention in the futures market, and the current status of the foreign exchange reserve. The Thai government once again failed to furnish such information, and the refusal brought the discussion to a stalemate.[21] The MOF mission came back to Tokyo without making any substantial progress, hoping only that the Thai government would offer the necessary information during their scheduled visit to Tokyo. As such, on condition of Thailand's disclosure of vital economic data to the MOF, it considered offering a total of $10 billion to support the baht. To account for the aid package, the MOF internally concluded that although Japan would be responsible for most of $10 billion, the MOF would also ask other Asian countries to contribute.[22]

The Thai delegation, headed by finance minister Bidaya, again volunteered no actual clear-cut information in Tokyo on the Thai economy.[23] The Thai government insisted on Japan's bilateral assistance but with no such information on the Thai economy. As was the case before (in May), it debilitated the sympathetic MOF Asianists. One MOF official said:

> Even though we had a general sense even at this point that the Thai crisis might result from a liquidity problem, we could not do anything with the Thai government's refusal. . . . Within the International Finance Bureau of the MOF, there were many who had been previously working with and at the IMF. Therefore their relationship with the IMF was good. So without the data, it was both politically and economically too risky for the MOF to act [independently] at the expense of the MOF relationship with the IMF.[24]

In other words, the Thai government's continued refusal led the MOF to retract its scheme for bilateral assistance for two important reasons. First, the refusal amplified the suspicion, held by many MOF officials, that IMF-type conditionality was now considered appropriate for resolving the Thai crisis, and the MOF understood well that it could not impose such conditionality on its Asian neighbor. Second, the refusal made the MOF wary of the possibility of seeing its bilateral bailout money repaid by the Thai government.[25] Because the MOF, unlike the IMF, does not have recourse (for example, conditionality or seal of approval) to force Thailand to do what is necessary to ensure repayment, the MOF felt it too risky to go ahead with bilateral assistance. Hence, the MOF finally decided to withhold its bilateral assistance and, as Sakakibara said, let the IMF play a "tough guy" role.[26]

The MOF's decision, however, did not mean that Japan would abandon its regional leadership role and take a backseat to the IMF. As was the case in May, the MOF was confident that it could at least equal the IMF in voicing its opinions on the Thai bailout operation.[27] Confidence derived largely from two factors. The first was Japan's financial willingness to contribute at least half of the total funds necessary for completion of the bailout package. Simply put, the MOF believed that money can talk. Perhaps related, the second factor had to do with U.S. indifference toward the Thai crisis from the outset. The United States understood that the Thai crisis was "an isolated incident and that the IMF package, with some help from Asian neighbors, would be enough to contain regional financial turmoil."[28] Moreover, congressionally imposed restrictions on future use of the Exchange Stabilization Fund (ESF) in 1995 following the Clinton administration's unilateral $20 billion bailout of Mexico kept the United States from engaging actively in the Thai rescue package.[29] The United States did not have financial resources available for extending bilateral assistance to Thailand. The unique absence of the United States as a serious player, which stood in stark contrast to the Mexican bailout in 1994, led the MOF to believe that it could fill the putative leadership gap. In other words, facing the enormous uncertainty emanating from the Thai government's refusals, the MOF chose a rather familiar pattern of implementing its foreign policy, "leadership by stealth,"[30] or "leadership from behind."[31] Sakakibara recalls:

> Without accurate information on the Thai economy, it was too risky for us to choose this [offering Japan's bilateral assistance]. Furthermore, it was out of the question for us to impose our thought on our Asian neighbors, like the U.S. and the IMF could do on others, given a strong relational norm called "Asian abstention" among Asian countries that precludes interfering in each other's affairs. Thus, we had no alternative but to ask the IMF to play a "tough guy" role. We came to the conclusion at that time that we would show Japan's strong leadership for Asia under the IMF cover. . . . However, putting the IMF leadership on the surface generated a big problem later. . . . [32]

Neither U.S. pressure nor domestic criticism of Japanese taxpayers' money going to foreign debt was present in the MOF's choice to support the IMF program. Nor did Japan's immediate economic gain seem to be much of a factor. On the contrary, the MOF could have extended bilateral assistance (possibly with some type of collaboration with other Asian countries) to Thailand had the latter given accurate economic information on *any* of the MOF's three requests. As will be discussed shortly, however, U.S. indifference turned out to be only a half-truth. It was indifferent to the Thai crisis in terms of monetary contribution, but the United States was active in terms of crafting austere IMF conditionality. This became a critical source of conflict with the MOF, together with the unfolding nature of the Thailand economic data.

STAGE TWO: THE MOF AND THE AMF PROPOSAL

After Japan's announcement that it would offer assistance only if the IMF participated in the bailout, the Thai government finally called on the IMF for help on July 28, 1997. The terms of the bailout package were soon negotiated between Thailand and the IMF, and the latter insisted that its loans would be contingent on Thailand meeting six conditions: raising taxes, cleaning up the finance industry, balancing the budget, ending subsidies to state companies and utilities, keeping a tight monetary policy, and continuing the current foreign exchange system to preserve currency stability.[33] A basic agreement was reached between Thailand and the IMF on August 5. The agreement stipulated that the Thai government was to reduce public spending, end public and quasi-public support for failing financial firms and banks (the Thai government thus suspended operations of forty-two finance firms; it had already suspended sixteen in May, from a total of ninety-one in the country), raise taxes (the VAT was raised to 10 percent from 7 percent), and remove the capital controls imposed in May 1997.[34] Japan hosted an IMF-led international conference in Tokyo for facilitating concrete terms for the Thai bailout package. The final agreement came on August 11, and the IMF approved a $17.2 billion bailout package under the Emergency Financing Mechanism, which was adopted for accelerated loan procedures in September 1995. The MOF actively supported Thailand throughout the entire process of negotiation; Japan became the first country to commit itself by agreeing to supply $4 billion through Japan Export-Import Bank (JEXIM Bank) untied loans to Thailand, which constituted the largest bilateral loans, equal only to the IMF contribution ($4 billion); the MOF made a considerable effort to mobilize other Asian countries to contribute to the bailout package; through Japan's presidency of the ADB, the MOF was also able to commit the ADB to contribute another $1.2 billion.[35] Asian countries (including Japan and the ADB) made an $11.7 billion contribution, while the United States failed to spare even a dollar on a bilateral basis. The Tokyo conference ended as a seemingly huge success.[36] Yet in less than forty days, Japan challenged the U.S.-led IMF bailout operation by proposing creation of a $100 billion regional fund, financed and run by "Asian" countries and excluding the United States from membership.

What happened? What influenced Japan's explicit policy shift from supporting to challenging the IMF? Why did Japan exclude the United States? To lay out a general sense of what happened, it is worth quoting an article describing Japan's AMF proposal on September 21, 1997, at the annual meetings of the World Bank and the IMF:

> Japan's AMF proposal has emerged from its experience of participating in the $17.2 billion IMF-led rescue package for Thailand this summer. The

> Japanese have indicated that they are concerned about being asked to play a bigger role in the world economy without any increase in their influence in the international organization. However, there was sympathy, outside the American delegation, that Japan had a genuine grievance about its lack of influence on the international economic stage, despite being an important contributor to the IMF's finances. Many also agreed that greater cooperation between Asian central banks and finance ministers would help prevent a repeat of the recent currency and stock market crisis—and might have been more effective than the *secret* IMF mission to Thailand in urging policy reforms. . . .[37]

As indicated in the article, Japan's AMF proposal derived from the MOF's critical assessment of the IMF bailout operation for Thailand. The MOF strongly felt the U.S. presence behind the IMF operation, which was *interpreted* to be working in the U.S. interest, bringing down the Asian model. It is not possible to make sense of this fundamental reinterpretation without reference to the MOF's historically developed sense of *who* the U.S. Treasury Department is. As the identity-intention analytical framework specifies, there is a strong connection between the MOF's identity conceptions, its situational understanding (related to its fundamental reinterpretation of the nature of the IMF bailout operation in Thailand), and its AMF decision.

Suspicion was aroused when MOF officials observed the great discrepancy between the unfolding nature of the Thai economic data and the U.S.-led IMF policy prescriptions (and implementations) for further liberalization and deregulation of the Thai economy. This in turn led to a power and legitimacy shift within the MOF in favor of the Asianists.[38] The Asian solidarity firmly evident in assembling the $17.2 billion Thai bailout package further encouraged the MOF to take independent action. Excluding the United States was, however, not an easy decision at all. It was not until early September that MOF officials finally made up their minds to exclude the United States, defining the nature and characteristics of the AMF in relation to the IMF.

The MOF's consideration of the AMF began shortly after the Tokyo conference drew to a close on August 11, 1997. It was partly in response to a study that came out as a result of the Shanghai Conference of the Executive's Meeting of East Asia-Pacific Central Banks (EMEAP), which was held on July 25. The Shanghai conference adopted a proposal for establishing a standby facility that would support member countries' economic restructuring. But the MOF had already conceived of the AMF, at least in embryonic form, around the time of the Thai crisis, for four major reasons:

1 Concerns about the possibilities that the crisis might result in contagion.
2 Awareness that there were no money sources available outside of Asia.
3 Awareness that there was limited access to the IMF fund, particularly for Asian countries due to their traditionally small IMF quotas.
4 Even though the Asian governments achieved agreement for the Thai rescue package, it proved difficult for some countries like Australia to justify bilateral support in domestic political arenas on a case-by-case basis. Thus it was thought easier to have an established regional fund for this purpose.[39]

The MOF wanted to set up a regional institution that was able to channel more funds to Thailand and other countries in Asia that could be affected by financial turmoil. In other words, the idea of the AMF was born with a mission to create more dispensable short-term money for the affected countries in the region while possible long-term ideas focused on fostering a framework for policy dialogue on various economic issues among the countries in the region.[40] In other words, from the outset the AMF was conceived of as a self-defense mechanism in the event of volatility in international markets, designed to initially ward off further hostile attacks (on Thailand) from hedge funds. The MOF's return to the AMF in the aftermath of the Tokyo conference was thus aimed at realizing a regional lender of last resort that would lend liquidity to countries with balance-of-payment difficulties. In Sakakibara's terms, the AMF proposal emerged from a simple conception that "like there is the ADB vis-à-vis the World Bank, why not have the AMF vis-à-vis the IMF?"[41]

Yet the AMF proposal was inherently destined to face two interrelated issues from the outset: who to include and exclude as members of such a regional fund, and how to position it in relation to the IMF. As to the former, the issue was whether to include the United States, given that country's abhorrence toward an Asian-only institution (for example, America's negative posture earlier on the Malaysian East Asian Economic Caucus proposal). The latter would depend on the former, as U.S. membership would mean that the new regional institution was likely to supplement and support the IMF without much autonomy. The MOF could not resolve these issues until early September, as it kept pondering the institutional purpose of the new regional facility. The MOF's understanding of the nature of the IMF bailout operation for Thailand significantly triggered its determination to make the AMF independent of the IMF to a sufficient degree.

The MOF's uneasiness with the IMF bailout operation in Thailand first emerged in late July, when the IMF started to declare that all was wrong and that fundamental surgery was needed.[42] In the eyes of most MOF officials, such an ostentatious declaration seemed contrary to what the IMF said about Thailand in its 1997 annual report, which praised the Thai government for its consistent record of sound macroeconomic management policies.[43] Even though the IMF claimed that its 1996 Annual Article IV Country Analysis of Economic Policy[44] indicated some macroeconomic problems in the Thai economy and warned the Thai government of the seriousness of its economic trouble in February and March 1997, it provided no official warnings in the weeks and months before July 2.[45] Rather, the IMF issued its "World Economic Outlook" in May but did not convey any clear signals that Thailand, or any other countries in Southeast Asia, were in serious trouble.[46] At the same time, however, wary MOF officials also thought that the IMF might be making a "sound" assessment of the Thai economy, because the IMF now had access to the country's economic data, which had been denied to the MOF on three occasions. By and large, MOF officials were waiting to see the IMF's economic prescription for Thailand before deciding how they could assist the Thai economy.

The basic agreement between Thailand and the IMF came out on August 5, 1997. As I have noted, in return for access to the IMF bailout package the Thai government agreed to a stabilization and structural adjustment program. The program stipulated that the Thai government would cut the current account deficit through maintenance of high interest rates. It targeted achievement of a small overall surplus in the public sector by 1998 through an increase in the rate of the VAT tax from 7 percent to 10 percent, expenditure cuts in a number of areas (ending subsidies on utilities and petroleum products), and greater efficiency in state enterprises via privatization. The main part of the structural reform was, as has been described, closing down insolvent financial firms (including Finance One, which was once the country's premier finance firm).

The MOF basically welcomed the agreement when finance minister Mitsuzuka expressed his endorsement for Thailand's bailout plan.[47] Nevertheless, quite a few officials questioned the soundness of such economic prescriptions, on two fronts: the government budget cuts could exacerbate deflation (questioning the stabilization program), and closing down finance firms too hastily might not instill confidence in the rest of the financial system (questioning structural reform program).[48] But MOF officials' questions never went beyond pointing out potential dangers that the IMF prescriptions might inadvertently generate. They still did not have access to the Thai economic data on which they could voice anything concretely. As a result, the MOF was not confident enough to go against the IMF, still believing that austere measures would engender market confidence in the Thai economy.[49]

The MOF finally secured Thai economic data sometime around the Tokyo conference,[50] ushering in a major turning point in its attitude toward the IMF bailout operation. Contrary to expectations arising from the Thai government's refusals, the Thai economy prior to the crisis had for a long time enjoyed strong "fundamentals" (see, for example, the table). Thailand had recorded strong economic growth for many years; its inflation rate was usually in single figures and much below the average for developing countries; and it had a high domestic savings rate. Moreover, Thailand enjoyed a healthy fiscal position. Public sector finances were either in surplus or had small sustainable deficits. The only significant blemish on this generally positive precrisis long-term economic record was the position of the current account balance. Thailand had experienced huge deficits, which in 1996 amounted to almost 8 percent of the GDP. Nevertheless, the MOF also learned that Thailand kept a relatively low ratio of debt service to exports throughout the 1990s. At the same time, the economic data revealed a sudden interruption and reversal of normal capital inflows in Thailand. The MOF thus concluded that the Thai crisis was not a crisis of the public sector but of the private sector, not a crisis of solvency but of liquidity (temporary), which was in stark contrast to the Mexican peso crisis in 1994. As MOF officials explain:

> We finally got the data. We found that fundamentals were more or less still in place, though we noted that Thailand had a problem with the current account deficit, as the deficit was being financed by bank borrowings. Then, we observed the amount of money coming and going out of Thailand in such a short period of time. Putting everything together, we thought that the Thai crisis was a private sector-led liquidity rather than a solvency problem. It was the problem arising from too much liberalization pressed by the United States, too little institutional support [to deal with huge capital inflows], and too early liberalization and deregulation in terms of economic development. Then, we looked at the IMF operation. We thought "something went fundamentally wrong."[51]

> We thought from the beginning that the IMF conditionality was too harsh. But once we received the Thailand economic data, it [the IMF operation] surprised us. How could the IMF decide to impose such harsh measures when economic fundamentals were not that bad? Some might think that that was the ordinary IMF operation. But we had a different thought. After all, the IMF might base its conditionality on the same economic data.[52]

In this vein, an IMF official recalled:

> Japan suddenly started to become very defensive [of the Asian model] shortly after the Tokyo conference. It puzzled the IMF, because Japan and the IMF had maintained such a close working relationship for the Thai bailout package. . . . According to our former boss [Mr. Saito, a former director of the IMF regional office in Tokyo], the Tokyo conference was one of the most successful conferences the IMF had ever had before. . . . The IMF thought Japan wanted to enjoy a leadership role. Like the U.S. did it for Mexico, Japan seemed to think that it was fine for Japan to do the same role. . . . At the same time, the IMF figured out that the IMF's attack on the so-called Asian model was a bit too harsh for Japan to endure, given its track record of selling the model to the rest of Asia.[53]

In other words, the MOF came to believe that "the most direct cause of the Thai crisis was in general the liberalization of the global financial market

Table 6.3 Key Indicators for Thailand Economy (% of GDP unless otherwise noted)

	1983–1989 (Average)	*1990–1996 (Average)*	*1995*	*1996*	*1997*
Real GDP growth[a]	8.1	8.6	8.7	6.4	0.6
Inflation[b]	3.1	5.1	5.8	5.9	6.0
Domestic savings	25.4	34.2	34.3	33.1	31.8
Fixed capital formation	27.7	40.4	41.8	40.8	35.8
Current account	–3.2	–6.9	–8.0	–7.9	–3.9
Fiscal balance	–3.0	2.8	2.6	1.6	–0.4
External debt service	5.8	4.5	5.0	5.4	7.1

SOURCES: IMF (1997, December); World Economic Outlook: Interim Assessment; World Bank. Table is adapted from Singh (1993, 13, table 1.3).

NOTES:

a Percentage per annum

b Average annual percentage change of consumer price index

and in particular the deregulation of the capital account that Thailand had undertaken in the preceding period."[54] The United States, the IMF, and the World Bank were instrumental in promoting these measures. The Thai crisis was therefore not entirely homegrown but occurred while the country's fundamentals were still sound. The sudden interruption and reversal of normal capital inflows in Thailand suggested that whatever the trigger for the crisis (external macroeconomic imbalances or liabilities of the Thai financial institutions), the foreign commercial banks grossly overreacted, giving rise to a panic-induced bank run. External creditors withdrew their funds before Thailand was about to default. As such, in the eyes of MOF officials the Thai crisis had almost nothing to do with any structural factors connected with the Asian development model. They wondered, "If Asia's (including Thailand) economic practices were so flawed, why did the region enjoy such an extended period of high growth before the crisis?"[55] MOF officials in fact argued that if Thailand had continued to follow the Asian model of state-guided investment and state direction of the financial system, there would not have been a crisis in the first place. The Thai crisis occurred directly as a result of liberalization and deregulation, with the Thai government relinquishing controls over the financial sector as well as corporate investment activities.[56]

This circumstance led to misallocation of investments as well as overinvestment, claimed by the United States and the IMF to be direct causes of the crisis. In Sakakibara's terms, the Thai economic turmoil represented "a crisis of *global capitalism*," not of Asian capitalism,[57] and it demonstrated that "the Washington Consensus was over."[58] Describing the turmoil in the Asian economies as "not an Asian crisis, but a crisis of global capitalism [thus angering Western policy makers]," Sakakibara argued at the World Economic Forum in Davos:

> The crisis had been caused primarily by a huge inflow of foreign capital. The Asian economy is not in meltdown. What we have seen is a bursting of the bubble, an end of the euphoria [about the market mechanism]. . . . The crisis was caused as much by reckless foreign lending to the region as anything else. . . . I am an advocate for deregulation and reform in Japan and everywhere, but the Asian crisis is primarily a capital account crisis. . . . Lots of people talk about the structural problem of the region now, but they have known about these things for years. . . . Before the crisis nobody said there was anything wrong with them, rather the reverse.[59]

The MOF defined the Thai crisis as a liquidity rather than a solvency problem, having seen Thailand's proven record of being able to sustain fast economic growth, sound fundamentals, export orientation, and the ability to service their debts in the long run. As a result, in the MOF's view an appropriate and effective strategy to deal with the Thai crisis was to pump money into Thailand, rather than fundamental restructuring of the Thai economy. In this sense, the MOF cast reasonable doubts on the effectiveness of the IMF's excessively tight fiscal and monetary prescriptions for the Thai economy. MOF officials initially thought that the IMF confused Thailand's capital account crisis, caused by massive international capital flows and a surfeit of short-term debt, with a traditional current account crisis caused by factors such as high inflation, low savings, and fiscal deficits. As is indicated in the interviews quoted here, however, it did not take long for these officials to make a conceptual change concerning the IMF bailout operation, from "confusion" to "intention."

The most significant factor that contributed to such a conceptual change on the part of the MOF was its recognition that the U.S. Treasury had spearheaded crafting of the terms of conditionality for the Thailand bailout package.[60] It was an unexpected call for the MOF, given that the United States had so far showed its reluctance in getting involved in the Thai crisis management. After all, the United States offered no money of its own to Thailand; its increasingly strong presence led the MOF to believe that the Treasury Department had control over the IMF operation—the United States had moved in under IMF cover. It was thus no coincidence that not only the Treasury Department but also the State Department did not hesitate to point out that the onset of the Thai crisis reflected deep-seated problems in economic fundamentals. Even before the Thai bailout package was completed in Tokyo, high-ranking U.S. officials had already started to mention "correcting" fundamentals:

> We are very pleased that Thailand has taken this step [the Thai government's basic agreement with the IMF on August 5, 1997]. We support the IMF program. . . . We think that focusing on correcting some of the fundamental problems that the Thai economy has is the best way to stabilize the baht.[61]

> We are obviously concerned with the economic and financial situation generally and that is why we have said we are prepared to support extraordinary IMF access for Thailand, if and when an appropriate program is agreed. . . . The crucial elements of such a program are strong fiscal adjustment, measures

> to reform the financial system and remove capital controls and achieve greatly improved transparency in economic management.[62]

It was not difficult for the MOF to decode what the U.S. Treasury meant by stressing "getting fundamentals right." It pointed to the case for "crony capitalism" on the understanding that the Thai economic crisis (later the Asian financial crisis) resulted from the basic economic and social structures of Thailand, and the crisis would continue unless these inherent structural problems were rectified. Since the Thai government's turn to the IMF for help on July 28, 1997, the Treasury Department, led by Summers, repeatedly advocated structural adjustment requirements for the Thai government's access to the IMF bailout package and generated neoliberal prescriptions for curing the ailing Thai economy.[63] Even though Treasury noted that there might have been various immediate triggers—a property price bubble, macroeconomic mistakes (for example, supporting for far too long a nominally fixed exchange rate), and a fall in the rate of growth of exports—the underlying root causes were structural and thus an integral part of the Asian model of development. The Thai crisis manifested itself in the form of overinvestment, misallocation of foreign capital inflows, and severe problems in financial sectors, for which the state-guided or state-centered financial system in Thailand was largely responsible. In drawing these conclusions, the U.S. Treasury adhered to the view that financial markets are fundamentally rational. The Asian economic crisis began because investors worldwide were "punishing" behavior and practices inconsistent with market principles.[64] In particular, Summers asserted:

> The problem with this model of economic development is that while it was built on the fundamentals—on high savings, high levels of education, and hard work, it favored centralized coordination of activity over decentralized market incentives. Governments targeted particular industries, promoted selected exports, and protected domestic industry. There was a reliance on debt rather than equity, relationship-driven finance not capital markets, and informal rather than formal enforcement mechanisms.[65]

Sakakibara recollected from his conversations with U.S. Treasury Secretary Robert Rubin and Summers:

> [I] was saying from the outset that this [the Thai crisis] was a crisis of global capitalism. But in 1997, Larry's view and Bob Rubin's view was that it was an Asian crisis, and especially, Asian policy management was the problem—

> Asian governments and Asian corruptions and collusions, the Asian structured economic system, which is close to the structure of the Japanese. I admitted that the problems had arisen both on the part of the borrowers and the lenders, and the lenders were mostly Wall Street, so it was a problem created by both the borrowers and lenders; it was a problem of the global economy.[66]

In the end, the MOF was unsurprised when the IMF echoed or presented similar views on the causes of, and prescriptions for, the Thai crisis. At the same time, however, the U.S.-led IMF decision to "regard the crisis as originating in problems of 'insolvency', and tackle them by insisting on major structural reforms and the virtual dismantling of the Asian model, has instilled in MOF officials 'the suspicion' that the IMF bailout operation overstepped the mark and made the blunder of converting temporary currency crises into full-blown economic ones."[67] The suspicion was ever-growing as the MOF was witnessing the nature of the IMF conditionality.

As it turned out, the IMF, in return for its financial assistance to Thailand, went much further than the usual conditionality requirements (cuts in money supply, high interest rates, fiscal retrenchment, and so on) aiming at stabilizing the currency, reducing current account deficits, curbing domestic demands, and restraining inflation (see the basic agreement between the IMF and Thailand on August 5, 1997). The IMF demanded far-reaching changes in the economic and social systems of Thailand, including still more liberalization of the financial sector. The Thai government had to allow a hostile takeover of domestic firms by nonresidents, remove all limitations on foreign ownership of Thai financial firms, and push ahead with liberal foreign investment legislation that would allow foreigners to own land, a practice that had long been taboo in Thailand.[68] The Thai government also had to make commitments to restructure public enterprises and accelerate privatization of certain key industries—including energy, transportation, utilities, and communications—by eliminating the tax, tariff, and credit privileges given to these industries. Furthermore, the IMF demanded changes in the system of corporate governance, in labor laws, in government-business relations, and in competition policy.

The MOF found no "rationality" in the IMF impositions other than feeling the powerful neoliberal drive of what Bhagwati calls the "Wall Street-Treasury complex."[69] After all, the MOF internally and externally defined and represented the Thai crisis not as one of the "public sector" but as one of the "private sector," not a "solvency" crisis but a crisis of (temporary) "liquidity," and not a crisis of "Asian capitalism" but a crisis of "global capitalism." From the MOF's point of view, applying the usual IMF austerity measures (which were tried and tested in Latin America and Africa, where the principle economic ills were a large budget deficit, high inflation, and massively indebted public sectors) in Thailand itself was controversial. This was because inflation was low and budget deficits did not exist in Thailand. Setting aside that the IMF's insolvency-busting methods were seen as simply inappropriate to deal with what was essentially a problem of liquidity, the extensive conditions the IMF imposed on Thailand, which went well beyond the usual IMF mandate and into what heretofore had been considered members' sovereign prerogatives, could not be understood as anything but an attempt to bring the Thai economy more into line with Anglo-Saxon-type economic practices. The insisted-on reforms appeared aimed at dismantling the Asian model of development. Forcing Thailand (and later all affected Asian countries) to undergo severe structural reforms as advocated by the IMF and the U.S. Treasury was "tantamount to punishing the innocent."[70] This was particularly so because IMF policies on high interest rates and the break-up of domestic corporations in Thailand were believed to have blocked the ability of the Thai economy to search for ways to boost exports, at the very time when it was under pressure to do so in order to overcome the liquidity crunch.[71]

Eventually, the MOF came to understand that the response of the IMF to the Thai crisis was largely dictated by an agenda drawn up by Washington and Wall Street to end the Asian model of development and replace it with a more open financial market because the United States and the IMF represented the crisis from the outset as the inevitable result of Thailand's failure to follow the norms and standards of global capitalism (see the three justificatory reasons for the AMF proposal later in this chapter). The IMF was seen to have been more interested in opening up the Thai economy through dismantling the very system that had ensured its success in the first place. Sakakibara answered questions regarding the role of the IMF in the Asian crisis:

> But the initial mistakes committed by the IMF in late 1997 and early 1998 were very crucial—they tightened the monetary policy, which was not necessary, imposed very rigid and sometime unrealistic structural reforms in a somewhat unreasonable manner. It was too hasty. Structural reforms in Asia may have been necessary but it should not have been imposed from outside with-

> out internal preparations for the change. . . . These are not the appropriate functions of the IMF. The IMF needs to concentrate on macro-policies and liquidity issues rather than on structural problems. . . . It was not the function of the IMF to impose those reforms on the countries in crisis.[72]

The MOF subsequently tried to lessen IMF conditionality, but to no avail.[73] The United States and the IMF justified such rigorous lending conditions in terms of a diagnosis of the crisis that placed heavy causal emphasis on features that were internal to Thailand and characteristic of the Asian model of development (citing "close ties between business and government, corruption and nepotism, banks that extended loans on political connections").[74] The U.S. and IMF's blunt refusal alienated the MOF and led it to critically reinterpret the entire structure of its interaction with the U.S.-led IMF bailout operation.

Despite the MOF's initial desire that Japan equal the IMF in managing the Thai crisis "both financially and intellectually," the monopolistic, unflinching power of the United States and the IMF in generating what Wendt calls "discursive conditions,"[75] in which the viability of the Asian model was "normatively" denied, and the privilege of market-based processes and outcomes was normatively endorsed, reminded the MOF of the familiar pattern of the U.S.-led IFIs' attitude toward Japan. Simply put, the attitude was that they needed "Japan's money but not its ideas." The flip side of this was that the United States cut its financial commitments (in the IFIs) while maintaining influence, which is "talking (or 'lecturing') without money" from the MOF's point of view.[76] The MOF felt that Japan's money was being used to promote a U.S. policy agenda.[77] It now came to see the IMF response to the Thai crisis as largely dictated by an agenda drawn up by Washington and Wall Street as a means to end the Asian model of development and replace it with a more open financial market. The U.S.-IMF representation of the crisis *from the outset* as the inevitable result of Thailand's failure to follow the norms and standards of global capitalism was now understood in this way.

In the meantime, the IMF program was failing to deliver on its promise. Not only was the Thai economy further deteriorating but the currency crisis was spreading more intensively to the Philippine peso, Indonesian rupiah, Malaysian ringgit, and Taiwan dollar, as financial speculators engaged in selling off stocks and local currencies, calling in debts, and buying dollars. The abrupt closure of forty-two financial firms in Thailand caused a panic run on the whole banking system.[78] The IMF's demand for a budget surplus, along with fiscal contraction and discount rate increases, bankrupted a number of local industries. Even exporters, who should have been able to compete on export price owing to a depreciation of the baht, were unable to obtain new loans as a result of the credit crunch. Moreover, high interest rates made investors fear growing domestic debt problems. The relentless attacks on the baht continued, and the unsuccessful IMF policies puzzled the Thai government. Thanks to the continued panic, the $17.2 billion IMF bailout package was easily depleted and became insufficient to address the falling baht. Frustrated with the severe IMF conditionality that exacerbated the crisis, by August 18, 1997, the Thai government called for establishment of an Asian fund (or an ASEAN Monetary Fund; the name was tentative) to support Asian currencies against foreign speculators.[79] All these developments called for Japan's response.

The MOF had three policy options available. The first was "nonaction," a (reluctant) maintenance of the status quo with the U.S-led IMF bailout operation. The second possibility was to offer Thailand bilateral assistance, something that could have been implemented earlier. The last option was to set up a standing regional institution (the AMF, a regional lender of last resort; multilateral assistance) through which Japan and other members could give Thailand swift emergency credits, and which would be a direct response to the Thai government's initiation already noted here.

The first option, nonaction, was unacceptable to MOF officials. It meant succumbing to the Wall Street-Treasury-IMF complex, according to the MOF's interpretation of its interactive structure with the U.S.-led IMF operation, whose primary purpose was understood as rolling back the Asian model of development Japan had thus far been so proud of. As such, both bilateral and multilateral forms of assistance were deemed sensible *only if* they could work outside the neoliberal IMF framework. In other words, both bilateral and multilateral policy options required Japan's independent regional leadership. The AMF prevailed in the end. MOF officials gave three main reasons for choosing multilateral over bilateral assistance:

1 Demonstrated Asian solidarity and demands for a standing regional institution to maintain monetary stability, which had developed since 1995[80] and intensified and consolidated throughout the Thai crisis management. The timing was right to realize it.
2 Out of strategic concern: The multilateral approach would be less likely to provoke the opposition of the United States and the IMF than Japan's independent bilateral approach would.

3 The MOF's need for multilateral cover for dispensing Japanese taxpayers' money, given Japan's own domestic economic and financial problems at that time.[81]

The MOF's decision to go outside the U.S.-led IMF framework simultaneously resolved the issue of membership (whether to exclude the United States) and the relationship of the AMF to the IMF, which were two sides of the same coin. As the MOF defined the *immediate* institutional purpose of the AMF in terms of ensuring speedy disbursement of funds to Thailand (and other affected countries) to weather a storm called "the IMF conditionality," and thus to get out of the liquidity crisis as early as possible,[82] exclusion of the United States was considered critical to running the AMF independent from the IMF to a substantial degree.[83] The MOF claimed that the AMF would not "be a subset of the IMF, but must retain some regional flavor and autonomy in spite of 'complementarity' with the IMF."[84] After all, the AMF's intended quick disbursement to Thailand would not be possible if its operation were to be contingent on IMF approval; how could AMF funds be disbursed without delay if the IMF would need time to formulate and negotiate the terms of conditionality with the Thai government again?[85]

After several consultations with Asian countries, the MOF decided to formally propose creation of the $100 billion AMF, financed and run by Asian countries, at the annual meeting of the World Bank and the IMF in Hong Kong in late September 1997. Japan would contribute $50 billion while the rest of the members would take responsibility for the other $50 billion. To finance the $100 billion, part of the foreign exchange reserves of each member state was pooled.[86] The AMF's membership was provisionally to include China, Hong Kong, Japan, Korea, Australia, Indonesia, Malaysia, Singapore, Thailand, and the Philippines. On September 10, Sakakibara unofficially informed Hong Kong, Singapore, Malaysia, Thailand, and Korea of Japan's plan to propose the AMF. On the same day, two high-ranking MOF officials visited China and Australia to explain Japan's AMF proposal. The MOF also proposed to these potential members convocation of an informal session to discuss Japan's AMF proposal when Asian finance ministers met in Hong Kong on September 12.[87]

Once the MOF's proposal to exclude the United States from the AMF, and the relationship of the AMF to the IMF, was circulated, the MOF faced strong opposition from both the United States and the IMF *even before* Japan's finance minister, Mitsuzuka, officially proposed the AMF at the annual meeting of the World Bank and the IMF on September 21. The United States and the IMF did not initially react unfavorably to the idea of establishing a standing regional institution in Asia. For example, Sakakibara met with Summers, deputy secretary of the U.S. Treasury Department, at the Organization for Economic Cooperation and Development (OECD) Meeting in Paris on September 8, 1997, where Sakakibara explained to Summers the basic framework of the AMF proposal during their lunch. He did not, however, tell Summers about two interrelated issues, exclusion of the United States and the relationship of the AMF to the IMF, because he was not yet sure of the latter (that is, how independent the AMF would be). Summers did not react negatively, believing that the United States would naturally be included and that the AMF idea was still in the "brainstorming" stage.[88] The IMF was even supportive of the AMF when the proposal first surfaced. Michel Camdessus, the IMF managing director at that time, was supportive in the sense that the new institution could supply more financial resources to the affected economies of Asia.[89] Stanley Fisher, the IMF deputy director who later became a vehement critic of the AMF,[90] went even further than that. He internally (within the IMF) proposed to study how the IMF could coexist with the AMF.[91]

All this changed completely with the arrival from Hong Kong (from the Asian finance ministers' meeting on September 12) of the news of "the exclusion of the United States" and "the AMF's substantial independence (almost complete)." This was precisely because a Japan-centered AMF meant that the AMF would apply "different" conditionality.[92] As such, in one IMF official's words, the IMF "withdrew the positive feelings about the AMF," and the United States was "infuriated," in Sakakibara's words.[93]

Summers called Sakakibara at his home in the middle of the night on September 14. The two-hour heated discussion began with Summers furiously remarking, "I thought you were my friend."[94] Summers severely criticized Sakakibara for his intention to exclude the United States and to create an AMF that was independent of the IMF. Even though Summers based his criticism of the AMF proposal on the grounds that the AMF would undermine the authority of the IMF (by reducing its leverage to compel reforms by means of conditionality) and the global efforts to ride out the crisis, he did not hesitate to express that the AMF proposal would constitute an Asian or a Japanese challenge to the United States.[95] Sakakibara did not back off. He responded by saying, "There's such a thing as the Asian Development Bank as against the World Bank. Why not an Asian Monetary Fund?"[96]

Summers's criticism was only the beginning of U.S. attempts to block the AMF proposal. Rubin called his counterpart, Mitsuzuka, to confirm U.S. opposition to the AMF proposal on September 17. On the same day, the United States sent a memo with joint signatures of Rubin and Greenspan to finance ministers of APEC, emphasizing U.S. willingness to cooperate with Asian countries in precipitating the increase of IMF quotas in Asia and creation of a new financing "window" that would permit more expeditious IMF responses to the crises. Nonetheless, the memo made clear that the IMF should be at the center of all these crisis management efforts. On September 20, a day before Japan officially put the AMF proposal on the table, Rubin met with Mitsuzuka in Hong Kong and urged Japan to give up on the AMF proposal. In addition, Rubin made a counterproposal to his Japanese counterpart on a cooperative effort to create a regional surveillance system that would include the United States. American efforts to block the AMF proposal were not confined to pressuring Japan. The United States attempted to persuade other Asian and European countries not to accept the AMF proposal. Among the potential members of the AMF, Australia became the first country to backpedal.[97]

Exclusion of the United States and the AMF's independence generated domestic critics as well. The most vehement critic was the MOFA, which traditionally puts highest priority on Japan's relationship with the United States. The MOFA reacted negatively to the idea of excluding the United States, anticipating the negative reaction from American officials. Even within the MOF, those officials with a close working relationship with the IMF tried to tone down the AMF proposal, even though they did not necessarily positively assess the IMF bailout operation. The pro-IMF officials' focus was not on nullifying the AMF but on adjusting the expected role of the AMF in terms of complementing the IMF (rather than supplanting it).[98]

The MOF also confronted some opposition from Japan's private sector. Despite many Japanese financial and manufacturing sectors' exposure to the Thai crisis (and later to other Asian economies in trouble), they were not entirely supportive of the AMF proposal, which would be a regional mechanism for disbursing quick funds to get Thailand out of the crisis. Initially, the private sector (financial and manufacturing) could not react, mainly because they did not know what the AMF was all about,[99] having had only limited consultation (mostly "information exchange" [*Johō Kōkan*]) with the MOF about it.[100] Eventually, however, the manufacturing sector opposed the AMF proposal on the grounds that "it would be dangerous to provide easy money in the name of an Asian rescue that could undermine the reforms and adjustments usually demanded by the stringent conditionality of the IMF."[101] They were, however, aware that "such action [creating the AMF] might result in the loss of golden opportunities for further liberalization of the Asian market."[102] Japan's financial sector opposed the AMF for a different reason. Those supporting the solutions through the IMF argued that "such a fund as the financial last resort creates a psychology of dependence."[103]

Such multidimensional opposition was offset by encouragement not only from Asian central bankers and finance ministers but also from Japanese Prime Minister Hashimoto, who had sought to develop Japan's independent policy on Asia.[104] The MOF went ahead without any modification in the membership, and Japan's finance minister, Mitsuzuka, officially proposed creation of the AMF on September 21, 1997, at the annual meetings of the World Bank and the IMF. Both Mitsuzuka and Sakakibara acknowledged that the plan was "not yet concrete." Nonetheless, they emphasized that the AMF would be "compatible" with the IMF, though with a "unique" focus on Asian countries' "specific" needs.[105]

The AMF ultimately was not realized; Japan finally retracted the proposal at a meeting of finance and central bank governors from fourteen Pacific Rim countries in Manila on November 18 and 19, 1997.[106] In Sakakibara's words, "I tried, Japan tried . . . but against the coalition of the United States, the IMF, and Germany, I was powerless."[107] Nonetheless, the idea of the AMF was never completely put to rest. It was first revived when Japan's new finance minister, Miyazawa, announced the New Miyazawa Initiative on October 28, 1998, which was officially known as "A New Initiative to Overcome the Asian Currency Crisis."[108] The original (potential) members of the AMF now constitute the ASEAN Plus Three (China, Japan, and Korea) and made a first step toward the AMF in the form of bilateral swap arrangements among central banks, called "Chiang Mai Initiative" on May 6, 2000. As recently as May 2007, the finance ministers from ASEAN Plus Three had a meeting to discuss establishment of the AMF.[109] Could it emerge as a standing institution in the foreseeable future?

ANALYSIS: IDENTITY-INTENTION VERSUS ALTERNATIVES

In the account given here, I have offered a causal argument of the identity-intention framework to Japan's AMF decision. To summarize, the most significant moment came when the MOF realized that the U.S. Treasury Department worked behind the IMF, crafting the terms of conditionality for the Thailand bailout package. This led MOF officials to fundamentally *reinterpret* the entire nature of the IMF operation as a way to bring down the Asian model of economic development. I argue that such meaningful understanding of the actions of the United States and IMF on the part of MOF officials could not have been substantiated without these officials' binary conceptualization of Japan and the United States as two rivals promoting different models of economic development. Such an identity-based situational understanding in turn led them to conclude that proposing an AMF without the United States would be the most compelling option in that political context (see Table 6.4 for a schematic summary).

Of importance here is that the AMF proposal was not destined to emerge in a pregiven fashion with certain *fixed* interests. The emergence was dependent on how MOF officials interpreted the situation, not on something inherent in material or ideational imperatives. Quite similarly, the "thin" rationalists[110] might explain this variation as resulting from the MOF's reflexive revaluation of the strategic situation under *changing circumstances*. I claim, however, that changing circumstances cannot be taken for granted, because ontologically they depend on, say, the MOF's reinterpretation of the nature of the U.S.-led IMF bailout operation. Where those changing circumstances come from (along with the question of how to capture the content of them) is a question for rationalism even in this thin sense. Yet, as noted at the outset, there are three major alternative explanations for Japan's AMF decision that stress material and ideational factors in the absence of identity factors. I now examine them to qualify the claim.

Table 6.4 Identity-Intention Analytical Framework and Japan's AMF Decision

Identity-Intention Logical Scheme	*Japan's AMF Decision*
A judged his situation to be C (interpretivist identity-dynamics works here)	The MOF interpreted the nature of the U.S.-led IMF operation as destroying the Asian model of economic development
A was resolved to achieve the end E in the context of C	The MOF was resolved to defend the Asian model in the context of its interpretation of the nature of the U.S.-led IMF operation
A judged that E could be achieved in C if he did x	The MOF judged that defending the Asian model of economic development could be achieved if the MOF created the AMF without the United States
Therefore, A did x	Therefore, the MOF proposed to create the AMF

Even though the MOF's AMF decision may have worked within the broadly defined boundaries of Japan's interest in the stability of the regional economy for its own sake (economic interdependence), the material (as defined in terms of immediate, short-term economic gains) explanation that derives the Japanese proposal from Japan's desire to rescue its private (including both financial and manufacturing) sectors in the crisis-affected countries does not account for the opposition of those very sectors to the AMF proposal. Opposition from private sectors invalidates the claim that Japan would use such a fund to help Japanese industrial and financial sectors withdraw from Thailand, and possibly from other financially troubled countries in Asia, without accruing significant losses. Who could calculate the utility of the AMF better than the Japanese private sectors that risked their assets in the troubled economies in Asia?

In addition, evidence shows that the MOF had only limited consultation with private sectors (mostly information exchange) about the AMF during its policy deliberation.[111] Counterfactually, if the MOF's main intention for the AMF proposal was to, say, protect the interests and needs of Japan's highly exposed private sectors in the crisis-affected countries, the MOF would have required extensive, not limited, consultation with Japan's private sectors in planning for the AMF.[112]

Related to this is another set of empirical conclusions drawn from the political dynamics of intra- and intergovernmental disagreements. An analysis solely focused on Japan's short-term gain would not offer an explanation for the MOF's divisiveness over exclusion of the United States. The material conception of interests would have dictated a united front rather than a disagreement within the MOF, let alone the MOFA's stiff criticism of the AMF excluding the United States. After all, given Japan's willingness to commit $50 billion to the multilateral AMF, the MOF's choice to extend bilateral assistance to the affected countries would have entrusted it with more manipulative leverage or power over use of the funds.

One version of ideational explanations centers on the causation of Japan's AMF decision on its interest in offering an alternative solution to the Thai crisis as the crisis deepened. Although this version of analysis is not theoretically advanced by previous studies,[113] what is underlying this can be captured in terms of the learning model of foreign policy.[114] This stresses how change in decision makers' beliefs due to certain experiences (particularly past foreign policies) shapes subsequent foreign policy decisions. Regarding Japan's AMF proposal, Haas's notion of "real" learning, or Nye's "complex" learning, which enables MOF officials to propose the AMF as an alternative through adoption of new causal beliefs (the Thai crisis as a liquidity, not a solvency, problem so that the MOF needed the AMF to quench the liquidity problem), indeed seems to be a powerful way to capture Japan's AMF decision processes.

Even though this alternative explanation may offer an account of Japan's proposal of the alternative solution, the learning model is ill-equipped (or underdetermined) to offer an account of Japan's decision to exclude the United States from the AMF. The MOF's implementation of new causal beliefs (pumping money into the crisis-affected region) could have been satisfied either with or without the United States when it delivered the AMF proposal. The logic of the learning argument might even expect the MOF to make an effort to involve the United States in the AMF as a source of additional funding. One might argue, in the vein of learning models, that the MOF's past experiences with the U.S. Treasury at, for example, the World Bank would shape the MOF's exclusion. If so, the current stage of learning models does not offer a theoretical and analytical mechanism of how these cognitive experiences are translated into decision-making processes, as suggested by the identity-intention analytical framework.[115] As such, this important alternative explanation for Japan's AMF decision is underdetermined at the theoretical and empirical levels.

Similarly, the second version of ideational explanations that account for Japan's AMF decision as a function of its desire to take a regional leadership role in dealing with the crisis is certainly important. It is undoubtedly true that ever since Japan got involved in management of the crisis, the idea of playing a regional leadership role on the part of the MOF was consistently strong, even after the demise of the AMF proposal. Nonetheless, the argument for regional leadership or responsibility is too general to account for the specificities of the AMF proposal, such as exclusion of the United States and the relationship of the AMF to the IMF. Two interrelated issues account for this insufficiency. On the one hand, the current status of this regional leadership role explanation does not specify the content of the role that would shape Japan's AMF decision (lender of last resort? leader of state-led economic development? both?). One is thus unable to locate the source(s) of constraints and opportunities (the question of what is at stake) presented to MOF officials who might be concerned with role enactments in their deliberation of the AMF. Invocation of mere regional leadership does not help much. On the other hand, even if one could identify a particular role enactment in the AMF decision, one has to show how that particular role identity became *salient*. Close examination of the evidence points to the absence of the role, for example, associated with the leader of state-led economic development at least in the beginning of Japan's involvement in the Thai crisis.[116] In the final analysis, no matter what regional leadership roles were in play, these role conceptions alone cannot empirically capture variation in Japan's policies from initial cooperation to conflict with the U.S.-led IMF bailout operation in Thailand without a theory of role (or identity) shifts. As such, this regional leadership role can at best be thought of as *a necessary condition* for Japan's policy choices. In sum, the suggested material explanation is not empirically defendable, while the ideational ones work on underdetermined causal mechanisms along with empirical uncertainties.

By contrast, the identity-intention analytical framework, which is the central theoretical position of this book, not only addresses specificities concerning Japan's AMF proposal but is also able to illustrate the interactions of two other major players concerned here: Thailand and the United States. On the one hand, the Thai government's intention to avoid the austere IMF conditionality by bringing in Japan's bilateral assistance could not have been conceived without its understanding of Japan's identity as the leader of an antiparadigmatic development approach that had developed through Japan's various confrontations with the United States. The Thai government's assumption that Japanese money would come without much conditionality could not be separated from Japan's identity in the realm of international finance and development. Otherwise, there would have been no appropriate reason for turning to Japan for help.

On the other hand, U.S. opposition to the AMF proposal could be understood in the context of the binary identity dimension.[117] The $100 billion AMF could have been a "blessing" for the United States in crisis management. Such financial contributions could have afforded America an opportunity to manage the crisis without using U.S. taxpayers' money. Instead, the United States took Japan's proposal as a Japanese challenge to U.S. authority and subsequently blocked the proposal. The Japanese "challenge" could not have been constituted without the United States's own binary understanding of itself and Japan as leaders of different modes of economic development.

From this identity-intention analytical framework, Chapter 3 theoretically anticipated the four major sequences of the social interaction processes between the U.S.-led IMF and Japan in the Thai bailout operation.[118] In what follows, I apply the expected sequences to the actual interaction processes discussed earlier. First, the U.S.-led IMF, acting on its definition of the Thai crisis as a problem generated by crony capitalism, engaged in an act that signaled to Japan (MOF officials) both its intention to fundamentally reform the Asian model of economic development and its desire for Japan to play a supporting role in managing the Thai crisis. Second, MOF officials interpreted the U.S.-led IMF action in relation to their own perception of the evolving nature of the Thai crisis, including the causes of the crisis. They defined the crisis as a problem of liquidity, not of solvency, generated by a huge amount of capital outflow in a short time period. As such, MOF officials interpreted the imposed, extensive conditions of the IMF on Thailand as aiming at dismantling the "innocent" Asian model of economic development. Third, MOF officials, on the basis of this interpretation, which involved the previously established collective meaning structures associated with the identities of the United States and Japan as leaders of different models of economic development, now engaged in an action of their own. The MOF defined Japan's national interest in terms of defending the Asian model of economic development. Japan proposed an AMF that excluded the United States from membership. This exclusion was a key factor realizing such an interest. It constituted a signal to the U.S.-led IMF in much the same way the U.S.-led IMF action (demolition of the Asian model) had signaled Japan. Finally, the U.S.-led IMF responded: it blocked establishment of the AMF.

7 CONCLUSION

After the Asian Monetary Fund

Whether an act should be described as a threatening, promising, or mocking action is determined by the perceptions, interpretations, judgments, commitments and shared meaning conventions of the parties involved. The correct description of a social action is thus more than a reliable convergence of coder and/or diplomatic judgments; its meaning and identity is constituted by the multiple interpretative perspectives of the principal actors in such events. Such interpretative complexities, I believe, are an appropriate emphasis for an increasingly historical, practical, institutionally aware and internationally constituted political science.[1]

BY EXAMINING THE TWO RESEARCH QUESTIONS that are designed to develop a holistic account of the Japanese challenge to the American neoliberal world order, I have not only explored the emergence and nature of the Japanese challenge but also offered a historically and theoretically informed analysis of Japan's AMF decision in the context of the Japanese challenge. I have specified a clear path of analytical steps necessary for this holistic account by connecting meaning-oriented discursive practices to actual policy choice. In terms of endogenization of interests, the identity-intention analytical framework provides an empirically testable, theoretical basis on which reflective human agents define their interests in sociohistorical contexts. What has been emphasized throughout this book is the constitutive power of human interpretation in shaping and organizing the political features of international relations; what matters is not so much objective conditions or realities but how actors understand them. In this constructivist vein, I have demonstrated the constitutive power of discursive practices (*words are deeds*) in constructing reality (who and what is normal in the history of the world economy?) that spawned such a social effect as the Japanese challenge, which was enacted domestically and projected internationally. I have also examined identity, a relational social construct, as a critical interpretive basis on which actors present various policy options to themselves as they meaningfully make sense of the threats and opportunities that obtain in a given situation.

In this concluding chapter, I summarize the main arguments of this book theoretically and empirically. I draw out the implications of the Japanese challenge for Japanese foreign policy toward Asian regionalism and the politics of a new global economic order (or governance), in the wake of the Asian financial crisis, which are not mutually exclusive of each other. They are also extensions of this book's arguments. The current status of the AMF is also discussed, and the major contribution of this book to the study of international relations is summarized. I conclude by introducing, as an epilogue, Murakami's proposal for a new international economic order that combines developmentalism and economic liberalism.

SUMMARY OF ARGUMENT, IMPLICATION, AND EXTENSION

In this section, the main arguments of the book are summarized along the lines of constitutive and causal analysis.

Constitutive Analysis

In explicating the constitutive question (what made it possible for Japan to challenge neoliberalism?), I have made two interrelated claims, one theoretical and the other empirical. Theoretically, I have shed light on the importance of constitutive analysis in explaining the emergence and nature of foreign policy. Empirically, I have demonstrated the role a deep-seated, collective meaning structure can play in shaping actors' conceptions of strategic feasibility and political legitimacy in developing a given foreign policy. The collective meaning structure informs actors what they can or cannot do, and what they will or will not do. With regard to the Japanese challenge, I have argued that a historically constructed understanding of normalcy enabled the Japanese developmentalists to challenge neoliberalism by offering a justificatory foundation for the international validity of state-led economic development. They have since the Meiji Restoration constructed a normalcy meaning structure by comparatively locating Japanese development experiences in the context of their views (or interpretation) on the role of the state in the developmental history of the world economy (or of Western developed countries; Asia was included later). In this case, normal means that state-led industrialization is a prerequisite for economic development, particularly for late-comers. On the basis of this historically informed normalcy meaning structure, the Japanese developmentalists delegitimated the neoliberal commitment to a universal development philosophy as nothing but a practice of hijacking the history of the world economy. They claimed that state-led economic development, rather than just an alternative possibility to economic development, was a *normal* practice for all the successful late-industrializers. In this sense, Japan challenged the very order of things constructed by uncritical neoliberal reading of the history of the world economy.[2] The analysis suggests that the Japanese developmentalists would not have conceived of challenging neoliberalism without their historically constructed normalcy meaning structure. Challenging neoliberalism, and the assertion of the international validity of state-led economic development model, does not follow from the Japanese understanding of the role of the state in their economic development experience as unique. The flip side of this is the unthinkability or unimaginability that the United States would promote state-led economic development, a position that derives from American historical construction of the magic of the marketplace as the source of successful economic development for itself and others.

In addition, this book suggests the contingent nature of how the Japanese challenge occurred. Had the fates of Asian and Latin American (and African) economies been reversed in the 1980s, the Japanese developmentalist version of normalcy would have been critically undermined. The contemporary Japanese developmentalists would have still had to wonder if Japan were normal, let alone question the universal validity of neoliberalism. A different version of normalcy would have been on the rise, given this book's findings that two other Japanese economic development discourses, Marxism and economic liberalism, have offered their own versions of historical normalcy and have been competing for relevance in Japan.

A major theoretical extension of this element of the book can be pursued in the form of comparative analysis. The discursive construction of economic development experiences is not limited to Japan. One may understand variations in states' responses (for example, Germany and France, arguably the two early developmental states) to neoliberal commitment to a universal development philosophy only by examining how a dominant discursive construction of each state's development experiences restricts or enhances the very thinkability and possibility of challenging it. Discourses do not exist independent of their ability to interpret unfolding events, both domestically and internationally. Rather, they always compete for relevance, as is the case with the rise of developmentalism in Japan. This connection between discourse and practice calls for a reflexive and historicized analysis of, for example, international political economy with sufficient scope for the importance of shared meanings of policy choice.[3]

Finally, the importance of historically constructed collective meanings in shaping the future course of policy practice suggests a plausible scenario about how the current dominance of neoliberalism in the politics of economic development can and cannot be changed in the future. This means there may not be a quick reverse for a surge of international regulations limiting the role of the state in economic development. As Wade convincingly demonstrates, developing countries face "the shrinking of development space." The World Trade Organization's regulations on investment measures, trade in service, and intellectual property rights combine to revitalize a modern version of Friedrich List's "kicking away the ladder."[4] The book's analysis suggests that the reverse course might require worldwide (not just Japanese) critical re-evaluation of the role of the state in economic development and its associated meaning in the history of the world economy. Can the Japanese challenge be further substantiated globally through the politics of normalcy (or universality) in the history of development of the world economy?[5]

Causal Analysis

As for the question of why Japan proposed to create an AMF that intentionally excluded the United States from membership in the middle of the Asian financial crisis, this book's main original claim is that the Japanese state officials' (MOF) conception of Japan and the United States as two rivals promoting different models of economic development formed the basis on which Japan proposed to create the AMF. Because Japan's decision to propose the AMF was not an isolated event but stood in relationship to previous events (clashes with the United States at the ADB, the World Bank, and the APEC, and so on), I have traced the AMF decision's intrinsic relations to them. In so doing, I have also illuminated the processes by which MOF officials have since the late 1980s internalized the binary conceptions of Japan and the United States, as they confronted the United States in various forums of international finance and development. I have paid particular attention to Japan's pushing the World Bank to publish *The East Asian Miracle* in 1993, because this event constituted a formative moment where Japan first officially established its identity as a challenger to U.S.-led neoliberalism at the international level (that is, going beyond Asia). The politics of economic development between Japan and the United States before and after publication of *The East Asian Miracle* played a crucial role in shaping Japan's fundamental reinterpretation of what the U.S.-led IMF operation in managing the Thai crisis was all about.

Focusing on the variation in Japan's policies toward the IMF operation in managing the Thai crisis, this book has explored the micro processes of Japan's decision to propose the AMF in the midst of the Asian financial crisis. I have demonstrated that Japan strategically chose to create the AMF as a regional financial mechanism for quick disbursement of funds to crisis-affected countries to be able to defend the Asian model of economic development against the U.S.-led IMF's imposition of a neoliberal economic order onto Thailand and other affected countries. For the AMF to work in the framework of an Asian conception of economic development, a U.S. presence would not help. The AMF proposal was thus launched, excluding the United States.

As demonstrated in Japan's AMF decision, the identity-intention analytical framework offers a nontautological understanding of the origins of an interest that is endogenous to the dynamic theoretical account of the relationship between identity and interest. As Hopf aptly puts it, the relationship of identity to interest "is nontautological because evidence of the interest and its content is not the interest itself. It is endogenous because the origins of the interest and the identity of the individual are both located within theoretical account of identity."[6] As such, the framework is not about material *or* ideational interests. The framework gives a theoretical account of how actors' identities inform actors of *reasoning* their goals for particular actions. Reasoning essentially manifests in the form of giving meaning to one's actions as well as others'. Identities are central to meaning making on the part of actors involved in the dynamic interaction of foreign policy. As such, the framework connects formation of meaning-oriented interests to actual policy choice. By analyzing historical actors' self-understood interests and motivations, the framework offers a better way of dealing with overdetermination of *given* interests as well as underspecification of the *kinds* of interests at stake to which rational theorizing of international relations is often vulnerable.

To put it differently, actors' interests themselves are social rather than rational, in the sense that interests cannot be detached from a social context woven from rules and meanings, which define relationships between the self and others and give interactions their purpose. In Onuf's words, "agency is a social condition."[7] The assumed context-free, timeless, and abstract model of the rational actor is ill equipped for capturing the importance of constitutive social forces in shaping actors' interests. The parsimonious elegance of rational theorizing of international relations tends to come only at the expense of more concrete, explicit, and historically informed studies of international relations. After all, the rational model does not offer a way to theorize actors' interests nontautologically; states do act according to their conception of self-interest. Because they act instrumentally on the basis of self-interest, they are called rational actors. By rational, what is meant is that states choose more (or most) attractive alternatives within the constraints of available information, the interests and strategies of other states (or nonstate actors), and the distribution of power. State officials (or decision makers), because they are assumed to be rational, are assumed to calculate costs and benefits, as rational model theorists suggest. Usually, it does not matter whether the actors concerned actually think and speak in ways consistent with rational model theorists.[8]

However, international constraints and opportunities, or strategic interests involving threats and opportunities, which are the primary conceptual tools that the rational approaches employ to account for states' *behavior*, must be understood *as such* by historical actors themselves in the first place. Otherwise, the rational approaches (away from actors' point of view) might end up inquiring into *what it should be* rather than *what it is*.[9] In other words, actors' preferences cannot be read off a material description of the world, because they live in a material world that they interpret, and it is on the basis of these interpretations that they present various policy options to themselves. Thus, "a study of action must always be undertaken as a study of the cultural resources through which people give meaning to the material worlds in which they live."[10] The logical and methodological rigor that rational approaches bring to political or social theory is purchased at the expense of losing contact with agency, which constitutes the root of social action. As I have empirically demonstrated, the analytical framework advocated in this book offers a better explanation *and* understanding of Japan's AMF proposal in comparison to those alternative explanations (variants of rational explanations) I have collected from the existing literatures on Japanese foreign policy, namely, economic interest group, state-centered, and systemic approaches (see Chapter 2).

Substantively, this book's findings reach beyond the AMF case in pointing to three new dimensions of postcrisis world politics. The first dimension is related to Japanese foreign economic policy. In the wake of the Asian financial crisis, many commentators have identified Japan's AMF proposal, independent of U.S. influence, as a defining moment for Japan's decision to "go Asia" in the sphere of Japanese foreign economic policy.[11] Japan has been conspicuous, for example, in shaping exclusionary Asian regionalism (the New Asian Regionalism, to be discussed in detail here) in the aftermath of the Asian crisis.[12]

The second dimension is emergence of the exclusionary New Asian Regionalism associated with East Asian regional identity. By "exclusionary," I mean exclusion of the United States from the institutionalization of Asian regionalization. The very practice of exclusion demarcates "new" from "old" Asian regionalism, of which the United States was a part (for example, the APEC).[13] Empirically, the advent of the ASEAN Plus Three (China, Japan, and Korea; APT) in 1997 was the first step toward the postcrisis exclusionary practice. For example, Higgott, Bergsten, Stubbs, Dieter and Higgott, Terada, and Yu all identify the APT process as a clear, institutional manifestation that reflects a deepening sense of regional "we" consciousness in a more tightly defined *East Asian* context.[14] They commonly point to the importance of these states' shared experience of the Asian financial crisis, which is inseparable from their shared resentment of the U.S.-led IMF response to the crisis.[15] The common experience that fostered a sense of common identity (East Asian identity) was East Asian states' shared "image of the region in adversity besieged by outsiders 'ganging up' in their attempts to exploit the difficulties that East Asian governments faced."[16] As Higgott aptly puts it in his discussion of the politics of resentment, "Most East Asians feel that they were both let down and put down by the West." At the center of this humiliation lies the Western replacement (or reconstitution) of *older* social forms, such as developmental states and East Asian miracles, with *newer* social forms, such as corrupt practitioners of crony capitalism. The IMF associated the Asian development model with crony capitalism, thus normatively, if not empirically, delegitimating the Asian model while normatively, if not empirically, privileging market-based processes and outcomes.[17]

As such, the U.S and IMF's discursive (and material) demolition of the Asian economic model in binary terms of *us* and *them* generated the reverse version of them and us on the part of East Asian states on the same grounds, which had been gradually fermenting through confrontations at the APEC (see Chapter 5). A remark by the Thai deputy prime minister, Supachai, reflects this binary structure of identities: "We cannot rely on the World Bank . . . [or] the International Monetary Fund but we must rely on regional cooperation."[18] Japanese finance minister Miyazawa firmly stated that "after the Asian crisis, Asian countries began to doubt the benefits of trade liberalization and that the APEC should answer this doubt."[19] Sakakibara goes even further by arguing that "if East Asia does not want to be divided and ruled as in the colonial days and in the *more recent* past, *we* need to form some type of regional cooperation of *our* own."[20] South Korea's President Kim Dae Jung claimed that the APT "would also be able to speak for the region in discussions with other major economic blocs, such as the European Union and the North American Free Trade Agreement. Why should Asia, alone among the 'three poles' of the global economy, not have its own grouping?"[21] In the fourth APT summit in Singapore in November 2000, Singaporean Prime Minister Goh Chok Tong also claimed in his statement that what was important was that the leaders of the thirteen countries were starting to think as "East Asian."[22] In terms of levels of "regionness," postcrisis Asia seems to have moved from a "regional complex" to a "regional society, regional community" capable of "articulating the transnational interests of the emerging region."[23]

Along these lines, there has been growing momentum for creation of an East Asian Community. A significant step forward was, for example, an official proclamation of the East Asian Community as a goal to be pursued in the declaration that followed the summit meeting of Japan and ten ASEAN members held in Tokyo in December 2003. In December 2005, the heads of ASEAN Plus Three met historically in Malaysia to translate this idea into a viable project. What is noticeable is that Asian states, for the first time in a long while, have started to define Asia or East Asia without the make-up of the Asia-Pacific that has included the United States. Japan's AMF proposal is at the root of all these later developments in the form of challenging the American neoliberal world order.[24]

The AMF itself has been taking small but important steps toward becoming a full-fledged, formal regional monetary institution. The AMF's first revival came through the New Miyazawa Initiative in 1998, which included establishment of backup facilities in the form of a swap arrangement with the central banks of Korea and Malaysia. It was followed by the Chiang Mai Initiative (CMI) in May 2000. The CMI arranged a network of bilateral swap arrangements among central banks of East Asian countries (ASEAN Plus Three) to give balance-of-payment support and "short-term liquidity support." As Amyx acutely notes, of importance is the latter support, which emerged out of the Asian financial crisis experiences. Unlike a balance-of-payment support linked to the recipient country's macroeconomic policy, in which the IMF plays a role through its conditionality principles on loan amounts, short-term liquidity support entails a liquidity injection into the recipient country where capital is exiting rapidly without particular macroeconomic mismanagement. This provision thus does not require any IMF intervention.[25]

Another major step was taken on May 6, 2005. The APT further strengthened the CMI at the ADB annual conference in Istanbul, not hesitating to point out that it would be a "step toward multilateralization"; "a de facto Asian Monetary Fund may eventually be created."[26] The Istanbul initiative doubled the size of currency swaps under the CMI from their current level of $39 billion,[27] increased the amount of emergency liquidity available without IMF conditions from 10 percent to 20 percent, and made bilateral swaps into two-way swaps, with the aim of making them multilateral in the future.[28] Japan led this initiative with China's support. Perhaps unsurprisingly, Kuroda, the new ADB president, who was among those to propose creation of the AMF in 1997 (Chapter 6), spearheaded the Istanbul initiative. In April 2005, Kuroda created the Office for Regional Economic Integration within the ADB to facilitate a regional monetary cooperation and appointed Kawai, another proponent of the AMF, as its head. At the ADB conference, Kawai went so far as to say that "the [strengthened] CMI has the potential to become an Asian Monetary Fund."[29] In this vein, the Asian finance ministers agreed to integrate and enhance the APT's Economic Review and Policy Dialogue (ERPD) process into the CMI framework at the APT Finance Ministers' Meeting in 2005. The 2006 meeting pushed the goal of CMI multilateralization further, adopting a collective decision-making procedure for the swap activation and initiating a study to examine possible options toward an advanced framework for the regional liquidity support arrangement.[30] On May 5, 2007, in Kyoto, finance ministers of the ASEAN Plus Three historically and unanimously agreed to make a joint effort to establish the AMF.

This book's analysis of the original AMF suggests that it would be likely to have its lending conditionality and prescriptions differ from those of the IMF when it is created in the near future. The regulatory mechanisms would be unlikely to encroach on the active role of the state in domestic economic governance. In Bowles's words, Asia's postcrisis regionalism is "bringing the state back in, keeping the [United] States out" as the flip side of the same coin.[31] Japan's two-step loan practice for its ODA policy, emphasizing the role of the recipient government in allocating loans to necessary places, may be a window on the shape of the AMF's regulatory mechanisms. This is gleaned from Seiji Kondo, who served as a Japanese "sous-sherpa" at the G-7 Köln summit, when he summarized the results of the summit:

> A fusion of the two viewpoints of globalism and regionalism is becoming necessary. Regional cooperation will be indispensable to Japan if it is to spread its *own* agenda in the future. It will also be important to bring about

a situation in which Europeans and North Americans will place more value on *Asian* cultures and senses, namely to infuse the global standard with *Asian* values. To put the matter more concretely, Japan has not given up the idea of the AMF.[32]

Lastly, the third dimension is Japan's active involvement in the politics of a new global economic order (or governance). On the basis of its understanding that the Asian financial crisis was mainly caused by defects in the deregulated financial markets of global capitalism, Japan challenged U.S.-led international financial systems in the debate over New International Financial Architecture (NIFA) at the G-7 summits in several areas: appropriate modes of financial crisis response, international financial institution reform, permissibility of capital control, hedge fund regulation, and regional financial and exchange rate mechanisms.[33] Warning against the U.S.-led "market fundamentalism" allegedly associated with global standards and universal values, Japan, in coalition with European countries, drew out of the 1999 Köln summit three important agendas for future discussion of the NIFA: (1) discussion of the adverse effect of policy biases in favor of short-term capital flows, (2) a caution against drastic capital account liberalization, and (3) examination of the justifiability of the use of controls on capital inflows.[34] In the 2000 Okinawa summit, Japan pushed further for IMF reform, urging it to focus surveillance more on abrupt large-scale cross-border capital movements, limit the IMF's structural policies to cases directly related to crises, and improve the IMF's transparency and decision-making process.[35]

Along these lines, on the politics-of-economic-development front, Japan established the Tokyo-based ADBI as "a center for alternative development and monetary paradigms," challenging the two Bretton Woods institutions' global prescriptions.[36] The Japanese challenge continues at bilateral (production and public-sector-oriented bilateral ODA practice), regional (protection of the ADB from neoliberal lending prescriptions and conditionality), and global levels (the aforementioned ADBI and reform politics at the IMF and the World Bank).[37] Going beyond Vietnam, Laos, and Myanmar in Asia, Japan now bilaterally promotes the Asian or Japanese model of economic development to Africa (in Tanzania, Ethiopia, and Ghana) through its close collaboration with the recipient countries' Poverty Reduction Strategy.[38] Japan does not agree with the World Bank's latest aid strategy, which takes poverty reduction as the ultimate goal of development. Japan claims that the World Bank

Strategy is not able to realize poverty reduction so long as it remains silent about how the recipient country successfully industrializes to make money on its own.[39] All in all, Japan does not regionally and globally embrace (at least in the politics of economic development and the NIFA) "the American Imperium."[40]

CONTRIBUTION TO INTERNATIONAL RELATIONS AND THEORETICAL EXTENSION

This book offers three types of contribution to studying international relations. Thematically, it presents concrete, historically informed conceptual and theoretical insights into one of the most provocative Japanese foreign economic policies in the postwar era: the Japanese challenge to the American neoliberal world order, promoting and defending the Asian (or Japanese) model of state-led economic development across the globe since the mid-1980s. In the broader field of International Relations, this book also contributes to expanding security-issue-related IR constructivist literature to incorporate international political economy. Theoretically, it shows the fruitfulness of a holistic approach to foreign policy analysis by combining constitutive and causal analysis. The holistic perspective not only permits richer understanding of the foundation of the Japanese challenge through constitutive analysis but also explains a particular policy choice reflective of the Japanese challenge through causal analysis. Relatedly and methodologically, this book suggests a way to systematically connect constitutive and causal analysis. Within each type of analysis, the book also specifies an empirically testable, clear path of analytical steps to ensure falsifiable research as well as to increase validity and reliability.

In addition, this book speaks to the critical theory of international relations that calls into question existing institutions (and orders) and social and power relations.[41] It does so by giving a Japanese reading of the history of the world economy. The Japanese alternative points to particular political and historical settings (or the historically, socially, and politically constructed nature) of the universalist foundation that undergirds neoliberalism and its associated institutional orders in world politics. As has been discussed, the study of the Japanese alternatives suggests both the constraints on, and prospect for, change in the global politics of economic development in the twenty-first century. The AMF case study also illustrates how "the institution of global standards" is politically produced and reproduced. At the same time, it (and later developments of New Asian Regionalism) suggests how the institution of global standards might change in the future. Taken together, the constructivist insights contained in this book make a contribution to the critical theory of international relations by offering the possibilities of both change and continuity in global economic governance.

As for theoretical extension, the holistic approach performed well enough to merit testing in the historical development of other foreign policies. In particular, the identity-intention analytical framework has a quality of "interpretivist generalization" concerning the structure of identity and interests in the action-reaction world of global politics (see Chapter 3 for discussion of scope conditions for this framework).[42] When it comes to future application of the framework to other cases, one further specification is worth noting on empirical grounds. More analytical attention may need to be paid to the process of domestic contestation of foreign policy making in issue areas where the distribution of decision-making authority is less concentrated. Regarding the AMF proposal, the MOF (particularly the Asian faction) was a dominant force with its expertise and jurisdiction over international finance and development issues in Japan vis-à-vis, say, the MOFA (and its pro-IMF faction), which tended to define Japan's national interests in terms of maintaining a good relationship with the United States. This might not be the case for other issue areas. In these cases, a richer and fuller account can be constructed by detailing domestic political struggles associated with competing identities and interests of a given state.

EPILOGUE: JAPANESE PROPOSAL FOR A NEW INTERNATIONAL ECONOMIC ORDER

I conclude this book by introducing Murakami's proposal for a new international economic order that resonates with Ruggie's notion of embedded liberalism in many ways. The heart of the proposal is to make a two-tier system of economic rules and orders that apply to developing and developed countries respectively in combining developmentalism and economic liberalism. I quote his proposal at length.

> We must reexamine the strengths and weaknesses of both economic liberalism and developmentalism from a broad perspective that goes beyond the viewpoint of economics. The strength of developmentalism is that it can sustain the benefits of decreasing costs, but its weaknesses are, first, that once

government intervention to implement developmentalism has begun, it tends to increase and become chronic. In particular, even when intervention has become unnecessary (that is, even when decreasing cost has come to an end in the targeted industries), the bureaucracy is reluctant to relinquish its power. At this point, developmentalism deteriorates into protectionism for stagnant industries, the economy as a whole loses its ability to grow, and the value of developmentalism is lost. A more fundamental weakness, however, is that developmentalism is effective only as long as there is a government able to implement both inter- and intra-industry coordination. Without a government to coordinate price-cutting and investment competition, developmentalism only creates a high-risk environment for firms. Furthermore, disparities between targeted and other industries, or distributive inequalities, occur under developmentalism. Unless these can be rectified by the government, developmentalism creates inequality [we should remember the dual structure that for a time became a problem in Japan] and invited political instability.

The central intent here, however, is to reexamine these issues from the perspective of the international economy. The conclusion is that *two rules* to deal with the two weaknesses are necessary. First, a "sunset" rule that terminates favorable treatment of follower countries needs to be adopted by international consensus. This will be difficult, but not impossible. The IMF and the GATT [General Agreement on Tariffs and Trade] have had similar rules for dealing with "exceptional" countries. Second, it is of decisive importance that developmentalism cannot become the fundamental rule for the global economy. This is because, given that there is no world government at present, there is no way of restraining international price-cutting and investment competition and there cannot be any international distributive policy to prevent disparities increasing among countries, or among industries that cross national borders.

Let us consider, for example, what would happen if the strongest economic power adopted developmentalism and raced ahead of its competitors. Increases in global inequality and political discontent would be even more likely than if developmentalism were forbidden to follower countries. That Japan is such a strong economic power is the substance of the criticism it is now receiving, even though the criticism is not based on coherently articulated theoretical analysis. Again, suppose that the United States became, in essence, a developmentalist country similar to Japan. Imagine how the competition and confrontation between the United States and Japan would destabilize economic and political order in the world. If developmentalism were taken as the only universal rule for the world economy, excessive competition on an international scale, more brutal than that under classical economic liberalism, would develop, crushing many countries' industries and distinctive firms. The result would be a world shaped by, and possibly resembling, Japan or the developmentalist United States. Surely nobody wants such a world.

These weak points of developmentalism are the strong points of economic liberalism. First, if economic liberalism is faithfully implemented, there will naturally be no government intervention or any difficult decisions as to when and how to terminate bureaucratic intervention. Second, given that economic liberalism should be a self-regulating mechanism, there will be no need for any world government or a similar global coordinating mechanism. Thus, economic liberalism has the qualifications to be a universal rule for the global economy, even in a world without a world government. These are important strengths of economic liberalism. Its weak point is of course that it cannot fully exploit the latent growth potential of decreasing costs.

It is difficulty to decide how these two models should be combined. In any case, we must first recognize that the trend toward decreasing costs is an undeniable fact. We must discard the groundless optimism about economic liberalism to which many of today's academic economists and others continue to give credence, uncritically and by force of habit. Accepting the reality of decreasing cost, we must reconsider how to combine the two rules and which institutions and practices of the two systems must be chosen. This choice between systems must be from a perspective that goes beyond merely economic issues. My own decision, for example, can be summarized in a proposed set of rules for *polymorphic economic liberalism.*

1. The leading industrial nations must adopt economic liberalism and discard developmentalism. The most important reason for this is that to adopt developmentalism as the universal rule for the world economy is equivalent to assuming the existence of a world government.
2. Developmentalism must be publicly approved for follower countries, and technology transfer should be promoted without hindrance. The key to this is the relaxation of patent rights. However, the "sunset" rule should be adopted to end such favorable treatment of follower countries.
3. A certain degree of distinctness in each country's market rules should be recognized. But as long as foreign firms and individuals obey such domestic rules, they must be allowed to enter the domestic market, without

exception, and must be treated in the same way that domestic firms and individuals are.

The third rule has a delicate relationship with the issue of universality in the first rule, but I consider this further in the following argument. The composite rule derived from these three is liberal but differs from classical economic liberal in its polymorphic nature. To repeat, classical economic liberalism advocated economic liberalism [minimizing restrictions on economic action] in all cases; in other words, it was a unifaceted economic liberalism.[43]

NOTES

Notes to Chapter 1

1. Carr 1964 (1939), 114.

2. The classic examples of antitheses to neoliberal generalization are found in List 1983 (1837), Polanyi 1944, Hirschman 1958, and Gerschenkron 1962. See also Kohli 2004 for a recent reformulation.

3. See Tickner 1990 for an excellent review. See also Gill 1989, Livingston 1992, and Toye 1993 for a similar point.

4. Killick 1995, 1998; Gold 1996. See also Chang 2003, 17–43 for a critique of the neoliberal historical generalization on the role of the state in economic development.

5. In terms of continuation of the Japanese challenge to neoliberalism, there has been concern among scholars about the impact of Japan's "lost ten years" (its own economic stagnation since the early 1990s) on its policy toward promoting state-led economic development. I expressed this concern at the end of every interview I had with MOF officials, academics, and researchers when I was in Tokyo in 2002. In a nutshell, they clarified that Japan's promotion of the Japanese model of economic development (which they believed was successfully applied in Asia) was, is, and will be for developing countries, not for developed ones. If the Japanese economy has a problem (lost ten years), it is Japan's problem as a developed country. Ultimately, they argued that Japan was the only (non-Western) country that made a successful transition from a peripheral to a core economy. In terms of current foreign economic policies, Japan still actively engages in promoting the state-led model in various ways.

6. Wan 1995/1996, Woo-Cumings 1995, Yasutomo 1995. Because of Japan's continuous resistance, the ADB is the only multinational development bank (MDB) that is unscathed by neoliberal doctrines in terms of lending prescriptions and conditionality.

7. Awanohara 1995, Wade 1996.

8. Higgott and Stubbs 1995, Rapkin 2001, Kim and Lee 2004.

9. Interview with an ADBI official, July 31, 2002, Tokyo. See also *Business Times*, May 31, 1999.

10. The word *only* needs some qualification. For example, developed European states such as France and Germany currently have their own economic practice not completely dominated by the market and show some reservations about advocating a market-only approach. Their approach is, however, far less assertive than that of the Japanese. Their acknowledgment of the role of the state in economic development is limited to a positive posture on state-run enterprises. On a spectrum, this is much closer to the neoliberal doctrine than the Japanese alternative is. Regarding a historical analysis of German development policy, see, for example, Messner and Nuscheler 2004. This point is further evident in Bronstone's in-depth study (1999) of the rules and norms of the European Bank for Reconstruction and Development (EBRD). Contrary to a story told by Steve Weber 1994 that the EBRD strongly reflects a distinctive European identity and goals, Bronstone demonstrates that in terms of lending policies, prescriptions, and conditionality the EBRD is even more reflective of the market-oriented neoliberal doctrine than is the World Bank's doctrine (Bronstone 1999).

11. By "neoclassical economic orthodoxy," I mean here an economic development approach espousing greater roles for market mechanisms and private sector initiatives. It prescribes elimination of subsidies to inputs, liberalization of product markets, and abolition of the state-run distribution system. It is often dubbed the "Washington consensus" (Williamson 1993). In this book, I use this term interchangeably with "neoliberalism." Conversely, by "state-led," I mean here that the role of the state in economic development or industrialization is not limited to provision of a basic legal framework, public order, and external security. The state *actively* encourages public services and other institutions favorable to industrialization and even undertakes direct organizational activities in production. See, for example, Kenichi Ohno 1998, 1–50 for a detailed comparison. For the role of the state in the history of economic development, see also Weiss and Hobson 1995.

12. See, for example, Scott 1991, Doty 1993, and Alker 1996. This is discussed in detail later.

13. Milliken 2001, 9.

14. The term *constructivism* was first introduced into International Relations by Onuf 1989.

15. Wendt 1992.

16. Ruggie 1998b, 884–885.

17. Cederman and Daase 2003, 5–6.

18. For an excellent discussion on the difference between "why" and "how possible," see Taylor 1989, 202–203.

19. Fearon and Wendt 2002, 63; Cederman and Daase 2003, 7–9. Both works relate this ontological deficit to the concept of "corporate identity," defined as "the intrinsic, self-organizing qualities that constitute actor individuality." See Wendt 1994, 385 for the definition.

20. Doty 1993, 298.

21. Reus-Smit 1999, 161.

22. The notion of thinkability can be linked to Bourdieu's *habitus*. Bourdieu 1984 refers to habitus as "a system of schemas for the production of particular practices." Similarly, see Hopf's exposition of the logic of everyday: 2002, 13–16.

23. Weldes 1999, 9.

24. Peter Hall 1989, 358.

25. Abdelal 2001, 18–21; Jefferson, Wendt, and Katzenstein 1996, 52–63.

26. According to Alker, "historicity" is "the sense of time-ordered self-understanding shared among members of a continuous human society." Personal communication with Hayward Alker (December 2002).

27. Ruggie 1998b, 871–874; Wendt 1999, 171–178.

28. Kowert and Legro 1996, 469.

29. One of the exceptions is Milliken. She heavily focuses on state interaction to account for "moves" that states made in the Korean War. See Milliken 2001.

30. Kowert and Legro 1996, 483–495.

31. Finnemore and Sikkink 2001. Similarly, see Helleiner 2005, 228–234 for sharing this concern when he reviews ideational analysis in international political economy.

32. Checkel 1998, 332. See Mearsheimer 1994/1995 for a similar critique.

33. Jackson 2003, 227–228. I discuss this issue in Chapter 3.

34. Jackson and Nexon 2004, 338–339.

35. Hopf 2002 might be an important exception. Yet this work is relatively modest in causal analysis because of the relative neglect of policy-making process. In addition, Hopf does not clearly spell out the rise and fall of the predominant discourse that affects foreign policy choice. This also leads to hindering causal efficacy. To be fair, poststructural (or critical constructivist) approaches do not produce causal accounts on epistemological grounds. Broadly, their analyses are focused on explicating constitutive research questions to uncover power relations hidden behind the politics of identity.

36. Abdelal, Herrera, Johnston, and Martin 2006.

37. Wendt 1999, 224.

38. Rodney Hall 2003.

39. This thread consists of intellectuals (mostly economists) and MOF officials. It is these intellectuals and MOF officials who have long been in charge of Japan's World Bank policies, of developing the Japanese alternative to neoliberal doctrines, and of drafting the AMF proposal. See Chapters 5 and 6 for detailed discussion.

40. Krasner 1985. By "authoritative" regime, Krasner refers to principles, rules, and procedures that increase the sovereign powers of individual states.

41. Gilpin 1987.

42. Derek Hall 2005, 124.

43. Lanciaux 1997, 473–479. From historical analysis of timings of economic model promotions by the United States and Britain, Lanciaux concludes that Japan's promotion of its model for economic development is not analogous to earlier attempts by those two countries to promote models for their own national interests. One of her vivid illustrations is that while promoting the ideas of free trade, Adam Smith was participating in the debate in Britain over whether the Americas should stay a colony of Britain. Free trade was promoted as an alternative to holding colonies that gave Britain the benefits of empire while relieving it of the responsibility and costs of governing and defending colonies. See Semmel 1970, 1993. See also Krasner 1976 and Gowa 1987 for the reasons a hegemon prefers a liberal, open economic order.

44. This means that all modern developed states in this century industrialized behind protective walls—the United States in the 1830s and most other developed states by the 1880s. As for the industrialization of the United States, many economic historians point out that direct government initiatives in transportation were a good example of the essential role played by the government in American economic growth and industrialization during the nineteenth century. Licht 1995, an economic historian, succinctly summarizes his view on American industrialization: "Developments in the nineteenth century were marked by America's passing from a mercantile to an unregulated and then to a corporately and state-administered market society." See also Tickner 1987 and Roy 1997. Taking one step further, some trace the idea of late industrialization back even further, to sixteenth-century Europe—especially the relationship between Britain (the late comer) and Venice. See Reinert 1994.

45. Uriu 2000, Gilpin 2003.

46. The first is Japan's "racial equality proposal" at the Paris Peace Conference of 1919. See Shimazu 1998 for detailed discussion of the rise and fall of the racial equality proposal of 1919. I borrowed the phrase "revolt against the West" from Bull 1984.

47. In December 1990, the Malaysian prime minister, Mahathir Mohamed, proposed to form an economic arrangement restricted to East Asian countries, excluding Australia, New Zealand, and the United States (the three Western APEC members). Malaysia's leader appears to have thought of the EAEC as being at a minimum a Uruguay Round lobbying group, and at the maximum a nucleus for a potential full-blown formal economic bloc in East Asia. See Low 1991 for the emergence of the EAEC idea. See also *Far Eastern Economic Review*, September 15, 1994.

48. Calder 1988.

49. Hirschman 1969, 13–40; Waltz 1979, 152–160.

50. Grieco 1997a, 111. See also Katzenstein 1997, 23–31.

51. *Asahi Shimbun*, September 20, 1997.

52. *Asahi Shimbun*, November 6, 1997, quoted in Katada 2001a, 196. It is an interview article with Mr. Hayami, former president of Nissho Iwai (a Japanese trading company).

53. Yasutomo 1995, 75.

54. According to Yasutomo, it was not until the successful Asian state-led development that Japan began to seriously engage in studying an alternative development model. Before that, Japan was passive about selling its development strategy. Even though this observation is generally true, Japanese exportation of its development model to Asia began in the early 1960s, at least at a moderate level. By the mid-1980s, Japan (the MITI and the MOF in particular) had already been advising many Asian economies on development of export-oriented industries. See Johnson 1992, 21–26 for this point.

55. Bennett 1999, 3.

56. Wade 1996, 12–14.

57. To be fair, it is not a major concern for Wade in his article. As such, he deploys these reasons rather descriptively.

58. Wade 1996, 14, footnote 22.

59. Wan 1995/1996.

60. Gilpin 1987, 48–49.

61. See, for example, Altbach 1997; Rowley 1997; Bergsten 1998; Higgott 1998; Amyx 2000, 2004; Hughes 2000; Cohen 2001; Green 2001; Katada 2001a; Kikuchi 2001; Rapkin 2001.

62. Ruggie 1998a lumps together neoliberalism and neorealism as "neo-utilitarianism" because they are variants within a rational choice model that takes actors and their interests as exogenously given.

63. In this way, this book differs from Wendtian systemic constructivism. See Chapter 3 for more detailed discussion. For some exemplar works on endogenizing a state's interests at the intersection of the domestic and the international, see Brubaker 1992, Price 1998, Rodney Hall 1999, Reus-Smit 1999, Weldes 1999, Abdelal 2001, Hopf 2002.

64. In this regard, Douglas 1986 provides a useful insight. She suggests that an institution is a configuration of ideas entrenched in "an intellectual process as much as an economic and political one."

65. Milliken 1999, 229.

66. Patterson and Monroe 1998, 325. See also Keeley 1990 and Price 1995 for genealogical discourse analysis for meaning production and reproduction.

67. The level of induction does not satisfy the atheoretical quality as set by "phenomenology" (letting the subject speak), because I already limited the discourse-space to the three main schools of thoughts. But the closure may be justified on the grounds

that no other serious Japanese economic discourse exists to the extent that it offers a contending interpretation of economic development of Japan, as well as that of other states.

68. Doty's 1993 discussion of the emergence of a "dominant" or "controlling" discourse that defines "subject," "object," and "relations" is relevant here.

69. Somers 1992, 607.

70. Patterson and Monroe 1998, 316.

71. Harré and Secord 1972, 295–297 in Alker and Hurwitz 2001, 1. This book's analytical emphasis on meaning underlying social actions distinguishes it from the "analytic narratives" tradition, which extracts explicit and formal lines of game theoretic reasoning in constructing historical narratives. For analytic narratives, see Bates, Greif, Levi, Rosenthal, and Weingast 1998. See also commentaries on this book by Carpenter ("What Is the Marginal Value of Analytic Narratives?"), Skocpol ("Theory Tackles History"), and Parikh ("The Strategic Value of Analytic Narratives") in *Social Science History*, 2000, *24*(4).

72. See, for example, Bennett and George 2001, 144–152, for uses of process tracing among historians and political scientists. See also Mahoney 2003, 360–367 for the discussion on pattern matching, process tracing, and causal narrative in the realm of "within-case analysis."

73. John Hall 1999, 210–216.

74. John Hall 1999, 99.

75. Abdelal 2001, 43–44.

76. Kratochwil 1989, 25.

77. In addition to MOF officials and IMF officials in the Tokyo office, I interviewed researchers and academics who extensively studied Japan's role in the Asian financial crisis. As a way to minimize the pitfalls often associated with elite interviewing (post hoc justification, subjectivity bias in giving an account of an event under study), I chose to use a semistructured interview technique. First, I developed a set of interview questions in a way that would help shed light on the processual, interactive development of Japan's AMF proposal (as shown in Chapter 6). Particular attention was paid to exploring how interviewees understood and defined the situation Japan faced. Second, I sent all interviewees the same set of interview questions ahead of our meetings. Lastly, however, I did not strictly stick with the interview questions during the actual interviews. Rather, I pragmatically changed the structure of the interviews (by developing open-ended questions) to draw out the situational understandings of interviewees (or their notion of what they thought relevant to Japan's AMF proposal) as much as possible. At the end of the day, however, the credibility of the interview data collected had to be adjudicated in relation to other forms of empirical data I gathered (the triangulation method). For discussion of elite interviewing, see, for example, Moyser 1987 and Lilliker 2003.

Notes to Chapter 2

1. Kenneth Bouling, quoted in Clinton 1994, 30.

2. Frieden 1999, 42.

3. Interestingly enough, in his most recent article Waltz 2000, 46 puts national honor on a level equivalent to survival as one form of national interest. In the realm of international political economy, Krasner 1978, on the basis of the acts and statements of central decision makers in the White House and the State Department, shows a persistent rank-ordering in the U.S. national interest (ranked in order of *increasing* importance): stimulating economic competition; ensuring security of supply; and promoting broader foreign policy goals, such as general material interests and ideological objectives. George and Keohane 1980 identify three types of national interest without a strict set of preference ordering: life, liberty, and property. Wendt 1999, 235–238 has four national interests, namely, physical survival, autonomy, economic well-being, and collective self-esteem.

4. Onuf 1998, 62–63.

5. Grieco 1997b, 167.

6. Morgenthau 1978, 5–6.

7. Morgenthau 1958, 54. See Clinton 1994, 25–35 for useful documentation of early debate on the conceptions and definitions of national interest in International Relations.

8. Waltz 1979, 134.

9. Wight 1995, 32.

10. Mearsheimer 1994/1995.

11. Morgenthau 1978, 8.

12. Waltz 1979, 126.

13. Krasner 1999.

14. This point is also noted by those rationalist scholars emphasizing the influence of domestic political structure on foreign policy making. See, for example, Milner 1991 and Fearon 1998, 293–295.

15. Rosenau 1972, 353. In this line of criticism of realists' assumption of national interest with fixed and transhistorical quality, Rosenau argues that national interest is "a pluralist set of subjective preferences that change whenever the requirements and aspirations of the nation's members change." Rosenau, quoted in Clinton 1994, 27. For a related line of argument, see Kratochwil 1982, suggesting that national interest is a construct emerging out of contingent historical, social, and rational processes that can vary considerably across states and points in time. See also Wolfers 1962 for an earlier critique of the realists' treatment of the relationship between power and national interest.

16. Tucker 1961, 463.

17. Weldes 1996, 277–279.

18. Waltz 1979, 71.

19. Bourdieu 1998, chapter 6. I use the term *more* here because this tendency of realist analysis is only *statistically* meaningful in comparison to other theoretical approaches. No social theorist, including constructivists, can be perfectly free of such a bias or fallacy. It lies in the nature of social inquiry to attribute the problems of theoretical understanding to people not engaged in theory as such.

20. As opposed to the ambition of rationalists to formulate a general theory of international relations regardless of historical epoch or differences in the internal complexion of states, most constructivists find pursuit of a general theory of international relations too ambitious. The constitutive forces constructivists emphasize, such as ideas, norms, and culture, and the elements of human agency they stress, such as corporate and social identity, are all inherently variable. There is simply no such thing as a universal, trans-historical, disembedded, culturally autonomous idea or identity. Thus most constructivists confine their analysis to compelling interpretation and explanation of discrete aspects of international politics, going no further than to offer a qualified contingent generalization. As such, constructivists repeatedly insist that constructivism is not a theory but rather an analytical framework. See Onuf 1989, 35–43; Finnemore 1996, chapter 1; Katzenstein 1996, chapter 2 and Conclusion. Maybe one exception to this is Wendt 1999, who has attempted to formulate a comprehensive social theory of international relations. In support of the Wendtian line, see Jackson and Nexon 2004.

21. Some constructivists are ideationally oriented in arguing that ideas broadly determine interests and that distribution of shared ideas matters much more than distribution of material capability. For example, see Haas 1990, 2 for discussion of the relation between interests and values. He argues, "Contrary to lay usage, interests are not the opposite of ideals or values. . . . Interests cannot be articulated without values. Far from values being pitted against interests, interests are unintelligible without a sense of values to be realized." In a more idealist vein, Sikkink 1991, 243, rejecting ideas as a kind of intervening variable that mediates between interests and outcomes, claims that "ideas are the lens, without which no understanding of interests is possible. . . . Ideas about economics and politics are present from the beginning in the very process of formulating interests, shaping not only actors' perceptions of possibilities but also their understanding of their own interests." More succinctly, "How a person chooses among potential alternatives is not only a matter of 'what he wants' but also of 'what he believes,' and for some kinds of choices an actor's beliefs or theories may play a most crucial role." See also Wendt 1994, 1999; Finnemore 1996; and Finnemore and Sikkink 1998. As will be discussed later, I think it is better to take such ideational arguments as a set of hypotheses to be empirically tested case by case. As is the case for brute materialism, the extreme version of ideationalism is not easily compatible with constructivist possibility ontology.

22. Smith, quoted in Sen 1998, 3.

23. Because all these alternative hypotheses are designed to answer the question *why* (not *how possible*), I make an effort to assess if they successfully offer insights into the question of *why* Japan challenged neoliberalism.

24. In addition to a material explanation that is critically examined in this chapter, previous studies suggest two specific ideational-based explanations, namely the "learning model argument" and the "leadership role model argument," for Japan's AMF decision. Because these two arguments do not directly correspond to how rationalists formulate the influence of ideas on policy choice, I scrutinize them in Chapter 6 *after* I empirically offer my identity-based analytical argument. In this way, this book's analytical leverage might be better measured in comparison to alternative explanations; readers themselves can evaluate the weight of each approach with evidence already in hand.

25. Lindblom 1977; Milner 1988, 1997.

26. This means that state or government institutions essentially offer an arena for group competition and do not exert a significant impact on the decisions that emerge. This point is, however, called into question by the Duke Project on Political Economy of Policy Reform in Developing Countries. From their research results, Bates and Krueger 1993, 454 claim that "one of the most surprising findings of our case studies is the degree to which the intervention of interest groups fails to account for the initiation or lack of initiation of policy reforms." Going further, they suggest that their studies reveal not just that interest groups do not drive the policy reform process but that they may in fact be unable or unwilling to act in support of policies that favor their interests. They argue that the fundamental problem with society-level analysis is that it wrongly assumes interest groups are organized in stable coalitions and such coalitions are dynamic sources of policy initiatives that best promulgate their own interests. Rather, it is the role of the state to set the agenda for the interest groups. See also Bates 1981 for the role of the state setting out options within which interest groups organize and influence policies and their implementation.

27. Yasutomo 1995, 50. For analyses that put more emphasis on society-state-level dynamics in determining Japan's foreign economic policies, see Pempel 1987, 1998; Muramatsu and Krauss 1987; Calder 1988, 1993; and Rosenbluth 1996.

28. Katzenstein 1978, 11.

29. Frieden 1988, 88.

30. See, for example, Calder 1993, Ramseyer and Rosenbluth 1993, and Rosenbluth 1996.

31. Pempel 1987, 286–287.

32. Finance is widely known to be the tie that binds the state to industrialists in the developmental state. In other words, financial controls are the nerves of the developmental state. See Woo-Cumings 1999, Introduction.

33. Calder 1993 and Ramseyer and Rosenbluth 1993.

34. Evans, Rueschemeyer, and Skocpol 1985; Sikkink 1991; Evans 1992, 1995. For a critique of this view, see Hamilton 1982.

35. Hatch and Yamamura 1996. However, one of the big problems with Hatch and Yamamura viewing Asian state-led economic developmentalism as an ideology (or thinly veiled justification of Japan-cum-Asian capitalists) imposed by an external force (Japan) is that they present a political world in which the Asian developing countries are treated as objects rather than subjects, debasing the validity of many Asian contributions to the global development debate. Along this line, Katzenstein and Rouse 1993, 238–239 conclude, through exploring Thai and Indonesian (the Asian countries they consider to be most dependent on Japanese trade, aid, and investment) economic relations with Japan, that Japan did not want to dominate its relations with these two and the host countries view Japan's involvement with them and their involvement with Japanese business in multilateral terms; they welcome Japanese capital, loans, and investment because they want to become more important and more diversified participants in the world economic system, not led by Japan.

36. The basics of the revisionist argument can be summarized here: U.S. economic policy (based on a neoliberal economic model) focuses on consumption as the primary engine of economic growth and seeks to maximize consumer welfare at any moment. Much consumption is either subsidized or taxed very lightly, while interest earned on savings, investment, and capital gains is taxed relatively heavily or otherwise penalized. National security is seen related to economic policy only in the narrow sense of managing the capability to manufacture weapons. Japan (based on a state-led economic model), by contrast, has emphasized production as the means of ensuring sustained economic growth. In Japan, consumption is taxed while production is treated favorably. The Japanese believe that promoting production is the best way to ensure long-term increases in standard of living; consumers will not be able to consume unless they produce. Moreover, Japan has firmly linked economic policy and national security. For example, the MITI's *Vision of Japan for the 1990s* speaks of achieving technological autonomy and bargaining power with other nations through technological and industrial leadership. See Prestowitz 1993, Introduction; and Gilpin 2001. The major revisionist works include Johnson 1982, Prestowitz 1988, van Wolferen 1989, Choate 1990, and Fallows 1994.

37. Prestowitz 1993, 16.

38. Shimada, quoted in Prestowitz 1993, 16.

39. *Washington Post*, March 1, 1992.

40. *Asahi Shimbun*, September 20, 1997.

41. *Asahi Shimbun*, November 24, 1997.

42. *Asahi Shimbun*, November 6, 1997.

43. The notion of state autonomy was first theoretically postulated by Max Weber

1978, 54 in his well-known definition. One of the most monumental books in marking the state-centered approach is Evans, Rueschemeyer, and Skocpol 1985. See also Ikenberry, Lake, and Mastanduno 1988, 1–14 for a compact summary of the state-centered approach in the making of foreign economic policy.

44. Lake 1988, 35–36. This notion of the state is similar to the neo-Marxists' reconceptualization of the state as the "material condensation of a relationship of forces among classes and class fragments." According to Sikkink, this reconceptualization rejects understanding of the state as a tool of the dominant class with no autonomy and as sealed off from social classes. On the basis of this notion of the state, neo-Marxist theories eventually argue that "because of the materiality of the state and the contradictions among various components within it, the state possesses a certain degree of relative autonomy from any given class fraction." Policies are therefore the outcome of class conflict mediated through a relatively autonomous state. Despite this acknowledgment of the relative autonomy of the state, in the final analysis neo-Marxist theories view the state as representing and organizing the long-term interests of the dominant class or capital as a whole. Therefore, compared to the statist position already discussed, the neo-Marxist version of the relative autonomy of the state is far more limited. See Sikkink 1991, 10 for her succinct discussion on Poulantzas 1978, 128–129 and Lindblom 1977. For a comprehensive survey of theorizing the role or agential power of the state in international relations, see Hobson 2000.

45. Biersteker 1990, 180.

46. Ikenbery 1986, 54.

47. Katzenstein 1978, 18.

48. Goldstein 1988, 217.

49. Katzenstein 1978.

50. Risse-Kappen 1991 develops a more nuanced, analytically rigorous version of typologies of state-society relationship in foreign policy making by adding insights from policy networks and coalition building to the existing strong-weak state literature.

51. Haggard 1988. In the case of Japan, Okimoto 1988, for example, makes an interesting observation based on the functional divisions of the state bureaucracy. He argues that each issue, and the ministry in charge of the issue, possesses a degree of politicization dependent on the type of political exchange between interest groups and the LDP.

52. Ikenberry 1986, 135.

53. Mikanagi 1996, 22. For the U.S.-Japan negotiation on Japan's market liberalization measures, see John Campbell 1993, Takatoshi Itō 1993, Schoppa 1993, Schwartz 1993, Rosenbluth 1996, Bullock 2000, Uriu 2000.

54. Okimoto 1988, 307.

55. Rosecrance 1986. See also Rosecrance and Taw 1990; Johnson 1995; Wan 1995; Heginbotham and Samuels 1998. Interestingly but ironically, the notion of Japan as a

trading state can be traced back to the so-called Yoshida doctrine, which laid the foundation for postwar Japanese foreign policy but has been taken as the root cause of the *reactive* nature of that policy. The doctrine is characterized by (1) a close and expanding alliance with the United States; (2) a minimalist security policy based on a security treaty with the United States and maintenance of strictly defensive military capability; (3) unflinching pursuit of economic growth through an export-oriented development strategy. The third characteristic is the primary reason Japan became a mercantilist state and is also why it is considered a strong state, while the first two characteristics help Japan continue to be characterized as a reactive state. Therefore, depending on which aspect of Japan one looks at, it can be seen in either way (even though reactive Japan and aggressive mercantilist Japan are poles apart!). Deriving from the combination of interdependence and economic statecraft literature, Inoguchi's notion of Japan as a supporter, not a challenger, stands in the middle. For the Yoshida doctrine, see Akaha and Langdon 1993, 6. For the reactive state thesis, see Calder 1988 and Miyashita 1999. See also Inoguchi 1986 for the notion of a supporter state.

56. Johnson 1982, especially chapter 1. However, some claim that by the mid-1970s the LDP politicians had gained increasing expertise and thus influence in policy making, even though the Diet, which is constitutionally the highest authority of Japanese state power, still remained passive and the bureaucracy continued to be the main source of policy making. See, for example, Muramatsu and Krauss 1984. In addition, there was a rising call among political, business, and intellectual leaders for administrative reforms in order to restrict the power of the bureaucracy. For the economic and administrative reforms, see Carlile and Tiltoneds 1998 and Mishima 1998.

57. Schmiegelow and Schmiegelow 1990, 507.

58. The rationale behind this is that, given its limited economic interest in Africa, why would a strategic (out of cost and benefit calculation) Japan run the risk of further exacerbating (given its trade friction with the United States) relations with America, the champion of neoliberalism, by not cooperating, for example, with the U.S.-led application of market-oriented structural adjustment policies? In his interviews with officials in a number of Japanese ministries, Stein confirms this. At a time when Japan began to question neoliberalism in the 1980s, Stein reports that there was apparently some concern about antagonizing the United States, which strongly supported the market-based adjustment packages that were very much seen as a product of the economics profession there. See Stein 1998, 40–42. Moreover, as evidenced in the Yoshida doctrine, Japan has since 1945 made Japanese-U.S. relations the highest priority of diplomacy, sometimes at the peril of relations with other states and areas. In this respect, Japanese relations with Africa have historically been a low priority (as one barometer, it was pointed out that no Japanese prime minister has ever visited an African country). The reverse of this is to expect Japan's intensive attempt at guarding Asia (where it has enormous economic stake) against U.S.-led market penetration. This presupposes

that a relatively closed Asian market (with protective walls, for example, to defend infant industries), which is the by-product of implementing a state-led Japanese alternative economic development model, would benefit Japan most and other competing industrial countries least (a Japan-dominated closed Asian market would even drive them out eventually). As is to be discussed, however, this line of reasoning is not empirically sustainable.

59. One of the best examples of these promotion efforts is the Overseas Economic Cooperation Fund (OECF) report 1991, from one of Japan's aid implementing agencies, which severely criticized the World Bank's market-oriented development programs in developing countries. The MOF is known to have strong influence over the OECF. See Hirata 1998 and Kenichi Ohno 1998. For a journalistic discussion of Japan's posture on development ideas, see *International Herald Tribune*, March 9, 1992.

60. *Bungei Shunjū*, April 1992, 176–193, quoted in Johnson 1993a, 59.

61. As discussed in Chapters 5 and 6, there exist factions even within the international bureau at the MOF, namely pro-Asia and pro-IMF. They differed on many points regarding the AMF. Interview with an MOF official, Tokyo, July 19, 2002.

62. Interview with an MOF official, Tokyo, July 19, 2002. The MITI had no jurisdiction over Japan's external financial and economic development affairs (including ODA policy), so it did not want to take sides with the MOF or MOFA. Simply put, the MITI had no wish to meddle in the conflict between the MOF and the MOFA over the AMF proposal.

63. Sudo 2002, 109–112. This was more or less a reflection of the emergence, since the late 1980s, of a growing cadre of younger Japanese politicians who felt that Japan should be more consciously proud of its accomplishment and more critical of the social and economic conditions currently found in the United States. They were in line with some of the younger bureaucrats who pointed out that the older generation had a bit of an inferiority complex toward that nation and therefore did not want to directly challenge the United States in international politics. Both groups grew weary of U.S. accusations concerning Japanese trade practices and openly criticized U.S. commercial policies. See Stein 1998, 40–47; and Wade 1996.

64. Although the MOF continued to work in the direction of excluding the United States from the beginning, exclusion was decided only just before Japan proposed the AMF on September 21, 1997, in Hong Kong. See Sakakibara 2000, 185–188 and chapter 4.

65. Kikuchi 2001, 164–166.

66. Sakakibara 2000, 186.

67. Stein 1998. Lehman also confirms Japan's consistent and strenuous efforts in promoting state-led economic development in Africa through its ODA policies since the late 1980s. Lehman 2005, 426 notes that "the conferences [the Tokyo International Conference on African Development] have often been discussed in the context of the Asian model of development."

68. On this point, Yanagihara, a leading Japanese development economist, makes a useful distinction between the Japanese alternative and neoliberalism. While dubbing neoliberalism the "framework" approach, emphasizing economic development and establishment of institutions and mechanisms for the appropriate functions of the market, he labels the Japanese alternative the "ingredient" approach, stressing that economic development is achieved through increasing real output (production). See Yanagihara 1998.

69. Wade 1996, 14, footnote 22 suggests that one way to nail down Japan's reason for challenging neoliberalism at the World Bank is to compare what it *wants* for the World Bank and what it *does* in the ADB.

70. Yasutomo 1995, especially chapter 2 on the ADB.

71. Wan 1995/1996.

72. In general, this approach is less strict than conventional rational choice theories by relaxing and allowing a pattern of interactions among bureaucrats, LDP politicians, and big business. Nonetheless, as the popular Japan, Inc. stereotype reckons, this approach tends to overemphasize the role of state bureaucrats in policy making while ignoring the importance of issue areas (for example, the domestic power configuration of international finance areas can differ from that of trade; security issues in general can have a domestic constituency different from that of economic issues). As a result, it can be said that this approach broadly underlies the assumption of the state as a unitary actor.

73. Ikenberry, Lake, and Mastanduno 1988, 12.

74. See empirical works in the same volume by Goldstein, Gowa, Ikenberry, Lake, and Mastanduno.

75. In other words, they were the most vulnerable to the Asian financial crisis. Facing the Asian crisis, Japan as a nation-state was not so much impending as were these private sectors that could go bankrupt any minute depending on how the crisis unfolded.

76. Generally speaking, analyses of Japanese foreign policy at this systemic level (including both reactive state and supporter state conceptions) tend to yield a less proactive definition of the Japanese state than the state-centered approach. On the continuum, Japan is a reactive state susceptible to outside pressure (mainly the United States), and Japan is a mercantile trading state unflinching in pursuit of economic gain in the world market. These are poles apart. In the middle stands the notion of a supporter, not a challenger. Important to note here is that all these characterizations of Japan work at their own level, which entails differing degrees of analysis and makes it virtually impossible to directly compare and contrast them. For example, reactive as well as supporter theses on Japanese foreign policy making are mainly discussed at the systemic level, while a mercantile trading state thesis, which comes along with the theory of grand strategy, mainly requires state-centered analysis. To complicate the

business further, a society-level approach has added another layer in understanding Japanese foreign policy making. The Japanese case clearly appears to reflect the classical debate on the level of analysis; to which level does one have to pay more attention to best explain and understand the Japanese foreign economic policies? See Hollis and Smith 1990 for an excellent summary of this debate in International Relations.

77. According to Calder 1988, 520, the essential characteristics of the reactive state are that (1) the state fails to undertake major independent foreign economic policy initiatives when it has the power and national incentives to do so; and (2) it responds to outside pressures for change, albeit erratically, unsystematically, and often incompletely.

78. Ever since Calder articulated the reactive nature of Japanese foreign policy in his 1988 article, there has been ongoing debate on the sources of Japanese reactiveness. In general, two sources have been identified as most effectual in reactive Japan: the external (mostly U.S.) pressure dubbed *Gaiatsu*, and Japan's immobile and highly fragmented domestic political process lacking strong leadership. Since this section's focus is on discussion of Japanese foreign economic policy at the systemic level, the first source (outside pressure) is the main subject. For discussion of external sources of Japan's reactiveness, see Islam 1991, Pyle 1992, Blake 1993, Lincoln 1993, Miyashita 1999. For discussion of internal fragmentation, see Hellmann 1969 and Calder 1988.

79. Waltz 1979, 65.

80. Mearsheimer 1990, 1994/1995.

81. Hirschman 1969, 13–40 and Waltz 1979, 152–160 causally link a weak state's accommodation of the will of a strong state to the asymmetric market and security relationship between the two states.

82. Yasutomo 1995, 50.

83. Keohane 1984, 32–34 suggests four prerequisites for a hegemon in the world political economy: access to crucial raw materials, control over major sources of capital, a large market for imports, and comparative advantages in high value-added goods. As opposed to this coercive-hegemon version, the liberal scholar Kindleberger puts forward the benevolent-hegemon hypothesis, maintaining that the hegemonic state, without employing coercive measures to pry open others' markets, will unilaterally open its markets with the expectation that other states reciprocate and open theirs. For discussion of the hegemonic hypotheses, see Kindleberger 1973; Krasner 1976; Gilpin 1981, especially chapter 3; Snidal 1985; and Ikenberry and Kupchan 1990. For a recent reassessment of Krasner's work, see Keohane 1997.

84. Keohane and Nye 1977, 7.

85. Inoguchi 1990, 419.

86. Wan 1995/1996. For security issues, see Pharr 1993, 235–237.

87. Viner 1948, Krasner 1978, Baldwin 1985, Moran 1996.

88. Vogel 1986. Some argue that the transition of Japanese diplomacy (from

passive-reactive to active) began with the return of Okinawa in 1972. See Buckley 1992 and Fukushima 1999.

89. Calder 1988, 520.

90. Krasner and Okimoto 1989, 117.

91. Sudo 2002, 110.

92. Stein 1998, 41. Wade 1996 suggests (just in passing) a possibility of this line of reasoning for the Japanese challenge. See also David Campbell 1992, chapter 8 for how Japanese economic power as a great national security threat to the United States was articulated throughout the 1980s.

93. See Uriu 2000 for the impact of the revisionists on U.S. trade policies toward Japan. On the notion that Japan is different, the revisionists in the Clinton administration pressured Japan to set a numerical import target to improve the U.S. trade deficit vis-à-vis Japan.

94. Krasner and Okimoto 1989, 129.

95. For example, Watanabe, a prominent Japanese economist for the state-led alternative, declares that adoption of a state-led development strategy is unavoidable for any country wishing to industrialize rapidly. See Watanabe 1998, 201–204.

96. Kenichi Ohno 1998, 32–34. On the basis of the experiences of Japan and the NIEs, they also claim that dissolution of the state-led industrialization regime is far from automatic. Successful dissolution must be supported by appropriate regime shifts. For example, they argue that domestic and international pressure for a more liberal system must be matched by appropriate government actions at the critical moment; private forces alone are not enough. Necessary policies include deregulation, decentralization, promotion of competition, enforcement of antimonopoly laws, downsizing of the government, external market opening, transparency of political and administrative processes, and political liberalization toward full democracy.

97. See, for example, Sakakibara and Tahara 1999, 151–159, among the most outspoken proponents of the state-led alternative, for comments and diagnosis on the staggering Japanese economy. See also Murakami 1996, chapter 8, an intellectual godfather of those proponents of the state-led alternative who essentially argues that developmentalism is suitable for latecomers, while classical economic liberalism is appropriate for mature industrialized countries.

98. Sakakibara and Tahara 1999, 133–150.

99. Gourevitch 1986.

100. Wendt 1999, 236.

101. What is interesting about all the theories reviewed here is that they rely either explicitly and implicitly on the concept of identities, such as "strong or weak state" and "reactive, supportive, and proactive state," which are inductively found.

102. Goldstein and Keohane 1993a, 8–24.

103. According to Goldstein and Keohane (1993a, 15), individuals are taught to be-

lieve in the cause-effect relationships posited by causal ideas. For example, those put forth by liberal trade ideas are persuasive to many people because they were taught classical economics in schools.

104. See the opposite view from Krasner 1991, who essentially argues that national power determines a focal point along the Pareto frontier, which is not necessarily the same as a functionally optimal point.

105. See Sikkink 1991 for the impact of institutionalized ideas on economic developmentalism of Argentina and Brazil.

106. John Hall 1993, 51.

107. Ruggie 1998a, 18.

108. Woods 1995, 171.

109. Adler and Haas 1992, 367.

110. Ruggie 1998a, 90.

111. Giddens 1979, 88.

112. See, for example, Odell 1982; Sikkink 1991, 1993; and Goldstein and Keohane 1993b. For the causal effects of ideas, see Woods 1995; Yee 1996, 1997. For general discussion of the contrasting view of neoliberal and constructivist ideas, see Ruggie (1998a, Introduction). For the epistemic community, see Haas 1992.

113. Peter Hall 1989, 383–384.

114. Woods 1995, 175.

Notes to Chapter 3

1. Giddens 1984, 43.

2. Wendt 1992, 398. Wendt 1999, 224–232 discusses four types of identity: (1) personal or corporate, (2) type, (3) role, and (4) collective. He further advances two general hypotheses in which identities are more important for actors facing identity conflict: (l) "In any situation the solution to identity conflicts within an actor will reflect the relative 'salience' or hierarchy of identity commitments in the Self, and (2) that hierarchy will tend to reflect the order in which I presented the four kinds of identity above." However, as Hopf 2002, 292 points out, it is questionable to specify a priori which are more fundamental if identities are constructed in relation to others.

3. Thus my adoption of Davidson's notion of primary reason as cause is meant to go outside the Humean "covering-law" model of causation.

4. Ruggie 1998b, 880.

5. Waltz 1979.

6. Axelrod and Keohane 1993, 86.

7. Keohane 1984, 64.

8. Krasner 1976, Gilpin 1981, Grieco 1990, Gowa 1994, Mearsheimer 1994/1995. See also Baldwin 1993.

9. Keohane 1984; Oye 1985.

10. Moravcsik 1997; Milner 1988, 1997.

11. Milner 1991.

12. Mercer 1995, using social identity theory (SIT) developed to explain experimental findings from the minimal-group paradigm, supports the neorealist assumption that states are a priori self-regarding or self-help, thus leaving constructivist arguments in disarray. But he himself makes a distinction between out-group and in-group competition: "Intergroup competition often will take the form of a preference for relative gains when dealing with out-groups and absolute gains when dealing with members of the in-group" (1995, 251). It is hard to render these conclusions congruent because the latter observation seems more in line with constructivists' focus on the process that determines identities and interests of actors in interaction. After all, his SIT-based research design, which predicts conflict with out-groups regardless of the content of the identity (thus only with the consideration of membership), is not appropriate for testing a constructivist notion of meaning-based identity choice.

13. Wight 1995, 25.

14. Giddens 1984, 213–226.

15. Downes 2001, 228.

16. Jackson 2003, 230. The irony is, in other words, inadvertent collapse of the distinction between rational individualism (or rational choice theory) and behavioralism on their treatment of intentions in theorizing human action. On the one hand, behavioralists do not include intention when they explain action on the grounds that intention is an empirically unobservable mental (internal) state. Rationalists, on the other hand, incorporate intention in their theoretical explication of human action by assuming that actors are intentional. Despite this important *theoretical* difference, both approaches to human action can be, in the end, lumped together as externalist in the sense that they empirically operate on the thesis that every action or event is brought about by a set of external conditions. For a view of "externalist," see McClellan 1996.

17. Ruggie 1998a, 19.

18. Downes 2001, 228–230.

19. Alker 1996, 355–360.

20. Onuf 1989, 163. Similarly, see also Hurd 1999, 399–403.

21. Wendt 1992, 405–406.

22. Bull 1977; Wendt 1999, 246–312.

23. Wendt 1992, 394.

24. Adler 1997, 322.

25. See Oakley 2000 for an excellent, ontologically informed reformulation of Popper's situational analysis. Oakley cites Popper in the vein of Giddens's double hermeneutics: "The world as we know it is our interpretation of the observable facts in the light of theories that we ourselves invent." Popper 1972 in Oakley 2000, 462.

26. See Vollmer 1999, 25–41 for a thorough review of debates on theories of agent causality.

27. Harré 2001.

28. *Nicomachean Ethics* 1985, 31–32.

29. Giddens 1984, 14.

30. Hopf 1998, 177.

31. Giddens 1984, 310.

32. Maoz 1990, 2.

33. A neorealist such as Snyder shares this view, saying with respect to how resources and capabilities are aggregated in the system, "If system structure (anarchy) only shapes and shoves, relationship patterns (alliance or not) give a more decided push." See Snyder 1997, 22.

34. Somers 1994, 620–627.

35. In International Relations, several ways are suggested for classifying variants of constructivism. For example, Onuf has strong and weak constructivism 2001, as is the case for Hasenclever, Mayer, and Rittberger (1998, 136). Ruggie has neoclassical, postmodernist, and naturalist constructivism (1998b, 880–882). Hopf 1998 makes a distinction between conventional and critical constructivism. Checkel 1998 divides it between thin and thick constructivism.

36. Harré and van Langenhove 2000b, 2.

37. Wendt 1992, 396–397.

38. Abdelal 2001, 38.

39. Max Weber 1978, 4. Italics added.

40. Wendt 1999, 329.

41. As opposed to the view of identity as reasoned choice, some communitarian approaches tend to claim that identity comes before reasoning for choice. A definitive communal identity is a matter of self-realization, not of choice. For example, Sandel 1998, 150 claims that "community describes not just what they *have* as fellow citizens but also what they *are*, not a relationship they choose but an attachment they discover, not merely an attribute but a constituent of their identity" (italics in original). See also Crowley 1987 for a similar line of argument. As is discussed later, however, it is hard to imagine that one can really have no substantial choice between available identities in a given context. There is always the possibility that one is constantly making choices. The "discovery" or "detecting" thesis runs the risk of establishing too deterministic a view of social action.

42. Bennett 1999, 5–12.

43. Kowert and Legro 1996, 469.

44. Florini 1996, 363–389.

45. This reminds me of the day I defended my dissertation proposal. One of the examinees said, carefully but nonetheless adamantly, it would be hard for him to

imagine that state officials would be asking each other what identities, but not interests, were at stake at the moment of deliberation of foreign policy. Additionally, he wondered if there exists a linguistically corresponding term of identity in both Korean and Japanese.

46. Davidson 2001, 5.

47. See, for example, Elman and Elman 2001, 20–27 for contrasting understandings of causation between historians and social scientists. Historians emphasize uncovering purposive and intentional behaviors of actors, while social scientists try to find a covering law behind such movements of actors.

48. Hempel 1966. In the world of the nomological-deductive (N-D) model of explanation, reasons cannot be causes. To give the reasons-explanation of action is to show the action's rationale from the actor's point of view, from the beliefs and objectives with which the actor started. But the N-D model aims to show how a statement reporting the occurrence of action being explained may be deduced from a statement describing the cause of the action together with a generalization backed by causal laws. The N-D model statistically establishes causation by subsuming the explanandum under a covering-law or lawlike generalization. Reasons can be treated neither deductively nor nomologically in the N-D model. This is because preferences are not given prior to practical reasoning. Searle 2001, 247–257 gives two features in the fact that there is in the philosophical literature no plausible account of a deductive logical structure of practical reason. He says (2001, 255):

> The first feature we might label "the necessity of inconsistency." Any rational being in real life is bound to have inconsistent desires and other sorts of motivators. The second we might label "the nondetachability of desire." Sets of beliefs and desires as "premises" do not necessarily commit the agent to having a corresponding desire as "conclusion" even in cases where the prepositional contents of the premises entail the prepositional content of the conclusion.

Similarly, see Alker 1996, 399–414 for the relationship between practical reason and scientific explanation.

49. Hacking's notion of "looping effect" (1999) is useful here.

50. Fay 1975, 85. See also Blumer 1969, 2.

51. Adler and Haas 1992, 367.

52. Wendt 1992, 396–403. As will be discussed in detail, this way of linking identity to a choice of action (an *interpretivist* notion of identity) is *one* of the three ways in which identity can affect behavior. According to a comprehensive literature review on the relationship between identity and action by Abdelal, Herrera, Johnston, and Martin 2006, there are two other ways an identity affects the choice of an action. They are SIT-based in-group and out-group identity action theory and role-identity theory. Each theory offers its own causal processes to choices of action. The SIT-based identity theory derives the central causal process in action from in-group and out-group dif-

ferentiation; the role-identity theory works on "role enactments" usually associated with "the logics of appropriateness." The interpretivist notion of identity advanced in this book employs identity as a cognitive heuristic for interpreting situations in which an actor finds himself or herself that determine the material or social incentives for a particular choice of action.

53. Operario and Fiske 1999, 41.

54. Similarly, Bloom (1990, 23) claims that people seek identity in order to achieve psychological security. See also Mead 1934, Berger and Luckmann 1966, and Stryker and Stratham 1985.

55. Simon 1982. See also March and Olsen 1989, 39–52 for a theoretical discussion of sense making in organizational studies.

56. Monroe et al. 2000, 423. This understanding of identity is in the vein of schema theory. As Mercer 2005 rightly points out, however, a major caveat found in schema theory in relation to its behavioral implication is the mistaken emphasis that the selective-perception element of schema theory explains only *mistakes* or *deviations* from rationality.

57. Stets and Burke 2000, 231. According to them, "accessibility" is "the readiness of a given (identity) category to become activated in the person. It is a function of the person's current tasks and goals, and of the likelihood that certain objects or events will occur in the situation" (230). "Fit" is "the congruence between stored (identity) category specifications and perceptions of the situation."

58. Markus, Smith, and Moreland (1985, 1494–1512) in Hopf (2002, 5).

59. Moscovici 1984, 7–8, in Hopf 2002, 6. See also Huddy 2001, 131–134 for a compact review for this categorization aspect of identity.

60. Foreign policy decision-making studies of cognitive biases in information processing that emphasize an inherent tendency toward consistency striving in human behavior are relevant here. See, for example, Finlay, Holsti, and Fagen 1967; George 1980; Larson 1997; and Herrmann 2003.

61. A pioneering work in this regard is Allport 1954.

62. Wendt 1999, 327.

63. Locke and Walker 1999, 178.

64. Abrams 1999, 221. See also Tajfel's original discussion of social identity (1981). Tajfel argues that the self-concept derives meaning from categorization of self and other within larger social units or groups, and social comparisons within and between groups motivate people's attitudes, appraisals, and judgment.

65. Adler and Haas 1992, 367.

66. Hopf 1998, 193. See also Frederick Frey 1985, 130–136 for the impact of the imputation of identity and interests on issue perception.

67. Weldes 1996, 282.

68. Ibid., 283.

69. Reicher and Hopkins 2001, 399.

70. See, for example, Walton 1990 and Audi 1993.

71. Elster 1983, 79.

72. In addition to this, critics of rational choice point out that human actors do not always reason according to the rules of probability and decision theory posited by the rationalist account. See, for example, Tversky and Kahneman 1982. Solomon 1992 demonstrates, through the example of the plate tectonics revolution in geology, that people make use of cognitive heuristics even in scientific decision making. See also Bloor's interest theory (1991) relying on a notion of personal motivation. Bloor basically argues that an appeal to personal motivation to explain behavior invokes intentions and a more elaborate psychological characterization of agency than rational choice suggests. In short, both schemes endorse Mercer's claim (2005, 89) that "in the absence of unique solutions, both rationalist and political psychologists must first establish an actor's desires and beliefs before judging behavior as rational."

73. Empirically, the issue is to make a genuine distinction between an actor's "real" reasons and merely justificatory ones. Reason is a cause only if it is in fact the real one that causes the action being explained. This is in line with scientific realists' notion of causal claim. According to scientific realist explanations in the social sciences, causal claims are made by way of explicating the causal powers of social agents that are conferred onto those agents by the social structures and relations that constitute them. See Weldes and Saco 1996, 373, footnote 47 for the notion of causation in scientific realism.

74. Donagan 1966, 155.

75. Elster 1986, 20–33.

76. Giddens 1984, 345.

77. Donagan 1966, 155. As discussed earlier, by assuming that an actor is rational in the sense of utility optimization this scheme is susceptible to the fallacy of imputed preference. In a similar vein, there are at least two strong objections to this scheme. First, there is no ultimate criterion of rationality that uniquely singles out one course of action as the thing to do. Second, there is no reason to believe that all historical actors are rational, in any of the several senses of rational that its proponents have explored. Human actors do not always reason according to the rules of probability and decision theory posited by the rationalist account. See, for example, Goldgeier and Tetlock 2001 for a recent explication of the relationship between rationality and psychology.

78. Of course, the framework potentially may address this caveat when the issue points to the question of whose rule or whose norm to follow or reject.

79. See, for example, Davidson 1993 and Dennett 1987, 1991 for the notion of "interpretivism," by which is meant that if an actor is interpretable then he or she is an intentional actor.

80. See Ringer 1997 and Hollis and Smith 1990, 71–82 for Max Weber's notion of

singular causal analysis on the basis of explanatory understanding. See also Davis 1979, 83–105; Giddens 1984, 345; Wendt 1992, 396–397; and Adler 1997, 329.

81. John Hall 1999, 99.

82. Cruz 2000, 282–284.

83. Rodney Hall 2003.

84. I make only preliminary claims or suggestions on this issue. A full discussion is beyond the scope of this part of the book, requiring another full article.

85. Jackson 2003, 13. Parentheses added.

86. Checkel 1998, 332.

87. Jackson 2003, 227–228.

88. Finnemore 1996; Keck and Sikkink 1998. Similarly, see also Finnemore and Sikkink 1998.

89. Sending 2002, 460.

90. In this regard, Rumelili 2004, 34–36, for example, calls for separation of the ontology of othering and its behavioral implication.

91. See Hollis and Smith's dramatic disagreement in their conclusion regarding the primacy of agent and structure in shaping human choice of action (Hollis and Smith 1990, 196–216).

92. See, for example, Ruggie 1983; Rodney Hall 1999; Reus-Smit 1999.

93. Max Weber 1949, 81, in Ruggie et al. 2005, 275.

94. Greenwood 1988, 97 in Vollmer 1999, 31.

95. Vollmer 1999, 30.

96. See Wallace 2004, 206–216 for an excellent discussion on this point.

97. Hollis 1987, 166. Italics added.

98. I rely on Schwartz's explication (2002) of Erikson's works (1958 and 1969). Although the two typologies refer to individual identity development, they are conceptually a useful baseline for collectivities.

99. See, for example, Hopf 2002 for a detailed exploration of this possibility.

Notes to Chapter 4

1. Polanyi 1944, 139–140.

2. Johnson 1993a, 63.

3. See footnote 9 in Chapter 1.

4. Searle 1995, 27.

5. Murakami 1996 (1992), 145–146 (trans. Yamamura). Murakami added the qualification of "intervention from a long-term perspective" in order to make it clear that the use of short-term policy to counter the business cycle—which is at the heart of Keynesian policy—does not alone qualify as developmentalism.

6. As discussed later, this does not mean that all Japanese developmentalists since the late nineteenth century shared the *same* intellectual and political interests

in contextualizing Japan's pattern of economic development in normal-abnormal meanings. Nonetheless, they have interpreted Japan's status by relating it to their understanding of the historicity of state-led economic development (the normal path of successful economic development). Additionally, the character of Japan's development experience (whether it would be regarded as normal in the history of the world economy) was particularly important to the early developmentalists in their struggle against economic liberals for the question of what Japan should do to survive Western imperialism. See, for example, Morris-Suzuki 1989a, 59–62.

7. How the Japanese developmentalists construct an alternative universalism (the normalcy claim) around the role of the state in economic development needs some qualification. They do not claim that there is only one method for state-led economic development. What they claim is the proven validity of the role of the state in developing and implementing appropriate development strategies for economic development. Theoretically, therefore, each country can have its own method of economic development. However, without developing and applying appropriate industrial policy (or completely relying on the function of the market), a given state cannot be hopeful for successful economic development, which is observed in the history of the world economy.

8. In a similar vein, Dessler 1989, 454 states that "policy not only relies upon physical capability, but it also requires a framework of meaning."

9. See, for example, Ōkita 1984; Hatch and Yamamura 1996, 130–145. Ōkita was a leading expert on Japan's economic relationship with other Asian countries; he was the first to explore in earnest the lessons of Japan's industrialization for developing countries. Ōkita can arguably be called the intellectual father of Japan's "specialist network." See Korhonen 1994, 102–104 for the emergence of the developmentalist thread.

10. See Akama 2000, 123–140 for an excellent explication of the history of Japanese Marxism.

11. Duus and Scheiner 1998, 151–159.

12. Kawakami 1965.

13. Morris-Suzuki 1989b, 15.

14. Hoston 1994, 221. See Ando 1998, 78–96 for a review of the debate on Japanese capitalism between the *Kōza-ha* and the *Rōnō-ha*.

15. Hoston 1986, 222.

16. The controversy over interpretation of Japanese economic development resulted from the Comintern's 1927 theses, claiming that Japan lagged behind Russia's own "backwardness" in February 1917. As such, the Comintern requires a two-stage (first bourgeois and then proletarian) revolution for Japan to achieve socialism. In December 1927, a group of Marxists who refuted the Comintern's theses left the Japan Communist Party (JCP), which accepted the theses. They established the Rōnō-ha (worker-farmer faction). The Rōnō-ha's efforts to refute the Comintern's theses gave rise to the

first Marxist debate on Japanese capitalism (*Nihon Shihon-Shugi Ronsō*). See Hoston 1986, 48–54. The *Rōnō-ha* later turned into the Japan Socialist Party (JSP).

17. Hoston 1994, 224. These four scholars are the editors of *Nihon Shihonshugi Hattatsushi Kōza* (Lectures on the History of the Development of Japanese Capitalism), where the name *Kōza-ha* originated.

18. Matsukata 1934, 75.

19. Noro 1983, 115–132.

20. This perspective was most clearly expressed in the "1932 Thesis" drawn up by the Kōza-ha in consultation with the Comintern. The theses stated that although the ultimate objective was establishment of a dictatorship of the proletariat, the way forward must first be cleared by a bourgeois revolution that would abolish the institution of emperor and redistribute the wealth of the land-owning class. See Morris-Suzuki 1989a, 82.

21. Moritarō Yamada 1934.

22. Ibid., 4.

23. In Moritarō Yamada's typology, the opposite ideal type of the Prussian model was the Anglo-American model, where the bourgeois-democratic revolution swept away all the feudal elements in the process of constructing a capitalist economic order.

24. Moritarō Yamada 1934, 70–71.

25. Noro 1983, 253–262.

26. Though the Kōza-ha theorists took the imperial institution as the representation of the remnants of semifeudal structure in Japan (thus bourgeois-democracy had not arrived yet), the Rōnō-ha Marxists defined the emperor as a "bourgeois monarchy" or a "mere appendage of a state apparatus based on a highly capitalistic industrial sphere." See Hoston 1994, 224–225.

27. Yasuba 1975, 62–63.

28. Sakisaka 1958, 113–114.

29. Tsuchiya 1937, 80.

30. Hattori 1955; Tsuchiya 1977, 158–160.

31. Sakisaka 1958.

32. See Hoston 1994, 402–420.

33. Barshay 1998, 250.

34. Toshio Yamada 1998, 158.

35. See Akama 2000 for development of "Marxism economics" in Japan.

36. I heavily draw on Toshio Yamada 1998, 154–155, 159–161 for the discussion on SMC.

37. Morris-Suzuki 1989b, 19.

38. Their SMC interpretation followed the Kōza-ha by taking up the definition of prewar Japanese capitalism as a "militarist and semi-feudalistic imperialism." See

Morris-Suzuki 1989a, 121–129 for an excellent summary of the emergence and development of SMC theory in Japan.

39. The SMC schema of history is as follows: general crisis → SMC → collapse of capitalism → socialism. This schema was based on two observations by the Japanese SMC theories. The first was that capitalism in the 1930s and the 1940s was in a crisis seemingly equivalent to its final crisis; the second was the growing role of the state in the advanced capitalist countries during and after the war. However, when SMC was first introduced in Japan in the late 1950s, it was criticized by more orthodox Marxists, who denied the existence of a distinct state monopoly stage of capitalism. Instead, they argued that the growth of state intervention was merely a transient reaction to the crises of war and economic recession. For this discussion, see Toshio Yamada 1998, 154.

40. Barshay 2004, 93–119 for Uno's analytical and conceptual contribution to Marxian political economy in Japan.

41. Uno's *Keizai Seisakuron* 1974 (1954). Uno, however, did not formally associate himself with the Rōnō-ha.

42. Uno 1946 in Barshay 2004, 130.

43. Toshio Yamada 1998, 159–161.

44. Ikumi 1958 in Toshio Yamada 1998, 159.

45. Ōuchi incorporated into his version of SMC Uno's analysis of capitalist developmental stages. See Barshay 2004, 126–131 for Uno's influence on Ōuchi.

46. Ōuchi 1970.

47. Ōuchi 1965, 9–10.

48. Ōuchi 1970, 150–151. See also discussion by Toshio Yamada (1998, 160–161) and Morris-Suzuki (1989a, 121–125) on Ōuchi.

49. Civil society is defined as "a society in which men free themselves of feudal or premodern communities in order to become independent individuals and enjoy liberty and equality legally and morally" (Moritarō Yamada in Hoston 1994, 443).

50. Uchida was heavily influenced by the "Ōtsuka historiography" from which he took the conceptions of the "modernized human type" and "mediocrity of fortune," which he elaborated into a concept of civil society. According to Toshio Yamada 1998, the heart of Ōtsuka historiography is its proposal of a new theory of the driving forces of capitalism. Previously, the historical school claimed development of commerce to be the driving force of capitalism. Against this historical school's claim, Ōtsuka came up with the concept of mediocrity of fortune (the intermediate producers' stratum and its later polarization) to capture the *real* driving forces of a *civilized* capitalism. To quote Toshio Yamada's interpretation (1998, 155–156):

> According to Ōtsuka, while the "path from above," or the progression from commercial (early capital) capital to industrial capital, was seen primarily in Prussia, the "path from below," or the progression from yeoman capital (intermediate producer's stratum) to industrial capital, was evident in Britain and America. The

"path from above" could not be truly revolutionary in the birth of capitalism. On the contrary, it was the "path from below" that constituted a pure and civilized capitalism that was sustained by a modernized human type and modern productive forces.

See Mitsunobu Sugiyama 1999 for Uchida's intellectual development. See also Koschmann 1999 for Ōtsuka's exploration of the notion of subjectivity (*Shuntaisei*) in relation to Japan's modern capitalist economic development. Additionally, see Kang 1999, 78–85 for the role of Ōtsuka historiography in creating Orientalism in Asia.

51. Uchida 1967, 119 citing Kawakami 1911 in Toshio Yamada 1998, 162.

52. Uchida 1970, 15–16 in Barshay 2004, 188.

53. Uchida 1981, 11 in Toshio Yamada 1998, 162.

54. Hirata 1994 in Barshay 2004, 192.

55. See Hirata 1989 in Hoston 1994, 443.

56. In this sense, civil society theorists argue that the Japanese model of economic development should not be a model to be followed by, say, other Asian countries. High economic growth may resolve unemployment and material poverty. However, precisely because high growth in Japan was achieved not really through strengthening human rights and civil society but instead by suppressing them, the Japanese way of economic development produces a new discrimination and poverty.

57. Toshio Yamada 1994 in Barshay 2004, 192.

58. Makoto Itō 1990.

59. Ibid., 45.

60. Ibid., 4–5.

61. Ikeo 1996.

62. See Ikeda (2002, 1–14) for a review of recent Marxist scholarship in Japan.

63. Chūsei Sugiyama 1994, 4. See also Mizuta 1988 for a history of Japan's reception of Western economic thought.

64. Kanda (1861) was the first to refute those in opposition to the land reform on the theoretical grounds of economic liberalism. Against those who were opposed to the idea of the free buying and selling of land, which was likely to increase inequality of property ownership, Kanda argued for the freedom of buying and selling land. He also wanted to replace tax in kind by a tax in cash by means of land bills to be issued by the proprietors according to the value of each piece of land. With both measures together, high land prices would be lowered and low ones raised so that an equilibrium was eventually reached. For this discussion, see Tsukatani 1986, 60–63.

65. Hoston 1992, 294–298.

66. Economic liberalism had some early success in influencing government policies. Two examples stand out. First, the ordinance issued by the Ministry of Agriculture and Trade in 1881 promoted freedom of economic activities for the people. Second, the government made a decision in 1880–81 to transfer government-owned industries to

private firms at very low prices, to lay the foundation for industrial growth. For the latter decision, some suggest that the government had nothing to do with the influence of economic liberalism. The decision was mainly to deal with financial problems facing the government. For example, the Meiji government had financial difficulties stemming from payment of samurai stipends in 1876, the cost of suppressing the 1877 Satsuma rebellion, and the unprofitability of many industrial projects under the government's direct operation. However, the government's recognition that long-term industrial expansion must rely on private sectors clearly reflected the idea of economic liberals at that time. See Norman 1975, 125–126.

67. Fukuzawa 1867 in Chūsei Sugiyama 1994, 4. During his lifetime, Fukuzawa shifted position toward foreign trade from liberal to protectionist (or nationalist) and then returned to liberal. According to Kumagai 1998, 30–32, Fukuzawa's positional shifts tended to reflect Japan's changing industrial and trade position in the world economy.

68. Mizuta 1988, 14.

69. Fukuzawa 1878 in Chūsei Sugiyama 1994, 60.

70. Fukuzawa (1881) in Chūsei Sugiyama 1994, 61.

71. Nishi in Chūsei Sugiyama 1994, 23–24. Nishi also enumerated five more restrictive elements: monopoly, guild, restrictive and prohibiting systems, usury law, and repression of luxury. See also Havens 1970, 172–177.

72. Katō (1869) in Chūsei Sugiyama 1994, 5.

73. This claim reflected on growing protectionist sentiment in Japan, whose origin was traced back to the unequal treaties negotiated with the Western powers in the 1850s. Even economic liberals detested the treaties, many of them agreeing with their archrivals (nationalist developmentalists) that the imposition unfairly and unduly deprived Japan of the opportunity to protect its own nascent industries from the onslaught of foreign manufactured imports.

74. Tsuda 1874 in *Meiroku Zasshi*, issue 5 (Braisted 1976, 58–59). See also Tsuda in issue 26 (Braisted 1976, 324–327) for not linking free trade to Japan's loss of specie on the logic of equilibrium. According to Morris-Suzuki 1989a, 53, apart from the belief in economic liberalism another reason for Tsuda to oppose tariff protection was that Tsuda did not have confidence in the ability of Japan to catch up to the West. As such, to Tsuda it was futile to attempt to generate the nation's economic growth through tariff protections.

75. Nakamura 1878 in Chūsei Sugiyama 1994, 7–8. Kanda 1874 also made a similar point in *Meiroku Zasshi*, issue 23 (Braisted 1976, 293–295).

76. Kanda 1875 in *Meiroku Zasshi*, issue 33 (Braisted 1976, 408).

77. Morris-Suzuki 1989a, 53–54.

78. Kanda 1875 in *Meiroku Zasshi*, issue 33 (Braisted 1976, 408).

79. Nishi in Chūsei Sugiyama 1994, 23–24.

80. Tsuda 1874 in *Meiroku Zasshi*, issue 5 (Braisted 1976, 58).

81. Tsuda 1874 in *Meiroku Zasshi*, issue 9 (Braisted 1976, 115–116).

82. Morris-Suzuki 1989a, 49–51.

83. This kind of debate among liberals, Marxists, and developmentalists on the direction postwar Japan should take (or on defining Japan's national interest) was redeployed during the early postwar era. See Gao 1998.

84. Sugihara 1980, 59–64.

85. See Komiya 1986, 22–24 for the alteration of generations among policy-oriented economists in Japan. According to Komiya, the older (or first) generation played a leading role in policy making during postwar economic rehabilitation, while the new (or second) generation was brought up with neoclassical economics, which was systematized and institutionalized in postwar America. See also Asahi Noguchi 2000, 255–280 for the debate between the two generations on Japan's external liberalization and industrial structure policy.

86. During the interwar period, Nakayama and Tanaka were two famous scholars in the tradition of economic liberalism. Their focuses were on theoretically improving on the existing neoclassical (Nakayama) and Keynesian (Tanaka) theories more than on engaging the debate on the nature of Japanese capitalism and industrialization. See Morris-Suzuki 1989a, 91–94.

87. Along with Shinohara, Shimomura was not strictly bound to neoclassical economic theories. He was not hesitant to point out the positive role of the state in economic development. He also emphasized the importance of production vis-à-vis consumption expansion as a leading factor for sustainable economic growth. On the continuum, however, Shimomura was closer to economic liberalism in the sense that he limited the appropriate role of the government to fostering economic conditions for efficient function of the market. In the final analysis, it is the dynamics of the market (not direct intervention of the state in the market) that enables sustainable economic growth.

88. Shimomura 1958, 1962.

89. According to Shimomura himself, he derived his approach to modern economics less from neoclassical economics than from Keynesianism.

90. Shimomura 1962, 294–295.

91. Shimomura 1967. This is the beginning of a virtual cycle for economic development: increase in productivity by increase in private fixed investment leads to economic growth and welfare.

92. Shimomura 1959, 189.

93. Shinohara studied under Kuznets in 1955 while he was visiting Johns Hopkins University. See David 1997, 119–124 for an excellent compact review of Kuznets's contribution to development economics. The two common denominators underlying the successes of all developed countries in the Kuznets schema were that the growth

of total product tended to accelerate as countries entered the epoch of modern economic growth (Kuznets's cycles) and that all successfully developed countries had "a system of industrial production based on the application of science and technology" (Kuznets's inverted curve). As will be discussed later, Shinohara heavily applied Kuznets's finding to explaining Japan's success.

94. See Morris-Suzuki 1989a, 141–143 for a theoretical review of Shinohara's critique of Shimomura.

95. Shinohara 1962. Shinohara is hard to classify. He comes closer to Japanese developmentalists in his emphasis on the role of the state in bringing about "dynamic comparative advantage" (as opposed to static comparative advantage) for economic development. As early as 1957, he suggested two industry selection criteria ("selective and target" industry promotion, such as "income elasticity" and "relative productivity growth"). He also appreciates for Japan's economic success the role of Japanese culture in work discipline, labor-management relationships, and industrial organization. However, his interpretation of the causes (or variables) of Japan's high economic growth still prioritizes in degree the role of private sectors over the direct role of the state in intervening in the market. As he put it, "In Japan's case, too, the success of guidance (industrial policies) from above was only made possible by dynamism in industrial circles." See Shinohara 1982, 23.

96. Shimomura 1982, 23.

97. See Hein 1994, 767–771 for the historical and theoretical basis for the concept of dual structure.

98. In traditional Western economic thought, this dualism stands for the relationship between the modern-industrial (or urban) and traditional agricultural (or rural) sectors. This difference was also pointed out by Minami 1973, 8. Since this subject of dualism was first made by Lewis 1954, however, the modern dualism debate has been replete with definitions and interpretations. See David 1997, 102–106 for a compact review of the dualism literatures.

99. Shinohara 1962, 17–21. Shinohara, like some of the Marxist theorists already noted, also put forward the theme of postwar recovery as an initial engine ushering in the era of high economic growth in Japan.

100. Some might argue that Shinohara's treatment of industrial dualism is in line with Hirschman's notion of "unbalanced growth." But there is no evidence at this point as to how much Shinohara was influenced by Hirschman. In his 1962 book, he does not make any reference to Hirschman's 1958 work.

101. Shinohara 1982, 50–52. Italics and parentheses added.

102. Komiya 1966a. See also Komiya 1980 (1975), chapters 1 and 2 in particular. Komiya did not completely reject some positive role played by the Japanese government supporting the growth. Nonetheless, he remained skeptical of claims attributing Japan's success to the policies of the state. He even treated such a claim as a sort of

"propagandizing." Komiya has also been famous in Japan as a vigorous critic of the government's cautious attitude toward opening the economy to foreign investment.

103. Komiya empirically traced the origins of Japanese frugality to a variety of peculiarities inherent in Japanese social structures, among them the age-related pay system, widespread payment of biennial bonuses to employees, and the underdeveloped state of consumer credit.

104. Solow 1956 is regarded as a pioneer who developed a "saving-investment" neoclassical growth theory. Neoclassical (even classical) economy postulates an automatic link between savings and investment. In contrast, Keynesian economy postulates that capital accumulation is determined by decisions to invest and not by decisions to save, thus negating the automatic link between saving and investment. Keynesians negate it on the grounds that households save and business firms invest for entirely different reasons.

105. Komiya defined industrial policy as "government policies taken in order to change the allocation of resources among industries or the level of some economic activity of the constituent firms of an industry." See Komiya 1990, 289.

106. Komiya 1980 (1975), 221.

107. Komiya 1988, 7–8.

108. Komiya 1980 (1975), 218–226. See also Friedman 1988 for a similar interpretation on the making of the Japanese miracle. He studied the development of the machine tool industry in Japan (taking up that industry as a representative case because it has been a part of almost every major regulatory effort in Japan since the 1930s) and attributes Japan's success to private initiatives resulting from dramatic expansion of smaller producers throughout Japan's economy.

109. Komiya 1990.

110. Ibid., 267–316.

111. Komiya 1988, 9.

112. Komiya 1990, 286.

113. Komiya 1980 (1975), chapter 10.

114. Komiya 1975, 5–6. See Calder 1993 for a similar observation, as opposed to that of Johnson 1982.

115. Komiya 1966b, 158–159, 169.

116. Ohkawa and Rosovksy 1973 depict Japan's high economic growth as "a trend acceleration." Ohkawa, who was known as the godfather of the Hitotsubashi School, also used Kuznets's cycle to describe the patterns of Japanese economic growth. For a summary of their findings, see Ohkawa and Rosovksy 1997, 203–238. See also Ohkawa and Shinohara 1979.

117. Fei, Ohkawa, and Ranis 1985, 35–64.

118. Ohkawa and Kohama 1989, xiv.

119. Ohkawa and Kohama 1989, 3–47.

120. Minami 1973, 89–223.

121. Minami 1994b, 47–56, 321–324. The first edition of the book came out in 1986. See also Minami 1994a.

122. Minami 1994b, 27.

123. Kosai and Ogino 1984, 120.

124. Nakamura 1981, 80. See also Nakamura 1985, 5–6, 74–75.

125. Shimada 1991, 5–8.

126. For excellent reviews of the genealogy of Japanese developmentalism, see Tsukatani 1986, 155–214; and Gao 1997, 18–66.

127. The idea of the state-controlled economy, however, had already emerged in Japan during the eighteenth century. Sato Nobuhiro and Honda Toshiaki were the prominent advocates of the view that political authorities should be directly involved in a nation's wealth-creating activity. I thank Berger for bringing this point to my attention. For the early Japanese vision of the state-controlled economy in the eighteenth century and a compact summary of the emergence of protectionism in Japan in the nineteenth century, see Morris-Suzuki 1989a, 34–40, 59–70; and Komuro 1998.

128. Biersteker 1993, 7–33. Economic liberalism came into being in reaction to mercantilism.

129. According to Braisted 1976, Kanda's translation of William Ellis's *Outlines of Social Economy*, which was published in Japan in 1867 under the title *Keizai Shōgaku*, was the first book that introduced protectionist ideas to the Japanese. Braisted 1976, 307, footnote 4.

130. Under the influence of the German historical school, the Japanese counterpart established the "Society for Social Policy" (*Shakai Seisaku Gakakai*)" in 1896, modeled after the German *Verein für Sozialpolitik*. The society consisted of the leading economists of late Meiji and early Taisho Japan and placed it between economic liberalism and socialism. The members of the society continued to increase their influence by reaching out toward the general audience through publications and by interacting with the government until 1927. Regarding the impact of the German historical school on Japan, see Pyle 1974; Cumings 1999; and Lehmbruch 2001. Regarding the rise and fall of the Society for Social Policy, see Fujii 1998.

131. Wakayama 1871 in Wakayama 1940. Interestingly, Wakayama was at that time an official of the MOF. As will be discussed later, the MOF has, since the 1980s, been an intellectual power house of exporting the Japanese model of economic development.

132. Ibid., 734–735.

133. Wakayama 1877 in Wakayama 1940, 769–771. This work was written immediately after Wakayama returned to Japan from Europe as a member of the Iwakura mission. See also Halliday 1975, 3–61 for the impact of the mission on the development of Japanese capitalism.

134. Sugi 1874 in *Meiroku Zasshi,* issue 24 (Braisted 1976, 304). Similarly, see in the same volume Sugi 1875 for a historical view of protectionism manifested in the title of the essay, "Conjectures on an Imaginary Closed Country." In issue 34 (Braisted 1976, 413–417).

135. Ushiba 1875 in Chūsei Sugiyama 1994, 9. Italics added.

136. Nishimura 1875 in *Meiroku Zasshi,* issue 29 (Braisted 1976, 356–358). Italics added.

137. Tsukatani 1986, 170–173.

138. Ōshima 1899, 101–102, in Tsukatani 1986, 171–172; italics added. Similarly, in his *Jōseiron* (On Present Situation, 1891), Ōshima also argues that engaging in free trade when a country is in an underdeveloped state is a practice that "liberates other nations at the expense of one's nation." See Chūsei Sugiyama 1994, 11–12, 102–104. Similarly, see also Sugihara 1988b, 241–246.

139. Okubo, for example, met with Bismarck and von Moltke in Berlin and heard directly from them about their experiences in founding the German Empire. See Sugihara 1988a, 219.

140. Okubo 1874 in Greenfeld 2001, 329. Italics added.

141. Okubo in Sugihara 1988a, 220.

142. Ibid., 221. For a lengthy partial quote of the memorial, see also Greenfeld 2001, 329–330.

143. See Dore 1999 and Derek Hall 2005 for the embeddednesss of economic nationalism in Japan's economic policy making.

144. Fukuda, under the guidance of Brentano, a leading member of the German social policy school, published his work in 1900 under the title *Gesellschaftliche und Wirtschaftliche Entwicklung in Japan* (Social and Economic Development in Japan). For the discussion of the normalcy claim that follows, I rely on Kang's interpretation (1999, trans. Lee and Lim) of Fukuda. Fukuda was also a leading figure of the Society of Social Policy mentioned in note 130.

145. Kang 1999, 94.

146. Ibid., 84.

147. Later in his life, however, Fukuda became a critic of the prolonged state-led economic development that suppressed the idea of full-blown individual rights. See Inoue and Yagi 1998, 64–65.

148. Kang 1999, 95.

149. Akamatsu's flying geese theory, a result of his synthetic approach to economics combining Hegelian dialectics and American empirical studies, was already famous in Japan during the 1930s, but Akamatsu continued to refine it until the 1960s. See Akamatsu 1962, 12, footnote 1 for his evolutionary refinements of his theory (Akamatsu 1935, 1937, 1945, 1956, 1961, 1962). I focus on his three works of 1945, 1961, and 1962 because they are most relevant for historicizing the development trajectories of late

industrializers, including Japan. For an empirical critique of the flying geese model in industrialization processes in East Asia, see Bernard and Ravenhill 1995.

150. The flying geese theory particularly refers to a situation where less advanced countries adopt the industries of more advanced countries, pursuing them on the road of economic development. At the heart of this theory lie levels of technological sophistication, on the basis of which countries are divided into two subgroups, leading (*Senshinkoku*) and follower countries (*Kōshinkoku*). There is also a middle category, newly rising countries (*Shinkōkoku*); these are countries that are developing more rapidly than others, and whose relative position is moving upward. The category of leading countries referred to the advanced Euro-American countries, and that of follower countries to the Asian countries. Japan moved as the first of the Asian countries to the position of newly rising country around the turn of the twentieth century. Yamazawa 1990, 69 rephrased it in a modern economic term called "the catching-up product cycle theory of development."

151. Akamatsu applied the flying geese theory to the growth of Asia's clothing industry and Japan's transistor radio industry after 1945 and confirmed that "the wild-geese-flying development completed its course from import to domestic production, and, further, to export in the short period of several years." See Akamatsu 1962, 23.

152. Akamatsu 1945, 305. He uses the United States as an example that exercised such a practice after its independence.

153. This optimistic view from Akamatsu reflects his embracing of Hegelian teleological philosophy. See Korhonen 1994, 98–99.

154. See, for example, Ōkita 1975a, 145–146 in Korhonen 1994, 101, 104–107; Hatch and Yamamura 1996.

155. See Ikeo 2000, 154–158. See also Okazaki 2005 (1996) for a detailed account of the government-industry relationship in postwar Japan.

156. See, for example, Ōkita 1975b, 33–58 for his enumeration of the elements that led to high economic growth: (1) technological catch-up, (2) high productivity and low consumption, (3) abundant supply of labor, (4) dual structure of the economy, and (5) high savings. Nonetheless, he emphasized the important role of the government. On the policy and planning side, the elements are (1) the "economy first" principle of government, (2) production-oriented policies, (3) expansion of heavy industries, (4) export promotion, (5) use of the price mechanism and planning, and (6) the financial system.

157. One major difference is that compared to their predecessors in the nineteenth century, who emphasized the role of the state (industrial policy) for the survival of Japan in the vein of economic nationalism, postwar Japan's developmentalists (particularly "government economists") have had an additional concern with legitimizing their role in Japan's economic success. This observation, however, does not deny their objective or sincere attempts to identify the real causes of Japan's economic success. See, for example, Komiya 1980 (1975), especially chapters 1 and 2.

158. Kojima 1958.

159. Ōkita started his career by joining the prewar Ministry of Communications and later, during World War I, became a research and planning officer in the Greater East Asia Ministry, where he learned the possibilities and the limitations of economic planning. In 1955, Ōkita became the director of the Research Division in the newly formed Economic Planning Agency (EPA). His main responsibility was to plan for ways of expanding Japanese exports. He was one of the chief architects of the 1960 National Income Doubling Plan. Embracing Akamatsu's flying geese theory of economic development, he became famous for his missionary role during his travels to East and Southeast Asian countries (in the 1960s and 1970s) in promoting the theory. See Ōkita 1961, 1975b.

160. He did not forget to include a favorable international environment led by the United States. See Ōkita 1975b, 58–63.

161. Ōkita 1980, 93–147.

162. Ibid., 246. Ōkita 1961, 98–128 criticized the logic of the Keynesian government intervention for allowing government intervention *only* in case of the immediate problems of deficient or excessive demand. According to Ōkita, governments (particularly those of developing countries) should be allowed to design longer-term planning for economic development.

163. Ōkita 1980, 105–148. See also Ōkita 1984, "Editor's Introduction" in *The Transferability of Development Experience*. The entire volume of the latter was about whether or not Japan's path to modernity and industrialization was unique.

164. Ōkita 1980, 246–247.

165. Ōkita 1992.

166. Ōkita 1994 in Woo-Cumings 1995, 241.

167. Murakami 1987, 33–90; 1998 (1992), 181–200. Murakami's posthumous book (1996, trans. Yamamura) is originally from his 1992 910-page book (in two volumes) titled *Han-koten no Seiji Keizai Gaku* (Anticlassical Political Economics, Tokyo: Chūō Kōronsha, 1992). For a short biography of Murakami, see Yamamura, "Translator's Preface" in *An Anticlassical Political Economic Analysis*, i-xxiv. Apart from his academic publications, Murakami was much involved in public service as well. For example, he was a senior research officer at the Economic Research Institute, Economic Planning Agency of Japan (1967–1970); expert member, Provisional Commission for Economic Reform (1973–1987); director, Japan Association of Economics and Econometrics (1975–1977); and chairman, Forum for Policy Innovation (1976–1989).

168. Murakami 1986. Murakami is also famous for his analysis of social values and their role in promoting or retarding industrial growth. In the case of Japan, he argued that successful industrialization was considerably indebted to its collectivism-based traditional family value, the famous "*ie*" thesis. On this basis, some scholars tend to categorize Murakami's explanation of Japan's high economic growth within

the unique thesis along with Morishima 1982, who stressed the collectivist ethos in Japan for its economic success. However, for Murakami such cultural variables as values are more or less "intervening" (but he did not depict the causal relation in this way). In the final analysis, it was the state that was able to "direct society as a whole toward industrialization" and foster and use the sense of group solidarity originally centered around the family (ie). The state was able to harness such a value to the common cause of competing with the West. See Murakami 1975; 1984, 281–363; 1986, 211–241. See Morishima 1982.

169. Murakami 1996, 144–182. Murakami acknowledges Marshall's contribution to originating the discussions of the increasing return. However, Murakami finds "Marshall's problem" (the inability to answer the question, "When costs are decreasing, why are markets not dominated by monopolists or collusive oligopolists?") resulting from the homeostatic character of neoclassical economic theory. Thus Murakami's "decreasing costs" argument, which is inexorably tied to technological progress (thus endogenizing such a traditionally exogenous variable as technology), was his theoretical attempt to remedy Marshall's problem.

170. Murakami's emphasis on technological progress as a leading factor for industrialization shows his intellectual debt to Akamatsu. For example, Murakami 1996 heavily bases his proposal for a new international world order on the flying geese pattern of economic development theory. Murakami 1996, 122–124, 302–309.

171. Ibid., 147.

172. Murakami 1998 (1992), 181; italics added. This decreasing-costs argument led Murakami to argue that two economic systems would be needed: developmentalism and economic liberalism. The former is suitable for late industrializers while the latter is appropriate for mature, advanced economies.

173. Ibid., 188.

174. This is a more specified form of the infant industry argument. See Murakami 1996, 151–154. See also the earlier discussion of sunset and sunrise industries.

175. Murakami 1987, 189–190.

176. Murakami 1996, 189–204. A similar argument is found in Kanamori (1970, 225–258 in Morris-Suzuki 1989a, 150). Modifying Shinohara's low-wage thesis for Japan's high growth, Kanamori argues that during the years of high growth Japanese wages had in fact been rising more rapidly than wages in most other industrialized countries. However, productivity in Japan was rising still faster, thus resulting in declining wage costs (wages divided by productivity). For a critique of Murakami's thesis, see Hamada 1997, 114–131.

177. Murakami 1996, 133.

178. Murakami 1992 in Yamamura 1997, 260–261, 268–269.

179. Ibid., 217.

180. Ibid., 233.

181. Takatoshi Itō, a Harvard-trained economics professor at the University of Tokyo, also served the government until recently (1998–2000) as director-general of the International Financial Bureau at the MOF. He is often regarded as a liberal thanks to his advocacy of "more" liberalization of Japan's economy. His liberalization advocacy, however, is premised on his conception of Japan as a developed country (not a developing country). As shown later, he advances the developmentalist idea of the role of the state in economic development when a country begins to industrialize.

182. Takatoshi Itō 1993.

183. Takatoshi Itō 1998, 27.

184. Ibid., 29–34. Reminiscent of Murakami, Takatoshi Itō maintains that government intervention is needed when it is difficult for the market to achieve an optimal allocation of resources *if technology has increasing returns to scale.*

185. Ibid., 31.

186. Ibid., 33.

187. Ibid., 18.

188. In particular, see the two chapters from Watanabe 1998, 201–219 and Maekawa 1998, 166–177 in the volume on comparative historical analysis.

189. Watanabe 1998, 201–202.

190. Kenichi Ohno 1998, 7.

191. There have recently emerged comparative institutionalist approaches as an explanation for the successes of Japan and East Asia. Taking up the "coordination problem," this literature tends to find the primary role of government not so much in directly intervening in resource allocation as in fostering development and interacting with private sectors. See, for example, Aoki, Kim, and Okuno-Fujiwara 2005 (1996); and Okazaki and Okuno-Fujiwara 1999.

192. The influence of Marxism in Japan, which once dominated economic discourse there, has declined since the 1960s, mainly because it was unable to account for Japan's continued high economic growth.

193. Yasutomo 1995, 27.

194. Ibid., 30.

195. See, for example, Kenichi Ohno 1998, Overview.

196. Regarding detailed analyses of the influence of the Japanese developmentalists in challenging neoliberalism in the ADB and the World Bank, see Chapter 5. Additionally, see Stein 1998, Amyx, 2004, and Katada 2004.

197. For careful analysis of the differences and similarities, see Kenichi Ohno and Kōjirō Sakurai 1997, 205–285. See also Pempel 1999.

198. *Interim Report of Asia-Pacific Economic Research* (Tokyo: Foundation for Advanced Information and Research, 1990, 64), in Bernard and Ravenhill 1995, 184.

199. Yasutomo 1995, 70–80.

200. See, for example, Morishima 1982.

201. See Ōkita 1975b, 119–159; Johnson 1992, 21–26. Similarly, see also Hatch 2002.

202. Since the 1960s, the MITI and the MOF have been inviting and training young bureaucrats across Asia on issues regarding economic development.

203. Fearon and Wendt 2002, 63; Cederman and Daase 2003, 7–9.

204. Doty 1993, 298.

205. Similarly, see Cruz 2000 for the concept of the "collective field of imaginable possibilities" that shapes the future actions of national collectivities.

206. Peter Hall 1989, 358.

207. Derek Hall 2005. Similarly, see also Leheny 2003 for the role of collectively held social meanings in institutionalizing modern tourism in Japan by the Japanese government.

208. Gilpin 1987, 48–49.

209. Ruggie 1998b, 871–874; Wendt 1999, 171–178.

210. See, for example, David Campbell 1992, 223–262 and Uriu 2000 for detailed documentation of the U.S.-Japan economic conflict.

211. Stein 1998.

212. As for exemplars in the field of International Relations, see, for example, Wendt 1987; Alker 1996, especially chapter 3; Weldes and Saco 1996; Weldes 1999; Milliken 2001; Hopf 2002; and Rodney Hall 2003. See also Milliken 1999 for a critical analysis of discourse-oriented empirical works in International Relations.

213. This reformulation is based on Kenichi Ohno's introductory chapter (1998) titled "Overview."

Notes to Chapter 5

1. Sakakibara 1993, v-vi, Preface to the English Edition.

2. See, for example, Somers 1994, and Neumann 1999. See also Chapter 3.

3. To capture this identity-based reasoning process, I discuss three specific analytical steps in Chapter 6 when I focus entirely on Japan's AMF decision.

4. On induction into the MOF, recruits are told that its earliest known incarnation dates from A.D. 678, when the ancient imperial court comprised three main components: an inner shrine for the gods, an outer shrine for the man-god (the emperor), and the treasure-store, or *Okura*. It is from this term that the MOF takes its Japanese name, the *Okurasho*—literally, great storehouse ministry. So it is that in Japan, after the deities of heaven and earth comes that of the MOF. As such, MOF officials claim to work under the assumption that politicians represent special interests; other ministries, which preside over particular sectors of society, are tainted by their interest in the health of their constituent industries. Only the MOF can claim to be a servant to none but the nation. See Hartcher 1998, 3.

5. The MOF enjoys a unique position as a generator of ideas about economic development in Japan. Its influence rests on (1) a jurisdictional hold over Japan's external fi-

nancial and economic development affairs, including Japan's policies for international financial institutions (IFIs), where international financial and development issues are debated; (2) the ability to influence the terms on which Japan's ODA policies, which are inseparable from development ideas, are implemented; and (3) a research and policy-design budget far greater than that of any development organization in Japan. As for the second, ODA loans are under the MOF's jurisdiction, while ODA grants are under that of the MOFA. See Koppel and Orr 1993 for the evolution of Japan's ODA policies. See also Katada 2002 for a recent update.

6. Yasutomo 1995, 231.

7. Brown 1999, 38–42. The notion of "directed credit" policies is further discussed later.

8. Fingleton 1995, 84–85.

9. Interview with Yuji Tsushima, a former MOF official who became a legislator in the ruling Liberal Democratic Party; *Wall Street Journal*, March 19, 1993, in Hartcher 1998, 105; italics added.

10. Interview with Sakakibara 1993, quoted in Hartcher 1998, 106.

11. Until 1990, the MOF ran an in-house training program for its young officials. The program offered them lectures, tutorials, and other work pertaining to economics. These young officials are now sent abroad for postgraduate studies for two full years, the favored subject being economics. The favored destinations are Princeton University and Cambridge University. See Hartcher 1998, 15–16; Fingleton 1995, 70–72.

12. Komiya and Yamamoto 1979, quoted in Hartcher 1998, 9. See also Komiya and Yamamoto 1981.

13. Interview with Komiya and Yamamoto 1995, quoted in Hartcher 1998, 9. See also Brown 1999, 24–31 for entry and promotion of MOF officials.

14. Interview with Komiya 1995, quoted in Hartcher 1998, 17.

15. *Shokun*, April 1994, in Hartcher 1998, 16–17.

16. Wade 1996, 31. Bruno Frey, Pommerehne, Schneider, and Gilbert 1984 claim that a major source of disagreement on macroeconomic policy between the economists in the five countries (United States, Austria, France, Germany, and Switzerland) surveyed can be attributed to their views and historical experiences of government intervention in their national economies. In comparison to American, German, and Swiss economists, French and Austrian counterparts tend to favorably view the role of the state in macroeconomic management.

17. Yasutomo 1995, 75.

18. Ibid., 79. Italics added.

19. Interview with an MOF official October 2, 1992, quoted in Yasutomo 1995, 76.

20. MOF officials do recognize that the level and type of state intervention differs among Asian countries. By the Asian model they mean the positive role of the state in general terms in Asia, in relation to neoliberal distrust of the role of the state

in economic development. See Pempel 1999. As for the main reason for this mistrust, Chang 1999 explains that "in the neoclassical economic orthodoxy, it is fundamentally wrong to believe that the objective of the state, which is fundamentally determined by certain individuals with self-seeking motives, will be commensurate with what is good for society."

21. In development economics circles in Japan, the Anglo-Saxon approach has normally been summarized this way: "The orthodoxy, represented by the IMF, the World Bank, and USAID, espoused greater roles for market mechanisms and the private sector and prescribed elimination of subsides to inputs, liberalization of product markets, and abolition of the state-run distribution system." See Yanagihara 1993.

22. Interview with a former MOF official (April 21, 1993), quoted in Yasutomo 1995, 77.

23. Interview with an MOF official (April 21, 1993), quoted in Yasutomo 1995, 78.

24. Interview with an MOF official (August 21, 1989), quoted in Yasutomo 1995, 93.

25. Interview with an MOF official (August 11, 1989), quoted in Yasutomo 1995, 93.

26. The IFB was later promoted to International Financial Affairs. See Brown 1999, 20–21 for historical development of the IFB.

27. This trend still continues today. Personal communication with Yasutomo (February 2005).

28. Yasutomo 1995, 143.

29. Ibid., 144.

30. See Wan 1995/1996, 516–517 and 521–522 for the personnel interconnectedness between the ADB and the MOF.

31. The finance minister (*Okura Daijin*), which is at the top of the ministry's hierarchy, is normally a political appointee. The administrative vice minister (*Jimu Jikan*) occupies the highest career post in the ministry. It is responsible for the entire operation of the ministry but concentrates on domestic matters. The vice minister for international affairs (*Zaimukan*), who normally comes from the ranks of the director-generalship of the International Finance Bureau, is the principal official in charge of external policy.

32. Both Chino and Nakahira had their first contact with the ADB when they were sent by the MOF to help it draft a charter in 1964–1965. Yasutomo 1995, 83. Chino became president of the ADB in the middle of the Asian crisis, replacing another Asianist president, Michio Sato.

33. Yasutomo 1995, 85.

34. See Wade 1996, 8–9. For short bios of Shiratori and Kubota, see footnotes 7 and 10 in that article. Both Shiratori and Kubota seem to have gone through the typical career paths envisioned by the MOF's revised personnel policy program. Both graduated from the Tokyo University Law Faculty. Shiratori studied economics at Columbia University (1964–1966), Kubota at Oxford (1967–1969). Later, Kubota became senior

deputy director-general of the International Finance Bureau, the same job Shiratori had before becoming executive director of the World Bank.

35. Interviews with MOF officials, Tokyo, July 15 and July 21, 2002. This was also confirmed in my other interviews with Japanese scholars and researchers who have been working closely with the MOF for a long time. As will be discussed later, these two factions had an initial disagreement on how to manage the Thai crisis and on the idea of the AMF. The rivalry seems to be a typical example of the long tradition of Japanese diplomatic polarity between *Ajia-ha* (Asian faction) and *Eibei-ha* (Western faction). See Berger 1996; Takahiko 1998; Kline 2002, 115–158. For the historical evolution of Asianism in Japan, see Koschmann 1997.

36. Hashimoto has been a long-time member of the Asia-Pacific club. The MOF organizes and runs the club to help Japan's political and policy-making elite build relationships with finance ministers from Asia-Pacific countries. See Hartcher 1998, 230.

37. Some analysts interpret the outspokenly antiorthodox Sakakibara's promotion to the powerful position of vice finance minister for international affairs in July 1997 as a reflection of Hashimoto's desire to craft a series of more ambitious foreign economic policy initiatives. In fact, prior to the birth of the AMF proposal, Hashimoto spoke of the need for a more vigorous Japanese foreign policy toward Asia during his visits to a number of Southeast Asian countries. See Altbach 1997, 8. Hashimoto's support was instrumental for Sakakibara to smooth over domestic disagreements on the issue of launching the AMF proposal.

38. Sakakibara sarcastically called the neoliberal approach "market fundamentalism" and criticized IMF and the World Bank style structural reform conditionality attached to their loans as "unrealistic." Given his emphasis on the role of the state in nourishing the undisciplined market, it is no coincidence that his favorite Western economist is Polanyi. See his presentation (the title is "The End of Market Fundamentalism") at the Foreign Correspondent's Club, January 22, 1999, which is downloadable from http://cei.haag.umkc.edu/institutional/Readings/Eisuke/fundamentalism.html.

39. Yukio Noguchi 1995, in Hartcher 1998, 185–188.

40. *Shukan Toyo Keizai*, July 8, 1995, in Hartcher 1998, 190–191.

41. Interview with Sakakibara (May 15, 2001), PBS, downloadable from http://www.pbs.org/wgbh/commandingheghts/shared/minitextlo/int_eisukesakakibara.html. The contents of this seventeen-page interview article are as follows: "A Portrait of Japan's Current Dual System Economy"; "Japan, Inc.: 1970–1990"; "Japan in Recession: 1990–2002"; "The Clinton Administration's Economic Policy Towards Japan"; "The Asian Boom of the 1990s" (where the quotation comes from); "The Asian Economic Crisis Unfolds"; "Global Consequences of the Asian Economic Crisis"; "Circumventing the 'Iron Triangle': The Need for Structural Reform"; "The Prospects for Recovery: Act One Begins"; "Re-enter China and India: How Japan and the U.S.

Will Approach Changes in Asia"; "Is There a Financial Panic Ahead for Japan?"; and "The Globalization of Japan, Again."

42. Funabashi 1992, 29.

43. Sakakibara 1993, Preface to the English Edition. The Japanese version of the book was published in 1990. The main argument of the book is that Japan is a market economy but not a capitalist one; he refers to the Japanese model as a "non-capitalist market economy." Although Japan's economy is based on market principles, it does not put the interests of the cigar-chewing capitalist at the center of the system. He claims that Japan's basic doctrine amounts to "anthropocentrism," by which he means that the Japanese people are at the center of the system. Following from this is the implication that the Japanese system is indeed superior to that of the neoliberal or Anglo-Saxon system.

44. *Shukan Toyo Keizai*, July 8, 1995, in Hartcher 1998, 191.

45. The MOF created the Institute of Fiscal and Monetary Policy (IFMP) in 1985 to serve as both a research institute and the MOF's window to the outside world. Originally set up to conduct research and policy studies and train MOF officials, by the 1990s IFMP had expanded its activities. It has hosted visiting scholars from abroad and increased the number of foreign trainees, especially government officials from the finance ministries of developing countries. Training sessions involve briefings by MOF officials and outside experts on Japan's economy and financial systems, and lectures and discussions by visitors on their financial systems. As such, the institute serves a dual role in internationalization of the MOF: it gathers information on the outside world that can be of use to ministry officials, and through its briefings to foreign officials it educates an international audience about Japan's own development experience and political economy. See Yasutomo 1995, 145.

46. *Shukan Toyo Keizai*, July 8, 1995, in Hartcher 1998, 191–192.

47. *Chūō Kōron*, August 1995, in Hartcher 1998, 192. See also Sakakibara 1993, 143–162, a chapter titled "Genealogy of Debates on the Japanese Economy" where Sakakibara traces Japanese intellectuals' representation of the Japanese economic system from "backwardness" and "specificity" to "universality."

48. Sakakibara, "Globalization and Diversity Inaugural Address," Development Thinking and Practice Conference, Washington, D.C., September 3–5, 1996, quoted in Altbach 1997, 6.

49. *Business Times* (Singapore), January 2, 1998. Italics added.

50. Sakakibara was also instrumental in inaugurating the ADBI, a think-tank for designing alternative models of economic development, and headquartering it in Tokyo after his AMF proposal eventually failed in the face of U.S. and European oppositions. Interview with an ADB institute official, August 3, 2002, Tokyo, Japan.

51. I do not deal with here the politics of economic development between the United States and Japan on their strictly bilateral disputes, where the U.S. Treasury and

MOF officials fought each other in the yen-dollar, structural, and framework talks from the mid-1980s to the early 1990s. In these debates, the United States demanded that Japan abide by supposedly universal rules—on transparency, market, and the limited role of government. Japan counterattacked by questioning the claimed universal validity of these rules. Surely Japan's later challenge to neoliberalism can be related to its riposte to U.S. pressure on these bilateral disputes. However, Japan's challenges at various international stages have their own substance and logic, which cannot be conceptually captured as just a mirror or extension of bilateral disputes with the United States in that MOF officials take pride in Japan's economic development model and wish to promote it for *developing countries*, with the conception of Japan as the leader of an antiparadigmatic development model.

52. Reagan, Address before the Annual Meeting of the IMF and World Bank, September 29, 1981, U.S. Department of State, Current Policy No. 322. See also Biersteker 1995, 118–121 for a review of the rise of neoliberal economic discourse.

53. Reagan, Address before the Board of Governors of the IMF and World Bank, September 27, 1983, Department of State Bulletin, *83* (2080; November 1983), 6, quoted in Tickner 1990, 59.

54. Reagan, September 29, 1981, quoted in Tickner 1990, 59. Compare it to that of the Japanese developmentalist interpretation (normalcy debate, Chapter 4). Interestingly enough, Asian NIEs countries such as Taiwan, Korea, Hong Kong, and Singapore were also classified as examples of economies that owed their success to free and open markets and minimal government regulation, which is in diametrical opposition to Japan.

55. Tickner 1990, 54.

56. Livingston argues that apart from the Reagan administration's ideological conviction of the magic of the market, the U.S. drive for the centrality of the market in international development was one of those efforts the United States made for "restructuring" the international agenda away from North-South relations. See Livingston 1992, 317–319.

57. Sprinkel (Cartagena, Colombia, March 30, 1982, Treasury News R703), quoted in Tickner 1990, 58.

58. See Gwin 1997 for the World Bank. With respect to the IMF, see Thacker 1999.

59. The United States and Britain also started to make substantial use of conditionality in their bilateral aid programs.

60. Included in regional MDBs are the Asian Development Bank, the African Development Bank, and the Inter-American Development Bank. The European Bank for Reconstruction and Development came into existence only in 1990.

61. See Killick 1998, 12–17 for how policy-based conditionality has been justified and legitimized. He points out three strands of justification: conditionality as a substitute for the collateral asset, which a private sector would require as a safeguard against

default by the borrower; conditionality as a safeguard against moral hazard; and aid effectiveness. See also Biersteker 1990, 484–486.

62. Killick 1995, 22–27.

63. Polak 1991, 40.

64. The IMF's changing tack into the area of economic development created tension with the World Bank; it played out in various instances since the 1980s. The tussle was observed, for example, in management of the Asian financial crisis. See McFarlane 2001, 220–221.

65. Danaher 1994, 3.

66. This convergence is evident in that the sectoral distribution of the lending portfolios of all MDBs then in existence was considerably identical. After all, up to the mid-1970s all MDBs gave primacy to resource input—particularly capital for investment—allowing recipient governments to take control of allocation of capital because it was relatively scarce in developing countries. It was assumed that more investment would lead to high economic growth. See Culpeper 1997, 37–44. See also Krasner 1981 for comparative aspects of the three regional MDBs.

67. See Scheman 1997 for the politics of development at the IDB and Strand 2001 for the AfDB. See also Culpeper 1997, 23–106.

68. Kappagoda 1995, 25–32.

69. Two-step loans refer to "funneling capital to the private sector through public agencies in recipient governments." As such, this practice does not deny a positive market-guiding role for the state by explicitly recognizing government leadership in forging a private and public sector cooperation. Debate between the United States and Japan over the legitimacy of two-step loans played out not only in the ADB but also in the World Bank.

70. Woo-Cumings 1995, 243.

71. *Treasury Report, U.S. Participation in the Multilateral Development Banks in the 1980s*, 1982. See also Dutt 1997, 2001 for the relationship between the United States and the ADB.

72. *Far Eastern Economic Review*, May 16, 1985, 63.

73. *Far Eastern Economic Review*, May 7, 1992, 49.

74. Woo-Cumings 1995, 245.

75. Traditionally, the ADB's strength lies in its diversity of well-designed and well-executed projects, particularly projects in the infrastructure and power utilities sectors, to which the ADB has historically allocated a significantly greater proportion of its lending resources (54 percent) than has, for example, the World Bank (28 percent). The World Bank, in contrast, has allocated considerably more to program and adjustment lending (24 percent) than has the ADB (3 percent). As such, the ADB's annual evaluation reports proudly suggest the ADB has a comparative advantage over the World Bank in project-based lending. See Culpeper 1997, 110–113. Similarly, see Kappagoda 1995, 157–158.

76. *Asian Finance*, April 15, 1988.

77. Yasutomo 1995, 91.

78. Interview with a former ADB staff member (June 14, 1990), quoted in Yasutomo 1995, 92.

79. Interview with an MOF official (former ADB staffperson, August 1, 1989), quoted in Yasutomo 1995, 93.

80. Yasutomo 1995, 88, 93.

81. During this crucial time, Japan's share of cumulative contributions increased from 41.9 percent in 1986 to 50 percent in 1993. In addition, Japan has been a crucial lender to the ADB, with 30.4 percent of the total in 1987–1993 compared to 11.7 percent from the United States. See Wan 1995/1996, 513, Table 1, Voting Powers vs. Contributions in the ADB of Key Members.

82. The portion of project loans at the ADB for 1986–1992 was above 50 percent annually. It even rose to 62.5 percent in 1992. See ADB annual reports 1988 through 1992.

83. Yasutomo 1995, 94.

84. See Stallings and Streeck 1995, 85–87 for a compact review of this conflict.

85. The World Bank's accommodation of Japan's push for publication of *The East Asian Miracle*, of course, reflected Japan's financial power. It became the second biggest shareholder in the World Bank in 1984. By 1989 it was the country with the biggest bilateral aid program in the world. In 1992, Japan equaled Germany as the second biggest shareholder in the IMF.

86. One of the first publications Japan made for promoting its development agenda was the MITI's *The New Asian Industries Development Plan* in 1987. It was written by MITI economists and Japanese academics with the purpose of setting out a regional strategy of industrialization for Southeast Asian countries. The publication illustrated the long-term nature of Japanese planning and the coordination between government and firms, stressing the potential benefits of the role of the state in directing sectoral industrial policies through financial policy (assisting some industries more than others).

87. Even though the Economic Planning Agency (EPA) has legal authority over the OECF, the MOF has a much stronger influence over the OECF than does the EPA. Most high-ranking OECF officials are former MOF officials who remain loyal to their home ministry. As such, the MOF is often called a parent ministry of the OECF. See Hirata 1998, 311–312.

88. Awanohara 1995, 168–169; Wade 1996, 7–8; Michael J. Green 2001, 236–239.

89. Quoted in Wade 1996, 8.

90. Woo-Cumings 1999, 10–11.

91. See Okuda 1993, 67–85 and Kubota 1993/1994 for the contrast between Japan and the United States on this issue.

92. Awanohara 1995, 168–169; Wade 1996, 9.

93. Biersteker 1990, 482–486.

94. The 1987 World Bank Report (titled *Trade and Industrialization*) set the conceptual framework for free trade policy as the engine of economic development. The 1989 report (*Financial System and Development*) emphasized financial deregulation for developing countries, urging removal of all interest rate controls and all subsidized targeted credit programs. See also *The Levy Report,* published by the World Bank in 1989, which took a strong view against government intervention in financial markets.

95. 1991 World Bank Report (*The Challenge of Development*), 3–4.

96. The paper was first published in Japanese in the *OECF Research Quarterly*, no. 73, 11–18, 1991. The English version was circulated at the annual meeting of the World Bank and the IMF in Bangkok in October 1991. The paper was initiated by Kubota, a senior MOF official then on loan to the OECF as managing director of the Coordination Department, who was also known as a hard-line Asianist, supported by the MOF; it was produced after five months of teamwork on the part of the OECF and outside academic economists. See Wade 1996, 10, footnote 14 for the detailed internal processes of producing the paper.

97. Wade 1996, 10.

98. OECF Occasional Paper No. 1, 16–17.

99. Ōshima 1891 in Morris-Suzuki 1989a, 61. See Chapter 4.

100. *Far Eastern Economic Review*, March 12, 1992.

101. World Bank, Press Release, No. 16, October 15, 1991. Mieno's statement was prepared by the International Finance Bureau of the MOF. Not surprisingly, Kubota, who directed OECF Occasional Paper No. 1 and had by now transferred back from OECF to a senior position in the IFB of the MOF, drafted Mieno's statement. See Wade 1996, 11.

102. Miller 1991, 1.

103. Awanohara 1995, 168.

104. Top management of the World Bank had already once attempted to block publication of a study report, later titled (when it was eventually published) *World Bank Support for Industrialization in Korea, India, and Indonesia*, because its conclusion gave "too strong an endorsement of government intervention." The report argued that the World Bank was unwarranted in discounting the positive role of the state's industrial strategy (especially for the Korean case) and urged the World Bank to "help governments design industrial policies" and "adopt a more differentiated, nuanced approach to recommending policy packages to individual government." Management called for the report not to be made available outside the World Bank until its conclusions were suitably revised. Masaki Shiratori, the Japanese executive director, in collaboration with several executive directors from borrowing countries pressed top management to allow publication. They prevailed, and the study was released in 1992.

See Wade 1996, footnote 17 for more detailed information on this matter. See also *Far Eastern Economic Review*, March 12, 1992, 49.

105. Once *The East Asian Miracle* study was initiated, it got much attention for political significance. On the one hand, it could invalidate neoliberalism. On the other hand, it could reject the dissenting, unorthodox Japanese development philosophy. As such, depending on the final outcome of the study it could trigger a complete change of principles of economic development, which might then influence all IFIs' lending prescriptions and policies. Japan anxiously awaited study completion; all the struggling developing countries aspiring to join the high-performing Asian economies looked forward to it as well. Japan's hope was that the World Bank would move away from the dogmatic, neoclassical position embedded in SAL policies toward one that embraced a more significant position for state-led economic development along Japanese lines. See *Far Eastern Economic Review*, February 10, 1992.

106. Mead 1934; Dittmer and Kim 1993, 13–31; Wendt 1999, 224–233.

107. Yasutomo 1995, 79; italics added. Shiratori also said that it was "Japan's duty to disseminate to developing countries the experience and development philosophy of Japan and Asian NIEs to developing countries through the World Bank." See Shiratori 1993, 243.

108. Summers, office memorandum to Kiyoshi Kodera, alternate Japanese executive director at the World Bank, regarding OECF Occasional Paper No. 1, April 3, 1992, quoted in Awanohara 1995, 174.

109. *Far Eastern Economic Review*, August 13, 1992 (titled *To Russia with Pride: Japan Offers Economic Model*).

110. *The East Asian Miracle: Economic Growth and Public Policy* (New York: Oxford University Press), 1993, vi.

111. Awanohara 1995, 177. Because the 1993 report validated (even if in a limited way) the state's interventionist role, one Japanese official said half-happily that the report would "constitute" the first step, to be followed by second and third steps.

112. Interview with former MOF officials (April 21, 1993), quoted in Yasutomo 1995, 79. See also OECF Discussion Paper No. 7, 1995 (*The World Bank's East Asian Miracle Report: Its Strength and Limitations*), prepared by the Research Institute of Development Assistance. To quote (2–3), "The report's analysis did not go beyond the framework of neoclassical economic theory. . . . There was a feeling that four broad issues remained unresolved: the role of government in economic development, the effectiveness of industrial policy, the need for greater attention to institutional dimensions of economic development, and the replicability of the East Asian experiences." See also Amsden 1994, 627–633 for a similar critique.

113. Interview with an MOF official, July 21, 2002, Tokyo, Japan. Japan's exclusion of the United States in the AMF scheme was inseparable from previous experiences with the United States in the politics of economic development so far discussed.

114. I heavily draw on Stein 1998, 42–46 for this discussion. Similarly, see also Lehman 2005, 430–435.

115. OECF Discussion Paper No. 6, 1995.

116. OECF Discussion Paper No. 7, 1995.

117. Inoue, Kohama, and Urata 1993 in Stein 1998, 43–44.

118. IDE (Institute of Developing Economies) 1995.

119. IDCJ (International Development Center of Japan), 1995.

120. IFIC (Institute for International Cooperation), 1995. See also JICA (Japan International Cooperation Agency), 1995 in Ohno and Ohno 1998, Chapter 14.

121. JIIA (Japan Institute of International Affairs), 1992 in Ohno and Ohno 1998, Chapter 12.

122. Nishimura 1994 in Ohno and Ohno 1998, Chapter 13.

123. *OECF Japan News Letter*, January 27, 1997.

124. Rapkin 2001, 386.

125. Funabashi 1995, 194–195.

126. Sakamoto, quoted in Rapkin 2001, 400.

127. Quoted in Oga 2004, 304.

Notes to Chapter 6

1. Bhagwati 1998, 12.

2. Rodney Hall 2003.

3. Katada 2001a, 173–174, footnote 5. In November 1995, Thailand, Indonesia, Malaysia, Hong Kong, and Singapore joined an agreement for mutual cooperation to cross-support their currencies. See *Nihon Keizai Shimbun*, May 15, 1997.

4. *New York Times*, October 24, 1997.

5. See MacIntyre 1999, 146–154 for the evolution of the Thai crisis from a political and institutional point of view.

6. *Economist*, July 12, 1997.

7. *Finance and Development* 1997, 8–11.

8. The Japanese bilateral aid program operates largely on the basis of developing country requests. Otherwise stated, Japanese aid personnel do not play nearly so active a role as their U.S. or European counterparts in proposing projects to recipient countries. The recipient countries are responsible for prioritizing their own needs when they request bilateral aid. See Carl J. Green 1994, 112 for the philosophical and political basis of the Japanese request-based aid program.

9. Michael J. Green 2001, 243.

10. *Asian Wall Street Journal*, July 18, 1997.

11. *Mainichi Shimbun*, July 12, 1997, quoted in Michael J. Green 2001, 244.

12. Perhaps hoping to get significant bilateral assistance from Japan, Thanong was

still explicit during his visit to Japan that "he did not intend to request financial support from the IMF." See Katada 2001a, 174, footnote 8 of Chapter 8.

13. Michael J. Green 2001, 244. See also *Daily Yomiuri*, August 5, 1997.

14. *Financial Times*, August 8, 1997.

15. Michael J. Green 2001, 244.

16. Sakakibara 2000, 167. *Nihon to Sekai ga Furueta Hi: Saiba Shihonsyugi no Seiritsu* (The Day Japan and the World Shivered: The Birth of Cyber Capitalism), Chūō Kōron Shinsha. Sakakibara wrote this book as a memoir six months after he retired from the MOF. I heavily rely on two chapters of the book, "Thai Baht Crisis" and "The AMF Proposal," for internal accounts of the MOF's decision making.

17. Sakakibara 2000, 168–169. Rerngchai Marakanond, president of the Thailand Central Bank, told MOF officials that if they could endure the next two or three months market fundamentals would take care of speculative attacks.

18. After returning to Tokyo, Watanabe secretly (without informing the Thai government) met with Stanley Fisher, deputy director of the IMF, in Tokyo on May 20, 1997. They exchanged information on the Thai economy and agreed to further cooperate in managing the Thai crisis. Sakakibara 2000, 169–170.

19. Interviews with MOF officials, Tokyo, Japan, July 19 and July 26, 2002.

20. Interview with an MOF official, Tokyo, Japan, July 26, 2002. See also Sakakibara 2000, 170.

21. Sakakibara 2000, 176.

22. Sakakibara 2000, 177. Note that even at this early stage the United States was excluded. Apart from Asian solidarity, claiming that an Asian problem must be solved by Asians, the MOF's exclusion of the United States resulted from its understanding of the Thai government's abhorrence of turning to the IMF. Going to the IMF meant inviting the United States to interfere in the bailout processes. Interview with an ADB Institute official, Tokyo, August 3, 2002.

23. The Thai government's refusal came from fear that MOF officials would renounce bilateral assistance once they realized the status of the Thai foreign exchange reserve. By this time, Thailand's foreign reserve was almost depleted in the process of defending the baht against speculative attacks. Interview with a Thai official, Washington D.C., September 11, 2003.

24. Interview with an MOF official, Tokyo, Japan, July 19, 2002.

25. I am grateful to Saori Katada for bringing this aspect of the MOF's deliberation to my attention.

26. Sakakibara 2000, 177; Michael J. Green 2001, 244. See also *Financial Times*, August 27, 1997 ("Mr. Yen's Delicate Dilemma"). In this interview, Sakakibara says, "We do not like imposing policy or interfering in each other's affairs."

27. Sakakibara 2000, 180.

28. Katada 2001a, 175.

29. Katada 2001a, 175.

30. Drifte 1996.

31. Rix 1993, 62–82.

32. Sakakibara 2000, 177.

33. *Ottawa Citizen*, August 6, 1997.

34. *New York Times*, August 12, 1997.

35. After finalizing the terms of the bailout package, Thai finance minister Thanong came up to Sakakibara to pay his gratitude for all the MOF had done for the negotiation. Thanong said that he was really disappointed when the MOF turned down his request on July 18, but that he now deeply appreciated the MOF for its efforts at facilitating the negotiation. See Sakakibara 2000, 181.

36. The IMF considered the conference one of the biggest successes in its history of formulating bailout packages. Interview with an IMF official, Tokyo, July 30, 2002.

37. *Independent*, September 23, 199. Italics added.

38. This does not suggest that there was serious policy competition between the Asian and pro-IMF factions. Throughout the entire AMF decision-making process, it was mainly the Asian faction, which constituted an unchallengeable majority (for example, almost the entire director-generalships of the IFB of the MOF were occupied by the Asian faction at the time), that decided to refuse to extend bilateral assistance to Thailand under enormous uncertainties resulting from the Thai government's refusal to disclose information on the economy; and it was the Asian faction that pushed through the AMF proposal. During this particular process, the most the pro-IMF faction could do was try to tone down the Asian faction's exclusionary version of the AMF in a way suggesting an alternative possibility.

39. Interview with an MOF official, June 1998, quoted in Katada 2001a, 196.

40. Interview with an MOF official, Tokyo, July 19, 2002. See also *Los Angeles Times*, October 2, 1997.

41. Sakakibara 2000, 182. But note that the ADB and the World Bank operate in differing modes of policy prescription and conditionality, as discussed at length in Chapter 5.

42. Interview with an MOF official, Tokyo, July 26, 2002. See also Sachs 1998.

43. The IMF report expressed some concern about the huge capital inflows; overall it gave Thailand high marks on economic management.

44. The IMF's Annual Article IV Country Analysis of Economic Policy cannot be publicized without governments' permission.

45. Winters 1999, 95; Rajan 2000, 14. After failing to anticipate the Mexican peso crisis of 1994–95, the IMF created a new "early warning system" to provide governments and capital controllers with more extensive and timely alerts on serious economic trouble on the horizon.

46. Winters 1999, 95.

47. *Ottawa Citizen*, August 6, 1997.

48. Sakakibara 2000, 179.

49. Sakakibara 2000, 179.

50. I failed to ask an MOF official whether the MOF got the information through the IMF or directly from the Thai government.

51. Interview with an MOF official, Tokyo, July 19, 2002.

52. Interview with an MOF official, Tokyo, July 26, 2002.

53. Interview with an IMF official, Tokyo, July 30, 2002.

54. Interview with a former JEXIM official, Tokyo, July 29, 2002. He said, "Almost everyone agreed that too much liberalization at least propelled the collapse of the Thai economy." Sakakibara 2000, 166–167, 170–175. See also Michael J. Green 2001, 239–242 for the U.S. and Japan's similarities and differences in interpretation of the causes of the Asian crisis. Green concludes that the differences partly derived from economic philosophies. Similarly, see also Wade and Veneroso 1998; Chang 1999.

55. Johnstone 1999, 131.

56. MOF officials euphorically call the Thai experience "Futago Kigi" (the twins crisis, by which they mean the Thai crisis resulted from the twins liberalization and deregulation).

57. Interview with Sakakibara, May 15, 2001, PBS.

58. Interview with Sakakibara, April 1999, quoted in Michael J. Green 2001, 247.

59. *Independent*, January 31, 1998. Sakakibara's argument drew a negative response from Rudi Dornbusch, professor of economics at MIT, who was at the meeting. Echoing the view of most Western governments, Dornbusch described the turmoil as "not a crisis in global capitalism, but in crony capitalism."

60. Interview with an ADB Institute official, Tokyo, August 3, 2002. See also, for example, *New York Times*, October 31, 1997, and Katada 2001a, 175, footnote 10 of chapter 8. Many IMF officials whom Katada interviewed endorsed U.S. involvement in crafting conditionality for the Thai bailout package.

61. Stuart Eizenstat, undersecretary of state, *Toronto Star*, August 11, 1997.

62. Lawrence Summers, deputy treasury secretary, *Toronto Star*, August 9, 1997.

63. See, for example, Rubin 1997; Summers 1997, 1998.

64. Johnstone 1999, 130–131.

65. Summers 1998.

66. Interview with Sakakibara, May 15, 2001, PBS.

67. Hughes 2000, 242.

68. Bello 1998, 435. See also Rapkin 2001, 394–395.

69. Bhagwati 1998.

70. Johnstone 1999, 131.

71. Hughes 2000, 243; Sakakibara 2000, 178–179, 181.

72. Interview with Sakakibara, January 13, 2000, *New Strait Times* (Malaysia).

73. Along with the United States, Germany opposed any modification. According to my interview with a former JEXIM official, Japan's number two position in the IMF is almost meaningless when it comes to the question of IMF conditionality. Japan's quota is relatively very small compared to that of the United States and Europe combined. Japan's number two position made it powerless against the coalition of the United States and Germany. Interview with a former JEXIM official, Tokyo, July 29, 2002.

74. Interview with Sakakibara, May 15, 2001, PBS. See also Rapkin 2001, 395.

75. Wendt 1999, 135.

76. See, for example, Ogata 1989 and Yasutomo 1995 on U.S.-Japan conflicts on the World Bank.

77. This point was noted by virtually every official whom I interviewed in Tokyo in July and August 2002.

78. See, for example, the IDE (Institute of Developing Economies) Spot Survey 1999, 67–70 for a detailed description of restructuring of Thai financial institutions under the IMF bailout operation.

79. Hiwatari 2002, 9. See also Katada 2001a, 175.

80. For example, Thailand, Indonesia, Malaysia, Hong Kong, and Singapore joined an agreement for mutual cooperation to cross-support their currencies from November to December, 1995. As was noted, the agreement was put into practice on May 14, 1997, when the central banks of these countries took part in defending the baht with a $10 billion contribution. In this vein, Japan convened the first central bankers' meeting of EMEAP (Executives' Meeting of East Asia-Pacific Banks) in July 1996. On this point, see Sudo 2002, 109.

81. Interviews with MOF officials, Tokyo, July 19 and July 26, 2002. One IIMA (Institute for International Monetary Affairs) official noted that the bilateral option was seriously considered. Interview with IIMA officials, Tokyo, July 23, 2002. For reason one, see also Sakakibara 2000, 182–183.

82. According to an MOF official (interviewed in Tokyo, July 19, 2002), there were three causes precipitating the AMF proposal: (1) the MOF's frustration with IMF conditionality (in his words, "There would be no uniform conditionality. Conditionality should be different, country by country."); (2) furthermore (perhaps expected), the IMF bailout operation was worsening the situation; and thus (3) the AMF was a mechanism to provide "more quick money." Compare and contrast these three reasons with the four reasons for the emergence of the AMF around the time of the Thai crisis that I discussed earlier.

83. Katada 2001b, 11, footnote 26 in particular. According to her interview with Sakakibara (Tokyo, July 19, 2001), Sakakibara noted that exclusion of the United States was intentional so that the Asian leaders could discuss regional financial problems without U.S. pressure. This point was also confirmed by my interviews with MOF

officials. Another interviewee, an IDE (Institute of Developing Economies) official (Tokyo, July 26, 2002), illustratively told me:

> I was not surprised when I first heard that the U.S. was excluded from the AMF. The U.S. did nothing on a bilateral basis. The U.S. would be an obstacle to implement quick money providing to countries in trouble. It [the exclusion] was rather natural, given the history of the MOF's confrontations with the United States in various multilateral settings. MOF officials always complained that the United States liked to use Japan's money for its own purpose.

Similarly, see Nordhaug 2000, 5; Sakakibara 2000, 184.

84. Interview with MOF officials, quoted in *Financial Times*, November 14, 1997.

85. This point was also noted by Rapkin 2001, 397.

86. Interview with Sakakibara, *South China Morning Post*, February 15, 2000.

87. Sakakibara 2000, 184–185. Perhaps before August 27, 1997, the MOF seems to have concluded substantial parts of the AMF proposal, such as the membership and the relationship of the AMF to the IMF. When Sakakibara was asked about Japan's preparation for leading to establish a new regional institution, he answered, "Japan is prepared to play a major role commensurate with its economic size. . . . I am ready for that. The Ministry of Finance is ready." See *Financial Times*, August 27, 1997.

88. Sakakibara 2000, 184.

89. Interview with an IMF official, Tokyo, July 30, 2002.

90. Fisher criticized the AMF proposal as a threat to the authority and effectiveness of the IMF itself. *Financial Times*, September 23, 1997.

91. Interview with an IMF official, Tokyo, July 30, 2002.

92. Interview with an IMF official, Tokyo, July 30, 2002.

93. Interview with Sakakibara, May 15, 2001, PBS.

94. Sakakibara 2000, 185–186. This incident gives fresh insight into the actual content of the AMF proposal, which was not clearly exposed until it was eventually aborted in November 1997. On page 185, Sakakibara wrote that "he [Summers] picked up a copy of our AMF proposal from a certain country and started to criticize the details of the proposal." One can infer from this passage the existence of a detailed AMF proposal, which was kept to only a handful of high-ranking MOF officials and circulated to Asian finance ministers in Hong Kong, September 12, 1997, as a "classified" document. In fact, one of my interviewees told me he heard a "rumor" from MOF officials that the detailed planning of the AMF was written in the MOF, which did not go public. Interview with IIMA officials, Tokyo, July 23, 2002.

95. Interview with Sakakibara, May 15, 2001, PBS. See also Sakakibara 2000, 186.

96. Interview with Sakakibara, May 15, 2001, PBS.

97. Sakakibara 2000, 186–190.

98. Another powerful ministry, the MITI, stayed neutral mainly because the issue was not in its jurisdiction. Overall the MITI was sympathetic toward the AMF

proposal. Interviews with MOF officials, Tokyo, July 19 and 26, 2002. See also Kikuchi 2001, 166 for the MOFA's opposition and Michael J. Green 2001, 247 for the pro-IMF officials' efforts to tone down the AMF proposal.

99. Interview with a former JEXIM official, Tokyo, July 29, 2002.

100. Katada 2001a, 196.

101. Ibid., 196.

102. Interview with a former president of Nissho Iwai, Japanese trading company, *Asahi Shimbun*, November 6, 1997, quoted in Katada 2001a, 196.

103. *Asahi Shimbun*, September 20, 1997, quoted in Katada 2001a, 196. For the same argument, see also *Asahi Shimbun*, November 8, 1997. Of course, there were some bankers supporting the AMF proposal on the grounds that the Japanese government would use such a fund to help them withdraw from Thailand and possibly from other financially troubled countries in Asia without accruing significant loss. According to my interviews, however, Japan's financial sector overall did not worry much about the seriousness of the Thai crisis around the time the AMF was proposed. Even though their investment was highly exposed to the Thai crisis, the total amount of the investment in Thailand was relatively small compared to their domestic nonperforming loans. As such, they were paying more attention to their domestic problems. In addition, like almost everybody they never expected the Thai crisis to become an Asian crisis at that point. Interview with an IDE official, Tokyo, July 26, 2002. Interview with a former JEXIM official, Tokyo, July 29, 2002.

104. Interview with a former JEXIM official, Tokyo, July 29, 2002. See also *Daily Yomiuri*, November 4, 1997.

105. See *Nihon Keizai Shimbun*, September 22 and September 24, 1997.

106. Hajime Shinohara, a former MOF high official and the managing director of the IIMA, argued that "throughout 1998 Japan had not disavowed the scheme [the AMF], nor had it accepted the Manila framework as the last word, considering it just a step in the direction of the AMF's establishment." *Business Times* (Malaysia), March 10, 1999.

107. Interview with Sakakibara, *Australian Financial Review*, September 5, 2000. Katada 2001a also noted that Japan's own worsened domestic and financial problems in November 1997 contributed to retraction. Interestingly, China also opposed the AMF (but now supports it). However, it was not that China reacted unfavorably to the AMF from the outset. According to my interview, the Chinese position shifted after Rubin's visit to dissuade China from supporting the AMF. Rubin's visit may have triggered the regional rivalry between China and Japan. Interview with a former JEXIM official, Tokyo, July 29, 2002.

108. The New Miyazawa Initiative was Japan's total of $30 billion in bilateral assistance to the Asian economies in crisis, half in the form of medium and long-term funding for Asia's economic recovery and half for short-term lending. Even then, the

United States initially did not react favorably to the initiative. The MOF had to insist that it was "the sovereign right of Japan to help countries in Asia and that the initiative should eventually benefit the U.S. as a whole." Interview with Sakakibara, *New Strait Times* (Malaysia), January 13, 2000.

109. See Chapter 7 for detailed discussion.

110. See, for example, Ferejohn 1991.

111. Katada 2001a, 196.

112. The MOF's interest in internationalizing the yen might be another possible factor (although it has not been suggested as such by commentators), because this could help strengthen the function of Tokyo as a financial center in the region. Two empirical problems readily arise. One is that the $100 billion in funding for the AMF was supposed to be dollar-denominated. The other is that there was no domestic consensus on increased use of the yen, at least at this point. Even the MOF was skeptical of this option that might reduce Japan's control of its own economic affairs, such as monetary supply. See, for example, Michael J. Green 2001, 260–262.

113. See, for example, Altbach 1997, Hughes 2000, and Rapkin 2001.

114. Nye 1987, Haas 1990, Levy 1994, Bennett 1999.

115. See, for example, Knopf 2003, 190–194 for this causally underspecified aspect of learning models. See also Ruggie 1998b, 16–18 for a critique of Goldstein and Keohane 1993b. Ruggie points out that rationalist treatment of causal beliefs (or ideas) tends to employ "ideas" as "intervening variables" between interests and policy behaviors in a sense that the role of ideas is reduced as a tool used for a process of elimination or selection to better execute the given interests. See Chai 2001, 43–45 for similar problems associated with the bounded rationality model (for example, the question of how "satisfying" alternatives emerge in the first place).

116. Japan's role as the lender of last resort offers empirically no clue to the exclusion of the United States, which could be an additional funding source for the AMF.

117. A conspiracy theory represented as the United States "buying off Asia" is beyond the scope of this book. However, at least around the time that Japan proposed the AMF, the United States did not anticipate the Thai crisis spreading to engulf almost the entire region of Asia (later spreading even to Russia and Brazil). As such, U.S. opposition to the AMF (from mid-September 1997 on) might not be solely designed to buy off Asia.

118. See Chapter 3.

Notes to Chapter 7

1. Alker 1991, 5–6 in Patomäki 2002, 48.

2. Bourdieu and Wacquant 1992.

3. In international political economy, one observes a recent surge of such calls ("historicized international political economy"). See, for example, Trentmann 1998;

Amoore et al. 2000; and Jacobsen 2003.

4. Wade 2003.

5. Amsden's claim (1994) resonates with this: "Why isn't the whole world experimenting with the East Asian model to develop?"

6. Hopf 2002, 16.

7. Onuf 1998, 60.

8. Elman and Elman 2001, 31. See also Walt's discussion (1999, 31–45) on the lack of empirical validity in formal rational choice works ("cult of irrelevance") in security studies. Another variant of the rationalist approaches pushes for a tighter connection between theory and observed outcomes by stipulating inquiry into whether the observed outcomes resulted from the actual decision-making process as the theory specifies. See, for example, Elster 1986.

9. Elster 1986, 1 observes that rational choice is, after all, a normative theory.

10. Ringmar 1996, 37.

11. Inoguchi 2002.

12. Terada 2003. In 2000, the MOF, through publication of *The Council on Foreign Exchange and Other Transactions*, made clear Japan's critical role in establishing a regional framework for finance and monetary cooperation.

13. Liu and Règnier 2002, xxiv.

14. Higgott 1999, Bergsten 2000, Stubbs 2002, Dieter and Higgott 2003, Terada 2003, Yu 2003.

15. For the politics of resentment, see Higgott 1998 and Hughes 2000.

16. Ravenhill 2002, 175.

17. Rodney Hall 2003, 3.

18. Supachai, quoted in Yu 2003, 284.

19. Miyazawa, quoted in Yu 2003, 284.

20. Sakakibara 2001, 7. Italics added.

21. *Asiaweek*, December 10, 1999.

22. Quoted in Soesastro ("Whither ASEAN plus Three?" *Trade Policy Forum*, June 12–13, 2001, Bangkok; http://www.pecc.org/trade/papers/bangkok-2001/soesastro.pdf).

23. Hettne and Söderbaum 2000, 3–4.

24. Interestingly, this is one reason that such renowned neo-Marxist and dependency scholars as Arrighi, Silver, and Brewer welcome the rise of East Asia (although they do not point to East Asian regionalism in particular). To quote them, "Even though at the moment little is visible of either [whether or not East Asia will attempt to influence of the rules of the global development game], the rise of East Asia seems to us the most hopeful sign that the extreme global inequalities created under European colonial imperialism and consolidated under U.S. hegemony will eventually give way to a more just and equal world." See Arrighi, Silver, and Brewer 2003, 27.

25. Amyx 2004, 211–212.

26. http://www.aseansec.org/afp/115.htm.

27. The network of bilateral swap arrangements and repurchase agreements under the CMI reached a total of $75 billion as of May 4, 2006.

28. *Asia Pacific Bulletin*, May 13, 2005.

29. *Asia Pacific Bulletin*, May 13, 2005.

30. The Joint Ministerial Statement of the 9th ASEAN Plus Three Finance Ministers' Meeting, Hyderabad, India, May 4, 2006 (http://www.aseansec.org/18390.htm).

31. Bowles 2002. Dieter and Higgott 2003, 435–444 also document Asian monetary cooperation along this line.

32. Kondo, quoted in Kunihiko Itō 2001, 139; italics added. Both Amyx 2004, 215 and Kunihiko Itō 2001, 137–138 recognize that the agreement among Asian countries over methods of surveillance of their economies stands as the largest barrier to, say, establishment of the AMF.

33. Katada 2004, 178. See Dobson 2004 for historical analysis of the change and continuity of Japan's G7/G8 diplomacy. Of particular interest is his discussion on the norm of East Asianism that has governed Japan's behavior as a spokesperson for Asia at the G7/G8 summits; Dobson 2004, 173–175.

34. Katada 2004, 191–192. Early in 1999 (before the summit meeting), Japan also promoted the idea of curtailing short-term capital outflows with two measures: countries in financial crisis should be allowed to suspend their external payment temporarily, and nonnational financial institutions have to maintain a certain level of outstanding claims to countries in crisis. Without much difficulty, one can recognize that the two measures reflect Japan's own understanding of the causes of the Asian financial crisis.

35. Katada 2001a, footnote 11, 124. In September 2002, the IMF revised its conditionality guidelines in the face of mounting criticism of its rigid, structural-reform-oriented conditionality. The most notable of the new guidelines on conditionality is inclusion of "national ownership," which emphasizes the role of a recipient country in formulating and implementing IMF programs. It is not clear whether or how much the IMF's revision is related to Japan's pressure. This is a good research topic to be pursued in the future. For the IMF's new guidelines on conditionality, see Statement of the IMF Staff on Principles Underlying the Guidelines on Conditionality (Washington, D.C., 2006).

36. Interview with an ADBI official, July 31, 2002, Tokyo, Japan.

37. For useful information on the current status of the Japanese challenge, visit the GRIPS Development Forum, operated by National Graduate Institute for Policy Studies in Japan (http://www.grips.ac.jp/forum-e/index.html).

38. Ishikawa 2005, Lehman 2005, Motoki 2005. See also Shirai 2004, 19–24 for discussion of Japan's "newly integrated" ODA policy coordinating ODA projects among

relevant ministries. Shirai also points out the Tokyo International Conference on African Development (TICAD) and the Initiative for Development in East Asia (IDEA) as the two important international forums Japan has been leading to disseminate Japanese as well as East Asian experiences and methods of economic development.

39. Kenichi Ohno 2003, Chapter 2.

40. Katzenstein 2005.

41. See, for example, Cox 1986.

42. The term *interpretivist generalization* comes from Hopf 2003.

43. Murakami 1996, 310–312. Italics and parentheses added.

SELECT BIBLIOGRAPHY

Abdelal, Rawi. 2001. *National Purpose in the World Economy: Post-Soviet States in Comparative Perspective*. Ithaca, NY: Cornell University Press.

———, Yoshiko M. Herrera, Alastair Iain Johnston, and Terry Martin. 2006. "Identity as a Variable." *Perspectives on Politics* 4. 4:679–94.

Abrams, Dominic. 1999. "Social Identity, Social Cognition, and the Self." In *Social Identity and Social Cognition*, edited by Dominic Abrams and Michael A. Hogg. Oxford, UK: Blackwell Publishers, 197–229.

Adler, Emanuel. 1987. *The Power of Ideology: The Quest for Technological Autonomy in Argentina and Brazil*. Berkeley: University of California Press.

———. 1997. "Seizing the Middle Ground: Constructivism in World Politics." *European Journal of International Relations* 3. 3:319–63.

———, and Peter M. Haas. 1992. "Conclusions: Epistemic Communities, World Order, and the Creation of a Reflective Research Program." *International Organization* 46. 1: 367–90.

Aggarwal, Vinod K. 1993. "Building International Institutions in Asia-Pacific." *Asian Survey* 32. 11:1029–46.

Akaha, Tsuneo, and Frank Langdon (eds.). 1993. *Japan in the Posthegemonic World*. Boulder, CO: Lynn Rienner.

Akama, Michio. 2000. "Marxian Economics." In *Japanese Economics and Economists Since 1945*, edited by Aiko Ikeo. London, UK: Routledge, 123–39.

Akamatsu, Kaname. 1945. Shinkōkoku Sangyū Hatten no Gankō Keitai. In *Keizai Shinchitsujo no Keisei Genri*. Tokyo: Shoko Geyosei-Sha, 299–314.

———. 1961. "A Theory of Unbalanced Growth in the World Economy." *Weltwirtschaftliches Archiv* 86, heft 2:196–217.

———. 1962. "A Historical Pattern of Economic Growth in Developing Countries." *Developing Economies* 1 (Mar.–Aug.):1–25.

Alker, Hayward R. 1996. *Rediscoveries and Reformulations: Humanistic Methodologies for International Studies*. Cambridge, UK: Cambridge University Press.

———, and Roger Hurwitz. 2001, Feb. 23. *Reasons, Causes, Games, Lessons, and Evolution in Inequitable Sequential Prisoner's Dilemmas*. Chicago (conference paper, International Studies Association).

Allport, Gordon W. 1954. *The Nature of Prejudice*. Cambridge, MA: Addison-Wesley.

Altbach, Eric. 1997. "The Asian Monetary Fund Proposal: A Case Study of Japanese Regional Leadership." *Japan Economic Institute Report* 47A:1–12.

Amoore, Louise, Richard Dodgson, Randall Germain, Barry Gills, Paul Langley, and Iain Watson. 2000. "Paths to a Historicized International Political Economy." *Review of International Political Economy* 7. 1:53–71.

Amsden, Alice. 1994. "Why Isn't the Whole World Experimenting with the East Asian Model to Develop? Review of the East Asian Miracle." *World Development* 22. 4:627–33.

———, and Kotaro Suzumura. 2001. "An Interview with Miyohei Shinohara: Nonconformism in Japanese Economic Thought." *Journal of the Japanese and International Economics*, 14:341–60.

Amyx, Jennifer. 2004. "Japan and the Evolution of Regional Financial Arrangements in East Asia." In *Beyond Bilateralism: U.S.-Japan Relations in the New Asia-Pacific*, edited by Ellis S. Krauss and T. J. Pempel. Stanford, CA: Stanford University Press, 198–218.

Ando, Takaho. 1998. "The Debate on Japanese Capitalism: the Kōza Faction and Its Perception of Society." In *Economic Thought and Modernization in Japan*, edited by Shirō Sugihara and Toshihiro Tanaka. Northampton, MA: Edward Elgar, 78–96.

Aoki, Masahiko, Hyung-Ki Kim, and Masahiro Okuno-Fujiwara (eds.). 2005 [1996]. *The Role of Government in East Asian Economic Development*. Oxford, UK: Oxford University Press.

Arrighi, Giovanni, Beverly J. Silver, and Benjamin D. Brewer. 2003. "Industrial Convergence, Globalization, and the Persistence of the North-South Divide." *Studies in Comparative International Development* 38. 1:3–31.

Audi, Robert. 1993. *Action, Intention, and Reason*. Ithaca, NY: Cornell University Press.

Awanohara, Susumu. 1995. "The U.S. and Japan at the World Bank." In *United States-Japan Relations and International Institutions After the Cold War*, edited by Peter Gourevitch, Takashi Inoguchi, and Courtney Purrington. San Diego: Graduate School of International Relations and Pacific Studies, University of California, San Diego, 155–82.

Axelrod, Robert, and Robert Keohane. 1993. "Achieving Cooperation Under Anarchy: Strategies and Institutions." In *Neorealism and Neoliberalism: The Contemporary Debate*, edited by David Baldwin. New York: Columbia University Press, 85–115.

Baldwin, David. 1985. *Economic Statecraft*. Princeton, NJ: Princeton University Press.

Barnett, Michael. 1993. "Institutions, Roles, and Disorder: The Case of the Arab States System." *International Studies Quarterly* 37. 3:271–96.

Barshay, Andrew E. 1998. "'Double Cruel': Marxism and the Presence of the Past in Japanese Capitalism." In *Mirror of Modernity: Invented Traditions of Modern Japan*, edited by Stephen Vlastos. Berkeley: University of California Press, 243–61.

———. 2004. *The Social Sciences in Modern Japan: The Marxian and Modernist Traditions*. Berkeley: University of California Press.

Bates, Robert. 1981. *States and Markets in Tropical Africa: The Political Basis of Agricultural Policy*. Berkeley: University of California Press.

———, Avner Greif, Margaret Levi, and Barry Weingast. 1998. *Analytic Narratives*. Princeton, NJ: Princeton University Press.

Bello, Walden. 1998. "East Asia: On the Eve of the Great Transformation?" *Review of International Political Economy* 5. 3:424–44.

Berger, Thomas U. 1996. *Cultures of Antimilitarism: National Security in Germany and Japan*. Baltimore, MD: Johns Hopkins University Press.

Bergsten, C. Fred. 1998. "Revising the 'Asian Monetary Fund.'" *Policy Briefs* no. 98–8. Washington DC: Institute for International Economics.

———. 2000. "Towards a Tripartite World." *Economist*, July 15.

Bernard, Mitchell, and John Ravenhill. 1995. "Beyond Product Cycles and Flying Geese." *World Politics* 47. 2:171–209.

Bevacqua, Ron. 1998. "Whither the Japanese Model? The Asian Economic Crisis and the Continuation of Cold War Politics in the Pacific Rim." *Review of International Political Economy* 5. 3:410–23.

Bhagwati, Jagdish. 1998. "The Capital Myth: The Difference between Trade in Widgets and Dollars." *Foreign Affairs* 77. 3:7–12.

Biersteker, Thomas. 1990. "Reducing the Role of the State in the Economy: A Conceptual Exploration of IMF and World Bank Prescriptions." *International Studies Quarterly* 34. 4:477–92.

———. 1993. "Evolving Perspectives on International Political Economy: Twentieth-Century Contexts and Discontinuities." *International Political Science Review* 14. 1:7–34.

———. 1995. "The 'Triumph' of Neoclassical Economics in the Developing World: Policy Convergence and Bases of Governance in the International Economic Order." In *Governance Without Government: Order and Change in World Politics*, edited by James N. Rosenau and Ernst-Otto Czempiel. Cambridge, UK: Cambridge University Press, 102–31.

Blake, Michael. 1993. "Evaluating Japan's Diplomatic Performance." In *Japan's Foreign Policy After the Cold War: Coping with Change*, edited by Gerald L. Curtis. Armonk, NY: Sharpe, 1–42.

Bloom, William. 1990. *Personal Identity, National Identity, and International Relations*. Cambridge, UK: Cambridge University Press.

Bloor, David. 1991. *Knowledge and Social Imagery*. Chicago: University of Chicago Press.

Bourdieu, Pierre. 1984. *Distinction*. Cambridge, MA: Harvard University Press.

———. 1998. *Practical Reason*. Stanford, CA: Stanford University Press.

Bourdieu, Pierre, and Loic, J. D. Wacquant. 1992. *An Invitation to Reflexive Sociology*. Chicago: Chicago University Press.

Bowles, Paul. 2002. "Asia's Post-Crisis Regionalism: Bringing the State Back in, Keeping the (United) States out." *Review of International Political Economy* 9. 2:244–70.

Braisted, William R. 1976. *Meiroku Zasshi: Journal of Japanese Enlightenment*. Tokyo: University of Tokyo Press.

Broad, Robin. 1988. *Unequal Alliance: The World Bank, the International Monetary Fund, and the Philippines*. Berkeley: University of California Press.

Bronstone, Adam. 1999. *The European Bank for Reconstruction and Development: The Building of a Bank for East Central Europe*. Manchester, UK: Manchester University Press.

Brown, J. Robert. 1999. *The Ministry of Finance: Bureaucratic Practices and the Transformation of the Japanese Economy*. Westport, CT: Quorum Books.

Brubaker, Rogers. 1992. *Citizenship and Nationhood in France and Germany*. Cambridge, MA: Harvard University Press.

Buckley, Roger. 1992. *US-Japan Alliance Diplomacy, 1945–1990*. Cambridge, UK: Cambridge University Press.

Bull, Hedley. 1977. *Anarchical Society*. New York: Columbia University Press.

Bullock, Robert. 2000. "Market Opening in Japan: Deregulation, Reregulation, and Cross-Sectoral Variation." In *New Perspectives on U.S.-Japan Relations*, edited by Gerald L. Curtis. Washington DC: Brookings Institution, 39–81.

Calder, Kent E. 1988. "Japanese Foreign Policy Formation: Explaining the Reactive State." *World Politics* 40. 4:517–41.

———. 1993. *Strategic Capitalism: Private Business and Public Purpose in Comparative and Historical Perspective*. Ithaca, NY: Cornell University Press.

Campbell, David. 1992. *Writing Security*. Minneapolis: University of Minnesota Press.

Campbell, John Creighton. 1993. "Japan and the United States: Games That Work." In *Japan's Foreign Policy After the Cold War: Coping with Change*, edited by Gerald L. Curtis. Armonk, NY: Sharpe, 43–61.

Carr, Edward Hallett. 1964 [1939]. *The Twenty Years' Crisis, 1919–1939*. New York: Harper Torchbooks.

Cederman, Lars-Erik, and Christopher Daase. 2003. "Endogenizing Corporate Identities: The Next Step in Constructivist IR Theory." *European Journal of International Relations* 9. 1:5–35.

Chai, Sun-Ki. 2001. *Choosing an Identity: A General Model of Preference and Belief Formation.* Ann Arbor: University of Michigan Press.

Chang, Ha-Joon. 1999. "The Economic Theory of the Developmental State." In *The Developmental State,* edited by Meredith Woo-Cumings. Ithaca, NY: Cornell University Press, 182–99.

———. 2003. *Globalisation, Economic Development and the Role of the State.* London: Zed Books.

Checkel, Jeffrey T. 1998. "The Constructivist Turn in International Relations Theory." *World Politics* 50. 2:324–48.

Choate, Pat. 1990. *Agents of Influence: How Japan's Lobbyists in the United States Manipulate America's Political and Economic System.* New York: Knopf.

Clinton, W. David. 1994. *Two Faces of National Interest.* Baton Rouge: Louisiana State University Press.

Coats, A. W. 1988. "From a Western Point of View." In *Enlightenment and Beyond: Political Economy Comes to Japan,* edited by Chūsei Sugiyama and Hiroshi Mizuta. Tokyo: University of Tokyo Press, 273–83.

Cohen, Benjamin J. 2001. *Essays in International Finance, International Finance Section.* Princeton, NJ: Princeton University Press.

Cox, Robert. 1986. "Social Forces, States, and World Orders: Beyond International Relations Theory." In *Neorealism and Its Critics,* edited by Robert Keohane. New York: Columbia University Press: 204–54.

Crowley, Brian L. 1987. *The Self, the Individual, and the Community: Liberalism in the Political Thought of F. A. Hayek and Sidney and Beatrice Webb.* Oxford, UK: Oxford University Press.

Cruz, Consuelo. 2000. "Identity and Persuasion: How Nations Remember Their Pasts and Make Their Future." *World Politics* 52. 3:275–312.

Culpeper, Roy. 1997. *The Multilateral Development Bank: Titans or Behemoths?* London: Lynne Rienner.

Cumings, Bruce. 1984. "The Origins and Development of the Northeast Asian Political Economy." *International Organization* 38. 1:1–40.

———. 1999. "Webs with No Spiders, Spiders with No Webs: The Genealogy of the Developmental State." In *The Developmental State,* edited by Meredith Woo-Cumings. Ithaca, NY: Cornell University Press, 61–92.

Curtis, Gerald L. 1999. *The Logic of Japanese Politics.* New York: Columbia University Press.

Danaher, Kevin. 1994. "Introduction." In *50 Years Is Enough: The Case Against the World Bank and International Monetary Fund,* edited by Kevin Danaher. Boston: South End Press, 1–5.

David, Wilfred L. 1997. *The Conversation of Economic Development: Historical Voices, Interpretations, and Reality.* New York: Sharpe.

Davidson, Donald. 1993. "Thinking Causes." In *Mental Causation*, edited by John Heil and Alfred Mele. Oxford, UK: Clarendon Press, 3–18.

———. 2001. *Essays on Actions and Events*. Oxford, UK: Clarendon Press.

Davis, Lawrence H. 1979. *Theory of Action*. Englewood Cliffs, NJ: Prentice-Hall.

Dennett, Daniel C. 1987. *The Intentional Stance*. Cambridge, MA: MIT Press.

———. 1991. "Real Patterns." *Journal of Philosophy* 88. 1:27–51.

Dessler, David. 1989. "What's at Stake in the Agent-Structure Debate." *International Organization* 43. 3:441–74.

Deyo, Frederic C. (ed.). 1987. *The Political Economy of the New Asian Industrialism*. Ithaca, NY: Cornell University Press.

Dieter, Heribert, and Richard Higgott. 2003. "Exploring Alternative Theories of Economic Regionalism: From Trade to Finance in Asian Co-operation?" *Review of International Political Economy* 10. 3:430–54.

Dobson, Hugo. 2004. *Japan and the G7/8: 1975–2002*. London: RoutledgeCurzon.

Donagan, Alan. 1966. "The Popper-Hempel Theory Reconsidered." In *Philosophical Analysis and History*, edited by William H. Dray. New York: Harper & Row, 127–59.

Dore, Ronald. 1999. "Japan's Reform Debate: Patriotic Concern or Class Interest? Or Both?" *Journal of Japanese Studies* 25. 1:65–89.

Doty, Roxanne L. 1993. "Foreign Policy as Social Construction: A Post-Positivist Analysis of U.S. Counterinsurgency Policy in the Philippines." *International Studies Quarterly* 37. 3:297–320.

———. 1997. "A Critical Exploration of the Agent-Structure Problematique in International Relations Theory." *European Journal of International Relations* 3. 3:365–92.

Douglas, Mary. 1986. *How Institutions Think*. Syracuse, NY: Syracuse University Press.

Downes, Stephen M. 2001. "Agents and Norms in the New Economic Science." *Philosophy of Social Sciences* 31. 2:224–38.

Drifte, Reinhard. 1996. *Japan's Foreign Policy in the 1990s: From Economic Superpower to What Power?* New York: St. Martin's Press.

Dutt, Nitish K. 1997. "The United States and the Asian Development Bank." *Journal of Contemporary Asia* 27. 1:71–84.

———. 2001. "The U.S. and the Asian Development Bank: Origins, Structure and Lending Operations." *Journal of Contemporary Asia* 31. 2:214–61.

Duus, Peter, and Irwin Scheiner. 1998. "Socialism, Liberalism, and Marxism, 1901–1931." In *Modern Japanese Thought*, edited by Bob T. Wakabayashi. Cambridge, UK: Cambridge University Press, 147–206.

Elster, Jon. 1983. *Explaining Technical Change*. Cambridge, UK: Cambridge University Press.

———. 1986. "Introduction." In *Rational Choice*, edited by Jon Elster. New York: New York University Press, 1–33.

Evangelista, Matthew. 1997. "Domestic Structure and International Change." In *New*

Thinking in International Relations Theory, edited by Michael W. Doyle and G. John Ikenberry. Boulder, CO: Westview Press, 202–28.

Evans, Peter. 1992. "The State as Problem and Solution: Predation, Embedded Autonomy, and Structural Change." In *The Politics of Economic Adjustment*, edited by Stephan Haggard and Robert R. Kaufman. Princeton, NJ: Princeton University Press, 139–81.

———, Dietrich Rueschemeyer, and Theda Skocpol (eds.). 1985. *Bringing the State Back in*. Cambridge, UK: Cambridge University Press.

Fallows, James. 1994. *Looking at the Sun: The Rise of the New East Asian Economic and Political System*. New York: Pantheon Books.

Fay, Brian. 1975. *Social Theory and Political Practice*. London: Allen and Unwin.

Fearon, James, and Alexander Wendt. 2002. "Rationalism v. Constructivism: A Skeptical View." In *Handbook of International Relations*, edited by Walter Carlsnaes, Thomas Risse, and Beth A. Simmon. London: Sage, 52–72.

Fei, John, Kazushi Ohkawa, and Gustav Ranis. 1985. "Economic Development in Historical Perspective: Japan, Korea, and Taiwan." In *Japan and the Developing Countries*, edited by Kazushi Ohkawa and Gustav Ranis. Oxford, UK: Basil Blackwell, 35–64.

Fingleton, Eamonn. 1995. "Japan's Invisible Leviathan." *Foreign Affairs* 74. 2:69–85.

Finlay, David, Ole Holsti, and Richard R. Fagen. 1967. *Enemies in Politics*. Chicago: Rand McNally.

Finnemore, Martha. 1996. *National Interests in International Society*. Ithaca, NY: Cornell University Press.

———, and Kathryn Sikkink. 1998. "International Norm Dynamics and Political Change." *International Organization* 52. 4:887–918.

Florini, Ann. 1996. "The Evolution of International Norms." *International Security* 40. 3:363–89.

Frey, Bruno, Werner Pommerehne, Fredrich Schneider, and Guy Gilbert. 1984. "Consensus and Dissension Among Economists: An Empirical Inquiry." *American Economic Review* 74. 5:986–94.

Frey, Frederick. 1985. "The Problem of Actor Designation in Political Analysis." *Comparative Politics* 17. 2:127–52.

Frieden, Jeffrey A. 1999. "Actors and Preferences in International Relations." In *Strategic Choice and International Relations*, edited by David A. Lake and Robert Powell. Princeton, NJ: Princeton University Press, 39–76.

Friedman, David. 1988. *The Misunderstood Miracle: Industrial Development and Political Change in Japan*. Ithaca, NY: Cornell University Press.

Fujii, Takashi. 1998. "The Japanese Social Policy School: Its Formation and Breakup." In *Economic Thought and Modernization in Japan*, edited by Shirō Sugihara and Toshihiro Tanaka. Northampton, MA: Edward Elgar, 44–59.

Fukushima, Akiko. 1999. *Japanese Foreign Policy: The Emerging Logic of Multilateralism.* New York: St. Martin's Press.

Funabashi, Yoichi. 1992. "Japan and America: Global Partners." *Foreign Policy* 86 (Spring): 24–39.

———. 1995. *Asian Pacific Fusion.* Washington DC: Institute for International Economics.

Gao, Bai. 1994. "Arisawa Hiromi and His Theory for a Managed Economy." *Journal of Japanese Studies* 20. 1:115–53.

———. 1997. *Economic Ideology and Japanese Industrial Policy.* Cambridge, UK: Cambridge University Press.

———. 1998. "The Search for National Identity and Japanese Industrial Policy, 1950–1969." *Nations and Nationalism* 4. 2:227–45.

George, Alexander L., and Robert Keohane. 1980. "The Concept of National Interests: Uses and Limitations." In *Presidential Decisionmaking in Foreign Policy: The Effective Use of Information and Advice* (by Alexander L. George). Boulder, CO: Westview Press, 217–38.

Gerschenkron, Alexander. 1962. *Economic Backwardness in Historical Perspective.* Cambridge, MA: Harvard University Press.

Giddens, Anthony. 1979. *Central Problems in Social Theory: Action, Structure and Contradiction in Social Analysis.* Berkeley: University of California Press.

———. 1984. *The Constitution of Society: Outline of the Theory of Structuration.* Berkeley: University of California Press.

Gill, Stephen. 1989. "American Hegemony: Its Limits and Prospects in the Reagan Era." *Millennium: Journal of International Studies* 15. 3:311–36.

Gilpin, Robert. 1981. *War and Change in World Politics.* Cambridge, UK: Cambridge University Press.

———. 2003. "Sources of American-Japanese Economic Conflict." In *International Relations Theory and the Asia-Pacific*, edited by G. John Ikenberry and Michael Mastanduno. New York: Columbia University Press, 299–322.

Gold, Joseph. 1996. *Interpretation: The IMF and International Law.* London: Kluwer Law International.

Goldstein, Judith. 1988. "Ideas, Institutions, and American Trade Policy." *International Organization* 24. 1:179–216.

———, and Robert Keohane. 1993a. "Ideas and Foreign Policy: An Analytical Framework." In *Ideas and Foreign Policy: Beliefs, Institutions, and Political Change*, edited by Judith Goldstein and Robert Keohane. Ithaca, NY: Cornell University Press, 3–30.

———, and Robert Keohane (eds.). 1993b. *Ideas and Foreign Policy: Beliefs, Institutions, and Political Change.* Ithaca, NY: Cornell University Press.

Goldstein, Morris. 1998. *The Asian Financial Crisis: Causes, Cures, and Systemic Implications.* Washington DC: Institute for International Economics.

Gourevitch, Peter. 1986. *Politics in Hard Times: Comparative Responses to International Economic Crises*. Ithaca, NY: Cornell University Press.

Gowa, Joanne S. 1987. "Rational Hegemons, Excludable Goods, and Small Groups: An Epitaph for Hegemonic Stability Theory?" *World Politics* 41. 3:307–24.

———. 1994. *Allies, Adversaries, and International Trade*. Princeton, NJ: Princeton University Press.

Green, Carl J. 1994. "Japan's Growing Leadership in Global Development." *SAIS Review* (Winter-Spring): 101–118.

Green, Michael J. 2001. *Japan's Reluctant Realism: Foreign Policy Challenges in an Era of Uncertain Power*. New York: Palgrave.

Greenfeld, Liah. 2001. *The Spirit of Capitalism: Nationalism and Economic Growth*. Cambridge, MA: Harvard University Press.

Grieco, Joseph M. 1997a. "Realism and Regionalism: American Power and German and Japanese Institutional Strategies During and After the Cold War." In *History, Cognition and Peace in East Asia*, edited by Dalchoong Kim and Chung-in Moon. Seoul, Korea: Yonsei University Press, 105–47.

———. 1997b. "Realist International Theory and the Study of World Politics." In *New Thinking in International Relations Theory*, edited by Michael W. Doyle and G. John Ikenberry. Boulder, CO: Westview Press, 163–201.

Gwin, Catherine. 1997. "U.S. Relations with the World Bank." In *The World Bank: Its First Half Century, Vol. 2*. Washington DC: Brookings Institution.

Haas, Ernst B. 1990. *When Knowledge Is Power*. Berkeley: University of California Press.

Haas, Peter M. 1992. "Introduction: Epistemic Community and International Policy Coordination." *International Organization* 46. 1:1–35.

Hacking, Ian. 1999. *The Social Construction of What?* Cambridge, MA: Harvard University Press.

Haggard, Stephan. 1988. "The Institutional Foundations of Hegemony: Explaining the Reciprocal Trade Agreements Act of 1934." *International Organization* 42. 1:91–119.

Hall, Derek. 2005. "Japanese Spirit, Western Economics: The Continuing Salience of Economic Nationalism in Japan." In *Economic Nationalism in a Globalizing World*, edited by Eric Helleiner and Andreas Pickel. Ithaca, NY: Cornell University Press, 118–38.

Hall, John R. 1999. *Cultures of Inquiry: From Epistemology to Discourse in Sociohistorical Research*. Cambridge, UK: Cambridge University Press.

Hall, Peter A. 1989. "Conclusion: The Politics of Keynesian Ideas." In *The Political Power of Economic Ideas: Keynesianism Across Nations*, edited by Peter A. Hall. Princeton, NJ: Princeton University Press, 361–91.

Hall, Rodney B. 1999. *National Collective Identity: Social Constructs and International Systems*. New York: Columbia University Press.

———. 2003. "The Discursive Demolition of the Asian Development Model." *International Studies Quarterly* 47. 1:71–99.

Halliday, Jon. 1975. *A Political History of Japanese Capitalism*. New York: Pantheon Books.

Hamada, Koichi. 1997. "Developmentalism and the Economics of Decreasing Cost." In *A Vision of a New Liberalism? Critical Essays on Murakami's Anticlassical Analysis*, edited by Kozo Yamamura. Stanford, CA: Stanford University Press, 114–31.

Harré, Rom. 2001. "Active Powers and Powerful Actors." In *Philosophy at the New Millennium*, edited by Anthony O'Hear. Cambridge, UK: Cambridge University Press, 91–109.

———, and Luk van Langenhove (eds.). 2000a. Introducing Positioning Theory. In *Positioning Theory: Moral Contexts of Intentional Action*, edited by Rom Harré and Luk van Langenhove. Oxford, UK: Blackwell, 14–31.

———. 2000b. *Positioning Theory: Moral Contexts of Intentional Action*. Oxford, UK: Blackwell.

Hartcher, Peter. 1998. *The Ministry: How Japan's Most Powerful Institution Endangers World Markets*. Boston: Harvard Business School Press.

Hatch, Walter. 2002. "Regionalizing the State: Japanese Administrative and Financial Guidance for Asia." *Social Science Japan Journal* 5. 2:179–97.

———, and Kozo Yamamura. 1996. *Asia in Japan's Embrace: Building a Regional Production Alliance*. Cambridge, UK: Cambridge University Press.

Hattori, Shisō. 1955. *Ishinshi no Hōhō*. Tokyo: Riron Sha.

Havens, Thomas. 1970. *Nishi Amane and Modern Japanese Thought*. Princeton, NJ: Princeton University Press.

Heginbotham, Eric, and Richard J. Samuels. 1998. "Mercantile Realism and Japanese Foreign Policy." *International Security* 22. 4:171–203.

Hein, Laura E. 1994. "In Search of Peace and Democracy: Japanese Economic Debate in Political Context." *Journal of Asian Studies* 53. 3:752–78.

Helleiner, Eric, and Andreas Pickel (eds.). 2005. *Economic Nationalism in a Globalizing World*. Ithaca, NY: Cornell University Press.

Hellmann, Donald C. 1969. *Japanese Foreign Policy and Domestic Politics: The Peace Agreement with the Soviet Union*. Berkeley: University of California Press.

Hempel, Carl G. 1966. "Explanation in Science and in History." In *Philosophical Analysis and History*, edited by William H. Dray. New York: Harper & Row, 95–126.

Herman, Robert G. 1996. "Identity, Norms, and National Security: The Soviet Foreign Policy." In *The Culture of National Security: Norms and Identity in World Politics*, edited by Peter J. Katzenstein. New York: Columbia University Press, 271–316.

Herrmann, Richard K., and Michael P. Fischerkeller. 1995. "Beyond the Enemy Image and Spiral Model: Cognitive-Strategic Research After the Cold War." *International Organization* 49. 3:415–50.

Higgott, Richard. 1998. "The Asian Economic Crisis: A Study in the Politics of Resentment." *New Political Economy* 3. 3:333–56.

———, and Richard Stubbs. 1995. "Competing Conceptions of Economic Regionalism." *Review of International Political Economy* 2. 3:549–68.

Hirata, Keiko. 1998. "New Challenges to Japan's Aid: An Analysis of Aid Policy Making." *Pacific Affairs* 71. 3:311–34.

Hirschman, Albert. 1958. *A Strategy of Economic Development.* New Haven, CT: Yale University Press.

———. 1969. *National Power and the Structure of Foreign Trade.* Berkeley: University of California Press.

Hiwatari, Nobuhiro. 2002. "International Arrangement After the Asian Crisis: Taking Seriously the Sources of Policy Preferences." (Unpublished manuscript.) Tokyo: Institute of Social Sciences, University of Tokyo.

Hobson, John M. 2000. *The State and International Relations.* Cambridge, UK: Cambridge University Press.

Hollis, Martin. 1987. *The Cunning of Reason.* Cambridge, UK: Cambridge University Press.

———, and Steve Smith. 1990. *Explaining and Understanding International Relations.* Oxford, UK: Clarendon Press.

Hong, Wontack. 1998. "The Catching-up: Lessons of East Asian Development." In *Contemporary Economic Issues: Regional Experience and System Reform*, edited by Justin Yifu Lin. New York: St. Martin's Press, 3–17.

Honjō, Eijirō. 1966. *Nihon Keizai Shisoshi Kenkyū, Vols. 1–2.* Tokyo: Nihon Hyōronsha.

Hopf, Ted. 1998. "The Promise of Constructivism in International Relations Theory." *International Security* 23. 3:171–200.

———. 2002. *Social Construction of International Politics: Identities & Foreign Policies, Moscow, 1995 and 1999.* Ithaca, NY: Cornell University Press.

———. 2003. "Interpretivism and Mainstream Political Science." (Unpublished mimeo.)

Hoston, Germaine A. 1986. *Marxism and the Crisis of Development in Prewar Japan.* Princeton, NJ: Princeton University Press.

———. 1992. "The State, Modernity, and the Fate of Liberalism in Prewar Japan." *Journal of Asian Studies* 51. 2:287–315.

———. 1994. *The State, Identity, and the National Question in China and Japan.* Princeton, NJ: Princeton University Press.

Huddy, Leonie. 2001. "From Social to Political Identity: A Critical Examination of Social Identity Theory." *Political Psychology* 22. 1:127–56.

Hughes, Christopher W. 2000. "Japanese Policy and the East Asian Currency Crisis: Abject Defeat or Quiet Victory?" *Review of International Political Economy* 7. 2:219–53.

Hurd, Ian. 1999. "Legitimacy and Authority in International Politics." *International Organization* 53. 2:379–408.

Ikeda, Satoshi. 2002. *The Trifurcating Miracle: Corporations, Workers, Bureaucrats, and the Erosion of Japan's National Economy.* London: Routledge.

Ikenberry, John G. 1986. "The State and Strategies of International Adjustment." *World Politics* 39. 4:53–77.

———. 1988. "Conclusion: An Institutional Approach to American Foreign Economy Policy." *International Organization* 42. 1:219–43.

———, David Lake, and Michael Mastanduno. 1988. "Introduction: Approaches to Explaining American Foreign Economic Policy." *International Organization* 42. 1:1–14.

Ikeo, Aiko. 1996. "Marxist Economics in Japan." *Kokugakuin University Economic Review* 3. 4:13–39.

———. 2000. "Economists and Economic Policies." In *Japanese Economics and Economists Since 1945*, edited by Aiko Ikeo. London: Routledge, 143–84.

———. 2001. "History of Japanese Economic Thought: The Present and the Future." *Annals of the Society for the History of Economic Thought* 39 (May):94–101.

Inada, Kenichi, Sueo Sekiguchi, and Yasutoyo Shoda. 1992. *The Mechanism of Economic Development: Growth in the Japanese and East Asian Economies.* Oxford, UK: Clarendon Press.

Inkster, Ian. 2001. *Japanese Industrialization: Historical and Cultural Perspectives.* London: Routledge.

Inoguchi, Takashi. 1986. "Japan's Image and Options: Not a Challenger, But a Supporter." *Journal of Japanese Studies* 12. 1:95–119.

———. 1990. "Japan's Politics of Interdependence." *Government and Opposition* 25. 4:419–37.

———. 2002. "Japan Goes Regional." In *Japan's Asian Policy: Revival and Response*, edited by Takashi Inoguchi. New York: Palgrave, 1–34.

Inoue, Takutoshi, and Kiichirō Yagi. 1998. "Two Inquiries on the Divide: Tokuzō Fukuda and Hajime Kawakami." In *Economic Thought and Modernization in Japan*, edited by Shirō Sugihara and Toshihiro Tanaka. Northampton, MA: Edward Elgar, 60–77.

Islam, Shafiqul. 1991. "Beyond Burden-Sharing: Economics and Politics of Japanese Foreign Aid." In *Yen for Development: Japanese Foreign Aid and Politics of Burden-Sharing*, edited by Shafiqul Islam. New York: Council of Foreign Relations, 191–230.

Itō, Kunihiko. 2001. "Japan, the Asian Economy, the International Financial System, and the G8: A Critical Perspective." In *New Directions in Global Economic Governance: Managing Globalisation in the Twenty-First Century*, edited by John J. Kirton and George Furstenberg. Aldershot, UK: Ashgate, 127–42.

Itō, Makoto. 1990. *The World Economic Crisis and Japanese Capitalism.* London: Macmillan.

Itō, Takatoshi. 1993. "U.S. Political Pressure and Economic Liberalization in East Asia." In *Regionalism and Rivalry: Japan and the United States in Pacific Asia*, edited by Jeffrey Frankel and Miles Kahler. Chicago: Chicago University Press, 391–422.

———. 1998. "Japanese Economic Development: Idiosyncratic or Universal?" In *Contemporary Economic Issues: Regional Experience and System Reform*, edited by Justin Yifu Lin. New York: St. Martin's Press, 18–37.

Jackson, Patrick T. 2003. "Defending the West: Occidentalism and the Formation of NATO." *Journal of Political Philosophy* 11. 3:223–52.

Jacobsen, John C. 2003. "Dueling Constructivisms: A Post-Mortem on the Ideas Debate in Mainstream IR/IPE." *Review of International Studies* 29. 1:39–60.

Johnson, Chalmers. 1982. *MITI and the Japanese Miracle: The Growth of Industrial Policy, 1925–1975*. Stanford, CA: Stanford University Press.

———. 1992. "Japan in Search of a 'Normal' Role." *Daedalus* 121. 4:1–34.

———. 1993a. "Comparative Capitalism: The Japanese Difference." *California Management Review* 35. 4:51–67.

———. 1993b. "The State and Japanese Grand Strategy." In *The Domestic Bases of Grand Strategy*, edited by Richard Rosecrance and Arthur A. Stein. Ithaca, NY: Cornell University Press, 201–24.

———. 1995. *Japan: Who Governs?* New York: Norton.

———. 1999. "The Developmental State: Odyssey of a Concept." In *The Developmental State*, edited by Meredith Woo-Cumings. Ithaca, NY: Cornell University Press, 32–60.

Johnstone, Christopher B. 1999. "Strained Alliance: U.S.-Japan Diplomacy in the Asian Financial Crisis." *Survival* 41. 2:121–38.

Kahneman, Daniel, Paul Slovic, and Amos Tversky (eds.). 1982. *Judgment Under Uncertainty: Heuristics and Biases*. Cambridge, UK, Cambridge University Press.

Kamarck, Andrew M. 1996. "The World Bank: Challenges and Opportunities." In *The Bretton Woods-GATT System: Retrospect and Prospect After Fifty Years*, edited by Orin Kirshner. New York: Sharpe, 106–27.

Kang, Sang-jung. 1999. *Beyond Orientalism* (translated by Kyung Duk Lee and Sung Mo Lim). Seoul, Korea: Isan.

Kappagoda, Nihal. 1995. *The Multilateral Banks. Vol. 2: The Asian Development Bank*. Boulder, CO: Lynne Rienner.

Katada, Saori N. 2001a. *Banking on Stability: Japan and the Cross-Pacific Dynamics of International Financial Crisis Management*. Ann Arbor: University of Michigan Press.

———. 2001b. "Japan's Counterweight Strategy: U.S.-Japanese Cooperation and Competition in International Finance." Paper presented at conference Beyond Bilateralism: U.S.-Japanese Cooperation and Competition in Asia, Tokyo, December 2–3, 2001.

———. 2002. "Japan's Two-Track Aid Approach: The Forces Behind Competing Triads." *Asian Survey* 42. 2:320–42.

Katzenstein, Peter J. (ed.). 1996. *The Culture of National Security: Norms and Identity in World Politics.* New York: Columbia University Press.

———. 1997. "Introduction: Asian Regionalism in Comparative Perspective." In *Network Power: Japan and Asia*, edited by Peter J. Katzenstein and Takashi Shiraishi. Ithaca, NY: Cornell University Press, 1–46.

———. 2005. *A World of Region: Asia and Europe in the American Imperium.* Ithaca, NY: Cornell University Press.

———, and Marin Rouse. 1993. "Japan as a Regional Power in Asia." In *Regionalism and Rivalry: Japan and the United States in Pacific Asia*, edited by Jeffrey Frankel and Miles Kahler. Chicago: University of Chicago Press, 217–48.

Kawakami, Hajime. 1965. *Bimbō Monogatari.* Tokyo: Iwanami Bunko.

Keely, James F. 1990. "Toward a Foucauldian Analysis of International Regimes." *International Organization* 44. 1:83–105.

Keohane, Robert. 1984. *After Hegemony.* Princeton, NJ: Princeton University Press.

———, and Joseph S. Nye. 1977. *Power and Interdependence.* Boston: Little, Brown.

Kikuchi, Tsutomu. 2001. "Japan and Multilateralism: The Regional Level." In *Japan and Multilateral Diplomacy*, edited by Philippe Regnier and Daniel Warner. Aldershot, UK: Ashgate, 153–74.

Killick, Tony. 1995. *IMF Programs in Developing Countries: Design and Impact.* New York: Routledge.

———. 1998. *Aid and the Political Economy of Policy Change.* New York: Routledge.

Kindleberger, Charles P. 1973. *The World in Depression, 1929–1939.* Berkeley: University of California Press.

Klein, Lawrence, and Kazushi Ohkawa (eds.). 1968. *Economic Growth: The Japanese Experience Since the Meiji Era.* Homewood, IL: Irwin.

Kline, Susanne. 2002. *Rethinking Japan's Identity and International Role: An Intercultural Perspective.* New York: Routledge.

Knopf, Jeffrey W. 2003. "The Importance of International Learning." *Review of International Studies* 29. 2:185–207.

Kohli, Atul. 2004. *State-Directed Development: Political Power and Industrialization in the Global Periphery.* Cambridge, UK: Cambridge University Press.

Kojima, Kiyoshi. 1958. *Nihon Bōeki to Keizai.* Tokyo: Kokugen Shobō.

Komiya, Ryūtarō. 1966a. "Editor's Preface." In *Postwar Economic Growth in Japan*, edited by Ryūtarō Komiya. Berkeley: University of California Press, vii–xi.

———. 1966b. "The Supply of Personal Savings." In *Postwar Economic Growth in Japan*, edited by Ryūtarō Komiya. Berkeley: University of California Press, 157–86.

———. 1975. "Planning in Japan." In *Economic Planning, East and West*, edited by Morris Bornstein. Cambridge, MA: Ballinger, 189–227.

———. 1980 [1975]. *Gendai Nihon Keizai Kenkyu*. Tokyo: Tokyo Daigaku Shuppankai.

———. 1986. "Industrial Policy's Generation Gap." *Economic Eye* 7. 1:22–24.

———. 1988. "Introduction." In *Industrial Policy of Japan*, edited by Ryūtarō Komiya, Masahiro Okuno, and Kotaro Suzumura. New York: Academic Press, 1–22.

———. 1990. *The Japanese Economy: Trade, Industry, and Government*. Tokyo: University of Tokyo Press.

———, Masahiro Okubo, and Kotaro Suzumura (eds.). 1988. *Industrial Policy of Japan*. New York: Academic Press.

———, and Kozo Yamamoto. "Japan: The Officer in Charge of Economic Affairs." In *Economists in Government*, edited by A. W. Coats. Durham, NC: Duke University Press, 262–90.

Komuro, Masamichi. 1998. "Trends in Economic Thought in the Tokugawa Period." In *Economic Thought and Modernization in Japan*, edited by Shirō Sugihara and Toshihiro Tanaka. Northampton, MA: Edward Elgar, 1–22.

Koppel, Bruce M., and Robert M. Orr (eds.). 1993. *Japan's Foreign Aid: Power and Policy in a New Era*. Boulder, CO: Westview Press.

Korhonen, Pekka. 1994. "The Theory of the Flying Geese Pattern of Development and Its Interpretation." *Journal of Peace Research* 31. 1:93–108.

Kosai, Yutaka, and Yoshitarō Ogino. 1984. *The Contemporary Japanese Economy*. London: Macmillan.

Koschmann, Victor J. 1997. "Asianism's Ambivalent Legacy." In *Network Power: Japan and Asia*, edited by Peter J. Katzenstein and Takashi Shiraishi. Ithaca, NY: Cornell University Press, 83–112.

———. 1999. "The Spirit of Capitalism as Disciplinary Regime: The Postwar Thought of Ōtsuka Hisao." In *Total War and Modernization*, edited by Yasushi Yamanouchi, J. Victor Koschmann, and Ryūichi Narita. Ithaca, NY: Cornell University Press, 97–115.

Kowert, Paul, and Jeffrey Legro. 1996. "Norms, Identity, and Their Limits: A Theoretical Reprise." In *The Culture of National Security: Norms and Identity in World Politics*, edited by Peter J. Katzenstein. New York: Columbia University Press, 451–87.

Krasner, Stephen D. 1981. "Power Structure and Regional Development Bank." *International Organization* 35. 2:303–28.

———. 1985. *Structural Conflict: The Third World Against Global Liberalism*. Berkeley: University of California Press.

———. 1991. "Global Communications and National Power: Life on the Pareto Frontier." *World Politics* 43. 3:336–66.

———. 1999. *Sovereignty: Organized Hypocrisy*. Princeton, NJ: Princeton University Press.

———, and Daniel Okimoto. 1989. "Japan's Evolving Trade Posture." In *United States and Japan in the Postwar World*, edited by Akira Iriye and Warren I. Cohen. Lexington: University Press of Kentucky, 115–40.

Kratochwil, Friedrich V. 1982. "On the Notion of Interest in International Relations." *International Organization* 36. 1:1–30.

———. 1989. *Rules, Norms, and Decisions: On the Conditions of Practical and Legal Reasoning in International Relations and Domestic Affairs*. New York: Cambridge University Press.

Kubota, Isao. 1993/1994. "The East Asian Miracle: Issues on Recent Economic Development Policy." *Finance* 29: 9–10.

Kumagai, Jiro. 1998. "Enlightenment and Economic Thought in Meiji Japan: Yukichi Fukuzawa and Ukichi Taguchi." In *Economic Thought and Modernization in Japan*, edited by Shirō Sugihara and Toshihiro Tanaka. Northampton, MA: Edward Elgar, 23–43.

Kunio, Yoshihara. 1979. *Japanese Economic Development: A Short Introduction*. Tokyo: Oxford University Press.

Lake, David A. 1988. "The State and American Trade Strategy in the Pre-Hegemonic Era." *International Organization* 42. 1:33–58.

Lanciaux, Bernadette. 1997. "Postimperialism and the Promotion of a Japanese Model of Economic Development." *Journal of Economic Issues* 31. 2:473–79.

Larson, Deborah W. 1997. *Anatomy of Mistrust*. Ithaca, NY: Cornell University Press.

Lee, Chung H., and Ippei Yamazawa (eds.). 1990. *The Economic Development of Japan and Korea: A Parallel with Lessons*. New York: Praeger.

Leheny, David. 2003. *The Rules of Play: National Identity and the Shaping of Japanese Leisure*. Ithaca, NY: Cornell University Press.

Lehman, Howard. 2005. "Japan's Foreign Aid Policy to Africa Since the Tokyo International Conference on African Development." *Pacific Affairs* 78. 3:424–42.

Lehmbruch, Gerhard. 2001. "The Institutional Embedding of Market Economies: The German 'Model' and Its Impact on Japan." In *The Origins of Nonliberal Capitalism: Germany and Japan in Comparison*, edited by Wolfgang Streeck and Kozo Yamamura. Ithaca, NY: Cornell University Press, 39–93.

Levy, Jack S. 1994. "Learning and Foreign Policy: Sweeping a Conceptual Minefield." *International Organization* 48. 2:279–312.

Lewis, W. Arthur. 1954. "Economic Development with Unlimited Supplies of Labour." *Manchester School* 22 (May), 139–91.

Licht, Walter. 1995. *Industrializing America: The Nineteenth Century*. Baltimore, MD: Johns Hopkins University Press.

Lilliker, Darren. 2003. "Interviewing the Political Elite: Navigating a Potential Minefield." *Politics* 23. 3:207–14.

Lincoln, Edward J. 1993. *Japan's New Global Role*. Washington DC: Brookings Institution.

Lindblom, Charles. 1977. *Politics and Markets: The World's Political-Economic System.* New York: Basic Books.

List, Friedrich. 1983 [1837]. *The National System of Political Economy* (translated and edited by W. O. Henderson). Totowa, NJ: R. Cass.

Little, Daniel. 1991. *Varieties of Social Explanations: An Introduction to the Philosophy of Social Sciences.* Boulder, CO: Westview Press.

Livingston, Steven G. 1992. "The Politics of International Agenda-Setting: Reagan and North-South Relations." *International Studies Quarterly* 36. 3:313–30.

Locke, Vance, and Ian Walker. 1999. "Stereotyping, Processing Goals, and Social Identity." In *Social Identity and Social Cognition*, edited by Dominic Abrams and Michael A. Hogg. Oxford, UK: Blackwell, 164–82.

Low, Linda. 1991. "The East Asian Economic Grouping." *Pacific Review* 4. 4:375–95.

MacIntyre, Andrew. 1999. "Political Institutions and the Economic Crisis in Thailand and Indonesia." In *The Politics of the Asian Economic Crisis*, edited by T. J. Pempel. Ithaca, NY: Cornell University Press, 143–62.

Mahoney, James. 2000. "Path Dependence in Historical Sociology." *Theory and Society* 29. 4:507–48.

Maoz, Zeev. 1990. *National Choices and International Processes.* Cambridge, UK: Cambridge University Press.

March, James G., and Johan P. Olsen. 1984. "The New Institutionalism: Organizational Factors in Political Life." *American Political Science Review* 78. 3:734–49.

———. 1989. *Rediscovering Institutions: The Organizational Basis of Politics.* New York: Free Press.

Matsukata, Saburo. 1934. "A Historical Study of Japanese Capitalism." *Pacific Affairs* 7. 1:71–76.

McClellan, Chris. 1996. "The Economic Consequences of Bruno Latour." *Social Epistemology* 10. 2:193–208.

McCloskey, Deirdre N. 1985. *The Rhetoric of Economics.* Madison: University of Wisconsin Press.

McFarlane, Bruce. 2001. "Politics of the World Bank-IMF Nexus in Asia." *Journal of Contemporary Asia* 31. 2:214–40.

McVeigh, Brian J. 2004. *Nationalism of Japan: Managing and Mystifying Identity.* New York: Rowman and Littlefield.

Mead, George Herbert. 1934. *Mind, Self, and Society.* Chicago: University of Chicago Press.

Mearsheimer, John. 1990. "Back to the Future: Instability in Europe After the Cold War." *International Security* 15. 1:5–56.

———. 1994/1995. "The False Promise of International Institutions." *International Security* 19. 3:5–49.

Mercer, Jonathan. 1995. "Anarchy and Identity." *International Organization* 49. 2:229–52.

———. 2005. "Rationality and Psychology in International Politics." *International Organization* 59. 1:77–106.

Messner, Dirt, and Franz Nuscheler. 2004. "Basic Outlines of German Development Policy." In *Global Governance: Germany and Japan in the International System*, edited by Saori Katada, Han W. Maull, and Takashi Inoguchi. Aldershot, UK: Ashgate, 161–77.

Michima, Ko. 1998. "The Changing Relationship Between Japan's LDP and the Bureaucracy: Hashimoto's Administrative Reform Effort and Its Politics." *Asian Survey* 38. 10:968–85.

Mikanagi, Yumiko. 1996. *Japan's Trade Policy: Action and Reaction*. New York: Routledge.

Miller, Rich. 1991. "Japan-U.S. Clash Looms on World Bank Strategy." *Journal of Commerce* 11 (December), 1–21.

Milliken, Jennifer. 1999. "The Study of Discourse in International Relations: A Critique of Research and Methods." *European Journal of International Relations* 5. 2:225–54.

———. 2001. *The Social Construction of the Korean War*. Manchester, UK: Manchester University Press.

Milner, Helen V. 1991. "The Assumption of Anarchy in International Politics: A Critique." *Review of International Studies* 17. 1:67–85.

———. 1997. *Interests, Institutions, and Information: Domestic Politics and International Relations*. Princeton, NJ: Princeton University Press.

Minami, Ryōshin. 1973. *The Turning Point in Economic Development: Japan's Experience*. Tokyo: Kinokuniya.

———. 1986. *The Economic Development of Japan: A Quantitative Study*. London: Macmillan.

———. 1994a. *The Economic Development of China: A Comparison with the Japanese Experience*. London: Macmillan.

———. 1994b. *The Economic Development of Japan*. New York: St. Martin's Press.

Minor, Michael. 1985. "Decision Models and Japanese Foreign Policy Decision Making." *Asian Survey* 25. 12:1229–41.

Miyashita, Akitoshi. 1999. "Gaiatsu and Japan's Foreign Aid: Rethinking the Reactive-Proactive Debate." *International Studies Quarterly* 43. 4:695–731.

Mizuta, Hiroshi. 1988. "Historical Introduction." In *Enlightenment and Beyond: Political Economy Comes to Japan*, edited by Chūsei Sugiyama and Hiroshi Mizuta. Tokyo: University of Tokyo Press, 3–33.

Moran, Theodore. 1996. "Grand Strategy: The Pursuit of Power and the Pursuit of Plenty." *International Organization* 50. 1:175–205.

Moravcsik, Andrew. 1997. "Taking Preference Seriously: A Liberal Theory of International Politics." *International Organization* 51. 4:513–53.

Morgenthau, Hans. 1958. "Dilemmas of Politics." Chicago: University of Chicago Press.

———. 1978. *Politics Among Nations: The Struggle for Power and Peace.* New York: Knopf.

Morishima, Michio. 1982. *Why Has Japan "Succeeded"? Western Technology and the Japanese Ethos.* Cambridge, UK: Cambridge University Press.

Morris-Suzuki, Tessa. 1989a. *A History of Japanese Economic Thought.* London: Routledge.

———. 1989b. "Introduction: Japanese Economic Growth, Images and Ideologies." In *Japanese Capitalism Since 1945: Critical Perspectives*, edited by Tessa Morris-Suzuki and Takurō Seiyama. Armonk, NY: Sharpe, 3–27.

Moyser, George. 1987. *Research Methods for Elite Studies.* Boston: Allen and Unwin.

Murakami, Yasusuke. 1975. *Sangyo Shakai no Byori.* Tokyo: Chūō Kōronsha.

———. 1984. "Ie Society as a Pattern of Civilization." *Journal of Japanese Studies* 10. 2:281–363.

———. 1986. "Technology in Transition: Two Perspectives on Industrial Policy." In *Japan's High Technology Industries: Lessons and Limitations of Industrial Policy*, edited by Patrick Hugh. Seattle: University of Washington Press, 211–41.

———. 1987. "The Japanese Model of Political Economy." In *The Political Economy of Japan. Vol. 1: The Domestic Transformation*, edited by Kozo Yamamura and Yasukichi Yasuba. Stanford, CA: Stanford University Press, 33–90.

———. 1992. *Han-koten no Seiji Keizai Gaku*, Vols. 1–2. Tokyo: Chūō Kōronsha.

———. 1996. *An Anticlassical Political-Economic Analysis: A Vision for the Next Century.* Stanford, CA: Stanford University Press.

———. 1998 [1992]. "Theory of Developmentalism." In *Japanese Views on Economic Development: Diverse Paths to the Market*, edited by Kenichi Ohno and Izumi Ohno. London: Routledge, 181–200.

Muramatsu, Michio, and Eric Krauss. 1984. "Bureaucrats and Politicians in Policymaking: The Case of Japan." *American Political Science Review* 78. 1:126–46.

———. 1987. "The Conservative Party Line and the Development of Patterned Pluralism." In *The Political Economy of Japan. Vol. 1: The Domestic Transformation*, edited by Kozo Yamamura and Yasukichi Yasuba. Stanford, CA: Stanford University Press, 423–68.

Nakamura, Takafusa. 1981. *The Postwar Japanese Economy: Its Development and Structure.* Tokyo: University of Tokyo Press.

———. 1985. *Economic Development of Modern Japan.* Tokyo: Ministry of Foreign Affairs.

Neumann, Iver B. 1999. *Uses of the Other: "The East" in European Identity Formation.* Minneapolis: University of Minnesota Press.

Noguchi, Asahi. 2000. "External Liberalization and 'Industrial Structure Policy.'"

In *Japanese Economics and Economists Since 1945*, edited by Aiko Ikeo. London: Routledge, 255–80.

Noguchi, Yukio. 1995. *1940 Nen Taise*. Tokyo: Tokyo Keizai Shinpōsha.

Norman, E. Herbert. 1975. *Origins of the Modern Japanese State: Selected Writings of E. H. Norman*. New York: Pantheon.

Noro, Eitarō. 1983. *Nihon Shihonshugi Hattatsu Shi, Vols. 1–2*. Tokyo: Iwanami Bunko.

Nye, Joseph S. 1987. "Nuclear Learning and U.S.-Soviet Security Regimes." *International Organization* 41. 2:371–402.

Oakley, Allen. 2000. "Popper's Ontology of Situated Human Action." *Philosophy of the Social Sciences* 32. 4:455–86.

Odell, John S. 1982. *U.S. International Monetary Policy: Markets, Power, and Ideas as Sources of Change*. Princeton, NJ: Princeton University Press.

Oga, Toru. 2004. "Rediscovering Asianness: The Role of Institutional Discourse in APEC, 1989–1997." *International Relations of the Asia-Pacific* 4. 2:287–317.

Ogata, Sadako. 1989. "Shifting Power Relations in Multilateral Development Bank." *Journal of International Studies* 22: 1–25.

Ohkawa, Kazushi, and Henry Rosovsky. 1973. *Japanese Economic Growth: Trend Acceleration in the Twentieth Century*. Stanford, CA: Stanford University Press.

———. 1997. "Capital Formation in Japan." In *The Economic Emergence of Modern Japan*, edited by Kozo Yamamura. Cambridge, UK: Cambridge University Press, 203–38.

———, and Hiroshisa Kohama. 1989. *Lectures on Developing Economies: Japan's Experiences and Its Relevance*. Tokyo: University of Tokyo Press.

———, Gustav Ranis, and Larry Meissner (eds.). 1985. *Japan and the Developing Countries: A Comparative Analysis*. Oxford, UK: Basil Blackwell.

———, and Miyohei Shinohara (eds.). 1979. *Patterns of Japanese Economic Development: A Quantitative Appraisal*. New Haven, CT: Yale University Press.

Ohno, Kenichi. 1998. "Overview: Creating the Market Economy." In *Japanese Views on Economic Development: Diverse Paths to the Market*, edited by Kenichi Ohno and Izumi Ohno. London: Routledge, 1–50.

———, and Izumi Ohno (eds.). 1998. *Japanese Views on Economic Development: Diverse Paths to the Market*. New York: Routledge.

———, and Kōjirō Sakurai. 1997. *Higashi Ajia no Hatten Keizaigaku*. Tokyo: Arma.

Okazaki, Tetsuji, and Masahiro-Fujiwara Okubo (eds.). 1999. *The Japanese Economic System and Its Historical Origin*. Tokyo: Oxford University Press.

Okimoto, Daniel. 1988. "Political Inclusivity: The Domestic Structure of Trade." In *The Political Economy of Japan. Vol. 2: The Changing International Context*, edited by Takashi Inoguchi and Daniel Okimoto. Stanford, CA: Stanford University Press, 305–44.

———. 1989. *Between MITI and the Market: Japanese Industrial Policy for High Tech-*

nology. Stanford, CA: Stanford University Press.

Ōkita, Saburo. 1959. Nihon Keizai no Seichō Ryoku to "Shin Chōki Keizai Keikaku." In *Nihon Keizai no Seichō Ryoku: Shimomura Riron to Sono Hihan*, edited by Kinyū Zaisei and Jijō Kenkyūkai. Tokyo: Kinyū Zaisei Jijō Kenkyūkai.

———. 1961. *Nihon no Keizai no Seichō to Kōzō*. Tokyo: Bungei Shunshū Sha.

———. 1975a. Akamatsu Sensei wo Tsuioku Suru. In *Gakumon Henro: Akamatsu Kaname Sensei Tsuitō Ronsū*, edited by Kiyoshi Kojima. Tokyo: Sekai Keizai Kenkyū Kyōkai, 145–6.

———. 1975b. *Japan in the World Economy*. Tokyo: Japan Foundation.

———. 1980. *The Developing Economies and Japan*. Tokyo: University of Tokyo Press.

———. (ed.) 1984. *The Transferability of Development Experience*. Nagoya, Japan: United Nations Centre for Regional Development.

———. (ed.) 1992. *Postwar Reconstruction of the Japanese Economy*. Tokyo: University of Tokyo Press.

Okuda, Hidenobu. 1993. "Japanese Two Step Loans: The Japanese Approaches to Development Finance." *Hitotsubashi Journal of Economics* 34:67–85.

Onuf, Nicholas Greenwood. 1989. *World of Our Making: Rules and Rule in Social Theory and International Relations*. Columbia: University of South Carolina Press.

———. 1998. "Constructivism: A User's Manual." In *International Relations in a Constructed World*, edited by Vendulka Kubálková, Nicholas Onuf, and Paul Kowert. New York: Sharpe, 58–78.

Operario, Don, and Susan T. Fiske. 1999. "Integrating Social Identity and Social Cognition." In *Social Identity and Social Cognition*, edited by Dominic Abrams and Michael A. Hogg. Oxford, UK: Blackwell, 26–54.

Ōtsuka, Hisao. 1951. *Kindai Shihon-shugi no Keifu* (Genealogy of Modern Capitalism), *Vol. 1*. Tokyo: Kobundo.

Ōuchi, Tsutomu. 1962. *Nihon Keizai Ron*. Tokyo: Tokyo Daigaku Shuppankai.

———. 1965. *Amerika Nōgyō Ron*. Tokyo: Tokyo Daigaku Shuppankai.

———. 1970. *Kokka Dokusen Shihonshugiron no Konponteki Hansei*. Tokyo: Tokyo Daigaku Shuppankai.

Oye, Kenneth A. 1985. "Explaining Cooperation Under Anarchy: Hypotheses and Strategies." *World Politics* 38. 1:3–24.

Patomäki, Heikki. 2002. *After International Relations: Critical Realism and the (Re)Construction of World Politics*. London: Routledge.

Patterson, Molly, and Kristen R. Monroe. 1998. "Narrative Political Science." *Annual Review of Political Science* 1: 315–31.

Pempel, T. J. 1987. "The Unbundling of 'Japan, Inc.': The Changing Dynamics of Japanese Policy Formation." *Journal of Japanese Studies* 13. 2:271–306.

———. 1998. *Regime Shift: Comparative Dynamics of the Japanese Political Economy*. Ithaca, NY: Cornell University Press.

———. 1999. "The Developmental Regime in a Changing World Economy." In *The Developmental State*, edited by Meredith Woo-Cumings. Ithaca, NY: Cornell University Press, 137–81.

Pharr, Susan J. 1993. "Japan's Defensive Foreign Policy and the Politics of Burden Sharing." In *Japan's Foreign Policy After the Cold War: Coping with Change*, edited by Gerald L. Curtis. Armonk, NY: Sharpe, 235–62.

Polak, Jacques J. 1991. "The Changing Nature of IMF Conditionality." *Princeton Studies in International Economics* 184: 1–76.

Polanyi, Karl. 1944. *The Great Transformation: The Political and Economic Origins of Our Time*. New York: Farrar and Rinehart.

Potter, David M. 1998. "Exporting a Japanese Model? Collusion in the Foreign Aid Program." *Journal of Economic Issues* 27. 2:403–9.

Prestowitz, Clyde Jr. 1988. *Trading Places: How We Allowed Japan to Take the Lead*. New York: Basic Books.

———. 1993. "Introduction." In *Beyond Capitalism: The Japanese Model of Market Economics* (by Eisuke Sakakibara). New York: Economic Strategy Institute, vii–xxi.

Price, Richard. 1995. "A Genealogy of the Chemical Weapons Taboo." *International Organization* 49. 1:73–103.

Pyle, Kenneth B. 1974. "Advantages of Followership: German Economics and Japanese Bureaucrats, 1890–1925." *Journal of Japanese Studies* 1. 1:127–64.

———. 1992. "Can Japan Lead? The New Internationalism and the Burden of History." In *Power, Economics, and Security: The United States and Japan in Focus*, edited by Henry Bienen. Boulder, CO: Westview Press, 189–225.

Rajan, Ramkishen S. 2000. "Examining the Case for an Asian Monetary Fund." *Visiting Researchers Series* 3 (Feb.): 1–29.

Ramseyer, J. Mark, and Frances M. Rosenbluth. 1993. *Japan's Political Market Place*. Cambridge, MA: Harvard University Press.

Rapkin, David P. 2001. "The United States, Japan, and the Power to Block: the APEC and AMF Cases." *Pacific Review* 14. 3:373–410.

Ravenhill, John. 2001. *APEC and the Construction of Pacific Rim Regionalism*. Cambridge, UK: Cambridge University Press.

———. 2002. "A Three Bloc World? The New Asian Regionalism." *International Relations of the Asia-Pacific* 2. 2:167–95.

Reicher, Stephen, and Nick Hopkins. 2001. "Psychology and the End of History: A Critique and a Proposal for the Psychology of Social Categorization." *Political Psychology* 22. 2:383–407.

Reinhart, Carmen M., and Vincent Raymond Reinhart. 1988. "Some Lessons for Policy Makers Who Deal with the Mixed Blessing of Capital Inflows." In *Capital Flows and Financial Crisis*, edited by Miles Kahler. Ithaca, NY: Cornell University Press, 93–127.

Reinert, Erik. 1994. "Catching-up from Way Behind: A Third World Perspective on First World History." In *The Dynamics of Technology, Trade, and Growth*, edited by Jan Fargerberg, Bart Verspagen, and Nick von Tunzelmann. Aldershot, UK: Edward Elgar, 45–70.

Reus-Smit, Christian. 1999. *The Moral Purpose of the State: Culture, Social Identity, and Institutional Rationality in International Relations.* Princeton, NJ: Princeton University Press.

Ringmar, Erik. 1996. *Identity, Interest and Action: A Cultural Explanation of Sweden's Intervention in the Thirty Years War.* Cambridge, UK: Cambridge University Press.

Risse-Kappen, Thomas. 1991. "Public Opinion, Domestic Structure, and Foreign Policy in Liberal Democracies." *World Politics* 43. 4:479–512.

Rix, Alan. 1993. "Japan and the Region: Leading from Behind." In *Pacific Economic Relations in the 1990s: Cooperation and Conflict*, edited by Richard Higgott, Richard Leaver, and John Ravenhill. Sydney, Australia: Allen & Unwin, 62–82.

Rosecrance, Richard, and Jennifer Taw. 1990. "Japan and the Theory of International Leadership." *World Politics* 42. 2:184–209.

Rosenberg, Justin. 1990. "What's the Matter with Realism?" *Review of International Studies* 16. 4:285–303.

Rosenbluth, Frances M. 1996. "Internationalization and Electoral Politics in Japan." In *Internationalization and Domestic Politics*, edited by Robert Keohane and Helen V. Milner. Cambridge, UK: Cambridge University Press, 137–58.

Rowley, Anthony. 1997. "International Finance: Asian Fund, Rest in Peace." *Capital Trends* 2. 1:1–3.

Roy, William. 1997. *Socializing Capital: The Rise of the Large Industrial Corporation in America.* Princeton, NJ: Princeton University Press.

Rubin, Robert J. 1997. "Remarks to the National Center for APEC" (Sept. 18; http://www.ustreas.gov/press/releases/pr1937.htm).

Ruggie, John G. 1983. "Continuity and Transformation in the World Polity: Toward a Neorealist Synthesis." *World Politics* 35. 2:261–85.

———. 1998a. *Constructing the World Polity: Essays on International Institutionalization.* London: Routledge.

———. 1998b. "What Makes the World Hang Together? Neo-Utilitarianism and the Social Constructivist Challenge." *International Organization* 52. 4:855–86.

———, Peter J. Katzenstein, Robert Keohane, and Philippe C. Schmitter. 2005. "Transformations in World Politics: The Intellectual Contributions of Ernst B. Haas." *Annual Review of Political Science* 8: 271–96.

Rumelili, Bahar. 2004. "Constructing Identity and Relating to Difference: Understanding the EU's Mode of Differentiation." *Review of International Studies* 30. 1:27–47.

Sachs, Jeffrey. 1998. "The IMF and the Asian Flu." *American Prospect* 37: 16–21.

Saito, Seiichiro, and Osamu Shimomura. 1984. "Setting Priorities for Asset Accumulation." *Japan Echo* 11. 4:11–17.

Sakakibara, Eisuke. 1993. *Beyond Capitalism: The Japanese Model of Market Economics*. New York: University Press of America.

———. 2000. *Nihon to Sekai ga Furueta Hi: Saiba Shihonsyugi no Seritsu*. Tokyo: Chūō Kōronsha.

———. 2001. "The Asian Monetary Fund: Where Do We Go from Here?" Paper presented at International Conference on Globalization, Feb. 26, Kuala Lumpur, Malaysia.

Sakakibara, Eisuke, and Soichiro Tahara. 1999. *Il Bon Jae Saeng* (translated by Sang Ho Lee and Kwang Min Park). Seoul, Korea: Hanul.

Sakisaka, Itsurō. 1958. *Nihon Shihonshugi no Shomodai*. Tokyo: Shiseido.

Sampson, Edward E. 1993. "Identity Politics: Challenges to Psychology's Understanding." *American Psychologist* 48. 12:1219–30.

Sandel, Michael. 1998. *Liberalism and the Limits of Justice*. Cambridge, UK: Cambridge University Press.

Scheman, L. Ronald. 1997. "Banking on Growth: The Role of the Inter-American Development Bank." *Journal of Interamerican Studies & World Affairs* 39. 1:85–100.

Schmiegelow, Henrik, and Michele Schmiegelow. 1990. "How Japan Affects the International System." *International Organization* 44. 4:553–88.

Schoppa, Leonard. 1993. "Two-Level Games and Bargaining Outcomes: Why Gaiatsu Succeeds in Japan in Some Cases But Not Others." *International Organization* 47. 3:353–84.

Schwartz, Frank. 1993. "Of Fairy Cloaks and Familiar Talk: The Politics of Consultation." In *Political Dynamics in Contemporary Japan*, edited by Gary D. Allinson and Yasunori Sone. Ithaca, NY: Cornell University Press, 217–41.

Schwartz, Seth. J. 2002. "In Search of Mechanisms of Change in Identity Development: Integrating the Constructivist and Discovery Perspectives on Identity." *Identity: An International Journal of Theory and Research* 2. 4:317–39.

Scott, James. 1991. "The Evidence of Experience." *Critical Inquiry* 17. 4:773–97.

Searle, John R. 1992. *The Rediscovery of Mind*. Cambridge, MA: MIT Press.

———. 1995. *The Construction of Social Reality*. New York: Free Press.

———. 2001. *Rationality in Action*. Cambridge, MA: MIT Press.

Semmel, Bernard. 1993. *The Liberal Ideal and the Demons of Empire: Theories of Imperialism from Adam Smith to Lenin*. Baltimore, MD: Johns Hopkins University Press.

Sen, Amartya. 1998. *Reason Before Identity*. Oxford, UK: Oxford University Press.

Sending, Ole J. 2002. "Constitution, Choice and Change: Problems with the 'Logic of Appropriateness' and Its Use in Constructivist Theory." *European Journal of International Relations* 8. 4:443–70.

Shimada, Haruo. 1991. "Is Japan's Economic System Different?" *Japan Close-Up* (Sept.):5–8.

Shimazu, Naoko. 1998. *Japan, Race, and Equality*. New York: Routledge.

Shimomura, Osamu. 1958. *Keizai Seichō Jitsugen no Tame ni*. Tokyo: Kōchikai.

———. 1959. Nihon Keizai no Seichōryoku to Seichō Riron. In *Shimomura Riron to Sono Hihan*, edited by Kinyū Zaisei Jijō Kenkyūkai. Tokyo: Kinyū Zaisei Jijō Kenkyūkai: 187–272.

———. 1962. *Nihon Keizai Seichō Ron*. Tokyo: Kinyū Zaisei Jijō Kenkyūkai.

———. 1967. Naze Seichō ni Jishin wo Motsuka? In *Nihon Keizai wo Miru Gan*, edited by Akira Koizumi and Miyazaki Yoshikazu. Tokyo: Tōyō Keizai Shinpōsha: 164–202.

Shinohara, Miyohei. 1962. *Growth and Cycles in the Japanese Economy*. Tokyo: Kinokuniya.

———. 1982. *Industrial Growth, Trade, and Dynamic Patterns in the Japanese Economy*. Tokyo: University of Tokyo Press.

Shirai, Sayumi. 2004. *Japan, the IMF and Global Governance: Inter-Disciplinary Approach to Human Security and Development*. Sept. 13–14, Kyoto, Japan (conference paper, Japan and Global Governance Workshop).

Shiratori, Masaki. 1993. *Sekai Ginko Gurupu: Tojokoku Enjo to Nihon no Yakuwari*. Tokyo: Kokusai Kaihatsu Janaru.

———. 1998. "Afterword to the Japanese Translation of the World Bank Report: The East Asian Miracle." In *Japanese Views on Economic Development: Diverse Paths to the Market*, edited by Kenichi Ohno and Izumi Ohno. New York: Routledge, 77–84.

Sikkink, Kathryn. 1991. *Ideas and Institutions: Developmentalism in Brazil and Argentina*. Ithaca, NY: Cornell University Press.

Simon, Herbert A. 1979. *Models of Thought*. New Haven, CT: Yale University Press.

———. 1982. *Models of Bounded Rationality*. Cambridge, UK: Cambridge University Press.

Singh, Ajit. 1999. "'Asian Capitalism' and the Financial Crisis." In *Global Instability: The Political Economy of World Economic Governance*, edited by Jonathan Michie and John G. Smith. London: Routledge, 9–36.

Snidal, Duncan. 1985. "The Limits of Hegemonic Stability Theory." *International Organization* 39. 4:579–614.

Snyder, Glenn H. 1997. *Alliance Politics*. Ithaca, NY: Cornell University Press.

Solow, Robert M. 1956. "A Contribution to the Theory of Economic Growth." *Quarterly Journal of Economics* 70. 1:65–94.

Solomon, Miriam. 1992. "Scientific Rationality and Human Reasoning." *Philosophy of Science* 59. 3:439–55.

Somers, Margaret R. 1992. "Narrativity, Narrative Identity, and Social Action: Rethinking English Working-Class Formation." *Social Science History* 16. 4:591–630.

———. 1994. "The Narrative Constitution of Identity: A Relational and Network Approach." *Theory and Society* 23. 5:605–49.

Stallings, Barbara, and Wolfgang Streeck. 1995. "Capitalisms in Conflict? The United States, Europe, and Japan in the Post-Cold War World." In *Global Change, Regional Response: The New International Context of Development*, edited by Barbara Stallings. Cambridge, UK: Cambridge University Press, 67–99.

Stein, Howard. 1998. "Japanese Aid to Africa: Patterns, Motivations and the Role of Structural Adjustment." *Journal of Development Studies* 35. 2:27–53.

Steinbruner, John D. 1974. *The Cybernetic Theory of Decision: New Dimensions of Political Analysis.* Princeton, NJ: Princeton University Press.

Stets, Jan E., and Peter J. Burke. 2000. "Identity Theory and Social Identity Theory." *Social Psychology Quarterly* 63. 3:224–37.

Strand, Jonathan R. 2001. "Institutional Design and Power Relations in the African Development Bank." *Journal of Asia and Africa Studies* 36. 2:203–23.

Stryker, Sheldon, and Anne Stratham. 1985. "Symbolic Interaction and Role Theory." In *Handbook of Social Psychology*, edited by Gardner Lindzey and Elliott Aronson. New York: Random House, 311–28.

Stubbs, Richard. 2002. "ASEAN Plus Three: Emerging East Asian Regionalism?" *Asian Survey* 42. 3:440–55.

Sudo, Sueo. 2002. *The International Relations of Japan and South East Asia.* London: Routledge.

Suganami, Hidemi. 1999. "Agents, Structures, Narratives." *European Journal of International Relations* 5. 3:365–86.

Sugihara, Shirō. 1980. *Nihon Keizai Shisoshi Ronshū.* Tokyo: Mirai Sha.

———. 1988a. "Economists in Government: Okubo Toshimichi, the 'Bismarck of Japan,' and His Times." In *Enlightenment and Beyond: Political Economy Comes to Japan*, edited by Chūsei Sugiyama and Hiroshi Mizuta. Tokyo: University of Tokyo Press, 211–21.

———. 1988b. "Economists in Journalism: Liberalism, Nationalism and Their Variants." In *Enlightenment and Beyond: Political Economy Comes to Japan*, edited by Chūsei Sugiyama and Hiroshi Mizuta. Tokyo: University of Tokyo Press, 237–53.

Sugihara, Shirō, and Toshihiro Tanaka (eds.). 1998. *Economic Thought and Modernization in Japan.* Northampton, MA: Edward Elgar.

Sugiyama, Chūsei. 1988a. "Fukuzawa Yukichi." In *Enlightenment and Beyond: Political Economy Comes to Japan*, edited by Chūsei Sugiyama and Hiroshi Mizuta. Tokyo: University of Tokyo Press, 37–58.

———. 1988b. "Nishi Amane and Tsuda Mamichi." In *Enlightenment and Beyond: Political Economy Comes to Japan*, edited by Chūsei Sugiyama and Hiroshi Mizuta. Tokyo: University of Tokyo Press, 59–73.

———. 1994. *Origins of Economic Thought in Modern Japan.* London: Routledge.

———, and Hiroshi Mizuta (eds.). 1988. *Enlightenment and Beyond: Political Economy Comes to Japan*. Tokyo: University of Tokyo Press.

Sugiyama, Mitsunobu. 1999. "Civil Society Theory and Wartime Mobilization: On the Intellectual Development of Uchida Yoshihiko." In *Total War and Modernization*, edited by Yasushi Yamanouchi, J. Victor Koschmann, and Ryūichi Narita. Ithaca, NY: Cornell University Press, 117–36.

Summers, Lawrence H. 1997. "Testimony Before the House Committee on Banking and Financial Services" (Nov. 13; http://www.ustreas.gov/press/releases/pr2062.htm).

———. 1998. "Emerging from Crisis: The Beginning of a New Asia. Remarks Before the Economic Strategy Institute" (Feb. 11; http://www.ustreas.gov/press/releases/pr2217.htm).

Tajfel, Henry. 1981. *Human Groups and Social Categories*. Cambridge, UK: Cambridge University Press.

Takahiko, Tennichi. 1998. "Debates on Japan's Foreign Policy." In *Challenges for China-Japan-U.S. Cooperation*, edited by Kokubun Ryosei. Tokyo: Japan Center for International Exchange, 71–89.

Taylor, Charles. 1989. *Sources of the Self*. Cambridge, MA: Harvard University Press.

Terada, Takashi. 2003. "Construction an 'East Asian' Concept and Growing Regional Identity: From EAEC to ASEAN + 3." *Pacific Review* 16. 2:251–75.

Thacker, Strom C. 1999. "The High Politics of IMF Lending." *World Politics* 52. 1:38–75.

Tickner, Ann J. 1987. *Self-Reliance Versus Power Politics: The American and Indian Experiences in Building Nation States*. New York: Columbia University Press.

———. 1990. "Reaganomics and the Third World: Lessons from the Founding Fathers." *Polity* 23. 1:53–76.

Toye, John. 1993. *Dilemmas of Development: Reflections on the Counter-Revolution in Development Economics*. Oxford, UK: Blackwell.

Trentmann, Frank. 1998. "Political Culture and Political Economy: Interest, Ideology and Free Trade." *Review of International Political Economy* 5. 1:217–51.

Tsuchiya, Takao. 1937. *Nihon Shihonshugi Ronshū*. Tokyo: Ikusei Sha.

———. 1977. *An Economic History of Japan*. Philadelphia: Porcupine Press.

Tsukatani, Akihiro. 1986. *Kindai Nihon Keizai Shisōshi Kenkyū*. Tokyo: Yūsankaku.

Tsuru, Shigeto. 1993. *Japan's Capitalism: Creative Defeat and Beyond*. Cambridge, UK: Cambridge University Press.

Tucker, Robert W. 1961. "Political Realism and Foreign Policy." *World Politics* 13. 3:461–70.

Tversky, Amos, and Daniel Kahneman. 1982. "Judgment Under Uncertainty: Heuristics and Biases." In *Judgment Under Uncertainty: Heuristics and Biases*, edited by Amos Tversky, Daniel Kahneman, and Paul Slovic. Cambridge, UK: Cambridge University Press, 3–20.

Uchida, Yoshihiko. 1967. *Nihon Shihonshugi no Shisōzō*. Tokyo: Iwanami Shoten.

———. 1981. *Sakuhin Toshite no Shakai Kagaku*. Tokyo: Iwanami Shoten.
Uno, Kōzō. 1946. *Keizai Minshuka to Sangyō Shakaika*. Tokyo: Shinsei (Dec.).
———. 1962. *Keizaigaku Hōhōron*. Tokyo: Tokyo Daigaku Shuppankai.
———. 1974 (1954). *Uno Kōzō Chosakushū Vol. 7*. Tokyo: Iwanami Shoten.
Urata, Shujirō. 1996. *Regionalization and the Formation of Regional Institution in East Asia*. Tokyo: Japan Center for Economic Research.
Uriu, Robert. 2000. "The Impact of Policy Ideas: Revisionism and the Clinton Administration's Trade Policy Toward Japan." In *New Perspectives on U.S.-Japan Relations*, edited by Gerald L. Curtis. Washington DC: Brookings Institution, 213–40.
van Wolferen, Karen G. 1989. *The Enigma of Japanese Power: People and Politics in a Stateless Nation*. New York: Knopf.
Viner, Jacob. 1948. "Power Versus Plenty as Objectives of Foreign Policy in the Seventeenth and Eighteenth Centuries." *World Politics* 1. 1:1–29.
Vogel, Ezra F. 1986. "Pax Nipponica." *Foreign Affairs* 64. 4:752–67.
Vollmer, Fred. 1999. *Agent Causality*. Boston: Kluwer Academic.
Wade, Robert. 1996. "Japan, the World Bank, and the Art of Paradigm Maintenance: The East Asian Miracle in Political Perspective." *New Left Review* 217: 3–37.
———. 2002. "U.S. Hegemony and the World Bank: The Fight over People and Ideas." *Review of International Political Economy* 9. 2:215–43.
———. 2003. "What Strategies Are Visible for Developing Countries Today? The World Trade Organization and the Shrinking of Development Space." *Review of International Political Economy* 10. 4:621–44.
———, and Frank Veneroso. 1998. "The Asian Crisis: The High Debt Model Versus the Wall Street-Treasury Complex." *New Left Review* 228: 1535–54.
Wakayama, Norikazu. 1940. *Wakayama Norikazu Zenshu, Vols. 1 and 2*. Tokyo: Tokyo Keizai Shinpōsha.
Wallace, R. Jay. 2004. "Normativity and Will." In *Agency and Action*, edited by John Hyman and Helen Steward. Cambridge, UK: Cambridge University Press, 195–216.
Walt, Stephen M. 1999. "Rigor or Rigor Mortis? Rational Choice and Security Studies." *International Security* 23. 4:5–48.
Walton, Douglas N. 1990. *Practical Reasoning: Goal Driven, Knowledge-Based, Action-Guiding Argumentation*. Savage, MD: Rowman & Littlefield.
Waltz, Kenneth. 1979. *Theory of International Relations*. Reading, MA: Addison-Wesley.
———. 2000. "Structural Realism After the Cold War." *International Security* 25. 1:5–41.
Wan, Ming. 1995. "Spending Strategies in World Politics: How Japan Has Used Its Economic Power in the Past Decade." *International Studies Quarterly* 39. 1:85–108.
———. 1995/1996. "Japan and the Asian Development Bank." *Pacific Affairs* 68. 4:509–28.
Watanabe, Toshio. 1998. "Designing Asia for the Next Century." In *Japanese Views on Economic Development: Diverse Paths to the Market*, edited by Kenichi Ohno and Izumi Ohno. London: Routledge, 201–19.

Weber, Max. 1978. *Economy and Society, Vol. 1.* Berkeley: University of California Press.

Weber, Steve. 1994. "Origins of the European Bank for Reconstruction and Development." *International Organization* 48. 1:1–38.

Weiss, Linda, and John M. Hobson. 1995. *States and Economic Development: A Comparative Historical Analysis.* Cambridge, UK: Polity Press.

Weldes, Jutta. 1996. "Constructing National Interests." *European Journal of International Relations* 2. 3:275–318.

———, and Diana Saco. 1996. "Making State Action Possible: The United States and the Discursive Construction of 'The Cuban Problem,' 1960–1994." *Millennium: Journal of International Studies* 25. 2:361–95.

Wendt, Alexander. 1992. "Anarchy Is What States Makes of It: The Social Construction of Power Politics." *International Organization* 46. 2:391–425.

———. 1994. "Collective Identity Formation and the International State." *American Political Science Review* 88. 2:384–96.

———. 1999. *Social Theory of International Politics.* New York: Cambridge University Press.

Wight, Martin. 1995. "Why Is There No International Theory?" In *International Theory: Critical Investigation*, edited by James Der Derian. New York: New York University Press, 15–35.

Williamson, John. 1993. "Democracy and the 'Washington Consensus.'" *World Development* 21. 8:1329–36.

Winters, Jeffrey A. 1999. "The Determinant of Financial Crisis in Asia." In *The Politics of the Asian Economic Crisis*, edited by T. J. Pempel. Ithaca, NY: Cornell University Press, 79–97.

Wolfers, Arnold. 1962. *Discord and Collaboration: Essays on International Politics.* Baltimore, MD: Johns Hopkins University Press.

Woo-Cumings, Meredith. 1995. "The Asian Development Bank and the Politics of Development in East Asia." In *United States-Japan Relations and International Institution After the Cold War*, edited by Peter Gourevitch, Takashi Inoguchi, and Courtney Purrington. San Diego: Graduate School of International Relations and Pacific Studies, University of California, San Diego, 227–50.

———. 1999. "Introduction: Chalmers Johnson and the Politics of Nationalism and Development." In *The Developmental State*, edited by Meredith Woo-Cumings. Ithaca, NY: Cornell University Press, 1–31.

Woods, Ngaire. 1995. "Economic Ideas and International Relations: Beyond Rational Neglect." *International Studies Quarterly* 39. 2:161–80.

Yamada, Moritarō. 1934. *Nihon Shihonshugi Bunseki.* Tokyo: Iwanami Shoten.

Yamada, Toshio. 1998. "Economic Development and Economic Thought After World War II: Economic Development and Marxian Political Economy." In *Economic*

Thought and Modernization in Japan, edited by Shirō Sugihara and Toshihiro Tanaka. Northampton: MA: Edward Elgar, 152–67.

Yamamura, Kozo (ed.). 1997. *A Vision of a New Liberalism? Critical Essays on Murakami's Anticlassical Analysis*. Stanford, CA: Stanford University Press.

Yamazawa, Ippei. 1990. *Economic Development and International Trade: The Japanese Model*. Hawaii, HI: East-West Center.

Yanagihara, Toru. 1993. "Japan's Foreign Aid to Bangladesh: Challenging the Dependency Syndrome." In *Japan's Foreign Aid: Power and Policy in a New Era*, edited by Bruce M. Koppel and Robert M. Orr. Boulder, CO: Westview Press, 188–202.

———. 1998. "Development and Dynamic Efficiency: 'Framework Approach' versus 'Ingredients Approach.'" In *Japanese Views on Economic Development: Diverse Paths to the Market*, edited by Kenichi Ohno and Izumi Ohno. New York: Routledge, 70–76.

Yasuba, Yasukichi. 1975. "Anatomy of the Debate on Japanese Capitalism." *Journal of Japanese Studies* 2. 1:63–82.

Yasutomo, Dennis T. 1995. *The New Multilateralism in Japan's Foreign Policy*. New York: St. Martin's Press.

Yee, Albert S. 1996. "The Causal Effects of Ideas on Policies." *International Organization* 50. 1:69–108.

Yu, Hyun-Seok. 2003. "Explaining the Emergence of New Asian Regionalism: Beyond Power and Interest-Based Approaches." *Asian Perspective* 27. 1:261–88.

Zehfuss, Maja. 2001. "Constructivism and Identity: A Dangerous Liaison." *European Journal of International Relations* 7. 3:315–48.

INDEX